DIXIE

A PERSONAL ODYSSEY THROUGH
EVENTS THAT SHAPED THE MODERN SOUTH

Curtis Wilkie

A LISA DREW BOOK

A TOUCHSTONE BOOK

PUBLISHED BY SIMON & SCHUSTER

NEW YORK   LONDON   TORONTO   SYDNEY   SINGAPORE

TOUCHSTONE
Rockefeller Center
1230 Avenue of the Americas
New York, NY 10020

First Touchstone Edition 2002

TOUCHSTONE and colophon are registered trademarks of
Simon & Schuster Inc.

A LISA DREW BOOK is a trademark of Simon & Schuster Inc.

For information regarding special discounts for bulk purchases,
please contact Simon & Schuster Special Sales at
1-800-456-6798 or business@simonandschuster.com

Designed by Colin Joh

Manufactured in the United States of America

1   3   5   7   9   10   8   6   4   2

The Library of Congress has cataloged the Scribner edition as follows:

Wilkie, Curtis.
Dixie/Curtis Wilkie.
p. cm.
"A Lisa Drew book."
1. Southern States—Civilization—20th century. 2. Southern States—Race relations.
3. Southern States—Social conditions—1945–. 4. Wilkie, Curtis. 5. Journalists—
United States—Biography. 6. Mississippi—Biography. 7. Wilkey family. 8. Mississippi—
Politics and government—1951–. 9. Mississippi—Race relations. I. Title.

F216.2.W55 2001
975'.043—dc21   2001020760

ISBN 0-684-87285-4
ISBN 0-684-87286-2 (Pbk)

To the memory of three good Mississippians:

My mother, Lyda Wilkie Stuart (1910–1997),
and my friends Aaron E. Henry (1922–1997) and
Willie Morris (1934–1999).
They all lived to see the promise of the South fulfilled.

Contents

★ ★ ★ ★ ★

Acknowledgments

The list of friends who encouraged me to write this book and offered generous assistance is long.

The late Willie Morris, Richard Ford, David Halberstam, Deborah Harris, and Howell Raines had faith in the idea of a book about Dixie before it became a reality.

Jere Hoar, William Winter, William Watkins, Eleanor Randolph, Jeanie Clinton, and Tom Oliphant read parts or all of the manuscript and offered helpful suggestions.

My children—Carter Wilkie and his wife, Allison; Leighton McCool and her husband, Campbell; and Stuart Wilkie—followed the work in progress and gave me wonderful support. Carter and Campbell also provided significant information about the Southern background of our families. I hope my grandchildren, Cameron, Davis, Morgan, and Merrick, will someday find the stories of their ancestors interesting.

Deborah Grosvenor, my agent, was a wise shepherd, as usual, in steering this book to publication. Lisa Drew, my editor at Scribner, enthusiastically embraced the proposal and lent a good and guiding hand. Thanks, too, to Jake Klisivitch, Lisa's assistant. I am very grateful to all.

As a child of Mississippi, a student at Ole Miss during the 1962 crisis, and a journalist for nearly forty years afterward, I was fortunate to witness a lot of history firsthand. *Dixie* is based primarily on personal memory, freshened and reinforced by more than seventy books and numerous magazine articles on the subject. Particularly valuable to me were old copies of the *Summit Sun*, which ceased publication in 1983, a quarter century's worth of my clippings from the *Boston Globe*, as well as stories of the 1950s and 1960s from the *Clarksdale Press Register*, the *McComb Enterprise-Journal*, the *Times-Picayune* of New Orleans, the *Clarion-Ledger* of Jackson, and the *Jackson Daily News*, which is no longer printed.

For their assistance during my research, I am especially indebted to Thomas Verich, Jennifer Ford, and the staff of the Department of Special Collections at the J. D. Williams Library at the University of Mississippi; to the staff of the Department of Archives and History for the state of Mississippi; to Charles Dunagin, Jack Ryan, and the staff at the *Enterprise-Journal*; to the Carnegie Public Library in Clarksdale; and to the library at Southwest Mississippi Community College in Summit.

Sean Mullin helped me overcome my neo-Luddite difficulties with new technology. My thanks to him and all my other friends at the *Boston Globe*.

Dozens of people responded to my questions about certain details, made available long-forgotten histories and records, and went out of their way to help. In no particular order, I'd like to thank Connie Curry, David Crews, Peyton Prospere, Will and Patty Lewis, Bob Black, Bob Fortenberry, Lynne Watkins, Ed Meek, Laura Magee, Nathan Cobb, William Paulk, Marty Nolan, Don Fortenberry, Franklin Holmes, Jack Dunbar, Taylor Branch, Bill Minor, David Sansing, Douglas Brinkley, Milly Moorhead, Elsie Milligan, Andy Carr, Bennie Gooden, Lucie Lee Lanoux, Walter F. Mondale, Lawrence Guyot, Ed King, Jack Thornell, Louis Sahuc, Jim Ingram, Hodding Carter III, Patt Derian, Ed Williams, Lew Powell, Jules Witcover, Myra MacPherson, Ron Goldfarb, Charles Overby, Jody Powell, Greg Schneiders, Tom Brokaw, Calvin Trillin, Pat Oliphant, Rick Hertzberg, Chris Matthews, Thad Cochran, Grady and Bettye Jolly, Butch and Pat Cothren, Jimmy and Meredith Creekmore, Raad and Karenna Cawthon, Jeff Price, Walter Edgar, Robert Khayat, Charles Reagan Wilson, Cheryl Thurber, Ann Abadie, Jerry Himelstein, Jerry Mitchell, JoAnne Prichard Morris, David Rae Morris, Malcolm White, Maude Schuyler Clay, Byron Seward, Louisa Williams, Marion E. Rodgers, George Shaddock, David Firestone, Walter Mears, and Chuck Zoeller. Forgive me if I have failed to name anyone who helped me flesh out events of sixty years.

In some instances, I have reconstructed conversations in which I drew upon my own memory and the recollections of others. In many cases, I was able to rely on contemporary accounts in newspapers or published histories for the quotes.

The judgments of *Dixie*, in the end, are my own. In using the terms *colored people* and *Negroes* early in the book, I tried to follow an approach that Taylor Branch settled upon for his magnificent histories of the civil rights movement: applying terms used by both blacks and whites during the period before *blacks* became acceptable. At some point in the 1960s, these various racial references became interchangeable; by the end of the decade, *blacks* became preferred. My decision to use racial epithets is based on my belief that no account of the twentieth-century South can be completely honest without them. If I have offended anyone, I apologize.

You who have waited for the angry resolution
Of those desires that should be yours tomorrow,
You know the unimportant shrift of death
And praise the vision
And praise the arrogant circumstance
Of those who fall
Rank upon rank, hurried beyond decision—
Here by the sagging gate, stopped by the wall.

—from Allen Tate's "Ode to the Confederate Dead"

CHAPTER 1

"We all knew Beckwiths"

★ ★ ★ ★ ★

The voice sounded faintly menacing, even though he spoke by telephone from hundreds of miles away.

At the beginning of our conversation, he used an old Southern pronunciation that fell just short of insult—"nigras"—but within a couple of minutes his manner degenerated. As he talked, the old man became more exercised, and his reedy whine bristled with malevolence. "Niggers," he told me, "are descendants of the mud people," unworthy of respect. Or life, for that matter.

Then he began ranting about "Babylonian Talmudists."

"Excuse me?"

"The Babylonian Talmudists. Don't you know what a Talmudist is?"

"I think I just figured it out."

"Babylonian Talmudists are a set of dogs," he explained. "If you read in the King James Version of the Bible, you'll see that a dog is a male whore. And God says kill them."

Racial mixing, he continued, "is a capital crime, like murder is a capital crime. But the Bible doesn't say, 'Thou shalt not kill.' It says, 'Thou shalt do no murder.'"

As he spoke, I took notes furiously, because the commentary was coming from Byron De La Beckwith, soon to be standing trial again for the murder of Medgar Evers, once the most prominent black man in Mississippi. Our talk took place in January 1994, more than thirty years after Evers had been shot in the back in the driveway of his home in Jackson. In connection with an article I was writing about the coming trial, I had called Beckwith at his home in Tennessee, where he had been living, free on bond, unrepentant and flying the Confederate battle flag from his porch. In the background, I heard his wife, Thelma, imploring him not to talk with me. But after Beckwith had determined that I had been born white and raised a Christian, he had agreed to an interview. Perhaps my own Southern accent had beguiled him, though I suspect he had simply seized on what would be one of his last opportunities to expound publicly on his racial theories.

By this time, Beckwith was seventy-three years old, cornered, yet still defiant. An erstwhile fertilizer salesman, he reveled in his reputation as an unconvicted assassin, a champion of white supremacy who had exterminated an upstart leader of the "mud people." After his first two trials had ended in hung juries, he had run for lieutenant governor of Mississippi in 1967, assuring his campaign audiences that he was a "straight shooter." He said it with a grin. But even then, he was becoming an embarrassment in a state worn down by the violence of the old guard. Beckwith finished fifth in a field of six candidates, though in losing, he won thirty-four thousand votes—sobering to think about.

Six years later, New Orleans authorities—acting on a tip—arrested Beckwith as he drove into the city. In his car they found a live time bomb and a map to the home of the regional director of the Anti-Defamation League of B'Nai B'rith. When a five-member jury found him guilty of participating in the plot against the Jewish leader, Beckwith declared that he had been convicted by "five nigger bitches." He served three years in the Louisiana State Penitentiary in Angola, but after the small size of the state jury was ruled unconstitutional, Beckwith had the conviction expunged from his record.

Now the Evers murder case was being resurrected, and Beckwith seemed pleased by his new notoriety. He told me he was "full of enthusiasm and adventure. I'm proud of my enemies. They're every color but white, every creed but Christian."

He alluded to his family's status in bygone days in Greenwood, when the Beckwiths had lived in a big house and circulated with those of importance in the Mississippi Delta. All that had faded; his relatives were dead, their fortune spent, their mansion in ruins. Nevertheless, Beckwith considered himself high-class, and he told me, "Country-club Mississippi is tired of this crap the Jews, niggers, and Orientals are stirring up."

My knowledge of "country-club Mississippi" lay on a par with my understanding of the Sorrowful Mysteries of the Roman Catholic Church, yet I had to suppress a snort at Beckwith's assertion. Country clubs might accept a WASP leper before welcoming Jews, blacks, and Americans of Asian descent, but I knew Beckwith had transmogrified into an even greater pariah. Despite his family pedigree, Beckwith represented a virulent element that had ultimately proved counterproductive to the Southern way of life.

For a few years in the early 1960s, it seemed that wily attorneys and buttoned-down movers and shakers in the white communities had found methods to delay integration indefinitely. They invoked states' rights and the doctrine of interposition, plotting their strategy in the backrooms of law offices rather than in clandestine meetings in piney woods. Throughout my boyhood, which coincided with the *Brown v. Board of Education* decision, the segregationists' plans succeeded.

Then, men lacking any subtlety, fanatics such as Beckwith, Bull Connor, the killers in Neshoba County, the bombers of Birmingham, as well as an array of reactionary governors—Orval Faubus of Arkansas, Ross Barnett of Mississippi, George Wallace of Alabama, and Lester Maddox of Georgia—created such a picture of hate and discrimination that the nation, and much of the South, finally began to say, Enough.

Because the segregationists' war had inflicted so much suffering on the region, I felt sure that not even "Kiwanis Club Mississippi" would want to sell Beckwith a ticket to a pancake breakfast.

Yet in some venues, I knew that Beckwith and his ilk continued to symbolize the South, and after we finished our talk, I was left with a question—not for the first time—of who really personifies the South.

There is no simple answer. The Southerner is an imperfect, conflicted character, not easily pigeonholed—though a stereotype invariably develops when the South attracts national attention. We have been stamped as curious people, with wits as slow as our speech and the odor of a segregationist heritage sticking to our clothes like stale tobacco smoke. For most of the twentieth century, we occupied a rural and poor society; it seemed as if our poverty served as Old Testament punishment for our racial codes.

We are reputed to be gothic in our behavior. Our own novelists and playwrights—recognizing the value of baroque characters—have helped perpetuate the mythic Southerner as someone a bit weird. James Dickey, a certifiable son of the South, assembled a cast of backwoods pig-fuckers for *Deliverance*, while Flannery O'Connor, a Georgian, created the crazy Holy

Roller Hazel Motes. William Faulkner had his Popeye, who favored a corn-cob as his sexual tool, and Erskine Caldwell built his books, which sold more than 80 million copies, around foolish cracker families.

In his popular 1998 novel, *A Man in Full,* Tom Wolfe, a native Virginian, came up with a modern version of Tennessee Williams's Big Daddy. Wolfe's character, Charlie Croker, was a onetime football hero at Georgia Tech who assured his rise from the gnat-infested bogs of south Georgia by "marrying up." Although Croker became a hard-charging Atlanta developer, he kept his uncouth ways. When Croker spoke, it was as though his words were strained through a portion of grits. ("I want'chall to know that this turtle soup comes from turtles rat'cheer at Turpmtine. Uncle Bud caught every one uv'em . . .") Like other pillars of Wolfe's Atlanta, Croker was happy to set his bigotry aside long enough to sit at the business table with a black man, but he didn't want his daughter to marry one.

Despite the great contributions that Southern blacks have made to our culture, the prototypical Southerner has always been a white male, and usually one with a white sheet in his background. The most messianic man of my lifetime, Martin Luther King Jr., lived and died in the South, yet one no more thinks of him as Southern than one considers the whites of Zimbabwe as African. Southern cult figures—Huey P. Long, George Wallace, Billy Graham, Bear Bryant, Elvis—have invariably been eccentric white men.

In a scene from Faulkner, a young man from Yoknapatawpha County, Quentin Compson, is asked by his Canadian roommate at Harvard to explain the South: "Tell me about the South. What's it like there? What do they do there? Why do they live there? Why do they live at all?" Compson kills himself before satisfactorily answering the question, but God knows Faulkner took plenty of swipes at the South over the years. In *Absalom, Absalom,* he called our homeland a "deep South dead since 1865 and peopled with garrulous outraged baffled ghosts." I like that description, because we deliberately set ourselves apart from the rest of America during the Civil War and continue, to this day, to live as spiritual citizens of a nation that existed for only four years in another century. We have defied assimilation—not so much out of an allegiance to the principles of the Confederacy as to a stubborn aversion to our conquerors.

Across the South, outward change has been profound. My generation experienced more disruption in our social order than any other demographic group in America. In a short span, we moved from enforcing segregation to accepting integration, from economic hardship to prosperity. We saw our politics turned on its head. Yet in the interior of our souls, I believe the Southerner remains unchanged, yoked to our history as surely as Quentin Compson one hundred years ago.

Pride may be one of the seven deadly sins, but I believe it is one of our finer characteristics. Sometimes we confuse pride with honor, but most Southerners are proud of the quirks that distinguish us from Middle America. We look upon the land mass below Richmond as a preserve for our customs and consider our difference our glory.

In the last half of the twentieth century, the country was homogenized by television, jet travel, and the Internet. Yet we maintained our own culture, our accent, our cuisine, our music, as if by giving them up we would finally admit defeat.

Rather than knuckle under to American conventions, we actually intensified our regional eccentricities. Like other down-and-out people, living in shtetlach beyond the Pale or in poor villages in Ireland, we cultivated a sense of humor that fed the stereotype yet served as something of a defense mechanism. Southern humorists, performing as professional rednecks, have thrived for decades as masters of self-deprecation. We would rather laugh at ourselves than be laughed at.

I love the South, yet for all of my own loyalty there was a lapse in my regional chauvinism. After Mississippi was plunged into a particularly hard period during the 1960s, I left my home state, overfed on the Southern experience. I felt we were digging our own grave with our racial policies. The decade had been a bad time, a period of intimidation and terror, of sorrow, guilt, and shame. Though I never renounced my roots, I was glad to escape them. I read *The New Yorker* and the novels of Cheever and Updike; their Eastern, urbane world sounded alluring. I particularly related to Willie Morris's autobiography, *North Toward Home*, in which the Mississippian wrote of turning his back "on the isolated places that nurtured and shaped him into maturity, for the sake of some convenient or fashionable 'sophistication.'" I was determined to join a band of expatriates on the East Coast, a group Morris described as "a genuine set of exiles, almost in the European sense: alienated from home yet forever drawn back to it, seeking some form of personal liberty elsewhere yet obsessed with the texture and the complexity of the place from which they had departed as few Americans from other states could ever be."

For nearly twenty-five years, I lived outside the South, but remained lashed to my home as surely as if I were a captive bound to a stake. I never lost my accent. When I opened my mouth as a reporter for the *Boston Globe*, those I interviewed sometimes asked, "Where in God's name are you from?" I never hesitated to say Mississippi. Never Boston or Washington or Jerusalem or any of my other harbors during that period, even though a claim on a different place might have made my passage easier.

Shortly after I arrived in the East, I visited Oscar Carr, a friend who had also fled the Mississippi Delta for Manhattan. An erudite man, Oscar was one of two brothers who had risked their place in Mississippi society by standing up for blacks. Though the Carr brothers were wealthy planters, they had sided with the underclass in a number of highly publicized fights for antipoverty funds and political equity. In 1968, Oscar served as a cochairman of Robert Kennedy's presidential campaign in Mississippi. After RFK's death, Oscar moved his family to New York, where, he told me with a laugh, he intended "to do the Lord's work—officially" at the national headquarters of the Episcopal Church. After dinner at the Carrs' apartment near Central Park, Oscar decided that I should meet Willie Morris, so we set off for one of Willie's haunts, Elaine's on the Upper East Side. We were met at the bar by the proprietor, a stout woman with a reputation for rude charming. She informed us that Willie was not there. Though Willie would apparently always be welcome, she added that "redneck assholes" (a description that may have fit me, but surely not Oscar) were not. So much for my first brush with the literary dens I had read about in *The New Yorker*.

As it turned out, Willie's career in New York proved as incandescent as a Roman candle, and by 1980 he had returned to Mississippi to live and write eloquently of the state's dreadful past and its happier contemporary times. Years later, I finally met him while in Jackson on assignment. As our friendship developed, he encouraged me to come home, too. A gentle man, Willie had a gift for practical jokes, preferably by phone. Among the telephone messages I got in Boston, I began to hear phony editorial requests for a profile of Leander Perez, the long-dead dictator of Plaquemines Parish below New Orleans, as well as earnest suggestions that it was time to return to the South. All from Willie.

During my years away, I found the South held no monopoly on racial or ethnic discrimination. The passions exposed during Boston's busing conflict the year I joined the *Globe* were as raw and unpleasant as any I ever witnessed, and the hatreds I encountered later in the Middle East made the segregationist rhetoric I had heard as a young man sound like the beatitudes.

During my trips to the South to visit family or cover stories for the *Globe*, I began to rediscover my home and my friends. Racial problems had not been solved, but many more people were working on them. Old pals who once waved the Confederate battle flag as if to stick a finger in the North's eye had cast the symbol aside after realizing that it grated on the sensitivities of fellow citizens who were black. White elected officials suddenly sounded far more thoughtful than the demagogues of my boyhood, and throughout the region, blacks held many leadership positions.

The South also exuded a metaphysical warmth. In contrast to Boston winters, when cold bites through several layers of clothing and darkness closes early in the afternoon, the South beckoned me with its sunlight and leisurely lifestyle.

In 1993, I finally followed Willie's advice and persuaded the *Globe* to let me spend that winter in New Orleans to enable me to make frequent visits to my mother, who lay slowly dying in nearby Mississippi. My editor, Matt Storin, gave the move his blessing. To most of our readers in New England, he said, Western Europe was more familiar than the American South. "Go and cover the place like a foreign country," he said.

Within a month, I had come full circle. My first major assignment, the third Beckwith trial, washed up memories of my first year as a journalist. In the spring of that year, 1963, I had covered a civil rights rally at a church in Clarksdale, a Mississippi Delta city where I had been hired as a reporter. The sanctuary was filled that evening with several hundred blacks, an assembly of day laborers and domestic workers, ministers and morticians, bracing for their challenge to the status quo with songs of freedom and speeches to fortify morale. I was the only white person in the crowd. One of the speakers was Medgar Evers. Following the rally, Aaron Henry, a local druggist who served as state president of the NAACP, invited me to his home to meet the visiting dignitaries. I had a beer with the group, which included Charles Diggs, a black congressman from Detroit. After an hour or so, Evers drove back to Jackson and I returned to my home on the white side of town.

When I stopped at the police station on my rounds two mornings later, an officer told me, with some satisfaction, that "your nigger buddy's house" had been firebombed before dawn. The congressman and members of the Henry family escaped without injury, but the Molotov cocktail had burned part of the Henrys' living room before the flames were put out.

A couple of months later, I arrived at work to learn that Medgar Evers had been murdered overnight. A rifle, abandoned near Evers's home, was eventually traced to Beckwith. There were two trials in 1964, when the climate in Jackson was controlled by right-wing politicians and the racist newspapers, the *Clarion-Ledger* and the *Daily News,* owned by the Hederman family. To impress the jurors, Ross Barnett, a former governor, showed up in the courtroom to be seen with Beckwith and his team of defense attorneys. Bill Waller, a young district attorney willing to run against the grain of those days, conducted a strong prosecution, but both trials ended inconclusively, and Beckwith went free.

In subsequent decades, several ironies helped revive the case. Waller was elected governor in 1971, partly on the new strength of grateful blacks who had been unable to vote and ineligible for jury duty in 1964. And in 1989, the *Clarion-Ledger,* now out of the hands of the Hederman family, obtained old files from the Mississippi Sovereignty Commission, a defunct segregationist agency. The documents showed that the Sovereignty Commission had screened the jury panel on behalf of the defense attorneys before Beckwith's second trial. The allegations of jury tampering, coupled with the demands of the black population of Jackson—which commanded 50 percent of the vote—put pressure on the district attorney's office to bring Beckwith back to trial.

A few days before the third trial, I went to see Waller at his law office in Jackson. I had known him since the 1967 gubernatorial campaign, when he had been a bold but unsuccessful candidate, and I occasionally saw him when I visited the state. A tall man, Waller had taken on weight and grown into a lumbering figure since our last meeting. He was still smarting from defeat in a 1987 election, when he had tried to make a comeback. He preferred to talk about the perfidy of rival politicians instead of the effort by the prosecutors to succeed in the Beckwith case where he had failed.

But Waller told me something interesting. Beckwith had been out of the public eye for years, a forgotten figure. Then he had showed up during the '87 campaign at a political rally and made an audacious gesture to shake Waller's hand. "It got in the papers," Waller said, "and got people talking about Beckwith again." The thought of a murderer walking around unpunished was no longer amusing to the people of Mississippi. The incident helped establish a public atmosphere that responded to the publication of the Sovereignty Commission papers and led to a decision to try Beckwith again. "I always thought he was a little nutty," Waller told me.

After many delays, the trial began in late January 1994 at the Hinds County Courthouse, a gray stone edifice in downtown Jackson, the same building where Beckwith had stood trial twice before. This time, a mixed jury— eight blacks and four whites, seven women and five men—was chosen. Three decades earlier, juries were all white, all male. This time, the court- room was integrated, and the state of Mississippi, represented by two white prosecutors, seemed determined to win.

The press sat in the balcony, looking down on a chamber where the defendant occasionally dozed or fiddled with his hearing aid. Some days Beckwith dressed in a jarring red sports jacket to complement his Confed- erate stickpin. A few feet away, the victim's widow, Myrlie Evers, followed testimony intensely, surrounded by her friends. A succession of aging faces from the first two trials reappeared in the witness chair; other veterans of the 1960s watched from the benches of the courtroom. It seemed a time warp—though this year events were not moving favorably for Beckwith.

A retired policeman recalled how the rifle had been retrieved from a thicket of sweet-gum trees and honeysuckle near Evers's home. Another witness related how he had seen a newspaper photo of the murder weapon, a rifle he had traded to Beckwith, and reported the information to authorities.

Delmar Dennis, an FBI informer and former chaplain for the White Knights of the Ku Klux Klan, told of how Beckwith addressed a 1965 Klan rally, "admonishing Klan leaders to become more involved, to be more vio- lent, to kill the enemy from the top down."

The case was sealed with a Perry Mason twist. A Chicago man named Mark Reiley had seen a television account of the trial and recognized the defendant as an inmate he had known while working as an orderly at a Louisiana prison. Reiley notified the prosecutors, and they flew him to Jackson as a surprise witness. He recalled that Beckwith had proselytized a religion that held blacks to be beasts of the field. "He told me, 'If they get out of line, you should kill them.'" More important, Reiley overheard Beckwith tell a black prison nurse, "If I can get rid of an uppity nigger like Medgar Evers, I won't have any problem with a no-account nigger like you."

After nearly two weeks of testimony, the case went to the jury early on a Friday afternoon. Most of the reporters covering the trial thought a guilty verdict would come quickly. But by nightfall, the jurors reported that they were still undecided, and when they appeared before the judge, the faces of some members of the panel seemed drawn with anger, as though they had been arguing. Deliberations were suspended for the night, and some of the journalists repaired to Hal & Mal's, a popular restaurant down the street, for drinks and dinner. My mood was disconsolate. I remember muttering, "I can't believe there's going to be another hung jury. I can't believe that old buzzard is going to walk free again."

Thinking the jury would be locked in debate for a long while, I took my time arriving for the vigil the next day. But when I got to the courthouse at midmorning, a bailiff, recognizing that I had been following the case for days, frantically waved me inside the courtroom before locking the doors.

I had nearly missed one of the most electrifying moments of my career. The verdict was guilty, and when I heard the word, I realized my arms were peppered with chill bumps. Below, Myrlie Evers shrieked with joy. As the single word—"guilty"—passed to a crowd standing outside the courtroom, haunting cheers reverberated in the marble corridors.*

During the days in Jackson, I had several get-togethers with classmates from my Ole Miss days as well as with newer acquaintances. One night was especially magical, and I wouldn't have traded it for a month of dinners at Elaine's. The hostess, Anne Winter, gathered a lively group. Two of her guests, David Crews and Peyton Prospere, had worked in the administration of her father, William Winter, a progressive governor in the early 1980s. Willie Morris and his wife, JoAnne, were on hand. And so was a special guest whom I had never met, Eudora Welty.

With the help of the younger men, Miss Welty had been ferried in a driving rainstorm from her home a few blocks away. Approaching eighty-five, she was frail and moved slowly. But her face glowed with the wonderfully wrinkled character of a long lifetime, and she carried on an animated conversation—with the help of a couple of fingers of whiskey. When I offered to get a refill, she instructed me to "make the next one a bit stronger."

Willie served as her interlocuter, drawing her out about Mississippi during the Great Depression and World War II, periods she infused into her novels. During our postmortem of the Beckwith trial, I asked a question I'm sure Miss Welty had answered many times: How was she able to write the

---

*Beckwith died in prison in January 2001.

short story "Where Is the Voice Coming From?" so quickly, and with such prescience?

The story had appeared in *The New Yorker* shortly after Evers's murder. It is a cold-blooded, first-person account of a racial murder:

"I'd already brought up my rifle, I'd already taken my sights. And I'd already got him, because it was too late then for him or me to turn by one hair. Something darker than him, like the wings of a bird, spread on his back and pulled him down. He climbed up once, like a man under bad claws, and like just blood could weigh a ton he walked with it on his back to better light. Didn't get no further than his door. And fell to stay . . ."

The narrator's hate resembled Beckwith's. The physical description a reader could infer matched Beckwith. Even the monologue sounded like Beckwith. Yet the story was completed before Beckwith had been arrested.

Miss Welty said she had written the piece in white heat, within hours of learning of Evers's death. With a cluck, she dismissed the notion that she had been remarkably foresighted.

"We all knew who did it" from the first moment, she said, "because we all knew Beckwiths. It wasn't necessary to know that man, Beckwith."

Just, I thought, as many people in the rest of the country continued to conjure up someone like Beckwith when thinking of Mississippians— rather than associating the state with my dinner companions.

The evening wound on, through courses of pasta and salad and bottles of wine, and after the rains diminished, Miss Welty was helped home. Flushed by the cheer of friendship and drink, the rest of us remained in the bosom of the dinner table past midnight.

Willie peered at me across the candlelight and posed a simple question: "Curtis, can you tell us why you came home?"

Though I had struggled with that question for months, I had never come up with a pat answer. I reflected, for just a moment, then a thought occurred to me: "Because people are kinder here."

But I didn't always feel that way.

CHAPTER 2

Natural Rebels

★ ★ ★ ★ ★

In the beginning, I assumed all the world to be Southern; nothing seemed unique about our racial customs, our religious beliefs, our reliance on King Cotton, our politics or pride. My birthplace was Greenville, a resolutely Southern place that held to Mississippi Delta tradition as if it were the Hope Diamond. Built against a levee, Greenville served as a plantation capital and also happened to be home to a literary circle that produced David Cohn, Shelby Foote, the newspaper editor Hodding Carter, the poet William Alexander Percy, and the nephew he raised, Walker Percy. The Percy home in Greenville, Walker Percy once said, was "a standard stopover for all manner of people who were trying to 'understand the South,' that perennial American avocation." The family lived in a mansion at the corner of Percy Street and South Broadway, and they symbolized a more attractive face of the Old South—an educated aristocracy practicing noblesse oblige and encouraging moderation in the teeth of a malignant strain of populism.

The Wilkies had little in common with this lifestyle; we represented the garden-variety white Southerners of the day, eluding poverty by a few steps yet satisfied with our standing. Both sides of my family had been part of the human tide that had cleared the swampy wilderness and settled the Deep South early in the nineteenth century, and our ancestors were similar to most of the people who had taken on the challenge of the wild region. The early Southern families had a pugnacious history, coupled with an inherent disregard of central authority, traits that were evident long before their descendants began objecting so strenuously to the dictates of the federal government in the twentieth century.

As best as my family can trace our origins, our ancestors left Scotland during the religious wars of the seventeenth century, refusing to pay fealty to either the English crown or Cromwell. I imagine that as Lowland guerrillas and partisans of the Scottish Kirk, they considered themselves soldiers in an army of resistance to the English. Others thought of them as merely malcontents. Writing of the cantankerous clans that spawned many Southern families, James G. Leyburn said that "every candid historian realizes that probably the majority of Scottish Presbyterians at the time were not of their persuasion, and that thousands regarded them as narrow-minded, unruly bigots who were not being 'persecuted' but were rightly being punished for causing a disturbance."

Unhappy in Scotland, these troublesome Celts crossed a narrow strait of the Irish Sea and landed unceremoniously in Ulster. A contemporary historian was scornful of the new arrivals. In his seventeenth-century chronicle of the Presbyterian Church in Ireland, the Reverend Andrew Stewart observed: "From Scotland came many, and from England not a few, yet from all of them generally the scum of both nations, who, from debt, or breaking and fleeing from justice, or justice in a land where there was nothing, or but little as yet, of the fear of God."

I gather we were not exactly blue-blood stock. But we were natural rebels.

Judging from accounts of the time, our ancestors thrived in their role as farmer-settlers, living and working on a vast "plantation" the British government established in Ulster in an effort to domesticate the wild Irish. But as Leyburn wrote in *The Scotch-Irish: A Social History*, efforts to dilute the Irish spirit with immigrants from elsewhere in the British Isles failed: "It almost always happened that these families before many years intermarried with the Irish, taking sometimes their language, often their customs, and generally their patriotism, and thus joined with the Irish in resistance to English domination."

So it was with my family. Several generations grew up in the northern counties of Ireland without any affinity for the British monarchy or the Anglican Church. When the New World beckoned, they joined a wave of emigrants setting out across the seas, years ahead of the potato famine. The *Belfast Newletter* of April 6, 1773, reported that it was "the very meanest of people that went off, mostly in the station of servants and such as had become obnoxious to their mother country." Perhaps they were drawn by the ideal of forming a democratic society in America, of joining another revolt against English rule. More likely, as talented settlers, they were attracted by the opportunity to open fresh land.

Arriving in the ports of Boston, Philadelphia, New Castle, and Charleston, these Ulster immigrants described themselves as Irish. They traveled in large, convivial groups made up of cousins and neighbors from the old country. Like the ancestors of so many Southern families, my forebears were among the pioneers who followed a wagon road into the Shenandoah Valley of Virginia, where they dwelled for a while, before moving to the Carolinas. There was a saying of immigrant patterns: "When the English moved to the New World, they founded towns and each built a brick house. When the Germans came to the colonies, they moved to good soil and each built a barn. And when the Scots-Irish moved to America, they all headed for the hills and each built a still."

When war broke out with England, the newcomers attracted more unflattering comment. A British officer, Patrick Ferguson, described the colonial upstarts in the Carolinas as "backwater men . . . a set of mongrels." One of my ancestors, Enoch Gilmer, had a patriot's role in the fight against Ferguson's forces at King's Mountain in 1780. According to *King's Mountain and Its Heroes*, written a hundred years ago by Lyman C. Draper, Gilmer was known as "the cunning scout . . . a stranger to fear." He spied on the Tories and determined the safest path for a charge by the American militia. His brother, William Gilmer, was wounded in the battle.

By the end of the American Revolution, my mother's ancestors, the Gilmers, were working their way westward with thousands of other Scots-Irish in a march that would eventually terminate near the banks of the Mississippi River.

During the 1830s, my father's family also arrived in Mississippi, claiming land that had been wrested from the Choctaw and Chickasaw by white authorities in the new state. My great-great-grandfather Sylvester Wilkie identified himself in the 1850 census of Yalobusha County as a "planter." He appeared to be overstating his position. His property was worth $1,000; planters usually owned land valued at no less than $10,000. But the early Southern settlers were not beholden to bureaucratic details.

In the decade prior to the Civil War, before he began his distinguished career as a landscape architect, Frederick Law Olmsted toured the South to write a series of dispatches for New York newspapers. The articles were later collected in a book, *The Cotton Kingdom*. For a Northeasterner who had attended Yale, Olmsted found a foreign country inside America, and he was generally appalled by what he saw.

The hotel where he stayed in Columbus, Georgia, was "disgustingly dirty; the table revolting; the waiters stupid, inattentive, and annoying." Long before H. L. Mencken turned his pen on the South, Olmsted offered trenchant commentary. In Georgia, "the operatives in the cotton-mills are said to be mainly 'Cracker girls' (poor whites from the country) who earn, in good times, by piece-work, from $8 to $12 a month . . . if temporarily thrown out of employment, great numbers of them are at once reduced to a state of destitution, and are dependent upon credit or charity for their daily food." When he found successful operations in the South, such as a railroad line running between Savannah and Macon, Olmsted noted with satisfaction that "it has been always, in a great degree, under the management of Northern men. . . ."

Olmsted also recounted long patches of dialogue in which he spoke precise English while his Southern subjects butchered the language. In one conversation aboard a steamboat between Mobile and New Orleans, Olmsted mentioned the possibility of freeing slaves. His Southern companion, who had emigrated from Ireland, responded:

"I wouldn't like to hev 'em freed, if they was gwine to hang round. They ought to get some country, and put 'em war they could be by themselves. It wouldn't do no good to free 'em, and let 'em hang round, because they is so monstrous lazy; if they hadn't got nobody to take keer on 'em, you see they wouldn't do nothin' but juss nat'rally laze round, and steal, and pilfer, and no man couldn't live, you see, war they was."

Olmsted obviously considered the South crude. But I'll bet his Southern hosts thought he was a fop.

The Southern pioneers gained renown as tough, ornery characters, contemptuous of authority and quick to resort to violence to settle a dispute. When the Civil War began, the Confederate ranks filled with Scots-Irishmen named Murphy, Dooley, Jackson, Riley, Regan, and Kelly, rosters that would bear no resemblance to the mythical American fighting units of World War II, made up of Grabowski, Antonelli, Rabinowicz, Demopoulos, and Smith.

My forefathers abandoned their push westward to put down roots in Mississippi before the Civil War. Along the way, I'm sorry to say, they acquired some slaves. My mother, a gentle, God-fearing woman, always insisted there were no slaves in our family. But my oldest son, Carter, who took an interest in our genealogy, discovered an 1860 slave schedule from Lafayette County, Mississippi, which shows that my mother's great-grandparents owned eighteen slaves, including nine children under the age of twelve. There is further proof of slaveholding in the handwritten will of another relative, Henry Gilmer, whose laconic catalog of human chattel is almost numbing:

"To my wife Mary Gilmer I give the following slaves. Lewis a man & Rosannah an old woman. To my son Robert Gilmer I give a Negro woman named Caroline. To my daughter Nancy G. Bryant I give a Negro girl named Silva 12 years old. To my daughter Mary Gilmer I give a Negro girl 20 years old named Margaret. To my son James E. Gilmer I give a Negro boy named George 17 years old. To my daughter Sarah Gilmer I give a Negro girl named Harriet 11 years old."

With this source of labor, my nineteenth-century relatives took over tracts of land in north Mississippi and became middle-class farmers. According to records, the Wilkies owned eleven slaves, who helped them operate a farm in the hills of Yalobusha County before the family resettled in the Delta, where the soil was more fertile.

My mother's ancestors tackled the terrain near Oxford. Though the land was not as rich as the Delta's, the Gilmers enjoyed greater prosperity than the Wilkies. They seemed better educated, too. In the will of Robert Gilmer, one of our Mississippi patriarchs, he divided his "library of reading books" among his heirs, indicating a level of literacy uncommon in the state at the time. Surveying the Oxford area for *The Industrial Resources, etc. of the Southern and Western States* in 1852, J. D. B. De Bow noted that "great attention has been given to schools and education, and here has been located the University of Mississippi; so amply endowed by the state, and now just going into operation under the auspices of some of the ablest professors from the eastern colleges. There is no overgrown wealth among them, and yet no squalid poverty; the people being generally comfortable, substantial, and independent farmers."

All that would be shattered by war.

In a paroxysm of anger set off by Abraham Lincoln's election and the prospect of losing regional autonomy and a workforce of slaves, virtually every able-bodied man in the South enlisted in the army of the Confederate States of America. For my family, it seemed merely an extension of their Scots-Irish nature to take part in yet another rebellion. The war record of my great-grandfather James Gilmer is easy to track because of an extensive history of his unit, the Lamar Rifles. Two weeks after the first shots were fired upon Fort Sumter, he left college to take up arms with more than one hundred men from the area. His brother, Robert, and cousin Billy Barr Gilmer enlisted in the Confederate army the same day.

"The members of this company," the history declares, "were some of them students of the University of Mississippi, and nearly all were sons of prosperous merchants, planters, and professional men, and of Revolutionary ancestors. They, as well as their fathers, believed absolutely in the doctrine of state sovereignty and the right to defend their homes and all constitutional rights against the aggressions of the Federal Union if it should become necessary."

James Gilmer was gone for four years. He fought in engagements at Seven Pines, Gaines's Farm, White Oak Swamp, Malvern Hill, Freeman's Ford, Thoroughfare Gap, the Second Battle of Manassas, Sharpsburg, Gettysburg, Falling Waters, Bristow Station, the Wilderness, Tolles Mill, Spotsylvania, and finally, Hanover Junction, where he was wounded and captured on June 1, 1864. He had to survive a Yankee prison with a high mortality rate at Elmira, New York, before he could come home.

As a measure of the lasting intimacy of the Southern experience, another member of the Lamar Rifles was a young man from Yalobusha County named Christopher C. Boyd. Severely wounded at Seven Pines, he returned to duty in time for Gettysburg, where he was captured. He rejoined the Lamar Rifles after an exchange of prisoners of war only to suffer another wound at Dobbs Ferry. More than 130 years later, Boyd's great-great-grandson Campbell McCool married my daughter, Leighton.

Christopher Boyd's brother, Addison, belonged to another Mississippi regiment. The devotion that these young volunteers attached to the Southern cause was reflected in a handwritten poem, "I Am a Rebel," Addison carried off to war in July 1861:

> I am a native of the South
> A youth yet young and small
> Honor and military fame
> Is not my wish at all
> But in the army of the South

I have a place to fill
And to the war I soon will go
A Yankee's blood to spill.

Two summers later, Addison Boyd was killed during the battle of Port Hudson, Louisiana.

It is not possible to measure the impact of the war on the South. Secession turned the region into a separate country for only four years, but hostile emotions boiled much longer. Regional rivalries persist into the twenty-first century. Today, Southerners speak the national language, but they do so in an accent that instantly marks them as different. I don't believe it's an exaggeration to compare the American North and South to Germany and France. In both instances, citizens of two regions waged bloody war on each other before accepting a form of union; their borders are peaceful now, but there are lingering animosities and suspicions.

Even in defeat, the Civil War is more important to Southern history than the invention of the mechanical cotton picker, more sacred than Sunday Communion. I know of no land where a Lost Cause is celebrated as fiercely, where scholars still debate Beauregard's tactics at Shiloh, where myths have been allowed to grow into heroic truths.

During my own lifetime, some towns in Mississippi refused to celebrate the Fourth of July, for it was on that day in 1863 that the Confederacy sustained epic defeats on two fronts. After a long siege, Vicksburg fell to Union forces, opening the Mississippi River to Yankee traffic. At the same hour, a thousand miles away, General Robert E. Lee's army was beaten into retreat on the plains of Gettysburg.

When the conflict was over, thousands of released war prisoners and bedraggled Confederate soldiers limped back to begin rebuilding their society. Though the South had been plundered and shorn of slavery, Southern civilization was still based on agrarian values and belief in states' rights, and these traditions would be maintained. For the most part, the Civil War veterans did not return to Tara; they came home to small farms and primeval forests that would be felled for timber. Existence would be hard; nothing would be remotely romantic in the Deep South for the rest of the century. But somehow, the South endured.

* * *

Sylvester Wilkie, the self-styled planter, died shortly after the war. All of his possessions were sold to pay off creditors, according to probate records in the state archives at Jackson, leaving his widow and children penniless. They moved to the Delta.

My mother's ancestors, meanwhile, resumed life in Toccopola, a farming village southeast of Oxford. During Reconstruction, the men in the Gilmer family helped found the Lafayette Springs Democratic Club. I suspect the organization sponsored a bit of night-riding. According to a monograph published by the Mississippi Historical Society in 1911, members of the Democratic club were also officers in the Ku Klux Klan. The document recounts an incident near Toccopola after the conclusion of the war, when a "vicious" band of former slaves attacked the home of Sam Ragland, a plantation overseer and Klan member. Ragland's wife was killed; he was gravely wounded. "This affair aroused the citizens to blood heat and they soon found the guilty parties, and they were justly dealt with," wrote Julia Kendel, the historian. "For a long time it was dangerous to go fishing in the Yocona River, provided one had a horror of coming in contact with a human skeleton when alone; for it was no uncommon thing to see a fish-hook fastened on the bones of a dead negro."

Terrorism became a respectable practice among Southern whites; they gave a religious name—Redeemers—to their movement to overthrow the forces of Reconstruction and reclaim authority for themselves. The Democratic club was also a sociopolitical statement against the Republican administration and its federal army of occupation. The activity led to a long line of Yellow Dog Democrats in our family. Across the South, generations grew up resentful of the party of Lincoln, swearing they would vote for a yellow dog before a Republican.

For decades, the South remained a poor and wounded region. I have a distant memory of a farmhouse near Oxford with the side of one room covered in Confederate dollar bills. Eighty years after the end of the war, the script was good for nothing other than wallpaper, yet the cause was still revered. And as a youngster, I learned the expression "Save your Confederate money, boys, the South will rise again."

There were fault lines in Southern solidarity, however, and religion caused one of the most profound cleavages.

When the region was settled, many of the newcomers imported a

Calvinistic faith from northern Ireland, establishing Presbyterian outposts in the new territory. After building homes for themselves with native oak, cypress, and pine, citizens of these new communities would erect a church in thanksgiving. In settlements lacking a city hall, a hospital, or a fire station, the churches became centers for religious services as well as quilting bees, picnics, and town meetings.

Presbyterians were pervasive across the region. I had always thought the term *redneck*—a rural, intolerant fool—derived from the blisters burned into the necks of dirt farmers plowing with a rope and a mule. But the historian David Hackett Fischer found records from North Carolina in 1830 indicating that *redneck* was "a name bestowed upon the Presbyterians" and had been used as a slang expression for religious dissenters in England.

During the nineteenth century, however, many Scots-Irish settlers gave up their staid Presbyterianism and responded to the call of Baptists and Methodists. In *Southern Cross,* Christine Leigh Heyrman's study of how the Bible Belt was created, the author wrote: "Southern whites recognized in evangelicalism a stark alternative to the region's traditional culture based on conviviality and competition. Baptists and Methodists modeled their churches on the primitive Christian communities of the New Testament, fellowships knit together by emotional intimacy and spiritual equality, godly discipline and self-abasement." Later, Heyrman noted, the two evangelical denominations cleverly set aside egalitarianism to appeal to attitudes developing in the postwar South. The Baptists, and to a lesser extent, the Methodists, asserted the supremacy of males and the white race, and the two denominations soon supplanted the Presbyterians. In fact, the Southern Baptist Convention grew into such a bastion that it influenced Southern elections—and ultimately, national politics—into the twenty-first century.

When I was growing up, the Baptists held the state of Mississippi completely in their thrall. Successful politicians were usually Baptists, ensured of the support of the largest congregations. Candidates adopted the pulpit styles of their ministers, braying nostrums of states' rights and segregation as if it were holy writ. When the nation gave up on Prohibition with the repeal of the Eighteenth Amendment in 1933, the Baptists refused to blink. The Church and its political allies maintained prohibition in Mississippi until 1966, when the legislature finally gave counties the right of local option to sell liquor. To this day, there are still predominantly Baptist counties across the Deep South where the sale of alcoholic beverages is outlawed.

The Baptists maintained strong views on race, too. When it became clear in the 1960s that federal courts would no longer tolerate segregated public schools, Baptist churches offered sanctuaries to obdurate whites by setting up their own private schools, which became known as seg academies.

The Southern Baptists and conservative Methodists controlled the establishment in much of the Deep South. But in some areas of Appalachia, which extended from the mountains of West Virginia and Kentucky to the hills of northern Alabama and Mississippi, an even sterner denomination, the Church of Christ, became a force for righteousness, frowning not only upon demon rum, but also on dancing and musical instruments. Gamier Pentecostal faiths, such as the Holiness Church and the "foot-washing Baptists," operated like sideshows in the Southern ecclesiastical circus, their devout writhing in the aisles, speaking in tongues, and wrestling with poisonous snakes.

At the time of President Clinton's impeachment, novelist William Styron, a native of Virginia, suggested in *The New Yorker* that the affair had been inflamed by the religious attitudes in the South, "where a strain of Protestant fundamentalism is so maniacal that one of its archetypal zealots, Kenneth Starr, has been able to nearly dismantle the presidency because of a gawky and fumbling sexual dalliance." Starr, the Whitewater prosecutor, was the son of a Church of Christ minister and briefly attended Harding College—now Harding University—in Searcy, Arkansas, a Church of Christ school that served as a training ground for the far right.

A century before, surrounded by a sea of fundamentalism, the Gilmers of Toccopola, Mississippi, and members of a family named Black, who had arrived there from North Carolina after the Civil War, remained steadfast Presbyterians. The union of those two families produced my mother, Lyda Black, and her younger brother, Scott. Like their neighbors, they lived on a small farm and suffered its perils.

When I was a child, I heard our own version of Grimm's tales. One time my uncle, as a small boy, ventured into a hog lot to play with a litter of newborn pigs. The sow, defending her offspring, attacked with astonishing ferocity. Before Scott could be rescued, the sow gnawed a deep wound behind his ear. Although he would grow up to play football at Ole Miss,

Uncle Scott had a hearing loss for the rest of his life. I was also told of the Christmas Eve the family homestead burned to the ground. Mother remembered only one item that had been saved, a red wagon for Scott, purchased with pennies saved in a jar, ordered from a mail-order catalog and hidden outside the house for a Christmas-morning surprise.

After the fire, the Blacks loaded a mule-drawn wagon and rode twenty miles—a trip that must have taken more than a day—into Oxford. The Lafayette County seat offered promise because it served as a north-Mississippi market and home of the state's only university. My grandfather Bob Black gave up farming for law enforcement. He became a town marshal, moving his family into living quarters in the jail. Once he was back on his feet, my grandfather bought for $1,800 a two-story frame house on Van Buren Avenue, two blocks off the courthouse square immortalized by William Faulkner.

Faulkner, of course, evoked that period brillantly in the town he renamed Jefferson and the county he called Yoknapatawpha. He was several years older than my mother, but Oxford was so small that all the white residents knew one another. She remembered him as "Bill" Faulkner, a curious fellow who had returned to Oxford from World War I with British airs and false claims of wounds he had never suffered. He inserted a *u* in his spelling of the Falkner family name, dressed in tweeds and a bowler, and carried a walking cane. Townspeople branded him Count No Count. But, God, could he write. My mother had a schoolmate who would approach Faulkner on the sidewalks of Oxford and taunt him for his pretensions. When he wrote *Sanctuary* in 1929, Faulkner named the madam of a Memphis whorehouse after his tormentor, my mother's friend Reba.

My father's family was doomed by early death and suicide, and I never learned a great deal about the Wilkies. Before he died at the age of thirty-five, Grandfather Edgar Wilkie lived with his wife and their three children in the town of Crenshaw on the eastern edge of the Mississippi Delta. He died of influenza and pneumonia in 1918. Four years earlier, his brother, Alvin Wilkie, also died in Crenshaw. Alvin was only twenty-seven. His death certificate attributes the cause to "injury by being run over with wagon."

My own memories of Crenshaw are as bleak as Dickens's darkest passages. It was a company town founded by the Crenshaws, though most members of that family had been wise enough to decamp by the time I began to visit my grandmother. During cotton season, the local gin's exhaust enveloped the town in a gray haze; a stench from sewage in open ditches lasted year-round. My fears of the place were compounded by cottonmouth moccasins that slithered from the Coldwater River bottom only to be mashed flat on the blacktop by passing cars.

My grandmother Carrie—I called her Mamaw—kept a henhouse in her backyard, a block from Crenshaw's business district, which consisted of a row of stores on one side of a county road. To celebrate my arrival, she always served fried chicken, a meal preceded by a grotesque scene in which she would scoop up one of her birds and twirl it by its neck until the head snapped from the body. The decapitated chicken, expending the last of its nerves, would perform a macabre dance before collapsing in a pool of its own blood.

Four years after the great flood of 1927, when the Mississippi River broke through levees and covered much of the Delta, my mother, a fresh graduate of the University of Mississippi, came to Crenshaw to teach. By this time, the flood disaster had given way to the Great Depression, which gripped the region just as severely. She met my father, they married, and I hope they were happy for a while. Shortly after my birth, the Southern economy revived a bit. Thousands of new jobs were created as the country geared up for World War II. My parents followed the work like migratory birds. When I consider a list of places where we lived in those years—Greenville, Memphis, Knoxville, Oak Ridge, El Paso, Oxford, and a small town in west Tennessee that has been lost by my memory—the itinerary of my early childhood looks like a fugitive's flight. But our life was always grounded in the South.

In east Tennessee, my mother held a clerical job in the defense industry; after Hiroshima, she was stunned to realize that she had worked in the plant that helped build the bomb. Because of security arrangements and the caution used with chemicals at Oak Ridge, she thought the project involved poison gas. We lived in a trailer in the makeshift city that had been thrown up almost overnight in the Smoky Mountains to service the secret program. We walked on sidewalks made of boards and took showers in a community bathhouse. Later, Daddy and Mother were rewarded with a tiny prefabricated house on a hillside. I remember little else about Oak Ridge, mostly fog and mud and a letter from Santa Claus, mailed from Knoxville at Christmas in 1943 by radio station WNOX. "Dear Little Friend," began the communiqué to children in the area, "Uncle Sam is using a lot of the things I make toys with, so this year there are many toys

I've had to leave out. So if you miss something you've wanted awfully hard, just remember I haven't as many helpers and toy-metals as I used to have."

As I grew older, I began to recognize a world outside the South where enemies lurked. During the war, they were personified by Hitler, Tojo, and Mussolini. Germans and Japanese were denigrated as "Krauts" and "Japs" in newspapers, films, and radio programs. But they became joined, in my consciousness, with another, more ancient, enemy: Yankees. Even as we battled overseas, I was gradually informed of a foe within our own country. The Yankees had beaten us in an earlier war, looted our fortunes, and imposed a dictatorial reign over the region by a bunch of half-wits until order could be restored after Reconstruction. Most of the South's hardships and indignities were blamed on Yankees, and no nouns were more vile than the names—brimming with onomatopoeia—given to their Reconstruction-era agents and collaborators, the carpetbaggers and the scalawags.

This was not something taught in my home, but acquired by osmosis. To my unsophisticated mind, Yankees meant anyone who lived north of Virginia; there was no distinction between real Yankees—the Protestants of New England who specialized in commerce—and others living outside Dixie. Yankees included the Irish cops of Boston, the Jewish diamond merchants of New York, the Latvian steelworkers of Cleveland, and the Italian bakers of Chicago. All Northerners were Yankees, and all Yankees were aliens, a threat to the Southern way of life.

I don't remember my father inveighing against Yankees, though I heard plenty of invective from his brother. Uncle Jimmy always used *goddamn* to precede the term; the "goddamn Yankees" were foisting regulations on us, ruining our schools, weakening our armed forces with integration, and trying to wipe out free enterprise. In the eyes of my uncle and others, the federal government was synonymous with Yankees.

Daddy seemed more easygoing. My recollections of him are reinforced by old photographs. In a Wilkie family picture, circa 1915, he is the child with a mischievous expression. An album contains later pictures of Curtis Carter Wilkie Sr. as an adult, dressed for business in a starched white shirt, tie, and vest, an average-size fellow with wavy, dark hair and an easy smile; his facial lines are softened by cheeks rounded with a trace of baby fat, as though he would always be young. During our days in Oak Ridge, I remember he tried to comfort me, his namesake and only child, during asthma

attacks when my breathing was labored. When he could borrow a car—
there were few autos in wartime and gasoline was rationed—he took me on
outings in search of ice cream, another scarce commodity. At home, he was
a benign presence, though it eventually became evident that Daddy had, as
my mother described it, "a drinking problem." When he held a job, he
worked as a bookkeeper, a term used for accountants who had no college
degree. Sometimes he would vanish from our little household, then materialize days later like a friendly ghost.

When I was four, my mother left him and took me to El Paso, ostensibly
to live in a dry climate to relieve my asthma. She became a schoolteacher
again; it was her calling. She looked like a teacher, wearing modest dresses
and braiding her long, black hair in coils around her head. She did not
drink or smoke or curse; when she was displeased with me, she would compress her lips into a thin line instead of shouting. She was a firm disciplinar-
ian and taught me the joys of learning. I was able to read children's books
and to recite all of Clement Moore's wonderful poem "The Night Before
Christmas" before I was five.

Then the war was over, and my parents reunited briefly on a plantation
near Memphis where my father kept the business books. We lived in a
drafty farmhouse; several of the rooms were empty because we had little
furniture. I was given a bird dog I named Pancho, drawing on my experience in El Paso. Within a few weeks, Grandfather Bob Black came to collect my mother and me. I remember Pancho chasing the car as we drove
away. We were leaving my dog and my father forever.

For an interval, my mother and I lived at the home of my grandfather
and stepgrandmother on Van Buren Avenue in Oxford. Then Mother was
hired to teach the fourth grade in Sardis, a Panola County town where the
hills begin to fall away into the Delta, halfway between Oxford and Crenshaw. It was the autumn of 1946. I entered the first grade, and from this
time my memories of race and class in the South grow more vivid.

Although Sardis's population was less than two thousand, it lay within the
sphere of Memphis, fifty miles to the north. In the rush of postwar activity,
with returning veterans and relative prosperity, there were no vacant apartments in the town, so the Ballentines, leaders of the Sardis school board,
felt obliged to take in my mother and me.

All towns, even those without a pronounced class structure, have at
least one prominent family, such as the Percys in Greenville; in Sardis, the

burghers were Bob and Ruth Ballentine. Mr. Ballentine, I would realize years later, had gone to Princeton with F. Scott Fitzgerald. Ruth was Zelda's contemporary; they had grown up in Montgomery and both gone away to Vassar. Despite their Fitzgerald connections, the Ballentines never flaunted any Roaring Twenties flair. They lived quietly, with two children a bit older than me, in a Victorian mansion, cooled with ceiling fans and framed with wide covered porches. Their home had an extensive library; Mrs. Ballentine reviewed books for a Memphis newspaper. Sheep grazed in a meadow beside the house, and in the early evenings the Ballentines gathered for cocktails—lemonade for the children—in the garden. They seemed content with the small-town setting, though I believe they could have fit in at the Algonquin roundtable. As major landowners in Panola County, they raised cotton as well as fresh produce, and in the summers the couple set up a roadstand on Highway 51 to sell tomatoes, plums, apples, and pears to tourists, who probably thought the Ballentines were country bumpkins.

After we had stayed with the Ballentines for several weeks, my mother located an apartment in the rear of another stately old house several blocks away. We moved, and shortly afterward, fire began to show up in my nightmares.

Although Sardis enforced segregation, the housing pattern of the town was a jumble of fine turn-of-the-century homes set near unsightly shacks where colored people lived. We passed their spare, unpainted cabins walking to school, but had little exchange with the occupants. We carried on our lives as though we inhabited different planets. Along with reading and writing, I learned the social conventions of the South. Whites enjoyed a higher station; we were not expected to lower ourselves to the level of our poorer neighbors. We were discouraged from playing with Negro children or visiting their homes, which were said to be filthy and unkempt—even though the women from these households often worked as servants, cleaning the homes of affluent whites. While whites were supposedly superior, we were not to exercise our advantage in insulting ways. If one had to deal with Negroes, we were to treat them evenly, as one might handle a valuable animal. Those who abused colored people and openly called them niggers were considered a subspecies, a class known as poor white trash.

One cloudless morning, a commotion interrupted the peace of our neighborhood. I could hear the beating of flames and see an angry orange flame against the blue sky. One of the shacks had caught fire. The little building was consumed within minutes, its corrugated-tin roof collapsed onto a heap of charred ruins. An infant, trapped inside, perished. As white neighbors milled around the scene, there seemed to be concern but no sense of great tragedy. The victim, said one of the neighbors, was "just a little colored baby."

In the spring of 1947, there was a final attempt at reconciliation between my mother and father. He had been working again in Greenville, living in a hotel. Daddy had shown up in the night a couple of times in Sardis, explaining that he had spent his last dollars for the taxi ride or claiming his money had spilled from a hole in his pocket. Mother seemed exasperated, but agreed to a family caucus on a Saturday in Memphis.

The setting was a café off Front, the street where dozens of cotton brokers had offices overlooking the river, but the scene could have come from an O'Neill drama. My mother brought me dressed in a miniature military jacket fashioned from the olive-drab uniform my uncle wore in the army. My father was accompanied by Uncle Jimmy as well as my aunt Virginia. We sat in a booth that smelled of stale beer, under a canopy of cigarette smoke. Mother disapproved of alcohol and tobacco and had little to say. Not only did efforts to reach an agreement between my mother and my father fail, an argument broke out between my father and my uncle, with my aunt offering shrill asides. Disgusted, my mother took me outside. The men followed, still quarreling. Daddy lurched into the street, and a passing car narrowly missed him. Mother led me away from the spectacle. But as we turned the corner toward Main Street, I looked back for a glimpse of my father. I had a childish premonition I would not see him again.

Several nights later, we were awakened by the ringing of our landlady's telephone. My mother was summoned; I drifted back to sleep. In the morning, we dressed and went off to school as usual, but before noon Mother appeared at my classroom and took me home. In the little bedroom we shared, she sat me down for a serious talk. The call in the night, she explained, had come from Greenville, where my father had been severely burned after falling asleep smoking in bed. She had received more calls at school that morning as his condition had worsened. The last call, she said, had informed her that my father was dead.

His body was brought to my grandmother's home in Crenshaw, where I saw firsthand the funeral rituals of the rural South. My grandmother keened with the grief handed down from her ancestors in Ireland. Her tiny house was overrun with weeping friends and relatives, bringing so many covered dishes, hams and chickens, sweet-potato casseroles and vegetable salads, that the icebox could not hold all the food. An open casket overwhelmed the living room. I rejected the sight of my father. His hair had been dark; the dead man had red hair. My mother explained it had been singed by fire.

There was no Presbyterian church in Crenshaw, so the services took place in a Baptist church. The Wilkie family sat in the front row, my mother stoic, the others stricken. Mamaw trembled, and I thought she might collapse. Aunt Virginia threw herself upon the coffin, shrieking for "Little Brother." Married but childless, she would eventually poison herself with liquor and barbiturates. Uncle Jimmy wept quietly in our pew. Years later, when I was an unhappy teenager, he would be very good to me, taking me to countless sporting events in Memphis. But he, too, would kill himself. He used a pistol, leaving me the last in our line of Wilkies.

It seemed that we were rehearsing for these tragedies on the day we buried my father. Punctuated by shouts of "Amen!" and "Praise God!" from the congregation, the preacher delivered a fevered eulogy, describing my father as a lost lamb. The choir, a group of working-class men and women, their faces scrubbed and their white cotton shirts starched, sang several hymns. One was the fundamentalist standard "When the Roll Is Called Up Yonder." After each verse, men with deep bass voices chorused, "When the roll is called up yonder, I'll be there." I wondered if my father's troubled life, ended nine days before his thirty-fifth birthday, would qualify him for entrance "up yonder." After he was put to rest in Longtown Cemetery, on a slope of the first hill rising out of the Delta, I noticed buzzards circling a nearby field. I asked my mother if they were after him. She managed a smile and assured me, "No, Son, they're not after your daddy."

CHAPTER 3

"We are the rednecks!"

★ ★ ★ ★ ★

Fifty years ago, the tracks of the Illinois Central Railroad and U.S. Highway 51 ran on a parallel course from Memphis to New Orleans, dividing Mississippi like a plumb line. Dozens of towns had grown up along the route before the Civil War, and tens of thousands of blacks, lured by the promise of a better life in Chicago, used the same path to flee the state in the twentieth century.

Northbound trains rolling out of New Orleans passed through miles of imposing swamp and communities with the lyrical names of Pass Manchac, Ponchatoula, and Tangipahoa before crossing into Mississippi and a strand of settlements at Osyka, Chatawa, and Magnolia. Just north of McComb, home for many railroad conductors and engineers, lay a point said to have the highest elevation on the line between New Orleans and Jackson: a little town called Summit, elevation 420 feet.

The rhythms of the South throbbed in places like Summit. In Southern cities, an air of hurried commerce diluted the essence, but rural towns retained the regional character and exuded a Caribbean languor. Without a dominant patrician class, the small communities were generally divided by race and church, though the people who lived in town and tended to have better educations looked down on those who dwelled farther out in the country. Conservative dogma was worshiped as ardently as the Christian faith, yet a collective spirit, almost utopian in its emphasis on good neighborly conduct and polite manners, existed in these places.

Summit thrived as a railroad town, with a couple of side tracks usually filled with freight cars picking up pulpwood and cotton produced in the area. The Illinois Central line bisected Summit; so did Highway 51, which was built to follow the railroad's trail through the state. Between the tracks and the highway, a distance one block long, lay "downtown"—a row of businesses on both sides of Robb Street: two drugstores, a barbershop, a mercantile store, a couple of small groceries, several ready-to-wear shops, a hardware store, a five-and-dime, the Progressive Bank, Jones Meat Market, Miss Geneva Lotterhos' Tea Room, and the Two Sisters Café.

Two blocks west, Robb Street dipped into a hollow known as the Bottom, a separate commercial area that served Summit's Negro neighborhood. It contained a knot of frame buildings housing a funeral home, a pool hall, and several cafés offering more beer than food. The colored people traded in the white-owned stores, but since they were not welcome at the white restaurants, they congregated in the Bottom, and on Saturday nights the scene pulsated with the sound of the blues and the peal of laughter. Though the Bottom looked livelier than downtown, white people rarely ventured there. The place seemed as mysterious as Conrad's "Heart of Darkness."

Summit had a single traffic light to regulate the flow of cars and trucks along Highway 51, the main north-south artery in the state. At the Robb Street crossing, the IC tracks were guarded by caution lights, a bell, and rickety wooden arms that descended with each procession of freights, local passenger trains, and cannonballing expresses. The *City of New Orleans* and its luxurious sister, an overnight Pullman called the *Panama Limited*, barreled through town twice a day. These great "through trains" never bothered to stop in Summit unless they plowed into automobiles blundering onto the tracks. Accidents happened, and the squeal of brakes and ripping metal would cut through the town like a clap of thunder during a summer storm.

From the window of a train, blowing past in a wink, the place looked no different from any other town along the way. But Summit's population was full of eccentrics, artists, romantics, more than its share of closet alcoholics, as well as a bona fide village idiot, and it seemed to me enchanted when my mother and I moved there in 1947. To be more precise, we moved to the campus of Southwest Mississippi Junior College, a mile outside town. The president of the school, a family friend with origins in Toccopola, had responded to my mother's widowed plight by offering her a multiple job as dean of women, registrar, and psychology teacher. The arrangement provided us a two-room furnished apartment with a private bath in the girls' dormitory.

I suppose I could paint a picture of deprivation. The rural South was beset with poverty and served as material for humorous punch lines. "Little Moron" jokes, for instance, played on ignorance in the Southern backwater. (Why did the Little Moron cut his outhouse in two? Because he heard his half-ass relatives were coming to visit.) We were piss poor. Mother and I took our meals in the school cafeteria, in the same building as the dormitory. At lunch on the Sabbath we were given a brown bag with an apple and a sandwich for Sunday dinner so the staff, a group of pleasant black women, could take the evening off. At least we never went hungry, which could not be said for everyone in the area. Our entertainment center consisted of a radio that broadcast mostly static; the McComb station shut down at dark, and signals from New Orleans rose and fell like waves.

In spite of the spare times, my recollections are invariably happy. As an only child, I suddenly gained a hundred big sisters in the dormitory and a host of other new friends. They spoiled me, the little boy who had lost his father. When I was hospitalized for asthma, the SMJC coach brought the great Ole Miss quarterback Charlie Conerly to cheer me; I'm told I croaked, "Who's Charlie Conerly?" Jerry Clower, a good-natured country boy who went on to become a Grand Ole Opry humorist, played center on the junior-college football team and practiced for his future profession by regaling the campus children with yarns. The faculty offspring served as my playmates, and we converted the lawn outside the cafeteria into an under-size football field. On trips into town, I marveled at the lush array of merchandise at the T.W.L., Summit's five-and-dime store. Batches of rubber bands and boxes of paper clips—products that had been unavailable during the war—could be purchased for pennies.

The junior college was part of a state-supported system for young people who either lacked the money or didn't have the desire to attend a four-year school. The student body was all white, of course, and drawn from several counties in the area. With a few notable exceptions. Every year, a youngster or two from Central America would show up, like rare flowers, on registration day. The story was always the same. Their parents, rich by the standards of Honduras or Guatemala, wanted an American education for their children, so they packed their sons and daughters off to south Mississippi after hearing of this boarding school near New Orleans. Sometimes the students were young teenagers—ready for junior high school, not junior college. It was too much trouble to send them back, so Southwest took the younger kids in as boarders and enrolled them in school in Summit. Others fit in marvelously. A Latin beauty, Orfilia Castaneda from Tegucigalpa, was crowned SMJC homecoming queen in 1948. That was as close as we came to integration.

My best friends were three girls who lived on campus. Laura Magee's dad taught science while her mother ran the home economics department. Like me, Laura was pint-size, a budding artist with a strong streak of youthful cynicism. We stayed in trouble for dumping the contents of salt shakers into the cafeteria sugar bowls or shooting arrows through open windows into classrooms. Our partners in these escapades were Wilda and Frances George. The George girls had come to live in the dorm with their older sister, Hazel, an English teacher, following the death of their mother. The girls and I roamed the grounds of the school like an urban gang.

We made "movies"—spools of paper with our own illustrations—which we would unwind in the common room of the dorm, extracting admission fees from the students. Since I was asthmatic and tiny for my age, the girls carted me around campus inside a pasteboard carton, which we described as a "juke box." Students were expected to put a nickel in a slot cut in the side of the carton. Thus primed, I would bellow one of the selections written on the top: "Oh, Buttermilk Sky" or "My Blue Heaven." Though we were known as the "campus brats," we considered ourselves the intelligentsia of the Summit school district.

I had spent most of my life in small towns, but not until we moved to Summit did I learn about a class of Southern whites known as country people. I encountered them each morning on the school bus that began its journey in the marshes of the Bogue Chitto River at dawn. By the time the bus reached Southwest, most of the seats were already occupied with boys and girls of all ages, sniffling with runny noses. Some of them came from homes with parents who could neither read nor write. They used slop jars hidden behind curtains or huts in the backyard for toilets. In some cases, their houses lacked not only running water but electricity. The country children were recognizable because they wore clothes fashioned from flour sacks stamped with patterns; flour companies knew packaging would be recycled, so they used cloth material that could be turned into colorful shirts or dresses.

After the stop at Southwest to load the clique of campus kids, the bus made a diversion at a cotton gin halfway to town, turning down a gravel road into deeper rough. At a country store, the bus picked up a boy we branded "Hitler" because a shock of black hair fell across his forehead in the manner of the late German dictator. Next the bus stopped for a pair of brothers who lived in a house by a creek. In times of high water they emulated Tarzan, swinging across the swollen waters on a thick vine hanging from a tree in their front yard. At the farthermost house on the road, we were joined by an older boy whose father eventually struck oil and became a sugar daddy for the Ku Klux Klan. But years before his family hit pay dirt, the son fascinated the school-bus crowd with tales of snakes that curled into his family's icebox for a cool resting place.

Our schoolmates were so poor that life on the Southwest campus seemed privileged. But as the school bus bumped over the rural roads, we could look from our windows and see living conditions that appeared even grimmer.

Clusters of black children, all ages and sizes, waved tentatively at the passing bus from cabins with dirt yards studded with broken glass and cast-off tires. Their shacks were usually set on the perimeter of cotton fields. To brighten the surroundings, the families decorated their front porches and tree branches with blue-glass milk-of-magnesia bottles. In the backyards, heavy cast-iron pots, heated by wood fires, bubbled with laundry. Water was drawn from wells or scooped out of ditches. We were told they used the woods for toilets, like animals.

In early autumn, when the landscape looked as though it had been littered with popcorn, entire Negro families would take to the cotton fields, moving methodically between the rows, stuffing the lint into large sacks they dragged behind them. The colored schools closed during cotton season to provide additional manpower to bring in the crop. Every little bit helped, even the small amounts gathered by the children. Cotton pickers were paid by the pound, and the rate in those years was $1.50 per hundred pounds. To me, it seemed impossible to pick a hundred pounds, but adroit workers were said to be able to pick at least a couple of hundred pounds a day. The families subsisted largely on seasonal earnings. To supplement their income, we were warned, they stole.

The gap between black and white cultures was enormous, but a pecking order existed among the white children, too. At the school in Summit, which housed all twelve grades, those living within the town's corporate limits felt superior to the kids from the country. We campus brats, however, believed we were the smartest of all. Asserting our intelligence, we made derogatory comments on the school bus concerning the country kids' inability to spell *Mississippi* or to obtain proper haircuts. I later learned that many of those children had a bright, native intelligence not yet developed at school. But I found out quickly they had pride. They reacted to our derision with fists and fingernails. We had ferocious fights, slugging and clawing at each other. Occasionally, Johnnie Woodall, the one-legged school-bus driver and father of two of our combatants, would have to pull off the road to separate us.

In a gesture to insinuate me peacefully into Summit's student body, my mother planned a seventh-birthday party for me at school. But on the day of the event, a deputy sheriff flagged down the bus before we reached town and sent everyone back home. The great hurricane of 1947 was bearing down on the Gulf Coast—this was before the weather service gave names to the storms—and all of south Mississippi was taking cover. The hurricane tore into Gulfport and Biloxi with a fury, ripping piers, demolishing homes, destroying the seawall, and killing scores. We lived far enough inland to escape significant damage and merely lost electricity. As the winds lashed the tall pines, the junior-college community rode out the storm in candle-light in the cafeteria. The Deep South might be blessed by mild winters, but the region seemed cursed by hurricanes, tornadoes that darted across the horizon with little warning, and frightening thunderstorms that boiled out of the Gulf on summer afternoons.

With stolid regularity, my mother shepherded the George sisters and me to church every Sunday. We rode into town on the junior-college bus. Most passengers were deposited at the First Baptist Church, though a few got off at First Methodist. Our little group stayed on board until the last stop, at the Summit Presbyterian Church, on the far side of the railroad tracks and the highway.

The location was appropriate because the Presbyterian congregation seemed distinctive from the rest of Summit. While the Baptists had much larger numbers, I thought the Presbyterians had a certain class. Members of our church included men and women from the town's oldest families—artists, bankers, builders, and well-to-do merchants—and I believed our services were comported with more dignity than those of the Baptists. This I knew from personal observation. Our elementary-school classes were routinely pirated by Baptist teachers taking us on "field trips" to swell the crowds at Baptist revivals on weekday mornings. The Baptists seemed terrorized by sermons warning of eternal damnation. Presbyterians did not dwell on these subjects. We worshiped with Calvinistic coolness; our songs were calm dirges and our services lasted less than an hour. The Baptists lingered past noon. As we waited in the bus for the Baptists to be dismissed, we could hear the strident voice of their minister, appealing to his flock to repent or burn in the fires of hell.

I thought Baptists peculiar. To baptize new members, the minister dunked their heads underwater in a glassed pool behind the pulpit. They called the practice "immersion"; we nonbelievers referred to the pool as a "dipping vat" better suited for livestock.

In their own way, the Presbyterians of Summit seemed as smug as the campus brats. Our church was a white frame building that had aged gracefully since its erection in 1848. We had tradition. After Robert McNair, a New Orleans educator, had settled in Summit and organized a Civil War company to fight the Yankees, the Presbyterians of Summit had hosted a celebration on October 3, 1861. The McNair Rifles were departing on what was thought to be a noble expedition. Luke Ward Conerly, writing a history of Pike County in 1909, described local enthusiasm for the war:

"Put it thus over the entire South, where there were four millions of negro slaves, equal in number to the whites, what was there under these circumstances for the Southern people to expect? With twenty millions of white people in the Northern States turned to be their enemies, sending their murderous emissaries among these four million slaves to incite them to massacre the four million Southern whites at the mercy of the twenty million Northern whites and the four million negroes in their midst, what can be said against the South seceding and Southern manhood asserting itself for its own preservation?"

Six months after he led his men from Summit, Captain McNair was mortally wounded at Shiloh. Dying, he sent a final message home: "Tell my wife that God will protect her."

God remained a powerful force across the South into the next century. I imagined Him a stern, older white male, Christian in His choice of religion and segregationist in His philosophy. It was simple to rationalize segregation: if God had wanted us all to be equal and alike, He would not have created a white race and a black race. There were ample biblical citations. Dr. G. T. Gillespie, president of Belhaven College, a Presbyterian school in Jackson, invoked passages ranging from chapter 4 in Genesis, dealing with the mark on Cain, to chapter 9 in the Book of Ezra, which described sorrow among the Jewish people after men from their community took heathen wives. ("For they have taken some of their daughters to be wives for themselves and for their sons; so that the holy race has mixed itself with the peoples of the lands.") When I was around ten, Ruth Atkinson, an enlightened lady who later became a well-known artist, dared broach the subject of equal rights during a Sunday-school discussion with her young class. I was dismissive. "They," I said of American Negroes, "didn't fight in our Revolution, so they don't deserve all our rights." That was a notion I'd picked up at school and parroted. I had learned other concepts that were equally absurd, such as the popular idea that blacks were genetically inferior and put on earth to perform menial tasks.

In one of his novels, Salman Rushdie wrote that "children are the vessels into which adults pour their poison." During my childhood, we were exposed to the white-supremacist doctrines that generations followed in the South. The theories were quietly practiced in our churches and propounded vigorously in our classrooms.

All Mississippi schoolchildren were expected to take a course in state history, and the textbook we used was quite remarkable. Written by a professor at Mississippi Southern College* named Richard Aubry McLemore and his coauthor, Nannie Pitts McLemore, *Mississippi Through Four Centuries* had some interesting descriptions of slavery: "The life the Negro lived as a slave was much better than that which he lived in Africa. It was said that his condition would continue to improve more rapidly in slavery than as a free man."

With the coming of the Civil War, the McLemores wrote, the value of slaves "was thought to be two and one-half times the value of all the lands and other property" in the South. "The loss of this slave property would make the people poor and reduce the value of their lands." Moreover, the authors contended that Northerners "did not know anything about the conditions in the South. This ignorance often led them to make false statements about the treatment of slaves."

The textbook duly reported the South's defeat, then turned to Reconstruction: "In this chapter, you will see how the Republicans ran the state. Their extravagance and their willingness to place untrained people in important places made the conservative whites unite against them." No wonder Mississippi helped anchor the Democratic Solid South for nearly one hundred years.

The history book also reported that Republican Reconstruction forces had a "difficult problem" in their handling of the Negro. "The war had given

*Now the University of Southern Mississippi.

him his freedom, but he was not trained to use it. Many of the Negroes refused to work. Others were guilty of petty crimes, especially stealing." To deal with the new Negro, "a number of secret organizations grew up," the textbook noted with approval. "The most important was the Ku Klux Klan. . . . Its members wore a disguise of long white robes" and exploited the superstitions among the black population. "A Negro who had been giving trouble in a community might awake some night to find a ghost-clad figure standing by his bed. . . . If these attempts to frighten them did not change the Negroes, the Klansmen would resort to whippings and in extreme cases to killing. The organization helped the South at a difficult time."

In our second year at Southwest, my life changed irrevocably.

We arrived at church one Sunday to discover that a guest minister, appearing to audition for an open pulpit, would be speaking. His name was John Leighton Stuart Jr., and we were told that he had been born and raised in China, the son and grandson of Presbyterian missionaries. Despite the China connection, his family had a strong Southern background.*

The visitor had been educated in Virginia and counted the crafty Confederate general J. E. B. Stuart as a relative. We learned of a further touch of celebrity. The minister's father had recently been asked by President Truman to set aside his job as president of Yenching University, a Western-oriented school in the city that was then called Peking, to become U.S. ambassador to China. I was not sure what an ambassador did, but it sounded impressive. When the guest minister finally spoke, his opening words lacked south-Mississippi diction; they resonated, instead, with such foreign erudition that I snickered. Mother pinched me.

His sermon was short and concentrated on love. The elders liked his brevity. Studious and somewhat shy, the minister displayed a style that contrasted with that of the Baptist preacher across town, who always seemed to be calling down hailstorms and locust invasions upon Summit. So Mr. Stuart, as I came to call him, was hired and moved to our town. He was a bachelor, four years older than my mother. As part of his ministerial duties, he began making calls on his handful of parishioners on the junior-college campus.

*Ninety years after the Civil War, Presbyterians in America were still divided into two denominations. Yankees belonged to the Presbyterian Church, U.S.A.; ours was the Presbyterian Church, U.S., or United South.

My mother's young colleague Hazel George, who had been named "most intellectual" at Mississippi State College for Women,* recognized a kindred spirit in Mr. Stuart and urged my mother to take an interest in the new minister. He had a marvelous vocabulary. When faced with a reference to something unmentionable, such as an undergarment, he would call it a "je ne sais quoi." He also possessed a corny wit that ran to puns. Bald by the age of forty, he said he had only two hairs left, named Pete and Repeat. He offered a quiz for me: If Pete and Repeat were sitting on a fence, and Pete fell off, who would be left? I answered, and he began the riddle again. He had wide-ranging tastes that included paperback detective novels with slightly racy themes. He lent these books esteem by calling them "commentaries." Hazel addressed Mr. Stuart as "Your Ecclesiastical Dignity." He responded by naming his car, a white Kaiser built in the postwar boom, The Ecclesiastical Chariot. Sometimes he took his Southwest flock riding in it.

On New Year's Day, 1949, I went fishing in the lake at Southwest, using a cane pole, string, and a hook baited with earthworms. Somehow I caught a bass that looked big enough to feed the multitudes. Clearly my catch called for a special dinner. During the Christmas holidays the dormitories were closed to save heat, so my mother and I were housed—along with others who had no place to go—in the home economics building, where we cooked our own meals. I invited Mr. Stuart to join us. Mother was embarrassed and instructed me to consult her before issuing invitations in the future. But Cupid's mission was accomplished.

Six months later, my mother married Jack Stuart in a ceremony that filled the Presbyterian church. The local newspaper described it as "one of the season's most talked about weddings" and gushed over my mother's "brunette loveliness." Mother's family drove down from Oxford, but my new grandfather, who was to have officiated, was unable to attend. The Communists were closing in on victory in the civil war in China, and he was being held under virtual house arrest at the American embassy by forces commanded by Mao Tse-tung and Chou En-lai, the revolutionary leaders who had known him at Yenching University. I knew little about Communists. They were supposed to be agents of a godless empire that threatened the security of the United States as well as the social structure of the Deep South. With my grandfather playing an active part in opposition to them, it all sounded very exciting. Not until August was Grand-

*Now the Mississippi University for Women.

daddy Stuart finally able to leave China safely, in an American exodus that Mao celebrated in an essay titled "Farewell, Stuart Leighton." By that time, my mother and I were ensconced in the Presbyterian manse next door to the church.

Mother suggested that I stop calling my new stepfather "Mr. Stuart" and use a less formal name, such as "Papa Jack." I had addressed him as Mr. Stuart for more than a year, and Papa Jack sounded like the name of a candy bar. So I called him Mr. Stuart for another ten years, a cold and formal title for a man who became a good and loving father. I finally began calling him simply Pa. Yet from my first night in the manse, I became for the first time in my life part of a family with a real house and an automobile. Even better, living there gave me the sophistication of a campus brat and the luxury of being able to live in town.

In the early fifties, Summit seemed extraordinarily pastoral and secure. No one bothered to lock their doors. Neighbors knew one another; in fact, I soon came to recognize practically every white person in town. Walking along Robb Street toward the Fox Theater, where I spent Saturday afternoons watching a bill including cartoons, a weekly serial installment, a western, and a thriller featuring Charlie Chan, I enjoyed the panorama.

On market day, Saturday, Robb Street was clogged with visitors from the country as well as Negro residents. There was no formal designation, but colored people tended to favor the north side of the street, thronging the sidewalk outside the T.W.L. and the storefronts of Richmond's Dry Goods and Calcote's Grocery. Across the street, a crowd of white men would gather on benches in front of Schluter's Hardware and Fortenberry's Barber Shop to exchange stories and listen to radio broadcasts of major league baseball games. The group included a fellow of indeterminate age who bobbed his head and giggled erratically. He wore coveralls and a tattered hat. According to local legend, his wits had been dimmed by congenital syphilis. He was widely known as Weewoe.

A more august collection could usually be found down the street at Barnes Furniture Store. The proprietor, Billy Barnes, was one of the drollest men I ever met. Instead of relying on a repertory of jokes, he delivered running commentary on personalities in Summit. He maintained a deadpan expression and rarely laughed at his own lines. His use of words reflected the influence of his grandparents, who had come to America from Wales and Scotland, and he drew upon their language to name Summit's simpleton. Weewoe roughly translated as "little trouble." Billy Barnes made pithy observations about others in town, especially the Baptists. Because of his informality, kids addressed him as Mr. Billy, or simply Billy. He held court in an office in the back of the store, scandalizing the Baptists by openly sipping from a bottle of beer and delighting his listeners with his biting humor. His confederates included a sardonic bachelor, Jack Covington, the bank president who doubled as mayor, and Billy's brother-in-law, Frank Watkins, who owned the Fox Theater. I was glad to know they were all Presbyterians.

Our congregation was dominated by Scots-Irish, though a few families had Welsh, German, or Swiss ancestry. The Barnes library contained many books printed in Edinburgh or London and brought across the Atlantic by Billy's family in the middle of the nineteenth century. He liked to display his grandfather's Psalter, written in Welsh and given by his minister "as a mark of approbation for good conduct" on his departure for America in 1848.

Despite their Calvinist training, the elders of the Summit church did not practice piety. Quite often they took a break between Sunday school and the 11 A.M. church service to have a beer at Ben Dickerson's Texaco station around the corner.

Other interesting characters flourished in the town. Three women, all mothers of friends of mine, took up painting in middle age. After winning regional recognition, they became known as the Summit Trio. Outsiders assumed Summit to be an artists' colony.

Women were treated with deference; even the kibitzers at Barnes Furniture toned down their commentary in the presence of women. On the street, men tipped their hats when women passed. Women held a special place in Southern society, honored and protected. But they were not expected to aspire to public office or to attain professional position beyond schoolteacher or secretary.

Yet in an era when many women listed their occupation as "housewife," Summit harbored a few feminist pioneers who had no reluctance about expressing opinions. Mother belonged to the local garden club, like most of the town's matrons, but she also attended meetings of the Business & Professional Women's Club and the American Association of University Women, organizations that supported the area's first faint stirrings for fair salaries for women. The teachers, the artists, and the ladies who ran their own businesses were in the vanguard, but no one was as out front as Mary Cain.

A. J. Liebling once said, "Freedom of the press belongs to those who own one." In Summit, Mary Cain founded the local newspaper, the *Summit Sun*, and exercised her First Amendment rights energetically, championing every far-flung, right-wing screed from the evils of federal aid to education to the injustices of the U.S. Supreme Court.

She lived a block from our house, and her newspaper office was around the next corner, on Robb Street, in a building the *Sun* shared with a garage operated by her husband, John Cain, a mechanic. He was a meek man who seemed uninterested in worldly events, but his wife was a fiery personality, a stomping, shouting, ass-kicking woman whose editorials had the kick of a double-barrel shotgun.

"The Federal government," she wrote, "is like a giant octopus with its eight arms reaching into the private lives of the people and threatening their liberties and their welfare." Or: "Purge present welfare department rolls, repudiate further Federal aid and make sure that only absolutely destitute people are aided by the Public Welfare Department."

The rest of the *Sun*'s pages were more subdued. Local news stories had a wry quality, such as the time Mrs. E. C. Wagner "was severely shocked but otherwise unhurt when her car's front end was clipped off as with giant shears by the onrushing City of New Orleans." Advertisements extolled the efficiency of laxatives, and a rendering plant in McComb offered to "move DEAD Useless and Helpless Animals for Nothing but the Animal Itself." The *Sun* also featured a regular column of social notes, recording the comings and goings of the townfolks.

Though a firm segregationist, Mary Cain devoted space to news from the Negro community. Originally titled "With Our Colored Friends," the section was later given a standing headline: "The Weekly Mirror, a Supplement of The Summit Sun, edited by Willye Mae Ayres exclusively for our colored readers." White people did not ordinarily use courtesy titles, such as mister or miss, when referring to Negroes, but the *Sun* permitted such items as "Mr. Jesse L. Zachary of Detroit is visiting with his sister, Mrs. Beulah Pinkney, and other relatives."

Mary Cain had no children, but she recruited a generation of young people to work with her at the *Sun*, where she printed gratis the Summit school paper, *The Bulldog's Bark*. In the sixth grade, I began acting as a sports-writer, continuing a Presbyterian hegemony in the *Sun*'s sports department established by "Scoop" Atkinson before he went away to Tulane and con-tinued by Jack Wardlaw, whose family's move to Jackson left me with the job.* With some editorial license, I wrote of Summit's contests with other high schools. After the visiting Bulldogs began the second half of a football game fourteen points behind in Gloster, I reported: "The stop watch broke and according to many we had probably the shortest half in history."

The editor thought me a prodigy and encouraged me to call her "Aunt Mary," the name used by other *Sun* apprentices. I preferred "Miss Mary." We were not, after all, related. But I admired her warmth and generosity, and it soon became apparent she had a widespread following outside Summit among those who shared her view that the federal government represented a bloated abomination.

In 1951, she became the first woman to run for governor of Mississippi. God forgive me, but I delivered Mary Cain literature during that campaign. Excited that a neighbor was running for high public office, I pedaled my bicycle through the streets of Summit, distributing announcements of her speaking engagements and tracts containing her diatribes against Washing-ton. My mother and father were not so enthusiastic about her candidacy. She was rarely a topic for dinner-table conversation, and when her name came up, they seemed slightly amused. Nonetheless, they never discour-aged my first adventures in political activism.

Before television commercials became the favored medium for politi-cians, we had political rallies, known as speakings. Candidates for every office from constable to governor would appear at these events. Given a few minutes to sound off, each successive speaker would try to raise the temperature of the oratory.

My knowledge of Mississippi politics was minimal. I heard someone say that our campaigns attracted demagogues like fruit drew gnats. When I asked Pa for a definition of a demagogue, he said, "One who has nothing to say, and says it very loudly."

I had actually first heard of a demagogue in 1947, an odd word I remem-bered because my mother expressed delight at news of the death of Senator

---

*Both Atkinson and Wardlaw went on to long careers at the *Times-Picayune* of New Orleans.

Theodore G. Bilbo of Mississippi. In the midst of Mary Cain's gubernatorial campaign four years later, as my interest in politics grew, I asked Mother about her reaction to Bilbo's demise. She denied making any happy exclamation, though I remembered it vividly. We were standing on the lawn of my grandparents' home in Oxford, and it seemed so out of character for her to express jubiliation over someone's death. Even someone she referred to as a "disgusting demagogue."

A little history is necessary to understand my mother's attitude. Bilbo—the name could have been invented by Faulkner—emerged from the mists of Pearl River County early in the twentieth century, a racist and scoundrel who latched on to the burgeoning populist movement.

In the years after the Populist Party had been crushed in its incipiency in Mississippi, the warriors for the masses shifted their political affiliation to the fin de siècle Democratic Party. They also let racism pervert their principles regarding the downtrodden.

Their leader at the time was James K. Vardaman, editor of the *Greenwood Commonwealth* and twice failed as a nineteenth-century gubernatorial candidate. Vardaman had two enemies: the corporate interests—represented by the powerful railroads—and the powerless Negro. With his piercing eyes, long mane of graying hair, and preference for immaculate white suits, Vardaman was known as The Great White Chief. Indeed. In one speech, Vardaman described the Negro as "a lazy, lustful animal which no conceivable amount of training can transform into a tolerable citizen." In another, he averred that the white man "would be justified in slaughtering every Ethiop on earth to preserve unsullied the honor of one Caucasian home."

Vardaman was finally elected governor of Mississippi in 1903, setting off a protracted struggle for power between Vardaman's forces and the Bourbons of the state, an upper class personified by the Percy family in Greenville. Although Bilbo, as a young legislator, had been accused of taking a bribe to side with the Percys in one battle, he threw in with the Vardaman crowd by 1911, when Vardaman and LeRoy Percy were dueling for a U.S. Senate seat.

Bilbo orchestrated the constituency of poor farmers as skillfully as Jimmie Rodgers yodeled a hillbilly anthem. Speaking on Vardaman's behalf in Pike County, Bilbo had the crowd cheering: "We are the lowbrows! We are the rednecks! Hurrah for Vardaman!"

When the general agent of the New Orleans, Mobile & Chicago Railroad Company distributed a leaflet counterattacking Bilbo's assault on big corporations, Bilbo called his adversary "a cross between a mongrel and a cur, conceived in a nigger graveyard at midnight, suckled by a sow, and educated by a fool." The railroad agent took umbrage. When Bilbo, campaigning via train, came to a stop in Starkville, the agent boarded and demanded an apology. Bilbo refused. The agent began whacking him across the head with the butt of a pistol, pausing after each stroke to demand a retraction before resuming the beating when Bilbo refused.

Bilbo suffered a concussion, two black eyes, and a cut in his scalp that required ten stitches, and he wore the wounds as proudly as a battle scar. Beatings came naturally to him. Bilbo was once caned by a retired military officer in Yazoo City and later poked in the face by the Kingfish, Huey P. Long, during a disagreement off the floor of the U.S. Senate.

So outrageous were Bilbo's antics that even the Mississippi press seemed appalled. During the 1911 campaign, Bilbo, as a Vardaman surrogate, was drawn into a debate with Vardaman's opponent, the patrician LeRoy Percy. According to a journalist who covered the event, Bilbo's remarks were "on a par with his low, depraved nature, seasoned with coarse expressions, strained efforts at rude wit, saturated with profanity, ribald jests . . . and slanderous remarks about his superiors." When it was Percy's turn to speak, he turned to Bilbo and called him "a vile degenerate" as well as a "low-flung scullion who disgraces the form of man."

Nevertheless, Vardaman won the Senate seat, and later in the decade Bilbo was elected governor. The two men ruled the state in tandem until Vardaman lost credibility in bellicose Mississippi by favoring neutrality at the beginning of World War I. When Vardaman tried a comeback, he appeared to be crippled by mental illness. The *Jackson News* said of Vardaman's candidacy: "It would be just as sensible to go out to the Mississippi Insane Hospital and pick out one of the unfortunate inmates and adorn him with a senatorial toga."

Bilbo had his own problems. Prevented by law from serving successive terms as governor, Bilbo helped assure the election of a protégé, Lee Russell, only to see the new governor snared by scandal. First, there were reports that Russell would reciprocate Bilbo's support by naming Bilbo president of the Industrial Institute and College for Women in Columbus, a move that one critic predicted would convert the campus into a "red-light district." The appointment was put off. Then a capitol secretary claimed that Russell had seduced her, and she sued the new governor for breaching a promise to marry her.

Governor Russell became convinced that Bilbo was behind a plot to embarrass him and subpoenaed his onetime cohort to testify at the trial. Bilbo went into hiding. The unfortunate secretary sought Bilbo out at his home in south Mississippi. A. Wigfall Green gave an account of her visit in *The Man Bilbo*:

"Bilbo, not wishing to see her, hid in the cowshed behind a young heifer, which threatened to reveal his proximity by loud mooing. Some people felt sorry for the girl, some for the governor, and some for the ex-governor, but most felt sorry for the heifer. The girl went to a hotel and tried to take her life by slashing her wrists."

The secretary was eventually discredited by testimony at the trial. But when Bilbo failed to appear as a witness, he was convicted of contempt of court and sentenced to ten days in the Oxford jail. His meals were brought to him by obsequious followers, a group said to include the Ole Miss chancellor. Bilbo handled his incarceration with aplomb. In his journal, he wrote: "Both profane and sacred history contains the names of great men who have gone to jail." He compared himself to Martin Luther and Saint Paul. When freed, Bilbo declared his candidacy for another term as governor from the jailhouse steps.

Elected again, he held the governor's office at the time of Mississippi's most horrific lynching. A Negro convict named Charley Sheppard escaped from the state penitentiary at Parchman, in the Delta, after killing a prison official and kidnapping his daughter. Following Sheppard's capture on New Year's Eve, 1928, the prisoner was paraded through the Delta prior to being burned at the stake.

Green's book carries a brief report of the incident: "A crowd estimated in the thousands gathered that night at the place of the burning. The funeral pyre was saturated with gasoline. . . . Sheppard's mouth and nostrils were filled with clay to prevent inhalation of the fumes and immediate death. The legs and feet of the victim, laved with gasoline, burned and fell from the body as the flames roared. . . . One spectator cut off the man's ears and afterward put them on public exhibit."

When Bilbo was called upon to investigate, he said it would be impossible to prosecute those responsible because too many culprits were involved.

After the 1934 election, he ascended to the U.S. Senate, where he proposed the use of relief funds to transport 2 million American Negroes back to Africa and sponsored a bill to outlaw interracial marriages, which produced a "motley melee of miscegenated mongrels."

After Bilbo was reelected to a third term in 1946, the Senate denied him his seat. An investigation had turned up evidence of kickbacks and illicit work by contractors at Bilbo's "Dream House" in Poplarville. Bilbo had dolled up the exterior of his Dream House with massive columns from the old state capitol, pillars that he had purchased for one dollar each. Bilbo had also established a slush fund in a bank account he controlled in the name of the Juniper Grove Baptist Church. When questioned about it, Bilbo replied, "When it comes to being a Baptist, I'm as strong as horseradish."

The month before my mother and I moved to Summit, he died at the Dream House before his claim to the Senate seat could be resolved. The cause of death was cancer of the throat.

When we heard of his death, my mother shouted, "Hallelujah!"

Though some Mississippi voters were embarrassed by Bilbo, his spirit lurked in our politics, and the 1951 campaign offered a lot of Bilboian bombast. It was the first gubernatorial race for a country lawyer from Standing Pine named Ross Barnett. He ran as a moderate conservative and promised voters that "the principles and Christian ideals for which I stand I believe to be most wholesome and constructive." With foursquare conviction, he added, "These principles will be announced and discussed at the proper time."

Other candidates in the race were already fixtures on the Mississippi political circuit or would become ones.

Although Mississippi was technically a one-party state, the Democratic Party had become so bitterly divided that its two factions effectively served as rival parties. On one side, rural populists attached themselves to a lineage that included the most obstreperous racists, Vardaman and Bilbo, the late governor Paul B. Johnson, and our senior senator in Washington, James O. Eastland. The other wing represented the "moderates," a business-oriented faction led by our other U.S. senator, John Stennis. The moderates preferred to play down race and trumpet economic development. In 1951, the two poles of the state Democratic Party were represented in the gubernatorial fight by Paul Johnson Jr., the son of the former governor, and Hugh White, a courtly old fellow who had served as governor in the 1940s and boasted of his program to induce Northern industry by waiving taxes and offering free land to Yankee-owned factories.

More than governmental experience, the most important prerequisite for holding high office in Mississippi appeared to be a gift for public speaking. The male candidates excelled in the art, but Mary Cain was the most memorable of the bunch. An attractive woman, she combed her dark hair into two balls at the crest of her forehead; in silhouette she appeared to be wearing Mickey Mouse ears. Her voice carried the pitch of an evangelist as she railed at the federal government, at the indignities of wage and hour laws, and at the inequity of public housing. She endorsed segregation in an odd way with a story demonstrating the beauty of racial purity. She told of a white man who teased an ebony-skinned lad for being "the blackest boy I've ever seen." After pausing for laughter, Mary Cain continued her tale: "The boy looked up at the man, and with every tooth showing in that black face, he said, 'I thank you, sir, I thank you. My mother was a lady. She didn't fool with no white trash.'"

Mary Cain finished fifth in a field of eight in the Democratic primary, a respectable showing for a woman in Mississippi politics, and she refused to give up her campaign against the federal government.

She played on an unusual dichotomy among white Mississippians. Though many were grateful for the New Deal programs of President Franklin D. Roosevelt that had brought electricity and running water to the rural countryside and offered subsidies to farmers, they embraced at the same time the philosophy of their forebears. They hated central authority and believed the federal government wasted money on programs, especially those that seemed to be designed to help Negroes.

Mary Cain saw no good in the federal system and opposed "all New Deal socialism." She detested the Tennessee Valley Authority, which provided cheap power to much of the mid-South, and she lashed out at farm subsidies, unemployment compensation, the concept of socialized medicine, and aid for the aged and needy. While the rest of the population still professed to be Democrats, Mary Cain began using a quote from Abraham Lincoln to start each column: "Let us have faith that right makes might, and in that faith let us, to the end, dare to do our duty as we understand it."

Social Security became her bête noire; she considered the program a dagger jabbed into American democracy by Communists. As her own employer, she refused to deduct $41.32 from her salary for Social Security in 1951. She began receiving threatening letters from a Mr. Enochs at the Internal Revenue Service. She shared her correspondence with *Sun* readers and returned one notice with her response scrawled across the face of the IRS letter: "This is not income tax and you know it." When the IRS persisted, she wrote back, "Come get your turnip, Mr. Enochs, I am all you can 'take' and it's up to you."

She sold the *Sun* to her niece for one dollar, closed her bank account, relinquished her joint holdings with her husband, and announced that he was not responsible for her debts. She intended to prevent the IRS from securing the payment.

"I don't want the government to take care of my old age. I prefer to take care of myself," she declared to her readers. "I suppose I may expect the Gestapo."

In the fall of 1952, when General Dwight D. Eisenhower defeated Adlai Stevenson, the Democrat nominated to extend the Roosevelt-Truman years, the *Sun* headline crowed: "New Deal Is Killed, Ike to Be President." Mary Cain thought she had won her lonely war against Washington. Within a year, she felt betrayed by Ike. Federal agents arrived in Summit to padlock the doors of the *Summit Sun*. Undaunted, Mary Cain rose from a sickbed, found a hacksaw, marched around the corner to the *Sun* office, and cut through the padlock. The action earned her the nickname Hacksaw Mary and enhanced her standing among the far right.

By the time I became a teenager, Summit was best known as the home of Mary Cain.

CHAPTER 4

"This Communist edict"

★ ★ ★ ★ ★

Sunday broke the pace of our town. Church services took precedence over sporting events, and Robb Street grew as still as a tomb. In the afternoon, the community withdrew behind the curtained windows of the old Victorian homes, abiding by Protestant doctrine that dictated a day of rest. Loud noise and games were discouraged.

The discipline made me restless. Even as a youngster, I suffered from loss of faith. Maybe I had never had much of it to lose. It was hard to believe in a God who robbed a boy of his father; difficult to think that a just God could accept the miseries of the world. Like one of Mark Twain's youthful agnostics, I didn't really believe in God, but I was afraid not to. So I spent Sabbath mornings at church with my family, marking time until the evening lineup of radio programs.

Beginning at five o'clock with Gene Autry, a medley of cowboy shows, comedies, and mysteries paraded through our kitchen, where I sat on a daybed, entranced: *Our Miss Brooks, The Jack Benny Show, Amos 'n' Andy, The Bing Crosby Show, My Little Margie, Hallmark Hall of Fame, Edgar Bergen & Charlie McCarthy*. All of the half-hour programs came from perspectives quite foreign to south Mississippi, but none of the personalities seemed remote.

It never occurred to me, for example, that Jack Benny was Jewish, even though his routine as a tightwad who celebrated his thirty-ninth birthday every year came straight out of Jewish vaudevillian tradition.

I didn't make any distinctions between Jews and Christians at the time, though Summit had been home to several Jewish families who played a role in its founding. A nineteenth-century resident, Captain T. Gracey, recorded that "the first store building was that of Louis Alcus and Isaac

Scherck, his nephew, who were second to none in contributing to the building up of the town."

According to other histories of the area, Jewish peddlers—immigrants from Alsace, the Ukraine, and Belarus—followed the Scots-Irish into the American South, eventually turning their vocation as mobile traders into that of local merchants. *Jews in Early Mississippi,* a book that traces their movement, identifies the first Jew in Pike County as Samuel Isaacs, who received a license to peddle in 1848.

Settling down in these villages, the peddlers built stores and small syna-gogues. Though their religious practices were obviously different, the Jews were generally accepted into the communities. One history identifies fam-ilies named Hyman, Meyer, Jacobowsky, and Lichtenstein as early residents of Holmesville, the area's first village. When the route of the railroad was drawn, "J. D. Jacobowsky and Jacob Hart and the Lichtensteins removed to Summit," according to Luke Ward Conerly's book, *Pike County, Mississippi, 1798–1876.* As esteemed citizens, their departure was a blow to Holmesville. Only because Christian businessmen named Felder and Nicholson moved to fill their vacancy was Holmesville "spared the mortification of a premature death and ultimate extinction from the map of towns."

When the Summit Rifles joined the Sixteenth Mississippi Regiment at the start of the Civil War, its ranks were made up of men named O'Calla-han and Collins as well as Moyse, Hiller, and three Hart brothers named Pincus, Morris, and Nathan. Among the 128 privates who tramped off to war in the Summit Rifles, nineteen were Jews. The unit suffered heavy casualties—sixteen men killed in action, many others wounded—and six died of illness while they were in service. According to the history, Isaac Dick, "the color bearer of the 16th Mississippi," was severely wounded at Cold Harbor, "shot down in the charge made on the Pennsylvania Buck-tails who were routed and driven from the field."

The Jews of Summit shared with their gentile neighbors the glory that Southerners managed to take from that terrible, failed enterprise, and they returned home to become leaders in the little town. They organized Con-gregation Ohaveh Shalom (Lovers of Peace) in 1870 and prospered for a period. But a tornado destroyed the synagogue fifty years later, and by the time I was a boy, all but a couple of Jews had abandoned Summit for New Orleans. One of those who had left, according to local lore, was a man named Samuel Aronson, whose son invented the Ronson cigarette lighter. The vestiges of their community in Summit were a Jewish cemetery tucked into a glade of trees—it served as a spooky location for games of hide-and-seek—and Hyman Mercantile Store, which still occupied downtown store-front space when we moved there.

Sometimes, when a former resident died in New Orleans, the remains would be returned to Summit for burial in the cemetery. In lieu of a rabbi, my stepfather would be asked to read from the Old Testament at the services. Joe Schluter, who owned the hardware store and fancied himself the town wit, nicknamed him Rabbi Stuart.

I never thought of Jews as particularly different. They were, after all, white and represented a tiny element in our religious stew. Besides the Baptists, Methodists, and Presbyterians, Pike County had a small Episcopal population, and I was vaguely aware of others who were not Protestants: families with Italian surnames and crypto-Arabs known as Assyrians, whose forefathers had emigrated from Lebanon when the land was still part of Greater Syria. Many of them worshiped at St. Alphonsus Catholic Church in McComb.

Even though the colored people of Summit embraced their own Baptist or African-Methodist faiths with vigor, they remained greater strangers to me than the Catholics. Negroes rarely figured in my life—except on Sunday nights. The *Amos 'n' Andy* show was my favorite. Each week, I followed the exploits of the Kingfish, the conniving president of the Mystic Knights of the Sea Lodge; his slippery running mate, Andy; the Kingfish's nagging wife, Sapphire, and his officious mother-in-law, Mama; the sly lawyer, Algonquin J. Calhoun; and their mild-mannered friend, Amos, a taxi driver. The Kingfish and Andy were lovable charlatans, getting into deep trouble, then extricating themselves, with harmless guile, before the thirty-minute program ended. On rare occasions they were earnest, such as the Christmas show when the cast rallied to find a present for Amos's young child.

Above all else, the characters were strong and lively, and I related to *Amos 'n' Andy* more readily than to the white situation comedies. The radio show took me, for the first time, into the homes and hearts of colored people. Instead of thinking of a race of people underfoot, I visualized the Kingfish & Co. as ordinary human beings with the same longings, schemes, and anxieties as whites. After listening to the program for a couple of years, I was astonished to learn that the voices, rich with black patois, belonged to two white men who had created *Amos 'n' Andy*, Freeman Gosden and Charles Correll.

Amos 'n' Andy was made into a TV show in 1951, and black actors and actresses were found to play the parts. They were riotously funny. Nonetheless, the program was sacrificed to the high priests of the Politically Correct. Pilloried as a modern blackface minstrel, reruns of the show were drummed off the air. At first, I felt guilty that I might have been laughing at the expense of colored people. Then I grew annoyed at being deprived of characters I had come, as a child, to think of as friends.

Not until years later, reading Henry Louis Gates Jr.'s memoirs, *Colored People,* did I feel vindicated. "Everybody loved *Amos 'n' Andy*—I don't care what people say today," wrote Gates, chairman of the Department of Afro-American Studies at Harvard. "For colored people, the day they took Amos and Andy off the air was one of the saddest days. . . . What was special to us about Amos and Andy was that their world was all colored, just like ours. Of course, they had their colored judges and lawyers and doctors and nurses, which we could only dream about having, or becoming—and we did dream about those things."

Outside of radio, the most popular forms of entertainment for a boy in Summit were movies, athletic contests, and pranks. Sometimes we even found the Baptist revivals entertaining. Every few months, a guest evangelist would be invited to spend a week in town, preaching in the morning and again each night, exhorting the faithful to repent their sins and renew their zeal. Like raiders from a hostile tribe, a couple of my Presbyterian pals and I would creep into the balcony of the First Baptist Church, where our Baptist schoolmates preferred to sit, to watch the pageant playing out beneath us. The hymns were rousing and the sermons powerful. The traveling preachers swept their hair in pompadours in the manner of Billy Graham, the most popular evangelist of the day. They tried to match his speaking style, too, barking and strutting around the pulpit. Tears fell when they told the familiar story—an allegory I figured was bullshit—of the high school couple who had made love in a car and immediately got run over by a train, damned by their lust to eternal perdition.

A hush fell over the sanctuary when it came time for the congregation to take part in group confession. "Every head bowed, every eye closed," the evangelist would admonish, invoking secrecy over the proceedings. Assuming a lowered, hissing voice, as if the conversation were now confidential between himself and each listener, the minister continued, "I want each of you who has committed a sin in the past month—maybe you think it's only a little sin—but if you've violated one of the Ten Commandments, if you've told a fib, if you've taken money that wasn't yours, if you've caused grief to someone you love, I want you to raise your hand."

I bowed my head and cupped my face with my hands, but peeked through my fingers to take a census of the sinful. It was revealing. Practically everyone in the congregation held a hand above his head. And the scene got more interesting as the evangelist began singling out such sins as coveting thy neighbor's wife.

At the climax of the evening, the choir led the congregation in verse after verse of "Just As I Am." Emphasis was put on the closing lines of each stanza, "O lamb of God, I come, I come," as dozens of penitents, tears wetting their cheeks, marched down the aisle to be born again.

When I delivered an embellished report of one evening's events, Mother warned me not to ridicule other people's religions. But making sport of the Baptists in those days carried the legitimacy of rooting against the New York Yankees, a team that won the pennant every year.* The Baptists treated Summit the same way the Yankees ran roughshod over the American League. They lorded over our town as if all citizens were serfs in their church's kingdom. Not only did they drag entire classes from the public school to their weekday morning services, they inflicted Baptist ministers on our weekly assembly programs when most of us—Baptist kids included—preferred an itinerant magician named Bobo or a pep talk by a football star from the junior college.

With impunity, from a loudspeaker attached to their church steeple, the Baptists blared recorded hymns early in the mornings to awaken their brethren for the first service of the day, held before the stores opened. I could hear the music in my bedroom across town. Grady Biglane lived near the church, and he could hear it much better. It is fair to say that Grady was a skeptic. He ran a pool hall for a white clientele, where grizzled men in overalls drank beer and played dominoes while the younger set shot billiards. Once I had a paperback copy of Henry James's *The Turn of the Screw*—a short, easy read for a book report—lodged in my hip pocket while I bent over the pool table to study the shot confronting me. A country fellow spotted the title and expressed immediate interest. "Where'd you get that there fuck book?" he asked. The air in the pool hall was always blue

---

*Even Faulkner, raised an Episcopalian, had fun at the Baptists' expense. To explain unusual behavior, a Faulkner character had a simple answer: "They're just Baptists."

with smoke and profanity. In the midst of one Baptist revival, the proprietor took strong exception to having been awakened by "Rock of Ages" minutes after dawn. "Goddamnit," Grady snarled, pounding an empty beer bottle on the counter for emphasis, "if those fuckers don't stop that music, I'm going to get my fuckin' deer rifle and blow those fuckin' horns off the top of that fuckin' steeple."

Revenge was taken before Grady could strike. Late one Saturday night, someone broke into the church and cranked up a recording of "Red Hot Boogie" on the sound system. Full blast. The song, which had risqué lyrics, pierced the postmidnight silence like a shriek in the dark. On our side of town, the words were incomprehensible, the noise a low moan. But inside homes in the shadow of the Baptist church, babies quailed and men and women bolted from their beds in terror.

To the Baptists, "Red Hot Boogie" constituted sacrilege most foul. I thought it was the best trick ever; even my parents couldn't suppress a smile when we discussed the incident at breakfast. The next day, after school, several of my classmates gathered around a pinball machine at the Two Sisters Café—which my parents considered a more wholesome venue than Grady Biglane's pool hall—to talk about the caper at the church. Gordon Covington Jr., a prominent Robb Street merchant and Baptist layman, saw us giggling and stomped over to remonstrate. He was a figure of authority in town, even though he was known as Gordon Junior all his life. "You all can laugh all you want," Gordon Junior said, "but we've got the FBI on the case." We quieted down until he left the café, then burst into more snickering. We knew his claim about the FBI was specious; they were too busy tracking the Communists to investigate the case of the "Red Hot Boogie." Besides, anyone with half a brain knew Lew Barnes was responsible.

Lew had been my friend for years; in many ways he was my idol, a role model for every boy in Summit with unconventional spirit. Quick-witted, daring, and exuberant, Lew helped develop a code called "backwards talk" that local teenagers put into use. Backwards talk was so distinctive that even the urbane students in neighboring McComb adopted the style. In backwards talk, a deceitful person could be described as an "honest John" or "a fine, outstanding human being," with heavy inflection on the adjectives. A boring movie became "the most compelling film of our time"; a tasteless hamburger "the most delicious thing I ever ate." If Lew intended to ignore an instruction, he might say, "That's the first thing I'm going to do." It became a way of bewildering our teachers and parents.

Lew also had a knack for assigning unshakable nicknames. He dubbed the town marshal, Clarence Brown, "Lawman," then shortened the title to "Man Brown." For the rest of his career, Summit's only law enforcement officer was popularly known as Man Brown. Once Lew tied the bumper of Man Brown's car to a light pole, then arranged for a speeding auto—filled with unrecognizable teenagers from McComb—to zoom by. Man Brown, tethered, was unable to give chase.*

Sarcasm came naturally to Lew. His father was Billy Barnes, the irreverent merchant, and his mother, Halcyon, belonged to the artistic Summit Trio. Visiting the Barnes home, a fine two-story structure with a wide yard and a gazebo, was like stumbling onto the set of a Greenwich Village revue. While other families might be content to muse at their meals over the weather, the Barneses strived to top one another's witty remarks with ripostes even funnier. When Mr. Billy mentioned the name of a scabrous individual, Lew would resort to backwards talk, adding, "He's an honorable citizen," with emphasis on each syllable of the word *honorable*.

Lew was small and looked so impish that he became a natural suspect for any misdeed. Deft with cards—woe betide anyone who played him for money—he could also blast coins out of the air with his rifle. He once won an old-fashioned turkey shoot sponsored by a local club by hitting all the targets. For first prize, he was awarded a live gobbler. After a respectable interval, Lew sneaked the bird into the balcony of the Baptist church on a Saturday night. When the organist struck up the first notes the next morning, the frightened turkey flew thrashing over the heads of the congregation.

By junior high school, Lew had a devilish reputation; while his parents slept, he escaped curfew by crawling down the roof from his second-story bedroom to spearhead excursions into the night. I was flattered when he took me along to swipe watermelons from a farmer's field or to push a stray dog inside the home of the music teacher, "Nip" Cain, who kept a dozen cats.

*Several years later, in a college paper on my hometown, I wrote: "The law enforcement in Summit is the brunt of a great deal of ridicule. Even the mayor laughs about it. The town marshal is Clarence Brown, who is elected and has a salary of $175 a month. Brown recently purchased himself a blue policeman's uniform and is keeping his fingers crossed for re-election so he can get full wear. The official police car is Brown's 1948 Chevrolet, the oldest white-owned car in town."

One of the most popular writers of the day was Mickey Spillane, a purveyor of hard-bitten detective novels with covers featuring seminude women. Lew and I thought we could collaborate on a mystery that fit the genre. We chose a title, *Gutter Gal,* and Lew came up with the opening line: "The night was as black as a sack of assholes. . . ." Despite this inspired start, our writing project got no further.

Lew was three years older than me, not a great gap in a small town. Besides, we had the bond of being Presbyterians. We were in the same Sunday-school class, which he often threw into convulsions with one-liners. When our teacher wondered why Jesus delayed approaching the tomb of Lazarus, three days dead, Lew supplied the answer: "I suppose because he didn't want to smell him." Once, Lew led me on an expedition in search of a possum in the attic of our church, disrupting Sunday services as we scrabbled across the planks above the ceiling of the sanctuary. I would follow Lew anywhere.

After Lew was banished from the Fox Theater, Summit's only movie house, for misconduct, it became au courant to join the list of exiles. Following Lew's lead, my friend Fulton Beck and I targeted a country couple who always sat in a front row, smooching their way through the Saturday matinee. We thought the fellow's name, Joab, humorous, and serenaded him with cooing, singsong taunts: "Jo-Abbbb, Jo-Abbbb." He twisted in his seat, mumbling threats while trying to locate the voices in the darkness. After he turned his attention back to the screen, Fulton and I fired several crab apples at the back of Joab's head. He rose, cursing, shaking his fist, and upstaging the western movie. The manager, spying on his audience from a back seat, evicted Fulton and me. Instead of feeling punished, deprived of Summit's most reliable source of entertainment, we were gleeful to have attained Lew's status.

Lew's chief sidekick was his classmate William Paulk, who grew up on a farm outside town. William's face had the alert features of a predatory bird, and he dispelled forever my idea that country kids were intellectually inferior. He excelled in backwards talk and could match Lew, phrase for phrase, in ladling out disdain for town officials and instructors at school. The colloquies were more crackling than the repartee on Sunday-night radio, and even though I was reduced to a bit player in their company, Lew and William kept me laughing for years.

When I was in the eighth grade, an accident jarred us out of our foolishness for a while, a reminder that death could come swooping down on our world at any moment. It happened early on a Saturday evening, when Pa and I were picking up clothes at the dry cleaner's. The sound of bells at the Robb Street crossing and the mournful wails of the approaching City of New Orleans were so regular to life in Summit that I rarely heard the passing train. But at nightfall that day, no one could miss the dreadful noise of the train's collision with a car.

For a few seconds, stillness descended on the town. Then people came rushing out of stores. Pa and I hurried to the railroad tracks. In a scene lit by rotating red lights on the halted express, several men were already tearing at the doors of a mangled automobile to rescue those inside.

I recognized the car. It belonged to Mr. Paulk, William's father. He had been my Little League coach, and members of our team had often ridden with him to games. William's sister was trapped inside the car. Though gravely injured, she survived. Mr. Paulk died before he could be pulled from the wreckage.

Summit was a baseball town, and in the early 1950s, our high school team was one of the best in south Mississippi. Lew held down second base while William played third. I was the scorekeeper and occasionally used my position to rule ground balls penetrating our infield as errors rather than hits; my rulings enhanced the earned run average of Summit's star pitcher, a crew-cut country boy named Elmer Smith. Once, I conferred with Lew after an ankle-high liner eluded his grasp. Lew told me to consider it an error. My scorekeeping decision ensured another no-hitter for Elmer, but the big right-hander rarely needed my help. He had a fastball that sizzled on its way to the plate, and a rainbow curve that threw batters off balance.

We fought Jackson Central, the only white public high school in the state's biggest city, to the last out in a play-off for the south-Mississippi championship in 1952. Central drew its roster from a student body comprising hundreds; a graduating class in Summit might have twenty boys and girls. We met Jackson Central in the play-offs again the next year. Down 4–0 in the final inning, Summit rallied, scoring one run and filling the bases. In my account in the *Summit Sun*, I described the game's last moments:

"J. W. Beck blasted one over the right field fence to win the game as the crowd went wild. J.W. was mobbed at the plate by the whole Summit team. Elmer Smith then set down the defending champions to end the game. The hysterical Summit fans carried Smith off the field on their shoulders.".

While we savored our baseball victories, it never occurred to us that there might be outstanding players in Summit among the colored students. They were not out of sight; we could see them during recess, competing on a playground at the colored school on a hill a block from our own ball field. But the thought of them as teammates never registered.

My only contact with the colored boys took place under a basketball hoop nailed to the top of our garage at home. After school during basketball season, I would play in our driveway for hours, dribbling behind my back, practicing set shots, and participating in imaginary games between the leading college teams I followed on the radio. Kentucky versus St. Louis or Marquette versus Indiana. Sometimes I would be joined by two or three Negro kids my age, who approached adventurously when they passed my house and saw me playing alone.

We had gritty contests, with plenty of fouls and body contact. One of my opponents was a boy named Solomon. Though he walked with a slight limp, he could outjump me when we tussled for rebounds. At the end of our games, I would go inside to get my playmates glasses of water. We understood that Southern mores prevented blacks from entering white people's homes socially. Solomon and his friends drank the water, said thank you, and drifted down the street toward their own homes, as if they were dematerializing.

When Little League baseball, with organized teams, uniforms, and umpires, came to McComb, practically every white boy in Summit enrolled in the program. We played at night, under spotlights fixed on creosote poles, and drew hundreds of spectators. Hardly anyone owned a TV, so the ball games were among the few evening diversions in Pike County.

The black children did not have Little League. I never knew how they spent their summer nights.

Several years after Jackie Robinson broke the color barrier in major league baseball in 1947, race eventually crept into the consciousness of national Little League officials. In a decision made shortly after I had passed through the system, Little League headquarters decreed that teams should be desegregated. Rather than submit to integration, the people of Pike County disbanded the baseball organizations that had given us such pleasure. They reconstituted the sport in new all-white leagues called Dixie Youth Baseball, but the games seemed to lose their magic.

When I was a Little Leaguer, I was already following major league baseball. I knew about Robinson and his Brooklyn Dodger teammates Don Newcombe and Roy Campanella; I also kept up with the exploits of a young gazelle from Alabama, Willie Mays; the dark-skinned Cuban Minnie Minoso; the ageless Satchel Paige; and other Negro pioneers, Sam Jethroe, Larry Doby, and Luke Easter. Without any racial references, they were mentioned in the same breath as the great white players Ted Williams, Joe DiMaggio, Hank Sauer, Ralph Kiner, and Robin Roberts. I learned of their derring-do over WNOE, a New Orleans radio station. The announcer, Al Helfer, traveled daily, like the mythical Flying Dutchman, from Fenway Park in Boston to the Polo Grounds in New York to Philadelphia's Shibe Park, broadcasting the Mutual Radio Network's "Game of the Day" from a different stadium every afternoon.

Despite this eclectic menu of daily games, primarily from the East Coast, I grew up a fan of the St. Louis Cardinals, like most Southerners. The Cardinals represented the nearest major league team, and their games were broadcast almost every night over the Cardinals' network by virtually every radio station in Dixie that stayed on the air after twilight. If those signals were unreliable, we could tune in after dark to the "clear-channel" station from St. Louis, KMOX.

Since we lived hundreds of miles from St. Louis, our only chance to see the Cardinals and their stars, Stan Musial and Red Schoendienst, came each spring when the major league teams completed the Grapefruit League season by barnstorming north from Florida, playing exhibition games in several Southern cities. When the teams came to New Orleans, we cut classes; fathers gladly abetted our truancy, taking carloads of boys on a two-hour drive to see the big leaguers.

The games took place at Pelican Stadium, the home of the Pittsburgh Pirates' farm team in the Southern Association. This dilapidated, segregated ballpark seated a few thousand, with a small section set aside for colored people.

In the first week of April 1954, two teams destined to meet in the World Series that fall, the Cleveland Indians and Willie Mays's Giants, came to New Orleans and the scene took on the trappings of a spectacle by DeMille. When we arrived at Pelican Stadium's gate, we saw that we had been preceded by a cast of thousands. Hours before game time, colored fans lined the sidewalk for blocks along Tulane Avenue in anticipation of seeing the Indians' Doby and Easter, as well as Mays and the estimable Monte Irvin, who were in the Giants lineup.

We were able to buy tickets at the "whites only" window as soon as the ballpark opened. Seated behind third base during batting practice, we watched as the Negro section filled. Ushers compressed our group—along with other white fans—into better seats behind home plate, turning over the rest of the ordinarily "whites only" grandstand to the colored spectators. To sell more tickets, the Pelican Stadium staff channeled an overflow of Negro spectators onto the field, filling patches of grass between the grandstand and the foul lines. When that was still not enough, dozens were backed against the fences in fair territory. By game time, the crowd had doubled the park's capacity.

Balls knocked into the fans standing in the outfield were declared ground-rule doubles. When one of the players—I think it was Whitey Lockman of the Giants—hit a weak pop fly on the edge of the outfield grass, the crowd surged forward from center field, fighting to catch the ball as if it were a talisman dropping from the sky. They engulfed the second baseman, and the batter was awarded two bases—the shortest double I ever saw.

The throngs reacted to good plays with thunderous cheers, as if the World Series were at stake. In his account in the *Times-Picayune* the next day, sportswriter Bill Keefe reported that the game "was hard-fought, and because the many Negroes on both teams did well—some of them playing starring roles—the unprecedented crowd of about 5,000 Negroes to a 'white' game got a big kick out of it."

I, too, was impressed by their enthusiasm. After I got back to Summit, I lapsed into local idiom and said to my parents, "You should have seen those coons jumping up and down." Mother snatched me from the dinner table and marched me into the kitchen for a lecture. *Coons,* she told me, was an unacceptable expression, as mean-spirited as *niggers* or *spades.* The terms were used by hateful people, she said, and were not to be heard in our house.

Mother's lesson in racial sensitivities was underscored a few weeks later. Summit had a "custard stand" along Highway 51—actually it was a hut housing a couple of machines producing soft ice cream—and the place served as the town's nocturnal hangout. I had a job as a carhop, earning princely wages of twenty-five cents an hour and what tips I could scrounge.

One evening, a truck parked off the highway and the driver, an affable-looking Negro man, walked to the front window to place an order. The custard-stand manager, a young fellow studying to be a veterinarian and by all appearances even-tempered, went apoplectic.

"I'm not going to serve you," my boss said, his voice rising. "We don't serve niggers. Get out of here."

The truck driver looked as if he had been slapped across his face. Without a word, he turned, walked back to his truck, and drove away.

For the first time in my life, without my mother's guidance, I felt real qualms about Jim Crow laws—mortified for the truck driver and ashamed to work at the custard stand. My boss's reaction seemed terribly rude and offensive to another human being. But I didn't have the courage to speak up or to quit in protest. Mississippi had a way of cosseting its white citizens in the comfort of the status quo.

We were preoccupied with baseball in May 1954. In a front-page story in the *Summit Sun*, the article being given better display than an epochal decision by the U.S. Supreme Court, I offered my finest Grantland Rice imitation:

"Saturday afternoon, on a sun-baked, oven-like Millsaps Field in Jackson, the Summit Bulldogs won their first state championship by downing the Shaw Hawks in a real thriller, 2–1."

The high court's ruling that segregated public schools were unlawful had been relegated to page 4. Although it had the force of a unanimous decision and stunned Southern society, I was too naive to see the earthquake coming. Lew Barnes was comically philosophical. Gesturing toward the colored school, he predicted the "boogies" would come marching down the street like an army of African savages to capture our school. That seemed absurd. I knew it would never happen.

Mary Cain perceived danger. Although she buried the news account, she offered editorial comment in her front-page column: "Fortunately, in America, it is the people who are, in the final sense, 'supreme.' The Supreme Court will learn, I think, that the people of the South will not even consider destroying their way of life by bowing to this Communist edict."

The morning newspaper in Jackson, the *Clarion-Ledger*, had an interesting variation of the story. Rather than describing the decision that grew out of a school case in Kansas, the *Clarion-Ledger*'s lead article from Washington began: "The Supreme Court of the United States today ruled that the constitution of Mississippi is unconstitutional." The Mississippi constitution, drafted in 1890 when Reconstruction was still a fresh memory, contained a number of measures to relegate blacks to second-class citizenship. Our constitution encumbered voter registration with poll taxes and literacy tests and restored features of a short-lived Black Code that had been aimed at the freedmen before Reconstruction began.

An editorial accompanying the *Clarion-Ledger*'s coverage of the decision noted that Mississippi faced a choice of accepting the verdict "or trying to find ways or means of legally evading the decision." The leadership of the state, of course, opted for the latter.

Recognizing that segregation would be challenged, the state had already instituted a plan—a couple of years before the *Brown* decision—to improve colored schools under the "separate but equal" theory upheld by the Supreme Court in the 1896 *Plessy v. Ferguson* decree. Before the state had taken this defensive action, public schools for Negroes had been a disgrace. Their schools were weather-beaten frame buildings badly heated in the winter. Libraries were as bare as the pupils' cupboards at home, and classrooms had worn-out textbooks discarded by white schools. The colored school in Summit had no science lab, and instead of a gymnasium, the students used a dirt basketball court outdoors.

At first, the politicians figured they could stave off integration by replacing the inadequate facilities. In 1952, before the *Brown* decision, the legislature shifted from its study of a controversial plan to offer tax-free loans to cattle farmers—a measure known around the capitol as the "bullshit bill"—to appropriate funds for Negro education. They reasoned that, given shining new schools, colored students would not demand to enroll at all-white schools. The mayor of Jackson, Allen Thompson, dedicated one of the new schools, the Lanier Junior-Senior High School for Negroes, on the week of the Supreme Court decision. He advised his audience to "count their blessings" instead of pushing for integration.

But with the "separate but equal" approach repudiated by the court, Mississippi legislators began considering a proposal to cut off all appropriations for public schools and divert the money into tuition grants for private schools—years before voucher plans became a topic of hot national debate. Diehards also drafted a constitutional amendment that would effectively abolish public schools in the state.

Reaction was not confined to government officials. In the Delta town of Indianola, a farmer named Robert "Tut" Patterson summoned a dozen of the area's leading businessmen to map a course of resistance at a meeting conducted at a cotton compress on July 11, 1954. They founded an organization and gave it a name: Citizens Council. Within months, the organization could boast of dozens of local councils and thousands of members in Mississippi and Alabama. To give the Council cachet, civic leaders in communities across the Deep South were encouraged to join. On the surface, the Council seemed as respectable as a Rotary Club, with membership rolls of bankers, lawyers, and merchants. But the organization had a sinister political agenda and gave its blessing to candidates making the loudest vows to defend the racial purity of Southern schools.

Behind the public display of concern over integration, the Council moved quietly to intimidate colored citizens. In most towns, Council members represented the major employers of the local Negro workforce, and they fired any janitor, maid, cook, or field hand suspected of integrationist tendencies. The group, my mother quickly concluded, smelled of the late Theodore G. Bilbo. In 1955, after *Look* magazine carried a critical article about the Council by the Greenville editor Hodding Carter, Mother suggested that I use the story, "A Wave of Terror Threatens the South," in a current-events report. A few days later, I stood before my ninth-grade class and delivered an unflattering assessment of this new Southern phenomenon. I'm not sure I fully understood the talk my mother helped me prepare; I know I failed to provoke any indignation among my bored classmates.

We didn't realize it at the time, but a more virulent group was being reactivated in southwest Mississippi, without publicity. The old White League Ku Klux Klan, a band that had roamed the region during Reconstruction, had died off years before. Though the Klan had flourished in scattered Northern locales in the early years of the twentieth century in reaction to Catholics, Jews, and immigrants in general, it had not been active in the South in decades. Suddenly, new klaverns sprouted in Pike County and spread to neighboring Amite and Walthall Counties. The Klan lacked the Council's prestige, drawing its membership from loggers, railroad workers, mechanics, and small farmers frustrated by their own poverty. But it did not lack teeth.

To recruit its men, the Klan relied on the vigilante tradition of the area. The nineteenth-century Klan had conducted raids and sparked race riots across southwest Mississippi. According to Conerly's Pike County history, the Klan members "were aglow with warmth and burning for action, and when it was seen that they would not submit to the efforts being made to Africanize their country, troops were stationed in every available locality to overawe them." Following a knife attack by a freed slave on the teenaged daughter of his former master, the history continued, "a body of determined men were ready to begin the work of extermination." County officials intervened to stop the lynching, the girl recovered, and the defendant escaped with a twenty-year sentence for assault and battery. The historian was unhappy with the verdict. "The public mind in Pike County has never been free from the stain it felt was left by not executing this negro at once," Conerly lamented.

The integration issue eventually split the Methodists in Summit. Because leaders of the national denomination, which would become the United Methodist Church, were considered wild-eyed liberals intent upon bringing Negroes into the fold, several prominent families in town broke away from the local congregation.

The group took over a house—conveniently located next door to their soul brothers at the First Baptist Church—that had once been used by the superintendent of the Summit school system. They joined a new, segregationist order called the Southern Methodist Church.

There would be no balm in any integrated Gilead.

The rhetoric in the 1955 governor's campaign in Mississippi became charged with visions of an impending apocalypse. The favorite in the race, a former governor named Fielding Wright—who was Strom Thurmond's running mate on the 1948 Dixiecrat ticket—invoked the theory of interposition, an approach advocated by James J. Kilpatrick, a Richmond newspaper editor, as part of Virginia's plan of "massive resistance." Wright thought it would work in Mississippi. In advertisements addressed as "A Message on Segregation to the Mothers of Mississippi," Wright asked, "Do you want to be sure that your boys and girls can continue to attend segregated schools, swimming pools, picture shows and other public places—as they now do?" He offered himself as "the only candidate with a practical plan to keep our segregated schools," promising that as governor he would stand as a buffer between local school boards and the Supreme Court. The court would be forced to remove the governor to reach the schools, Wright said. "They'll never be able to do it."

Other candidates relied on emotion rather than strategy. Paul Johnson Jr., running a third time for the office his father had held, depicted himself as the sworn enemy of the "initials' organizations." His voice oozing contempt, he spelled them out: the AFL, the CIO, the ACLU, and the group representing the plaintiffs in the *Brown* case, the NAACP. "We all know what that stands for," Johnson shouted. "Niggers! Apes! Alligators! Coons! Possums!"

Ross Barnett ran again, polishing a plaint against the federal government that would become a staple in his speeches. Mary Cain came back for an encore, too, but won only sixteen thousand votes, a figure far below her numbers in 1951. The times seemed to call for strong men with strong language.

Although Johnson led in the first Democratic primary, he fell in the runoff to J. P. Coleman, a member of the Stennis faction of the party. A big, broad-chested man, Coleman talked sensibly. Instead of shouting about the niggers, he suggested that integration could be circumvented by lawful means. All it took, he implied, was the will of the white people of Mississippi and a wise leader. He had a reassuring manner and seemed to possess enough cunning to lead the resistance.

We were left with the impression that integration would never come to Mississippi in our lifetime.

CHAPTER 5

"Forget, Hell!"

★ ★ ★ ★ ★

O le Miss.
The two words used by nineteenth-century servants to refer to the matriarch of the plantation became shorthand over the years for the University of Mississippi, the most Southern of schools in the most Southern of states, an institution unreconstructed a century after Appomattox. The grounds of the school were drenched with the legacy of war. After the battle of Shiloh, a classroom building that had been turned into a morgue became known on campus as the Dead House. Behind Fraternity Row, the remains of unknown soldiers from both sides lay in a common grave, victims of skirmishes in the region.

In 1861, the entire student body enlisted in the Confederate army, rejecting the pleas of the school's chancellor and the advice of Confederate president Jefferson Davis, who compared the specter of sending boys off to war to the "grinding of seed corn of the republic." My great-grandfather's company, the Lamar Rifles, suffered heavy casualties. The other campus unit, the University Greys, was decimated at Gettysburg, cut down to the last man during Pickett's charge. Not even the college town, Oxford, escaped; it was looted and burned by Union troops. A Yankee correspondent traveling with the invading army wrote: "Where once stood a handsome little country town now only remain the blackened skeletons of houses and smouldering ruins."

Midway through the next century, resentment still simmered there. The campus store specialized in Confederate battle flags and other icons of the Lost Cause. One popular item, a decal, featured the symbol of Southern aristocracy, a civilian "colonel" with planter's hat and drooping white mustache and goatee, declaring, "Forget, Hell!" No, Ole Miss did not forget. In 1936, the football team took the name Rebels, and a couple of years later, students began electing a Colonel Rebel to reign with Miss Ole Miss.

In 1958, when it came time for me to go off to college, no questions clouded my judgment. Though my parents suggested that I look at Pa's alma mater, Washington and Lee, or consider a Presbyterian school, Southwestern at Memphis, my heart was committed to Ole Miss. I would be the fourth generation of our family to have Ole Miss connections, following my Civil War–era great-grandfather; my grandfather, the Oxford town marshal, who went on to serve as chief of the Ole Miss campus security; and my mother. In 1947, the summer after my father's death, Mother and I had lived in an Ole Miss dormitory while she completed requirements for her master's degree, so I had explored the school's nooks and crannies as a youngster and felt completely at home there.

From my first Ole Miss football game in 1946, I had been a devout partisan. When the Rebels upset Maryland, breaking a long winning streak by one of the nation's top teams, in 1952, I rejoiced as if the South had won the war; when Ole Miss lost a game, a rare occurrence in my youth, I would take to bed as if stricken by disease. My allegiance ran deep.

I thought the grounds of Ole Miss lovely, a compact campus centered around the Lyceum, a redbrick Greek Revival building dating to the school's founding in 1848. Classroom buildings were set off by long, rectangular lawns, and an expanse of grass and trees, known as the Grove, stretched east toward town, past a statue of a rebel soldier. When I enrolled, it was easy to walk to class or to stroll to the town square in Oxford, where shops surrounded a whitewashed courthouse.

It was not unusual to see William Faulkner on the square, as unapproachable as God. He stood out in a field of blue denim, dressed as he was in herringbone jackets or sometimes in threadbare khakis. But I was surprised by the tiny size of the great man. He seemed far too short and slight to have composed such sound and fury. Faulkner had himself attended Ole Miss and later served as postmaster at the school until an inspector fired him for inattentiveness in 1924. As he stalked away from the job, Faulkner delivered a peroration we were taught in English class: "I reckon I'll be at the beck and call of folks with money all my life, but thank God I won't ever again have to be at the beck and call of every son of a bitch who's got two cents to buy a stamp."

Ole Miss dripped with mystique. Though the school offered enrollment to any graduate of a white Mississippi high school, and tuition, room, and board cost less than $2,000 a year, Ole Miss had the aura of an exclusive club for the planter class. Wealthy Delta families sent their sons and daughters to Ole Miss as surely as they harvested cotton each fall. Ole Miss functioned as a clearinghouse for the state's political power structure as well as a finishing school for the young women who would marry the elite and preside over their mansions.*

Nestled in the Mississippi hills, sixty miles from the nearest city, Memphis, Ole Miss stood as a bastion of the state's establishment, and in my freshman year, the school seemed impregnable.

Upon arrival, I submitted to freshman ritual. Upperclassmen shaved my head, topping it with a blue Ole Miss beanie, but nothing could humble me. After years of vicarious experience, I had become, at last, a member of the Ole Miss community. I quickly pledged myself to a fraternity and hitched a ride to Memphis, where our football team claimed victory in the first game of the season. Because of Oxford's remote location, we played several home games each year in the Tennessee city, and the student body flocked there to cheer the Rebels and enjoy pleasures forbidden in Mississippi.

Oxford was the county seat of Lafayette County, a jurisdiction as dry as the Gobi Desert. The Baptists, with assistance from other hard-shell denominations, controlled politics in the region and outlawed the sale of alcoholic beverages in a wide swath of counties around Oxford, from the hills of northeast Mississippi to the Delta.

Beer had been voted out in a referendum. The outcome occurred, Faulkner declared in a broadside he privately published, "because too many voters who drank beer or didn't object to other people drinking it, were absent in Europe and Asia defending Oxford where voters who preferred home to war could vote on beer in 1944."

Faulkner wanted his message to appear in the *Oxford Eagle*, but the editor, Colonel Eldon Hoar, a teetotaler, told the novelist that he didn't dare publish it. Instead, Colonel Hoar agreed to print copies of the letter, headlined "To the voters of Oxford," and Faulkner handed out the leaflets on the square himself. Responding to a Baptist charge that money squandered

---

*In 2000, Endesha Ida Mae Holland, a black playwright who'd grown up decades earlier in the Delta, spoke at the Oxford Conference for the Book, an annual event cosponsored by the university. She expressed delight at the invitation: "Ole Miss was always a gleam in our eye, but we knew we couldn't go there."

on beer should be spent on food and clothing, Faulker argued, "By this precedent, we will have to hold another election to vote on whether or not the florists, the picture shows, the radio shops and the pleasure car dealers will be permitted in Oxford."

Despite Faulkner's intervention, Oxford remained dry. Under local option, some counties permitted beer sales, but liquor was illegal throughout the entire state. Enforcement of prohibition in Mississippi, however, was arbitrary. In the river counties of the Delta and along the Gulf Coast, with polyglot populations composed of wayward Cajuns, Italian contractors, Lebanese traders, and Greek restaurateurs plus a sprinkling of Chinese grocers thrown in for good measure, local authorities simply ignored the ban on booze. Stores with neon lights advertising "package goods" flourished in these areas, and bars operated openly along the Gulfport-Biloxi strip. The liquor dealers paid a semiofficial black-market tax to local sheriffs, who doubled as county tax collectors. The state tax collector also got a share of the booty.

But in places such as Oxford, alcohol had been proscribed for years; as a result, students were forced to deal with bootleggers or to drive more than thirty miles to counties permitting beer sales. A third alternative was Memphis.

Our opening football game coincided with my eighteenth birthday. Afterward, I observed the milestone in a nightclub, knocking back shots of cheap bourbon and chasing it with Coke. Like many students, I had obtained a fake Selective Service card with a birthdate showing I was over twenty-one, ensuring a right to alcohol. By the time I found my way back to Oxford, nausea had replaced my freshman exuberance and I missed a day of classes.

But I soon slipped into the mainstream of the school, learning the technique of composing a news story in journalism class and writing a term paper about the nefarious Bilbo for English 101. ROTC was mandatory for freshmen and sophomores, so each Thursday I was required to wear an army uniform and spend the afternoon on the drill field, presenting arms with a vintage M1 rifle. Though we were issued no ammunition, the weapons were dangerous. One drill called for us to insert a thumb into the rifle breech to disengage a bolt; if the movement was maladroit, the bolt action would spring forward and smash the thumb.

The military was one Southern tradition I followed badly. I disliked the regimentation, perspired inside the heavy, scratchy uniform, and could never master the spit shine that was supposed to make my government-issue shoes glisten. I was a lowly private, and "gung ho" upperclassmen—who planned to go into the service as officers upon graduation—took delight in hectoring me. Our rifles were stored in the ROTC hut, and once a week we were expected to go there, disassemble the firearm, oil the parts, and put the thing back together before Thursday drills. To retaliate against the routine, I was part of a band of disgruntled freshmen who poured handfuls of sand down the barrels of rifles assigned others.

ROTC classes were sometimes amusing. Taught by career master sergeants with bulging beer guts, the courses offered instruction in the nomenclature of weapons. Many of my classmates were football players who couldn't distinguish a cannon from Chaucer. The athletes occupied a curious position on campus, heroes on Saturday, but "meatheads"—a term generally applied to linemen—the rest of the week. They shared my dissatisfaction with ROTC. Lifting their rear ends above their seats, they cut outrageous farts in class. The instructor, a veteran of General George Patton's Third Army, would grin and pause in his lecture to observe, "Goddamn, gentlemen, I believe someone has shit in his pants." The sergeant delivered more obscenities when a defused rifle grenade was passed around the room. The meatheads would attach the weapon to the front of their trousers and stroke it with masturbatory gestures.

Outside the classroom, I hung out at the SAE house, where I took meals and played countless rubbers of bridge. The fraternity house was built to look like a plantation home, but it had the ambience of a speakeasy. The SAE brothers lounged around the living room in shades of undress, watching TV. The favorite show was *The Three Stooges*, which appeared each afternoon.

Our "houseboy," a dashing colored man in his thirties named Miller P. Burk, moonlighted as a bootlegger, competing with Johnny's Tin Shack, an industrious operation several miles north of Oxford, across the Marshall County line. Johnny's did big business, with a stock as impressive as a big-city liquor store. On Fridays, the flow of cars from the campus created such a jam on the gravel road that a deputy sheriff, whose boss was on the take, directed traffic.

Students without transportation turned to sources closer to home, such as Miller P. He kept quart bottles of beer iced down in the mop sink of a closet at the SAE house and dabbled on the side as a brewmeister, storing volatile concoctions of home brew in the same closet. On more than one night the brothers' sleep was shattered by exploding bottles of Miller P.'s home brew.

Several passions are important to Southern men. The love of a good woman ranks slightly ahead of the exhilaration that comes from a sip of sour-mash whiskey. Other pleasures include greeting the chill dawn in a deer stand, debating the merits of barbecue from North Carolina, Tennessee, or Texas, expanding on stories that improve with age, and enjoying the bonhomie of friends. Then there is football.

In my years at Ole Miss, football transcended almost all else. Though I had given up my dreams of becoming an all-American by the tenth grade— I had a low tolerance for pile-driving tackles—I never lost enthusiasm for the game. Its requirements for speed, brute force, and strategy seemed an extraordinary combination of brains and muscle, and the regional rivalries fought out each autumn Saturday in front of tens of thousands of spectators were like wars without fatalities.

Seasons that began in sultry heat ended in the sleet and numbing rain of late November, yet weather never deterred us. If the game was not in Oxford, we traveled in automobile caravans to Memphis or Jackson or took student trains to Baton Rouge and Knoxville. Fall weekends were built around football, and I would sooner flunk an exam than miss a game.

From its inception, the Southeastern Conference featured powerhouse football. When I was a student, two members of the SEC, Ole Miss and LSU, dominated the national rankings, and the annual contest between these archenemies unleashed primal emotions. Because Tiger Stadium could hold the population of ten Oxfords, the game was usually played in Baton Rouge on misty Saturday nights in bayou country. Thousands of Mississippians would descend on the Louisiana city like Crusaders, and bloody pregame fistfights in Baton Rouge barrooms served as preludes to larger scuffles in the stadium, where chaos was king.

Before the opening kickoff, LSU cheerleaders would parade around the track with a cage containing Mike, a Bengal tiger. They elicited fearsome roars from the mascot, stirring the Louisiana faithful, and they provoked howls of disgust from us. When the cage rolled toward the Ole Miss side, we rose, thousands of middle fingers lifted, and pelted the tiger's cage with a fusillade of ice, wadded plastic cups, and an occasional bottle. Mayhem spread through the stands: fans grappled in the aisles in drunken disorder, and thunderous noise was said to have set off readings on the Richter scale.

Seven games into the 1959 season, LSU held the country's number one rating; Ole Miss, ranked number three, was also undefeated and had allowed only seven points all year. The showdown came on Halloween night. Lew Barnes, my friend from Summit, tracked me down in the Ole Miss student section. Though he had attended LSU, he squeezed in beside me. Nipping from a couple of pints of Old Crow, we watched, spellbound, as Ole Miss clung to a 3–0 lead into the fourth quarter. The night was wet, and rather than risk a fumble in its own territory, Ole Miss began kicking the ball back to LSU on third down, putting reliance on the staunch Rebel defense. In the closing minutes, LSU's Heisman Trophy winner, Billy Cannon, scooped up a bouncing punt on his eleven-yard line and began racing down the sideline. He evaded two tacklers. Hit a third, fourth, and fifth time, he recoiled and kept running. Cannon disappeared from my view for a moment, shielded by the Ole Miss reserves standing in front of the bench. My eyes darted to the opposing stands, where the LSU fans were leaping like berserk waves. In a split second, I realized the terrible truth. Cannon reemerged into sight in full gallop, and when he crossed the goal line, Lew swallowed the last of his bourbon and pitched the empty pint into the air. The bottle tumbled on a downward arc for twenty rows, striking a man on the shoulder. In the tumult, no one but Lew and I and the bruised spectator noticed.

While we followed the fortunes of our athletic teams, another set of students from the South—motivated by values far different from ours—were triggering a revolution. Their activities started with sit-ins in Greensboro, North Carolina, three months after the Ole Miss–LSU game that I thought would be the seminal event of my college career.

On February 1, 1960, four colored freshmen from the Agricultural and Technical College of North Carolina took seats at a Woolworth's lunch counter and asked for cups of coffee. Denied service, they kept their seats until the store closed. The next day, twenty students showed up. While dithering Greensboro officials considered whether to arrest the students, the demonstrations spread to other stores.

The tactic jumped like a forest fire to another city, Nashville, where students at Fisk University met sterner resistance when they challenged segregation at downtown lunch counters. As soon as one group occupying the white-only sections were arrested, more students replaced them. Angry whites pounded the demonstrators with their fists and kicked them when they were knocked to the floor. The students refused to fight back. They employed a technique little known in the South, the philosophy of Mohandas Gandhi that called for passive resistance. It was a principle they had learned from Jim Lawson, a pacifist minister in Nashville. And out of their movement came men and women every bit as capable as the future leaders of Mississippi being produced at Ole Miss.

"They did not think of themselves in those days as being gifted or talented or marked for success, or for that matter particularly heroic," David Halberstam wrote years later in his book *The Children*. But he noted that the tiny Nashville group produced John Lewis, a future congressman from Georgia; Marion Barry, who went on to become mayor of Washington, D.C.; Diane Nash, a prominent figure in the civil rights movement; James Bevel, a key lieutenant to Martin Luther King Jr.; and Gloria Johnson, the first black woman psychiatrist to be tenured at Harvard Medical School.

When the protests spread to Mississippi, young men and women had sugar and ketchup poured on their heads after they had the effrontery to sit at a Jackson lunch counter. The sit-ins failed to win service, but the demonstrations opened a new dimension in a struggle that had enjoyed few breakthroughs in the years since Rosa Parks had refused to sit in the back of the city bus in Montgomery in 1955.

I followed the events with remote curiosity, watching film clips on network news shows or reading reports in newspapers. The uprising was given little credibility by the Mississippi press, which dismissed the demonstrations as the work of a handful of misguided Negro Communists. With the Cold War in full flower at the time, our region was afflicted with more than a touch of xenophobia, and it became standard practice to brand anyone sympathetic to the Negroes' dilemma as a "fellow traveler" orchestrated by Moscow.

Undeterred by the South's attempt to suppress the sit-ins, the students turned to other methods to confront Jim Crow. A Congress of Racial Equality (CORE) leader named James Farmer revived a tactic, first used by Negroes traveling to the South in 1947, to test a Supreme Court decision that had struck down segregation on interstate buses. In the troubled spring of 1961, passengers in two integrated groups bought tickets on separate Greyhound and Trailways buses to travel from Washington into the Deep South. They called themselves Freedom Riders. Southern authorities had their own name for the visitors: "outside agitators." The term had the ring of Red provocateurs.

The travelers encountered their first trouble in Rock Hill, South Carolina, where a gang of whites attacked a group including John Lewis. Violence flared again in Alabama. Outside Anniston, dozens of white men pursued the Freedom Riders down a highway in a honking line of cars. After overtaking the Greyhound bus, the mob beat out its windows with bricks and an ax. A firebomb was pitched through a shattered back window, forcing the terrified passengers to flee the burning bus and fall into the hands of the mob. A contingent of state troopers rescued the Freedom Riders before any were killed, but police protection broke down a couple of weeks later in the capital of Alabama.

To prevent a recurrence of the frightening incident near Anniston, the Justice Department thought it had negotiated safe passage for the next group. But the Freedom Riders were greeted by a discomforting scene when they arrived at the Montgomery terminal on May 20. The policemen who had been stationed there had disappeared, leaving only a group of reporters to meet the bus. As soon as the demonstrators disembarked, local white men popped out of hiding places and set upon the group with baseball bats and lead pipes.

Dixie bristled.

At first, the trouble seemed far away, but the conflict was drummed home to me when the Freedom Riders arrived in Pike County in an attempt to integrate the McComb bus station. At the fraternity house, I watched the black-and-white images on TV as a gang assaulted the unwelcome visitors. I recognized someone I had known when we were both teenagers, punching a colored man and flinging him against the concrete wall of the bus station. Others were knocked through windows. Blood was drawn that day, and Pike County earned its first battle stripe on the way to its reputation as "the church-burning capital of the world."

Determined to keep the Negro community from being aroused by the visitors, whites in Pike County responded to the Freedom Riders in vigilante style. There was local precedent for operating outside the law. A century earlier, a guerrilla band affiliated with the renegade Confederate captain Charles Quantrill had ambushed a train and killed the Pike County sheriff to free a prisoner. By 1961, law enforcement officers were in league with the night riders, and the hardiest nucleus of these neo-Redeemers rallied to the call of the reconstituted Pike County Ku Klux Klan.

The streets of my home ran with the blood of unwanted visitors. One of the victims was a young white student named Tom Hayden, beaten savagely during a confrontation. But the Klan's main target was a young Negro, Bob Moses, an organizer for the Student Nonviolent Coordinating Committee, a new civil rights group known by its acronym, SNCC, as Snick. Moses set up shop in McComb to aid a handful of local blacks recruited for the uprising. On paper, Moses seemed too mild to handle the situation. He had studied philosophy at Harvard, where he embraced gentle Quaker tenets and Zen Buddhism. His background seemed as foreign to Pike County as Mao Tse-tung's. He appeared to be the ultimate "outside agitator."

The vigilantes were armed with firebombs and guns; Moses conducted his battle in Gandhian style, with no weapon stronger than moral authority. When he accompanied two men in neighboring Amite County to register to vote, the three Negroes were beaten on the courthouse steps by a gang of relatives of the sheriff. Moses pressed charges, but succeeded only in attracting another hostile crowd. As a group of whites milled outside the office of the justice of the peace, where Moses hoped to testify, gunshots were fired, and the sheriff deported Moses back to Pike County.

A month later, Herbert Lee, a Negro farmer helping Moses in his voter registration drive, was shot and killed by an Amite County state representative. The official, E. H. Hurst, said he had been defending himself when he hammered Lee on the head with a pistol during a disagreement. The gun went off accidentally, Hurst explained. The legislator was quickly exonerated, and authorities left Lee's body lying outside a cotton gin for several hours to emphasize the futility of aspirations of men such as Moses and Lee.

In 1961, my views on race began to change significantly. Although I had been taught by my parents to eschew racial epithets and to treat colored people respectfully, our household abided by segregationist codes. While I made a point of shaking hands with Negro men—and felt self-satisfied that I was making a generous gesture because many whites felt it beneath their dignity to do so—I never thought of inviting a colored person to my home; I knew no one well enough to do so, anyway. I hope I never insulted a

Negro personally, but in school, I succumbed to the environment. I laughed at nigger jokes and told my share of racist tales.

But something gnawed on my conscience. Part of my unease I attribute to my mother's influence. She had been brought up in old Mississippi, yet recognized the worst of its characteristics. If she could do nothing to change the society into which she had been born, at least she could inculcate in her son a sense of fairness. I was also reacting to the abuses in Pike County—from the insult by the custard-stand manager to the beatings at the McComb bus station. Even as I practiced it, I knew that segregation was mean and wrong.

When the Negro students launched their challenge of the system, I realized that even though we called ourselves rebels at Ole Miss, the kids at North Carolina A&T and Fisk were the real rebels of my generation. And though I was still too timid to give them public support, I wanted to believe that I, too, was a rebel at heart.

In the summer of 1961, I had a seasonal job in upstate New York, my first extended venture to the Northeast. As the only Southerner among two hundred college students working at a Lake George resort, I found myself outside the psychological boundaries of Mississippi. For the first time, I ate at tables with Negroes. I did not feel contaminated. In fact, I enjoyed the novelty. It seemed liberating.

As the token Southerner, I was put on the defensive by probing questions from my new friends from Colgate, Bates, and Barnard. They had the grace not to accuse me of racism, but they pressed me about segregation and reduced me to weak explanations about the system. "I guess you need to be from there to understand," I would mumble, hoping they might change the subject. I knew segregation was indefensible.

I did not acknowledge my shifting beliefs to anyone, not even my family, but at Lake George, in my twenty-first year, I finally accepted the idea that my homeland's customs were unjust, and I began to see the senselessness of Southern resistance.

The recognition came at a time when other new vistas were opening for me. At Ole Miss, I had discovered literature: not just Faulkner, but Steinbeck; early Dos Passos and his radical trilogy, *U.S.A.*; Mailer, the hipster manqué; the nineteenth-century Romantic poets; the voices of the American Beat generation, Ferlinghetti, Ginsberg, Kerouac; as well as Suzuki, the Zen master.

Even as the ground was shifting under my feet, the South was digging in.

Returning to Mississippi that fall, I found that Summit lay in an epicenter of violence. Fathers of my childhood friends were enlisting in the Klan as well as an offshoot organization called Americans for the Preservation of the White Race. *Nigger,* a word once left to the province of poor white trash, had become part of the popular vocabulary. In response to a wave of civil rights demonstrations earlier in the year, Pike County had grown more obstinate, its white citizens mobilizing as if for war. Taylor Branch would write extensively about Pike County in his prize-winning history *Parting the Waters.* In one passage, he quoted a Justice Department official who toured the McComb area in 1961 and "felt the climate of fear as a prickly sensation under his collar."

By this time, Ross Barnett, a clownish also-ran in the political campaigns of my childhood, had become governor of Mississippi. As the son of a Confederate veteran and the most unremitting segregationist, Barnett had won election in 1959. With the support of the Citizens Council, Senator Jim Eastland, and the remnants of the Bilbo faction, Barnett had prevailed over Carroll Gartin, the candidate of the moderate wing of the Democratic Party.

Years later, I learned some of the details of that bitter race.

Eastland was a stealthful power broker. No matter that he had served as senator from Mississippi for nearly twenty years; he rarely made public appearances in the state. Instead, he manipulated events from his office in Washington through a network of cronies back home. Eastland had been smarting ever since Gartin challenged him for his Senate seat in 1954. Though a "moderate," Gartin attempted to score points that year by saddling Eastland with the *Brown v. Board of Education* decision, reminding Mississippi audiences that Eastland held high office in Washington yet had done nothing to stop the Supreme Court. After Eastland won reelection, he vowed to send Gartin to political oblivion.

To hedge his bets against Gartin in the 1959 governor's race, Eastland encouraged a third candidate to join the field, a flamboyant lawyer from the Delta named Charlie Sullivan. Running an unorthodox campaign, Sullivan advocated putting an end to prohibition, and he captured the imagination of many progressive voters. Sullivan's candidacy bled Gartin of support and helped assure Barnett's election.

After losing two previous races for governor, Barnett made sure the public understood his position this time. "I am a vigorous segregationist," he announced. "I will work to maintain our heritage, our customs, constitutional government, rights of the states, and segregation of the races."

His enemies were not so much the colored people, who could not vote, but the moderates. A Barnett supporter, a circuit judge in Scott County, informed one audience, "Segregation is right, it is Christian, and it ought to be taught from the homes and preached from every pulpit in the state and nation. There is no place for moderation in the matter of segregation. A moderate is a fellow who will take a little of it, an occasional mixer; a fellow who will now and then mix the blood of a white boy and colored girl, and a white girl with the blood of a colored boy."

Barnett employed a campaign anthem tweaking the line of succession among Mississippi moderates. The song dubbed Hugh White, the gubernatorial victor in 1951, "Big Daddy," and J. P. Coleman, who had won in 1955, "Tall Daddy." Gartin, their lineal descendant, became "Little Boy Blue." While Barnett stood on the stage, smiling oafishly, his hillbilly band sang his praises:

> He's for segregation, one hundred percent,
> He's not a moderate, like some other gent.
> Big Daddy, Tall Daddy, Little Boy Blue!
> Climb on the wagon, it's rolling along.
> Climb on the wagon, you cannot go wrong.
> Shout from the rooftops, this victory song:
> Roll with Ross, roll with Ross, he's his own boss.

Barnett's sponsors described him as a country lawyer with a fox's cunning. I thought he was a fool of the highest order, a living caricature of a bumbling Southern politician. He spoke with an elaborate accent, pronouncing the word *Mississippi* as if it were spun from a gruel of grits, molasses, biscuits, and red-eye gravy, and he flapped his arms while speaking as though fighting fire in his side pockets. His face resembled a tufted owl's and his speech made Mrs. Malaprop sound like a scholar. Addressing a congregation at Beth-Israel Temple in Jackson, he began, "There is nothing finer than a group of people meeting in true Christian fellowship."

During a flying trip across the state early in the campaign, he exited a small plane and walked into a whirling propeller, suffering deep gashes in his left shoulder and great wounds to his dignity. When his press secretary, Erle Johnston, sought helpful comment from several pilots, hoping they might have a logical explanation for Barnett's carelessness, he was told that "only a goddamn fool" would walk into a propeller.

Though he seemed hopelessly provincial, Barnett injected foreign policy into his campaign. Americans, he told the crowds, could not afford to "let our country become as mongrelized as Egypt, where a cultural nation allowed itself to integrate with inferior races that brought about its downfall."*

Stories of Ross Barnett's miscues multiplied like the biblical loaves and fishes. Some of the tales proved to be parables. One oft-told anecdote had Barnett responding to a press conference query about the disputed Pacific islands Quemoy and Matsu with his own question: "Are those the two fellows from Tishomingo County I put on the Game and Fish Commission?" My friend Bill Minor, who covered the Mississippi statehouse for more than fifty years, says the incident never happened. But Minor has his own stories. Such as the time he offered an extra bed in his room to the campaigning Barnett, who had no place to stay in a little Delta town. Late that night, a knock awakened Minor. Opening the motel room door, the journalist beheld a strange trio: the candidate, Barnett's son, and the campaign driver. The son and the driver took over the extra bed. To Minor's horror, Barnett stripped down to a ghastly white union suit and crawled into the reporter's bed.

Senator Ernest Hollings of South Carolina swears that another legendary Barnett tale is true. The event took place when Hollings was governor of South Carolina and a member of a delegation of Southern leaders on a trade mission to Brazil. The governors alternated the job of responding to their hosts' welcome at each stop on the trip, and Barnett's turn came one night at a regional airport where hundreds of Brazilians had gathered to greet the yanqui visitors. Barnett had no clue of the location and fumbled through his oration by asserting "the great affinity the people of Mississippi have with . . . your fine country." He was waiting for a cue from his fellow governors, Hollings recalled, but no one bailed him out. Finally, the Mississippi governor spied a sign on the airport hangar and felt he had the information to conclude his remarks: "Oh, yes, the people of Mississippi wanted me to deliver special greetings to the great people of Cinzano!"

*A decade later, Barnett's patron, Senator Eastland, was called upon to escort Egyptian president Anwar Sadat to a congressional appearance. In a conversation with his staff afterward, Eastland reflected on Sadat's dark skin and confided, "I didn't know he was a nigger."

Barnett may have been the people's choice in the election of 1959, but he became a butt of ridicule at Ole Miss. He was lampooned at Stunt Night, when various fraternities competed to produce the most outlandish skit. For the SAE revue, I assumed the role of Barnett, alluding to his propeller wounds by cavorting about the stage in a Quasimodo limp, hollering malapropisms and mispronunciations.

When the governor came to Oxford to crown the homecoming queen during one of his first autumns in office, the booing at the halftime ceremony was so unmerciful that university officials discouraged him from returning the next year.

Then a man named James Meredith said he wanted to enroll at Ole Miss, and attitudes toward Barnett began to change dramatically.

CHAPTER 6

Never!

★ ★ ★ ★ ★

For eight years, Mississippi managed to evade the *Brown v. Board of Education* ruling while our neighbors were forced into compliance. Ugly crowds in Alabama succeeded in chasing Autherine Lucy from campus after she became the first black student to register, under court order, at the University of Alabama in 1956, but not before she had breached the walls of the all-white institution. The following year, President Eisenhower responded to defiance in Little Rock by sending a thousand paratroopers from the 101st Airborne Division to ensure the enrollment of nine black pupils at the city's Central High School after the Arkansas governor, Orval Faubus, used the National Guard to turn back the children. In the other surrounding states, Tennessee and Louisiana, officials accepted the inevitable and approached the desegregation of their public school systems with relatively little panic. But Mississippi said, Never!

When a Negro man named Clennon King applied for admission to Ole Miss in 1958, officials spirited him away to a mental institution. The next year another colored man, Clyde Kennard, appeared at the registrar's office at Mississippi Southern College in Hattiesburg. Before he could leave the campus, police stopped Kennard for reckless driving; the charges grew more serious after bottles of whiskey were allegedly found in his car. Later, Kennard was accused of stealing several sacks of chicken feed. The case had all the appearances of a setup; nevertheless, Kennard drew a prison sentence of seven years—even though he was suffering from colon cancer. The fates of Clennon King and Clyde Kennard became the subject of jokes, rather than concern, among members of the Mississippi establishment. Citizens were assured that white sanctity would be preserved in our schools, that Mississippi would never surrender its sovereignty, and heaven help those who might challenge the system.

As a result, we were disbelieving in the summer of 1962 when the Fifth Circuit of the U.S. Court of Appeals ordered Ole Miss to admit James Meredith, more than a year after he had applied for admission in a letter explaining, "I am an American-Mississippi-Negro citizen." Inspired by the promise of John F. Kennedy, Meredith had sent his first communication to the school on the day the new president was inaugurated.

If segregated education in Mississippi was to be broken, Meredith had the credentials to act as the instrument. He was an air force veteran, nearly thirty years old, with perseverance as well as maturity. Instead of acquiescing to a rebuff from the school, he won support from the NAACP Legal Defense and Educational Fund, which had tons of experience in desegregation cases. His was not a routine action. Rather than targeting an inconspicuous country school or an insignificant institution that could be shut down before submitting to integration, Meredith's lawsuit struck at the cradle of the state's power structure.

Until then, our biggest culture shock at Ole Miss had come at the movies. During my sophomore year, a Civil War romance, *Band of Angels*, had played at an Oxford theater. In one scene, Sidney Poitier, in the role of an educated slave, slapped Yvonne De Carlo after the actress—cast as a planter's daughter whose light skin did not betray her mother's black background—vowed to "keep on living a white life." Murmurs of disbelief swept through our college crowd, and we were astounded when black spectators cheered Poitier's blow from their segregated seats in the balcony.

Ole Miss was not accustomed to impertinence from blacks. The school's ideal Negro had long been "Blind Jim," a lovable old man with a white beard and milky eyes who had hung around the campus for sixty years, selling peanuts, dispensing folk stories, and cheering its athletic teams. He liked to boast that he had never seen Ole Miss lose a game. On Saturdays, when a hat was passed around the football stadium for Blind Jim, it overflowed with greenbacks from alumni warmed with bourbon and goodwill.

In his sesquicentennial history of the school, David Sansing wrote:

"The relationship between Ole Miss students and Blind Jim Ivy was genteel racism in its purest form and it broke none of the codices of white supremacy, but their fondness for him was genuine. When he died on October 20, 1955, Ole Miss students and alumni raised more than a thousand dollars to endow a scholarship in his honor. The Blind Jim Scholarships would enable 'Mississippi Negro youngsters to attend Negro institutions of higher learning.' Because of the terrible complexities of race, the young African Americans who would benefit from the affection Ole Miss students had for Blind Jim could not attend the school he loved and had been a part of for so long."

Over the years, there may have been other slight transgressions of racial lines; there were rumors that a couple of black students—so light they passed for white—had managed to attend classes in post–World War II veterans programs. In the 1950s, Stuart Purser, chairman of the art department at the university, was so impressed by a bust sculpted by M. B. Mayfield, a Negro living near Oxford, that he arranged for Mayfield to take informal instruction. The professor secured Mayfield a job as a janitor at Ole Miss, and he was allowed to sit in a broom closet near the art classrooms for several years, listening to lectures and taking notes.*

But when a black man openly sought to become a student, Ole Miss officials balked. At first, they informed Meredith that he had applied too late. Then they ignored his follow-up inquiries. After he persisted, Meredith was told the credits he hoped to transfer from Jackson State College,† a black school, would be unacceptable because Jackson State lacked the accreditation of the Southern Association of Colleges and Secondary Schools. A requirement that new students provide letters of reference from five Ole Miss alumni also hindered his attempt to enroll. So did a federal judge, sympathetic to Ole Miss, who granted numerous delays for attorneys representing the school.

The Fifth Circuit, which had a no-nonsense record in issuing school-desegregation orders, observed that the Ole Miss case was being argued "in the eerie atmosphere of never-never land" and instructed the lower court to get moving. When a trial was finally held, school officials testified that race had not been a factor in considering Meredith's application. Asked if any Negro had ever attended Ole Miss, the officials swore that they could not answer because, in the words of the dean of student personnel, "I don't know the genealogical background of every person I meet." The district judge, a Mississippian named Sydney C. Mize, ruled on February 3, 1962, that "the University is not a racially segregated institution." He also found that Meredith "was not denied admission because of his race."

---

*Four decades later, Mayfield's art was featured by the school's Center for the Study of Southern Culture and exhibited at Southside Gallery on the Oxford town square.

†Now Jackson State University.

It took a Fifth Circuit panel only four months to overturn Mize's decision and order the school to accept Meredith. But Ben Cameron, a member of the Fifth Circuit who had not served on the panel, a Mississippian with a segregationist background, intervened by issuing a stay in implementing his colleagues' decision.

On September 10, 1962, as a new school year was beginning, Justice Hugo Black, speaking for the entire U.S. Supreme Court, enjoined Ole Miss from further delays. An ecstatic Constance Baker Motley, the NAACP attorney who had handled the case, said that day, "This is the end of the road for the university."

I was still not so sure. After flunking feature writing my senior year—I had been tardy turning in stories and Professor Jere Hoar taught me a lasting lesson about deadlines—I had dropped out for a semester. Under the influence of Kerouac, I went "on the road" to California for a while, then returned to Summit, where I wound up working in a quilt factory.* The hard manual labor quickly persuaded me to return to school. As a result, I was back at Ole Miss that fateful fall, needing only to pass the feature-writing course to graduate. As the Meredith case mushroomed into a gigantic struggle between the state of Mississippi and the federal government, I thought it quite conceivable that the school would be closed forever and my diploma denied. Even wild talk of secession was in the air.

After enduring more than two years of ridicule as a bumbling figure, Ross Barnett seized the opportunity to redeem himself. "We will not surrender to the evil and illegal forces of tyranny," he thundered in an address telecast across the state three days after the Supreme Court order. Mississippi, the governor said, "must either submit to the unlawful dictates of the federal government or stand up like men and tell them, 'Never!'"

The old fellow must have been pleased when he saw the headline in the *Clarion-Ledger*: "Place Assured in History for Fearless Ross Barnett." The piece began in prose as purple as a storm cloud. "The humble plowboy from

---

*My take-home pay was $77 every two weeks. It seemed okay to me since I lived with my parents and ate out of their refrigerator. But my coworkers had limited educations and families to feed. Once during a break, I asked a fellow if the quilt workers ever thought of organizing a union. "Hell, we don't need a union here," he said. "We get all the union benefits—a week's paid vacation and a nice picnic on Labor Day—and we don't have to pay no union dues." Unions were viewed with suspicion and often looked upon as Communist fronts.

Standing Pine, leader in his refusal to yield principle to compromise, stands assuredly today on the blazing pages of American history awaiting a challenger to his order to resist." The author of the article, worked into a personal frenzy over the case, died of a heart attack five days later.

Barnett was assuring a place in history for himself, all right, and the Jackson newspaper and its sister publication, the *Daily News*, were pounding a drumbeat that would climax in armed revolt in a couple of weeks.

The Jackson papers were owned by the Hederman family, a righteous band of brothers and cousins who served as propagandists for the Citizens Council. Stalwart segregationists and laymen in Jackson's First Baptist Church, the Hedermans appointed themselves moral arbiters for the state. During the Ole Miss crisis, their editorial writers referred to the Fifth Circuit judges as "the nine judicial baboons in New Orleans," while their columnists continued to tickle their readership with an unremitting litany of racist jokes involving watermelons and chicken thefts.*

As far as our household in Summit had been concerned, the Hederman papers might as well have been written in Sanskrit. When I was a child, my mother wouldn't allow the *Clarion-Ledger* or the *Daily News* on our lawn, much less inside our home. The papers represented everything she opposed in Mississippi. My social views were not clearly formed at this time, but I knew a bad newspaper when I saw one. I liked the name that detractors had for the state's biggest newspaper: the *Carrion-Lecher.*

I grew up reading a New Orleans newspaper, the *Times-Picayune.* After giving up my youthful infatuation with Mary Cain, I adopted Bill Minor, the *Times-Picayune* correspondent in Mississippi, as a journalistic model. Writing under the byline of W. F. Minor, he captured the essence of Mississippi politics and regularly scooped his rivals in Jackson. Minor cut a striking figure, with prematurely white hair and the bluest eyes I've ever seen. He seemed to know everyone in the state. A. J. Liebling, a press critic for *The New Yorker* with a fine appreciation for Southern politics himself, singled out Minor for praise for a series of articles in the 1940s concerning a secret police force named the Mississippi Bureau of Investigation. After the *Times-Picayune*'s exposés concerning the MBI—Minor quoted one source

---

*In "Mississippi: The Closed Society," published two years after the Meredith affair, the liberal Ole Miss history professor James W. Silver wrote: "The Mississippi press mounts vigilant guard over the racial, economic, political, and religious orthodoxy of the closed society. . . . To read the Hederman press day after day is to understand what the people of the state believe and are prepared to defend."

who compared the operation to the Gestapo—the bureau was disbanded.

But another agency, the Sovereignty Commission, was later created to perpetuate segregation and spy on Mississippians, and the commission worked hand in glove with the Hederman papers. Years afterward, Minor was still angry over the arrangement. "The Sovereignty Commission," he told me, "would send copies of its investigative reports to Tom Hederman, the editor, and he would feed that stuff to one of his columnists, Jimmy Ward or Tom Ethridge, or to a favorite reporter who would write stories accusing people of subversive activities. The Hedermans did the hatchet jobs for the Citizens Council and the Sovereignty Commission. They were part and parcel of the establishment that maintained the system of segregation, and they helped whip up the violence. They were a bunch of mean racists, and during the Ole Miss crisis, you could see Bob or Tom Hederman slipping out of the back door of the governor's office."

Other than for Minor, however, there was little enterprising journalism in the state. The Hedermans' hegemony covered most of Mississippi. Competition came from the *Times-Picayune* in south Mississippi; in parts of north Mississippi, a Memphis daily, the *Commercial-Appeal*, was read. A few small, respectable dailies were scattered around the state, and a brave woman, Hazel Brannon Smith, operated an antiestablishment weekly in Lexington. But the Hedermans and their corps of right-wing columnists fed paranoia in the state and popularized the mantra "Never!"

When the Hedermans, who already owned the *Clarion-Ledger*, gained control of the *Daily News* in the mid-1950s to establish a newspaper monopoly in Jackson, a group of moderate businessmen founded an alternative daily, the *State-Times*. They hired my parents' friend Oliver Emmerich, editor of the *Enterprise-Journal* in McComb, to run the *State-Times*. For the duration of the *State-Times*'s existence, Mother permitted a Jackson newspaper in our home. But the *State-Times* had been driven out of business by the time of the Ole Miss crisis, and Mississippi was left to rely upon the wisdom of Charlie Hills, who wrote a political column for the *Clarion-Ledger* that suggested that the state government was fighting "the unleashed furies of the Congo." Another *Clarion-Ledger* columnist, Tom Ethridge, upped the ante. Ethridge said Mississippi had come under attack by "Asiatic cow-worshippers and African semi-savages not far removed from cannibalism." Florence Sillers Ogden turned from her society beat to praise Barnett for his stand; her column observed that white and colored people "are not and never can be equal."

The *Clarion-Ledger* did not confine its disgust with the Kennedys to its editorial columns. In a front-page article headlined "Robert Kennedy, Jackass Compared," the newspaper reported state attorney general Joe Patterson's support of Ben Cameron, the lone Fifth Circuit judge who kept blocking progress in the Meredith case. "Robert Kennedy criticizing a judge of Judge Cameron's stature," Patterson said, "is like a jackass looking up into the sky and braying at a great American eagle as it soars above."

Not to be outdone, Mary Cain saw Communists involved in the Ole Miss plot. In an editorial, written as the crisis deepened, she demanded—in all caps—to know, "WHO IS BACK OF THIS EVIL NEGRO MEREDITH?" That week, "The Weekly Mirror," the *Summit Sun*'s supplement for its colored readers, did not appear.

Meredith made his first appearance on campus on September 20—my twenty-second birthday—accompanied by a Justice Department official and a carload of U.S. marshals. He did not look threatening. Dressed neatly in a dark suit, Meredith carried a small attaché case, as if he had come to close a business deal. He went inside a building where Governor Barnett waited, out of sight of hundreds of curious students. Espousing the doctrine of interposition, Barnett assumed the role of registrar and told the black man that he should forget about coming to Ole Miss.

The federal agents drove Meredith away. Jeering rustled the leaves of the oaks in the Grove. Moments later, Barnett came out of the building. For the first time, an Ole Miss crowd cheered him. But the exhilaration did not last long. Within hours, several members of the university's administration were cited for contempt of court. The endgame had begun in earnest.

After fitful negotiations between Barnett and U.S. attorney general Robert Kennedy, Meredith was brought to Jackson in an effort to register him there, away from the growing hubbub at Ole Miss. The governor refused him again, and thousands of whites who had gathered around the capitol complex hailed Barnett like Caesar.

Meredith reappeared in Oxford the next day. This time he was met by a wall of state troopers who blocked the federal convoy before it could reach campus. Barnett remained in Jackson, prevented from flying to Oxford by bad weather, so Lieutenant Governor Paul Johnson took his place, reading from the interposition script and handing Meredith a document denying him entrance to the school. After a brief shoving match between Johnson and the chief U.S. marshal, a beefy man with a weather-beaten face named James McShane, the federal delegation returned to Memphis. Photos of the confrontation would prove invaluable to Johnson when he ran for governor the following year.

We did not know it at the time, but Barnett had begun to negotiate the terms of surrender. Faced with his own contempt-of-court citation, the governor began to try to cut deals with the attorney general late in September. According to Arthur Schlesinger Jr.'s *Robert Kennedy and His Times*, the attorney general remarked "that he regarded Governor Barnett . . . as genuinely loony—that he had been hit on the head by an airplane propeller . . . and had never been the same."

In one telephone conversation, Barnett told Kennedy, "We have been part of the United States, but I don't know whether we are or not."

"Are you getting out of the Union?" Kennedy asked.

"It looks like we're being kicked around—like we don't belong to it."

One of Barnett's advisers, a Jackson lawyer named Tom Watkins, attempted to arrange a face-saving solution for the governor. Watkins assured the Justice Department that if one federal marshal pulled a pistol, Barnett would stand aside at the entrance to Ole Miss. Later, the governor decided that one gun would not be sufficient. Barnett appealed to the U.S. attorney general to order dozens of marshals to draw their guns so that it would appear the governor was yielding to a superior force. Kennedy was queasy about a massive display of firearms.

With the details of the staged showdown incomplete, Meredith embarked on another trip to Oxford, traveling in a motorcade from Memphis. Hearing of the imminent confrontation, I joined hundreds of other students gathered along University Avenue at the east entrance to the school. It was a lovely autumn afternoon, and the crowd seemed more festive than unruly. But Barnett was back on the phone to Washington, warning of violence. "A lot of people are going to be killed," Barnett told Kennedy, according to audiotapes of the conversation that were revealed later. "It would be embarrassing to me." The Justice Department turned back Meredith's motorcade before it reached Oxford. The students, who thought they were about to see history made, were told to disperse. "Y'all go back to your dorms," instructed Johnson, the lieutenant governor, riding in a highway patrol car and speaking through a bullhorn. "Y'all go back to your dorms. The nigger ain't coming today."

The next day, a Friday, the Fifth Circuit ordered Barnett to begin paying a daily fine of $10,000 if he continued his obstruction. Finally, the governor agreed, in a series of secret telephone calls to Washington, on arrangements to enroll Meredith. President Kennedy took part in the conversations over the weekend; he was nonplussed when Barnett told him, "I appreciate your interest in our poultry program." After completing details for Meredith's registration, the president turned to his brother and remarked, "You've been fighting a sofa pillow all week."

Barnett may have capitulated, but Mississippi had not.

The state was on war footing. Dozens of sheriffs and their deputies, hundreds of self-styled auxiliary policemen, and aspiring vigilantes were prepared to come to Oxford to defend Ole Miss. In a "bulletin," the Clarion-Ledger reported from Tuscaloosa, "A large number of out-of-state cars was reported grouping here . . . as rumors spread across Mississippi that many Ku Klux Klansmen were planning to descend upon Oxford and/or Jackson."

Shrill alarms echoed across Dixie. The tocsin was sounded by no less than Major General Edwin A. Walker, a superpatriot who had left the army after being reprimanded for excess in his indoctrination of American troops in Europe on the evils of Communism. Walker had commanded federal forces during Little Rock's desegregation in 1957, and he was sorry for his part in that drama. After retiring from the army, he came home to Dallas and was used as a mouthpiece for the John Birch Society. The federal government, for years his employer, became his enemy. In a radio interview broadcast throughout Mississippi in late September, the general attacked "the Antichrist Supreme Court" and delivered a ringing call to arms:

"Rise to a stand behind Governor Ross Barnett," he urged listeners. "Now is the time to be heard. Ten thousand strong from every state in the Union! Rally to the cause of freedom! The battle cry of the Republic! Barnett, yes! Castro, no! Bring your flags, your tents, and your skillets. It is time. Now or never." Walker recalled that he had been "on the wrong side" in Little Rock. "This time I am out of uniform, and I am on the right side, and I will be there."

Mississippi was marching toward insurrection. Recognizing the gravity of the situation, my mother sent me a letter in which she was uncharacteristically brusque and economical in her words:

"Son: Your great-grandfather Gilmer set out to fight the federals from Ole Miss with the University Greys, called the Lamar Rifles, nearly a hundred years ago. He didn't accomplish a thing! See that you don't get involved!!!!" She signed it simply "M'ur," a contraction of the word *mother* I had used as a child. Mother had muddled her history. There were two Confederate units from Ole Miss, the University Greys and the Lamar Rifles. My great-grandfather Gilmer belonged to the latter. But the wisdom of her message was soon evident.

Weeks later, I shared the letter with the historian Walter Lord, who had come to Oxford for research on his book *The Past That Would Not Die*. As a "liberal" student, I had been paired with a couple of reactionary classmates for an interview with the historian. I spoke with Lord freely, on the condition that my family and I remain unidentified. Excising my great-grandfather's name, Lord used my mother's letter in his book. "It was a voice of sanity in what had now become a madhouse," he wrote.

On the last Saturday night of September, the football stadium at Jackson was filled beyond capacity. The regularly scheduled game between Ole Miss and the University of Kentucky had become a sideshow to the desegregation crisis, and the grandstand stirred with tens of thousands of Confederate battle flags. For years, the Ole Miss band had featured an enormous Confederate flag, so large that it covered most of the field, in halftime performances. But there had never before been many banners in the stands; flags blocked views and fans were discouraged from twirling them. But in the midst of the struggle with Washington, the flag had become de rigueur. The Stars and Bars flew on the radio antennas of cars and fluttered from windows of homes and office buildings across the state. The stadium was a red-and-blue sea.

In his book, Walter Lord quoted a student describing the din: "It was like a big Nazi rally. . . . It was just the way Nuremberg must have been." The student was me.

At halftime, Ross Barnett came onto the field, and the noise level reached a maniacal pitch as the crowd was informed of the lyrics for a new state anthem. The tune had been taken from Barnett's campaign song, "Roll With Ross," but fresh verses had been written and were flashed on the scoreboard:

> States may sing their songs of praise,
> With waving flags and hip-hoo-rays;
> Let cymbals crash and let bells ring,

'Cause here's one song I'm proud to sing:
Go, Mississippi, keep rolling along,
Go, Mississippi, you cannot go wrong,
Go, Mississippi, we're singing your song,
M-I-S, S-I-S, S-I-P-P-I!

As the thousands howled, Barnett lifted his arms in triumph. It was an incredible instant. Even as a dubious spectator, I could feel flesh curdling on my arms. I harbored strong misgivings about the governor; I thought he was an idiot. I did not wave a flag and I did not cheer. But I would not have traded my seat for a million dollars. I knew I was witnessing the final convulsions of the Civil War. All the crowd lacked were pitchforks and rifles. That would come the next night.

Unknown to his followers, Barnett had betrayed the resistance earlier in the day, agreeing with the Kennedys on a plan to bring Meredith to the campus that weekend. But the Saturday-night mob knew nothing of this agreement. Quite giddy, the crowd broke into song again, following words printed on leaflets passed through the stadium:

Never, never, never, never,
No, never, never, never.
We will not yield an inch of any field.
Fix us another toddy, ain't yielding to nobody.
Ross is standing like Gibraltar, he shall never falter.
Ask us what we say, it's to hell with Bobby K.
Never shall our emblem go
From Colonel Rebel to Old Black Joe.

Like most of my classmates, I woke the next day in Jackson a tad hungover, exhausted from the political passions of the previous evening, not knowing that Sunday's false peace would explode within hours. The first inkling of trouble came during the three-hour trip to Oxford. Driving back with my friend Franklin Holmes, we were passed by scores of speeding police cars.

When we arrived on campus late in the afternoon, we saw the administration building, the Lyceum, surrounded by several hundred U.S. marshals, wearing white battle helmets and bulletproof vests. The protective gear looked incongruous over their dark business suits.

I'd like to think my journalistic instincts drew me into the crowd gathering on the grass circle in front of the Lyceum; perhaps it was a student's inquisitive nature. At any rate, I was about to get a lesson in mob psychology that had not been taught in the classroom.

Before sundown, the atmosphere had the feel of a pep rally; there were chants of the school cheer, "Hotty Toddy," punctuated by random rebel yells. But as the evening grew darker and more people arrived, the mood grew nasty. A federal force had been allowed to invade Ole Miss and capture the antebellum building that symbolized the school, and I detected both a growing sense of betrayal, directed for the first time at Barnett, and heightened rage at the Kennedys.

Students who had merely been heckling the marshals moved to more disruptive tactics. Though dozens of state troopers were on hand, the officers did little to discourage the taunting. I had the impression the state police felt they had been sold down the river by the governor, emasculated at a time when they had been spoiling to make a stand against the federal marshals.

A student flicked a burning cigarette on the canvas top of one of the military trucks that had conveyed the marshals to campus. When a marshal moved to extinguish the spark, he was pelted with eggs and debris. Another student produced a knife and began jabbing at a tire on one of the trucks. A state trooper helpfully pointed out an air valve as the most vulnerable spot. Rocks sailed and a couple of bottles broke into shards at the feet of the marshals. Still, the Mississippi troopers did nothing to restore order; some of them laughed at the marshals' discomfort.

From across the circle, I heard smashing sounds. A television cameraman had been attacked, his equipment flung away, and the windows of his car broken. The mob had grown fangs. I saw another photographer knocked to the ground. Someone snatched his camera, banging it against the pavement again and again. Blood gushed from a cut on the photographer's head. When a young faculty member attempted to stop the attack, I heard the sickening noise of fist striking skull, a sound I knew from roadhouse fights. The instructor fell, defended by no one. It was nightfall, and with a cover of darkness, more curses and rocks rained on the marshals.

Suddenly, a noise of scattered poppings, muted explosions, broke over our heads, followed by swirls of smoke. The marshals had fired tear gas into the crowd. Like schools of fish, hundreds of students darted in different directions, shouting in panic. To escape, Franklin Holmes and I scampered across the Lyceum circle, now wreathed in noxious fumes.

The first campus riot of the 1960s was under way. Unlike the dozens to come later in the decade, ours was a right-wing uprising.

Fleeing, I got my first dose of tear gas. It scorched my face and burned my lungs. I could barely breathe. Coughing and crying, I found refuge in the lobby of a girls' dormitory, joining a group of stunned classmates. On a television set in the lobby, I saw the visage of President Kennedy, delivering an address to the nation on the Ole Miss crisis. James Meredith was safely on campus, he announced. "This has been accomplished thus far without the use of National Guard or other troops." Invoking a theme he knew was dear to the South—its "honor and courage"—Kennedy talked of the valor "won on the field of battle and on the gridiron." He said there was no reason "why the books on this case cannot now be quickly and quietly closed," and he concluded with a message to the students of Ole Miss:

"You have a new opportunity to show that you are men of patriotism and integrity, for the most effective means of upholding the law is not the state policemen or the marshals or the National Guard. It is you. It lies in your courage to accept those laws with which you disagree as well as those with which you agree. The honor of your university and state are in the balance. I am certain that the great majority of the students will uphold that honor."

The president did not know that, minutes before, all hell had already broken out on the Ole Miss campus.

Neither did the faithful at the First Baptist Church back home in Summit. At that hour, they turned their Sunday-evening service into a referendum on the Meredith situation. The congregation unanimously adopted a resolution:

"Whereas, it is our firm conviction that the Word of God endorses the idea of segregation of races. . . . Whereas, it is our firm conviction that integration of the school system in Mississippi would open an era of bloodshed, immorality, and crime unmatched in the history of our nation. . . . Therefore, be it resolved that we stand solidly with our governor, Ross R. Barnett, in this solemn hour and pledge to him our loyalty throughout this great ordeal."

Instead of firing a few volleys of tear gas to disperse the crowd, the federal marshals, their patience exhausted, triggered hundreds of rounds. That stirred a wasp's nest. Rumors swept the campus, as insidious as the gas: a popular young woman had been struck and killed by a tear-gas canister; the grounds of Ole Miss were littered with many other student casualties; over the fallen Mississippi bodies, marshals were bringing Meredith to the Lyceum to be registered that night.

Already burning from the tear gas, students were stoked into venomous wrath by the various reports, especially by the word of the young woman's death. As soon as the first rounds of gas dissipated and Kennedy's brief speech ended, crowds surged back toward the Lyceum. The mob's numbers increased exponentially. Within a half hour of the outbreak of fighting, the state troopers—who had maintained roadblocks at the gates of the school to keep troublemakers away—withdrew, leaving the campus open to posses of night riders. Cars filled with students from other schools in the state, eager to join the rebellion and unwilling to let Ole Miss enjoy all the glory of the insurrection, poured onto the campus. So did pickup trucks, driven by seething men armed as if for a deer hunt. Hundreds of others flowed in on foot along University Avenue, carrying shotguns, sticks, rocks, and bottles. A construction project near the Lyceum provided a supply of bricks.

In the center of the Lyceum circle, the Confederate battle flag had been hoisted to the top of a flagpole.

By 9 P.M., control of the riot had passed from the students to the hands of an adult gang. From my vantage point at the foot of the circle, I watched as disorganized rioters made wave after wave of assaults on the Lyceum. I could hear ham radio units broadcasting appeals across north Mississippi for reinforcements.

Rioters commandeered the university fire truck, using the vehicle to charge the Lyceum. The scene looked like a distortion of a western movie: instead of Indians galloping around an embattled wagon train, the fire truck sped around the circle in front of the Lyceum like a toy out of control. Each time the truck passed the Lyceum, its passengers—clinging to the running boards—threw rocks and bricks and were met with broadsides of tear-gas canisters that struck the truck like heavy hail. After several circuits, the marshals captured the truck and some of its occupants.

Others picked up the fight. Uncoiling fire hoses, they sprayed the marshals' position with powerful jets of water. Although the mob was driven back again, the abandoned hoses continued to thrash and spew about the circle like giant, dying snakes.

Rioters requisitioned a bulldozer from the construction site. A man who looked as though he had just come from a job clearing the backwoods fired the ignition and steered the grinding machine toward the marshals' redoubt. A cluster of insurrectionists marched behind him, pitching bricks into the blackness. They were met with fresh rounds of gas. The bulldozer barged into an oak.

The next assault was by car. Roaring across the grass circle, the driver collided with one tree and caromed into another, disabling the vehicle.

I thought it impossible, but the night grew more surrealistic. Gangs uprooted concrete benches from the campus lawns and tumbled the debris onto the streets in an effort to block any convoys that might be coming to rescue the marshals. Inside the Lyceum, Robert Kennedy's press secretary, Ed Guthman, reported on the phone to his boss, "It's getting like the Alamo."

A layer of choking fog enveloped much of the campus. In my role as budding journalist and student voyeur, I wandered the fringes of the war zone, racing away when caught in pockets of gas and returning when it ebbed. I heard the rattle of gunshots and concluded that a firefight was taking place between the marshals and the mob.

Afterward, the federal government insisted that the marshals never resorted to firearms during the long night, a claim supported by a post-riot investigation. But if they had fired back, I would not have blamed them. Their situation, to use a newsman's cliché, was deteriorating rapidly. Through a veil of gas, I could see shadows, men crouching, firing pistols at the Lyceum. Marksmen with rifles climbed into trees to get better angles. Wounded members of the federal force fell at the foot of the building, exposed to further fire until they could be dragged inside by other marshals. Some in the mob dropped, too, struck by stray bullets.

Because no ambulances could fight their way onto campus, private cars were used to carry the wounded to the Oxford Hospital. I saw the mob block one car containing a bleeding marshal. The group finally allowed the vehicle to pass after determining the passenger might be dying. Such were the rules of war that night.

Nearly four hours after the riot began, the first reserves came to the marshals' rescue. A convoy of Jeeps and trucks loaded with men in military gear tore out of the smoke along University Avenue and rounded the circle leading to the Lyceum. They were showered with bricks and bottles. A Jeep bounced off one of the concrete barricades, but kept moving. The next day, we learned the members of the relief unit belonged to the Oxford National Guard; they were local merchants, insurance salesmen, and mechanics who had been put under federal orders to reinforce the marshals.

News of the coed's death proved to be untrue, but other reports were verified. The body of a foreign reporter had been found behind the campus YMCA. Another man, identified for posterity as a "jukebox repairman" from Oxford, was shot to death while watching events from the edge of the Grove.

When the melee began, several cars had been abandoned at the Lyceum circle. Thwarted in their attempts to storm the administration building, the mob directed its fury on the cars. They turned the vehicles upside down, then torched them. Flames licked from the windows, and burning wires caused the car horns to bleat mournfully.

Next, I feared, they would set fire to our buildings.

Ole Miss, a seat of Southern hospitality where the student motto had been Everybody Speaks, was being sacked by vandals from our own state.

I was not wise enough to perceive my own risk and stayed on the perimeter of the action for hours, enthralled by the bloody battle. During an interval in the fighting, Franklin Holmes and I spotted a face that had become familiar in the days leading to the riot. It was General Walker, standing near the Confederate monument, wearing a Texas cowboy hat and a dopey expression. In fact, he looked a bit dazed, as if he had swallowed a handful of tranquilizers. "Hell," I said to Franklin, "let's go talk to him."

We introduced ourselves to Walker and asked his assessment of the night. The general responded genially, saying the riot represented a great public outcry against the Kennedy administration. All the blood that would be spilled this night, Walker said, would be on the Kennedys' hands.

The old soldier asked us if the marshals were using bullets or buckshot to fight back. Since I was an ROTC washout, I knew little about weapons or military strategy and pleaded ignorance. "The marshals are clearly disorganized," the general offered, suggesting that they were probably running out of tear gas. If the mob wanted to overrun their position, he said, they should employ a flanking movement and attack from the south side of the Lyceum instead of constantly throwing themselves into a line of tear-gas fire at the front of the building.

Before the marshals could be overwhelmed, thousands of soldiers began arriving after midnight. Army trucks carrying troops in battle gear began lumbering onto the campus from different directions. They came down University Avenue and they came up Sorority Row, weathering barrages of rocks and bricks and Molotov cocktails. Bearing rifles with bayonets, helmeted soldiers swarmed through a western gate near a dormitory where Meredith had been sequestered throughout the night. Few of the rioters realized Meredith was there, or they might have redirected their attack from the Lyceum to his dormitory. Overhead we could hear the drone of a massive airlift, as troop transports descended, one after another, on the Oxford airport.

Franklin and I decided it was time to go back to the SAE house. Inside, there was bedlam. Many of our classmates were waiting to use the lone telephone to let their anxious parents know they were not among the casualties. In the distance, we could still hear the crump of tear gas, coupled with unearthly howling.

After dawn, platoons of paratroopers, working at bayonet point, finally drove the rioters off the campus. Skittering through side streets, the mob tried unsuccessfully to regroup in downtown Oxford. In the mopping-up operation, scores of men with no connection to the university were arrested. One of them was General Walker.

By the time the battle was over, the campus reeked of tear gas. I expressed my dismay in a disconsolate letter I wrote home a few hours later, on Monday evening: "Dear Folks: It is rumored that we are now under martial law and that a 7 P.M. curfew is to be imposed." I gave a detailed ten-page account, written on lined notebook paper, of the riot the night before. I illustrated my story with a map showing the major points of conflict.

Thousands of troops were now on campus, I noted. "About a third of the campus population has evacuated. Others are leaving all the time. Classes have been forgotten. The semester is irreparably damaged."

I made my judgment: "No one is guiltless. Neither Barnett, the Kennedys, the Federal marshals, the Mississippi law officers, the NAACP, the Citizens Council. I hope they are happy because they have all contributed greatly to the ruin of our university. . . . Right now it is impossible for me to attempt to salvage an education out of this mess. The mood is generally one of despair here. The campus is blockaded at all entrances as is downtown Oxford and all roads leading to the town."

After assuring my parents that I would not get involved in further trouble—I pledged to stay inside "because a gun battle between rednecks and troops might explode at any minute"—I added a postscript as though it were a news bulletin:

"I can hear tear gas bombs exploding across the campus. No one seems to know why. . . . Jeeps incessantly patrolling the streets by the dozens. One tear gas bomb exploded in front of our house for no apparent reason. The troops are surely getting nervous. Planes, planes, planes overhead."

The final toll was two dead, countless wounded. Newspaper accounts simply said that "hundreds" were hurt. Various figures were published for the number of soldiers used to put down the riot, perhaps as many as thirty thousand. They never called it martial law, but Ole Miss lived under military occupation for my final semester. Despite my gloomy prediction, I completed my requirements and Meredith attended classes without further violence.

The might of the federal government had prevailed. The back of resistance in Mississippi had been broken, just as it had a century earlier when Vicksburg fell. But the state would continue to lash out, like a wounded animal, for several more years of blood and fire and terror.

CHAPTER 7

"You can pronounce hero, can't you?"

★ ★ ★ ★ ★

With a college diploma I expected doors to open, but not even the armed services wanted me. Summoned during final examinations for a preinduction physical—there had been a draft call because of the Berlin Wall crisis—I left the army hospital with a 4-F classification. Asthma. The military rejection didn't trouble me, but my prospects looked equally dim elsewhere. My only job offer—available to anybody with a journalism degree from Ole Miss—came from the *Clarion-Ledger*. Described as a "rewrite" slot, the job was to copy stories verbatim from outlying dailies in Mississippi, add a dateline, and reprint them in the Jackson newspaper as though *Clarion-Ledger* correspondents had filed the dispatches. I would have tried selling Bibles door-to-door before going to work for a Hederman paper, so I kept looking.

After a futile month, I found a job as a rookie reporter at the *Press Register* in Clarksdale, a city with a population of twenty thousand in the heart of the Mississippi Delta. Although I had been born in the Delta and had occasionally visited the place with friends from Ole Miss, it was still terra incognita to me. *The Most Southern Place on Earth* is the title that historian James C. Cobb chose for his 1992 book on the Mississippi Delta, and that was an excellent description of the region when I moved there.

In 1963, the Delta maintained the country's last feudal system. A distinct class structure was in place. Prosperous white families reigned over thousands of acres of plantations while blacks served as their vassals, working in their fields and their homes. For the planters, life was a high-stakes crapshoot, betting against bad weather and boll weevils and hoping the price of cotton would go up. In good years, when substantial profits from the crop were assured, the planters might take their families to Manhattan for Christmas shopping sprees or overseas for vacations on the Continent. They spent money as though each season would be their last. Sometimes they lost it all—their land, their homes, their fortunes—a contingency that put an edge to existence in the Delta.

Myths grew up there as quickly as weeds. Everything seemed exaggerated, from the extremes in wealth and poverty to the lush accents that placed a broad pronunciation on the letter A. A cosmopolitan population, including many Catholics and not a few heathens, the people of the Delta enjoyed a hedonistic society beyond the Baptist pale. Parties lasted late, and mornings often included eye-openers for breakfast. Tennessee Williams spent his childhood in Clarksdale and set several plays in the Delta. Although scores of novelists and playwrights have made attempts to capture the place, *Cat on a Hot Tin Roof* best caught the Delta's strange ethos: the eccentric manners, the flow of bourbon and braggadocio, the stylized way of speaking, the sense of doom that kept springing out of the closet despite every attempt to keep it contained.

Geographically, the Delta consists of an arc of rich, flat land beginning just below Memphis and winding two hundred miles along the Mississippi River, its breadth no wider than the sixty miles between Greenville and Greenwood. Spiritually, according to David Cohn, one of the many writers from the region, "the Mississippi Delta begins in the lobby of the Peabody Hotel in Memphis and ends on Catfish Row in Vicksburg." Cohn's terminal points were, of course, places of good times and liquid cheer.

Despite the outward gaiety, the Delta had a foreboding background. The land had not been taken from the Choctaws until well after Mississippi became a state in 1817, and the low-lying terrain threw up many natural barriers to the white man. "Rumors of the Delta's unhealthiness and reasonably accurate depictions of its junglelike vegetation and climatic unpredictability may have delayed settlement of the area," Cobb wrote in his book. Only the fertility of the soil enticed cotton growers, who were wearing out the land in the hills of north Mississippi. Shortly before the Civil War, the prospect of unimaginably rich land at cheap prices finally convinced these entrepreneurs to clear the new wilderness and move their farming operations closer to the great river.

The Delta's planter class had emerged relatively late in the history of the Old South, but once the cotton farmers acquired wealth, they spent lavishly.

As Cobb wrote of their society in the mid-1800s: "Younger members of the Delta aristocracy gave so many parties that such entertainment was often available several nights a week. These elaborate affairs served to acquaint 'eligible' young adults of comparable social standing, and the Delta's gentry thought nothing of a forty-mile round-trip if a good party awaited them in the middle of it. . . . Their lifestyles and material wealth seemed to encourage some members of the Delta's plantation elite to indulge in considerable social pretense."

In the 1960s, colored people provided manpower to sustain the joie de vivre, though there was little joy in their own environment. Blacks outnumbered whites two to one in most counties, yet lived far below the poverty level in the squalor of plantation shacks and rows of sagging frame houses at dusty crossroads. As farmworkers, they were exempt from federal minimum-wage requirements and depended on the mercy of the "boss man." Although the Negro population had escaped the shackles of institutionalized slavery—and many had moved to Chicago and Detroit in the years following World War II—those remaining in the Delta lived in de facto bondage.

In Coahoma County, where Clarksdale was located, the 1960 census determined that Negro families had a median annual income of $1,406. The per capita income for colored males was $758; Negro females earned exactly half that amount. Most Negroes in the county had gone to school for less than five years.

It was no coincidence that the soulful music known as the blues had risen out of the Delta, producing hundreds of musicians, including B. B. King, Robert Johnson, Son House, Sam Cooke, John Lee Hooker, Muddy Waters, W. C. Handy, Howlin' Wolf, and Ike Turner.

Joe Ellis owned the *Clarksdale Press Register*, acted as its editor and publisher, and signed our checks each Thursday with a regal flourish. I will always remember my first paycheck—$63.71 after deductions. Joe had taken over the newspaper after coming home from World War II with a journalism degree from Washington and Lee and service as a naval officer. Though he was a member of a respected Clarksdale family, Joe represented something of an anomaly. He was a Republican.

At that time, the Republicans could have held their county caucus in a bathroom stall. The few I knew were moderately conservative, pro-business mavericks who seemed to enjoy their powerlessness.

Joe was an intelligent, nervous man who chain-smoked cigarettes and drank countless cups of overcooked coffee from an urn that burbled all day in the pressroom. When I arrived, he was just beginning his scrap with civil rights activists who had organized a boycott of white-owned businesses. He seemed far more concerned over his feud with the mayor, W. S. "Kat" Kincade, a gruff arriviste.

While white Clarksdale stood united in its opposition to cries for equity from the black community, the population split over the operation of city hall. The "cut-glass set," which included Joe, considered the mayor a boor. Kincade drew his following from the working classes who ran the service stations, delivered the laundry, sold the groceries, and followed a lifestyle dramatically different from the Delta aristocracy. Kincade had started as a contractor and wound up a millionaire by manufacturing a device to keep car engines warm overnight. Despite his riches, he had few social graces. Kat Kincade wore khaki shirts, cursed, and scratched his ass in public, and Joe's crowd feared he would put the city under his crass dominion.

The week I went to work for the *Press Register*, Joe fired off a blistering editorial, accusing Kincade of cronyism and suggesting that a number of "lounge lizards" were on the city payroll. The editorial voice was not exactly magisterial, but I figured my new job would be fun. My enthusiasm was hardly diminished when the mayor didn't deign to return my phone calls and dismissed me with curt remarks after I approached him for comment at city hall. Even as a green *Press Register* reporter, I considered myself in the camp of enlightenment, arrayed in combat against the armies of ignorance.

Just as the state Democratic Party was divided between the moderates and the Eastland-Barnett axis, the Delta establishment had two schools. In Clarksdale, the upper class—which is to say many of the planters and their friends in the banking and legal communities—went about repression quietly; they might listen politely to a black man's entreaty to register to vote or to be hired for a good job, but the answer was usually "Never." Kincade and his uncouth crowd were not so subtle. They practiced overt racism and followed an old maxim: keep the nigger down. Kincade threw the word around a lot and surrounded himself at city hall with minions who shared his views. Not only would they say no, they were prepared to rap the heads of insolent blacks.

Besides the mayor, Clarksdale's city government had two commissioners. Both quarreled constantly with Kincade. Despite the commissioners' antipathy to the mayor, the *Press Register* held the pair in low regard, too. At one point, feelings ran so high that Commissioner J. W. McKellar and Kincade agreed to resign and run against each other, though McKellar chickened out in the end. The other board member was a jackass named Hudson Bell, who insisted that the *Press Register* refer to him as "police commissioner" because he had nominal jurisdiction over the police department. Bell liked the title because his hero was Bull Connor, and he did his best to pattern himself after the blustering police commissioner of Birmingham. Bell carried a pistol in a holster strapped to his chest, kept his coat open to expose the weapon to an admiring (he thought) public, and denounced niggers in almost every breath.

By this time, the racial flashpoint had moved from Oxford to Alabama, where George Wallace became governor the winter I took my job in Clarksdale. A former bantamweight, Wallace campaigned as "Alabama's fighting judge" and promised to keep the races separated in the state. In his famous inaugural address—"segregation now, segregation tomorrow, segregation forever"—Wallace picked up Ross Barnett's worn gauntlet and flung it back at the federal government. "We will tolerate their boot in our face no longer," Wallace vowed while a crowd of thousands in front of the Montgomery capitol cheered and shook their fists. Wallace attacked black atrocities ("The Belgian survivors of the Congo cannot present their case") and accused the federal government of overkill at Ole Miss. "No wonder Communism is winning the world," he lamented.

That spring, Birmingham blacks began a series of sit-ins at lunch counters, outraging Eugene "Bull" Connor, the city's top cop. According to Dan T. Carter's biography of Wallace, *The Politics of Rage,* Connor had been a prominent figure in Alabama's racist-populist alliance long before the fighting judge enlisted. "Connor ran the police department like a plantation (he called his favorite cops 'my nigguhs') and he tolerated blacks only if they were willing to grovel or to assume the role of 'Sambos' and 'Aunt Jemimas.'" Although Connor had failed in a bid to become mayor and was finishing his term as a lame-duck commissioner when the demonstrations rolled into the streets of Birmingham, he earned himself a place in history with his strong-arm tactics.

The Birmingham protest movement, led by a local activist, Fred Shuttlesworth, and Martin Luther King Jr.'s Southern Christian Leadership Conference (SCLC), deployed hundreds of black schoolchildren in a new strategy. At first, the children filled the streets in chanting masses; arrested, they overwhelmed the city jail. Frustrated by his inability to cope with the demonstrators, Connor unleashed police dogs and fire hoses on the crowds. Shuttlesworth was hospitalized after being knocked against the brick wall of the Sixteenth Street Baptist Church by a high-pressured blast of water. Connor expressed regret that he had not seen his adversary in pain: "I'm sorry I missed it. I wish they'd carried him away in a hearse." Pictures of the melee galvanized much of the nation in support of the Birmingham blacks, but across the South, Connor was deified by people like Clarksdale's Commissioner Hudson Bell.

As Birmingham quaked, demonstrations spread through Dixie like the yellow fever epidemics that had enervated the South in the nineteenth century, and the Delta, with hundreds of thousands of blacks, became a logical setting for a racial Armageddon.

The first confrontations with the white establishment in Clarksdale were hesitant, probing operations. In an effort to exert economic pressure, local Negroes had been encouraged by the NAACP to boycott white-owned stores as early as 1961 after the city fathers decreed that colored citizens could no longer participate in the annual Christmas parade. Because their buying power was relatively limited, the boycott had little impact other than to convince other blacks that white interests could be challenged without resulting in a lynching.

Trying another tack, groups of Negroes began showing up at the Coahoma County circuit clerk's office to register to vote. To look presentable, they dressed in their Sunday best, the men in dark, frayed suits, the women in worn, flowered dresses. Although Kincade controlled city hall, the county courthouse was in the hands of the planter class, whose leaders had enough sense to know that pigheaded resistance would be counterproductive. As a result, some Negroes were allowed on the voting rolls. But the officials also recognized that whites were heavily outnumbered in Coahoma County, so many other applicants were turned down to keep a solid white majority. Usually, the circuit clerk, a cranky old man named J. W. Smith, cited a failed literacy test, in which Negroes were asked to interpret arcane provisions of the state constitution.

Officials used more brutal measures in other places in the Delta. Shortly after my arrival in Clarksdale, police in Greenwood, sixty miles down the road, hammered participants in a voter registration march and hauled many of them to jail. Comedian Dick Gregory, who took part in the demonstration, had a one-liner to assess the situation: "This is worse than Russia."

Gregory was a frequent celebrity guest at civil rights rallies in Clarksdale, one of a growing number of nationally known Negroes who began coming to town to inspire the population to rise up. But the most important figure in the local movement was a pharmacist, Aaron Henry, the state president of the NAACP.

As half of the *Press Register*'s two-man reporting team, I was expected to know the newsmakers in the community, so in the first days of my career the paper's senior reporter, Bill Skelton, took me across the railroad tracks to the Fourth Street Drug Store to meet Aaron. From that first encounter, I knew I would get along much better with the NAACP leader than the mayor.

With the civil rights movement gaining momentum, whites were beginning to complain about "militant" blacks, yet nothing about Aaron appeared threatening. He had a gentle face, expressive, smoky eyes, and wore a sports shirt and slacks like an ordinary Delta merchant. He spoke with uncommon eloquence, and he welcomed me to Clarksdale with a man-to-man greeting, showing no trace of the deferential manner most Delta blacks used when dealing with whites. During his conversation with us, Aaron softly pushed a grievance he had with the newspaper, directing his remarks at Bill Skelton rather than picking on the new reporter. For some time, Aaron had been calling on the *Press Register* to use courtesy titles—Mr., Mrs., Miss—for blacks just as the paper did for white people.

Throughout the South, the refusal to couple a black man's name with the word *mister* was a common practice to keep the colored population a notch below whites. The tradition was not only demeaning, it created awkward journalism. If I had been writing a story about Bessie Smith, the legendary blues singer who had died years earlier in Clarksdale from injuries suffered in a car wreck, I would have been required to refer to her as "the Smith woman" in the second reference rather than call her Miss Smith.

Aaron's complaint had the support of Bill Skelton as well as Harry Abernathy, the managing editor. But Joe Ellis shared a dilemma with many Mississippi editors. Though he understood that Negroes deserved better treatment and realized that ground should be yielded on certain issues, Joe faced condemnation from his peers if he appeared to be caving in to black demands. Joe was grudging on the courtesy-title issue. But after a couple of in-house arguments with Bill and Harry, he changed the *Press Register*'s policy.

Aaron Henry never crowed over the victory; he accepted it as a just resolution to a problem. That was his style. During my early assignments covering the racial scene, I found that many of the local leaders in the civil rights movement, especially the ministers, were demonstrative and long-winded. Aaron rarely raised his voice, but his determination was so obvious he didn't need to shout.

Because Bill Skelton had his hands full covering the courts, schools, business developments, and the Byzantine machinations of city and county governments, I drew assignments to cover the civil rights rallies and began spending more time at Aaron's command post. From the time I'd read Camus in college, I had wanted to cover a revolution.

The Fourth Street Drug Store was an old-fashioned pharmacy with an ice cream counter near the front door. Shelves stocked with pomades, hair straighteners, and laxatives lined the aisles, and in the back, Aaron filled prescriptions and offered advice on the telephone. He kept me posted on prospective visits of "dignitaries"—a word he used and the *Press Register* did not—such as Roy Wilkins, the national head of the NAACP, Martin Luther King Jr., and James Meredith.

In polite conversation, the term *blacks* was not widely used at the time. We talked, instead, of *colored people* or *Negroes*. I favored *colored*, and when I used the latter term, I applied the standard Mississippi pronunciation, *Nigras*. Aaron objected. I said *Knee-grow* sounded affected and claimed it was difficult to pronounce. "Hell, Curtis," Aaron said, "you can pronounce *hero*, can't you?" I cleaned up my pronunciation.

Aaron had been born near Clarksdale, served in the army, and graduated from Xavier College—now a university—in New Orleans before coming home to open a drugstore and begin the real work of his lifetime, civil rights. Since he was self-employed, Aaron was in a position to challenge the system without losing his job. Other than the ministers, who answered to their congregations, and a handful of men who owned funeral parlors or other small businesses, the Negro community depended upon white employers. In this inhibiting atmosphere, it seemed miraculous that Aaron had not only organized an NAACP chapter in Clarksdale, but had recruited hundreds of members.

The year before I met Aaron, he had been arrested after a hitchhiker told police that Aaron had made a sexual pass during their drive down a Delta highway. Aaron was convicted of disturbing the peace, sentenced to sixty days in jail, and fined $250. The case, which had attracted widespread attention because of Aaron's status, was on appeal. I assumed he had been framed by white authorities.

Aaron was married, had a young daughter, and lived in a modest home in a colored neighborhood—the house that was firebombed in my first spring in Clarksdale. Two white men were arrested within hours, charged with pitching bottles filled with gasoline through the windows of the home. Though Joe Ellis disapproved of Aaron's activities, he published a front-page editorial deploring the attack. "Every decent Clarksdalian regrets last night's incident," he wrote.

The same week, coincidentally, the NAACP filed suit in federal court seeking to desegregate Clarksdale's city hall, its parks and playgrounds, swimming pools, the Coahoma County Courthouse, the Carnegie Public Library, and the Coahoma County Hospital. Within a month, a mysterious blast knocked a hole in the roof of Aaron's drugstore. The sheriff attributed the damage to a bolt of lightning. Aaron told me it was nitroglycerin.

A few weeks later, several shots were fired into the Henrys' home. Six days later, the city's board of mayor and commissioners rejected a request for a biracial committee to consider complaints of discrimination. Preston Stevenson, a white Presbyterian minister who supported the proposal, was summarily fired from his volunteer position as city hall chaplain. That night, Medgar Evers was murdered in Jackson. Congressman William Colmer, who represented the Mississippi Gulf Coast and served as Trent Lott's mentor, called Evers's murder "the inevitable result of agitation by politicians, do-gooders, and those who sail under the false flag of liberalism."

Less than a year after the disaster at Ole Miss, we were marching head-long into another series of bloody battles, and the great-grandson of the man who had left the university to fight the Federals a hundred years ago no longer knew which side he was on.

Most of my friends in Clarksdale came from moderate circles, men and women who observed segregationist customs but disapproved of blatant bigotry. When I moved there, I was practically adopted by the Maynard family. The two Maynard daughters, Elsie and Lucie Lee, were Ole Miss graduates and friends of the girl I was dating, Jane Pelegrin. In a burst of Southern hospitality, they introduced me to their parents and treated me like a reclamation project; they helped furnish my rented digs, plied me with nutritious meals, and saw to it that I met the proper people in town.

The Maynards were Brahmans in the community; their large home was lit by a sunroom, and their Oriental rugs radiated warmth. The father, George Maynard, had attended Washington and Lee with Pa. Ten years earlier, he had been the only attorney in Clarksdale willing to represent Aaron Henry and other members of the black community in an effort to obtain an indictment against two white men charged with raping a pair of Negro teenagers. Mrs. Maynard, whose name was Lucie Lee, too, could have been a model for any of the mannered Southern wives in Eudora Welty's novels. I called the Maynard home often on the phone. When she answered, I would say, "Hello, Mrs. Maynard, this is Curtis Wilkie." Mrs. Maynard always giggled. I shouldn't have bothered identifying myself, she later told me; no one else had a voice as deep and raspy as mine.

The Maynards were accustomed to dealing with their daughters' friends. After a party one night, young Lucie Lee decided her parents would enjoy meeting a colorful character from another Delta city. So she took the visitor, who happened to be quite drunk, into the Maynards' bedroom. Her slumbering parents rose and greeted the midnight guest cordially, but the next day Mr. Maynard remonstrated, "Lucie Lee, sometimes I think you'd bring a goddamned baboon home." I was in the stray-dog category myself, but no one treated me better than the Maynards, and as racial tensions built, their home became something of a sanctuary.

They had loyal, long-standing servants who seemed like members of the family. One ancient retainer, Marion Jackson, had worked for the Maynards for years before moving to Chicago. Later, he came home, disillusioned with the big city, and asked for some kind of job. Though he was approaching eighty, the Maynards gave him a permanent assignment: to take Elsie's young son, Jay, on strolls through town each day.

The Maynard household was a study in Southern respectability in the segregationist era. They deplored the state's race-baiting politicians; it seemed unimaginable that any member of the Maynard family would use derogatory terms to describe colored people. Yet it would have been just as unthinkable for them to entertain Negroes in their home. Like me, they abided within the system.

The Maynards were moderates. In Clarksdale, moderates were outnumbered but not without influence. From the outset of the NAACP boycott, it was apparent that some of the most important people in town were willing to make accommodations with the Negro population. It was in the moderates' interest to keep the peace, while at the same time maintaining the basic system. As descendants of Coahoma County's founding fathers, leaders of the Ole Miss alumni network, lawyers and doctors, ministers and teachers, the local moderates were not without political clout. Allied with the Stennis wing of the Democratic Party, they sometimes supported victorious candidates. But on the increasingly paramount question of race, they found themselves torn by conflict, unable to make a break with American apartheid. So they counseled moderation on racial matters. Their amorphous position, taken totally without passion, afforded them little leverage.

The hard-core segregationists, on the other hand, were rabid, and their vigor gave them the upper hand. The exponents of "Never!"—ranging from bankers and wealthy but barely literate planters to surly restaurateurs and shade-tree mechanics—seemed to have a visceral aversion to blacks. Though Clarksdale did not have a functioning Citizens Council, the policies of the organization were carried out, de facto, by well-connected people who acted on the advice of a couple of local lawyers.

Like a photograph slowly developing in the chemical basin of a darkroom, the situation gradually became clear to me: our elected officials were essentially front men. Public policy followed the dictates of powerful unelected segregationists who provided private leadership. The arrangement was perfectly acceptable to the city fathers. Because the race issue transcended their petty spats at city hall, the mayor and the two warring commissioners were willing to put aside their personal differences to implement a program of unadulterated racism.

Their most notorious agent was Clarksdale's police chief, Ben Collins. Long before hippies began to call cops "pigs" later in the decade, Collins had the misfortune to look porcine. Red-faced and overweight, he had large, upturned nostrils that flared with excitement at the prospect of pounding someone. "There's nothing I like better than whipping niggers' asses," he once told me in a moment of reflection.

As part of my beat, I stopped at the police department each morning to review the docket of overnight arrests and incidents. To avoid alienating my police sources, I kept my opinions to myself. Journalism school would call that maintaining objectivity; at the Clarksdale PD, it was a matter of self-preservation. Some of the police officers were funny fellows, and I often joined them for coffee. They specialized in nigger jokes, and I duly chuckled at the punch lines. The chief especially liked the one about the stolen pig disguised as a Negro named Oink Jones.

Ben Collins was not a man of great sensitivity. He worked as a referee at high school football games on Friday nights and seemed as fond of the striped shirt and white knickers as he was of his police uniform, which was adorned with badges and gold braids. When President Kennedy's assassination disrupted a football weekend—high school and college games were canceled and the networks preempted the professional schedule that terrible Sunday—Collins waxed his displeasure. "The next time they shoot one of those sons of bitches," he said, "I hope they do it in hockey season."

While racial animosity drove the gang at city hall, some local conservatives dwelled on a farther shore. Reasonably well-educated and economically well-to-do, these individuals were troubled by Communists as well as Negroes. Convinced that the two forces were conspiring to bring down democracy as practiced in Mississippi, they assembled a strange coalition of activists, including the leaders of the United Daughters of the Confederacy and Rabbi Benjamin Schultz of Temple Beth Israel, whose congregation came from throughout the north Delta.

The anticommunists had a euphemism—Citizens for Freedom or something like that—for their organization. That it was a cover for the John Birch Society was one of the poorest-kept secrets in Clarksdale. They donated stacks of extremist "literature" to the public school libraries and attracted out-of-town speakers from a collection of circuit-riding right-wingers who included the famous columnist Westbrook Pegler and Summit's own Mary Cain.

Since I had no seniority at the newspaper, I got to cover most of the night meetings in town, a schedule that veered wildly from civil rights rallies in black churches to forums sponsored by the anticommunists at the City Auditorium. When Mary Cain came to preach to the converted, I was there.

Our friendship had been strained in recent months. On my first visit home after the Ole Miss riot, I stopped by the *Summit Sun* to discuss the situation with her. The right was rallying behind General Walker, portraying him as an innocent victim of a plot by the Kennedys. Not only had Walker been arrested, an Associated Press news story had accused him of leading a student charge on the federal forces at Oxford. I was still annoyed over the clumsy handling of the showdown by everyone concerned, and I volunteered that I had not seen Walker involved in any kind of assault.

The next week I was horrified to read her column:

"Curtis Wilkie, one of our Summit students at Ole Miss, tells me that he personally talked with Gen. Walker and that the general was in no way inciting the students to rebellion. 'We were not sure who he was,' said Curtis, 'and some of us walked up and asked him who he was. He told us, and added that he had come to help us. We told him we certainly appreciated his interest and shook hands with him. I never did see him inciting the students.' On the other hand, he aided in keeping the students good-humored, as Curtis saw it."

That was not quite the way I saw it, nor the way I had told it to Mary Cain, who took no notes and never said she intended to quote me. I was peeved that she had misconstrued my remarks. During her speech in Clarksdale months later, she branded a couple of public figures in Mississippi Communist dupes. Afterward, she asked me not to report the slander. "I wouldn't want them to read that," she said with a tentative smile. I said I was sorry, but I considered her allegations newsworthy.

It was the last time I ever talked with Mary Cain, the neighbor who had published my first stories, the bylined accounts of a sixth-grade sportswriter, a dozen years earlier.

Of all the Mississippi editors, I most admired Hodding Carter, the iconoclast at the *Delta Democrat-Times* in Greenville. After his *Look* magazine article, which I had appropriated for my oral report in the ninth grade, Carter was denounced as a liar and censured by the state legislature for "selling out the state for Yankee gold." The vote was 89–19. He responded with an editorial:

"I hereby resolve by a vote of 1 to 0 that there are 89 liars in the state legislature, beginning with Speaker Sillers and working way on down to Representative Eck Windham, a political loon whose name is fittingly made up of the words 'wind' and 'ham.' . . . Those 89 character mobbers can go to hell collectively or singly and wait there until I back down." Carter went on to win a Pulitzer Prize for his attacks on the Citizens Council, and he regularly flogged Ross Barnett and other officials in the state.

After General Walker sued Carter for a million dollars in libel damages in the aftermath of the Ole Miss fiasco, I was contacted by the editor's attorneys about my encounter with the old soldier. They came to my house in Clarksdale to interview me and seemed bemused by one piece of pop art I had created and tacked to my kitchen wall. Originally, the poster had been an advertisement for the movie *Cleopatra*. I had obliterated the faces of Richard Burton and Elizabeth Taylor, replacing the heads of the loving couple with likenesses of George Wallace and Martin Luther King, cut from the covers of *Time* magazine.

The lawyers were interested in my observations of Walker. Among other things, Carter had called the general a "seditious psychopath." Satisfied that my sympathies lay with their client, one of the attorneys confided that Carter's comment "may have been a fatally alluring alliterative." The lawyers were reaching out for anyone with information about the general's activities on the night of the riot, so I told them of my talk with Walker and his tactical suggestions. To be truthful, I said, Walker had appeared more dreamy than wild-eyed, and that he led no charge, so far as I knew. I wanted to be helpful, but doubted my testimony would be valuable.

Fortunately for Hodding Carter, I wasn't needed. The U.S. Supreme Court threw out a judgment Walker had won earlier against the Associated Press on the grounds that the general had deliberately thrust himself into the public eye and had thus became legally vulnerable. As a result, his case against Carter was dropped before it ever went to trial.

After the NAACP sued the city of Clarksdale, Aaron Henry announced that his organization intended to attack every segregated law on the books, and he promised to do it with local people. A few days after Medgar Evers's assassination, the demonstrations began in earnest. In the first public protest, four pickets appeared near city hall. One carried a placard saying, "To Ignore the Pleas of Negro Citizens Is Tyranny." All four were arrested.

Demonstrations occurred daily. Aaron would call the *Press Register* to alert our staff to the latest target, which might be a lunch counter, the bus station, or city hall. In an air already charged with tension, new currents crackled. Blacks would individually drift into the white commercial district, then suddenly merge into small groups at an appointed location, breaking out posters hidden inside their shirts. Police would rush to intercept them, as if the Negroes belonged on the FBI's Ten Most Wanted list. The charge against the demonstrators was usually the same: parading without a permit. Even when the protesters were thirty children carrying American flags.

Martin King came to town for an Independence Day "freedom rally." He urged a crowd that filled a church around the corner from Aaron's store to keep the marches peaceful. "Our aim is to win the white man's friendship and understanding," he said. Aaron recommended the same course. But a new, truculent voice was among the speakers that evening. Charles Evers had returned to Mississippi following his brother's murder to take Medgar's job as field secretary of the NAACP. Though he shared with Aaron a goal, Charles Evers was competing with him for power within the organization, and he clearly did not agree with Aaron's conciliatory remarks. To demonstrate his disregard for an injunction issued against the two-year-old black business boycott, Evers held the document over his head and ripped it into pieces. He heaped further insult on the officials of Coahoma County by vowing, "One of these days Negroes will occupy the sheriff's office, and those now holding the job will be back on the plantation where they belong."

The demonstrations continued, and the arrests mounted. Hearings were held twice a week in a small courtroom above the police station in city hall. Once, when friends and relatives of the Negro defendants gathered to watch the disposition of the cases, Police Chief Ben Collins dispatched his men to spray Lysol over their heads to "disinfect" the crowd.

The incident took place several minutes before the city judge, Ed Connell, entered the room. I felt sure he would not have tolerated it. Ed was a few years older than me, an outstanding graduate of the Ole Miss law school and a member of an old Clarksdale family. He was much admired because, as a childhood victim of polio, he gamely moved about on crutches. Because I considered Ed a moderate, I approached him privately to suggest that he consider mercy for some of the defendants, especially the youthful ones. Ed's job as judge was part-time, but he took it seriously. He lectured me sternly on the law. The demonstrators were deliberately breaking the law, he said, and to uphold the law they had to be punished. Implicitly, he reminded me of my own status: a young reporter, new to town and naive about racial matters.

When Aaron Henry was brought before Ed on charges of parading without a permit—Aaron had carried a sign that said "We Protest Until Freedom Comes"—Ed fined him $101 and sentenced him to thirty days in jail. The state president of the NAACP joined the city's work gang. On his first day of incarceration, the *Press Register* dispatched a photographer to take

Aaron's picture. I was not sure whether the newspaper wanted to humiliate Aaron or to illustrate the story of another civil rights leader in jail. Aaron gladly posed for the picture, a shovel in his hand.

There were more arrests. A youngster wearing a T-shirt saying "Love Yes, Hate No" was thrown in jail for parading without a permit. Another young man in a shirt bearing the words "Freedom Now" drew additional charges of vagrancy and resisting arrest. He said he was beaten inside the jail by a Negro employee of the city. "It didn't happen," the police chief told me. The chief also denied charges that he had turned on the heat—it was August—in a small cell where a number of women were held.

After a police sweep put another two dozen Negroes in custody, I went to the jail to make a firsthand report. "There was an air of joviality about the proceedings," I wrote, "as police jokingly made requests for the group to sing. One song which the Negroes were singing—not a request, incidentally—had these words: 'Ain't gonna let nobody turn me 'round, turn me 'round, turn me 'round; Gonna keep on a-walking, keep on a-talking, talking about freedom land.'"

Events oscillated between tragedy and farce.

On a Sunday afternoon in the middle of September I turned on my television to watch pro football and heard numbing news instead. A bomb had ripped through the Sixteenth Street Baptist Church in Birmingham, and four little girls, wearing white dresses for Youth Day services, were dead.

Looking back after nearly four decades, I believe the South began to change inexorably that day. Our transition in racial attitudes would take years, and a long period of bitter resistance lay ahead. But the consciences of many white people were shaken badly that Sunday. We had been willing to ignore the indignities, the bogus arrests, and the intimidation heaped upon our black population, but the murder of their innocent children was unacceptable.

That autumn it seemed the only colors were black and white.

I attended a party with an Ole Miss crowd at a cabin on a lake near Clarksdale and discovered that a blues band led by the SAE houseboy-cum-bootlegger Miller P. Burk had been hired to furnish the entertainment. Miller P. and I toasted our reunion, knocking back a beer together, but around midnight the party's atmosphere took a nasty turn. One of the guests objected to the presence of a Negro band and punched Miller P. I leaped into the brawl, taking a couple of swings in Miller P.'s defense while others struggled to separate the fighters. Folding chairs, drumsticks, and a guitar skittered across the floor in the confusion. I felt a beer bottle hit the back of my head. Blood spilled over my shirt from a cut behind my ear. When one of my erstwhile SAE brothers expressed delight over the sight of blood, I cracked him in the jaw. As I was being driven to the hospital to get stitches for my head wound, I looked at my right hand. My little finger was cocked at an unnatural right angle. I would carry a crooked digit for the rest of my life as a token of the night.

I had to go about my work with my head bandaged and my hand in a sling for several days, enduring caustic comments at the police station, remarks that were usually reserved for civil rights workers.

As I scanned the police report one morning, the desk sergeant gave me a tip. "We had an interesting case last night," he told me in considerable confidence, the arrest of "a bunch of New York Jews" at Aaron Henry's house for breaking curfew. Clarksdale's curfew called for everyone to be off the streets by midnight, but it was only applied to Negroes and civil rights workers. The latest group of miscreants had been clapped in jail a few hours earlier, though the desk sergeant assured me they had been treated fairly. "We give them their one phone call, and you know who this son of a bitch Lowenstein called?" He pronounced it *Lowen-stine*.

I glanced at the report and saw three names, including Allard K. Lowenstein's. He went on to become a Pied Piper for the antiwar and civil rights movements. Another of the "Jewish" suspects was Stephen Bingham, the nephew of a Manhattan congressman.*

"You know who that son of a bitch Lowen-stine called?" the desk sergeant said again. "He called Franklin Fucking Delano Roosevelt Jr. Can you imagine that?"

Though President Roosevelt's wife, Eleanor, had been derided as an integrationist—Bilbo crowned her "queen of Greater Liberia"—FDR's memory was still honored in much of Mississippi for his New Deal programs, and the Clarksdale police were impressed by the name of his son, practicing law somewhere in the North. "Franklin Fucking Delano Roosevelt Jr.! We thought, 'Holy shit! We better let these sons of bitches go,'" the officer said. The three men were charged with loitering and released on a $16 bond.

* * *

*Bingham later spent thirteen years as a fugitive, suspected of smuggling a gun into a California prison to precipitate a bloody, attempted jailbreak, before being exonerated.

Lowenstein, I learned in a subsequent conversation with him, was in town to help organize a campaign that sounded foolish to me. Aaron had decided to run for governor on something called the Mississippi Freedom Democratic Party ticket. The party had no legal standing, no place on the ballot that fall, and not many blacks could vote. It appeared to be a waste of energy.

For all intents and purposes, the election had already been decided in the Democratic primaries in August, where the campaign had been as absurd as ever.

The gubernatorial race had developed into another contest between the moderates and the hard-core segregationists, enlivened by revelations that Ross Barnett had secretly dealt with the Kennedy brothers. Barnett's lieutenant governor, Paul Johnson, was favored by the Eastland crowd. His chief opponent was former governor J. P. Coleman, a champion of the moderates.

Another candidate, a Clarksdale lawyer named Charlie Sullivan, had finished third with Eastland's blessing four years earlier and figured to be formidable again. I knew Sullivan as a spellbinding orator who attracted dozens of spectators to the Coahoma County Courthouse to watch his performances as a trial lawyer. I also knew Charlie drank too much and had heard that he no longer had Eastland's support because he had recently insulted the senator.

As an ardent exponent of states' rights, Sullivan felt Eastland was forsaking Mississippi's principles in Washington by maintaining good relations with the Kennedy brothers. He announced his sentiments at a Delta party where the guests were expected to fawn over Eastland. Red-faced with whiskey, Sullivan confronted Eastland, calling him a hypocrite. Within days, Eastland had spread word through his network in Mississippi: Sullivan was to be destroyed politically.

Charlie Sullivan was eliminated in the first primary,* setting up the match between Johnson and Coleman in the second primary.

The two men sounded as though they were running for kleagle of the Ku Klux Klan instead of governor. Johnson presented himself as a man who had stood tall against the U.S. marshals at Ole Miss. Coleman attacked that position in full-page newspaper ads: "Let's tell the whole truth, Paul. . . . What part did you play in this secret deal that led to the tragedy at

---

*Sullivan was killed some years later when his private plane crashed.

Ole Miss? If you base your claim to the governorship on your three-minute stand at Ole Miss, then the voters are entitled to know about the three days of negotiation with the Kennedy administration." Coleman added, "Is it not a fact you voted for the Kennedy ticket in the 1960 election?"

Coleman was under fire himself for allowing John F. Kennedy, who had visited Mississippi while a U.S. senator, to sleep in a bed in the governor's mansion. In Johnson's ads, Coleman was also accused of being the favorite of the few black voters. Results from the first primary showed that Coleman carried a couple of all-Negro towns in the Delta. It was evidence, Johnson said, that "once Mississippi's resistance is silenced, Kennedy will have a smooth road to a one-world government under socialism."

Coleman, the alleged moderate, declared he didn't want black votes. "We have never sought this kind of support," he said, "and would not accept it if offered."

Johnson won the runoff, assuring his election over a sacrificial Republican candidate in November. The Republican, Rubel Phillips, used his own anti-Kennedy theme, lining the highways with billboards linking the Democrats with the president. The message was simple: "K.O. the Kennedys!" In the days after November 22, workmen scurried across the state to paper over the signs.

In the meantime, the state Democratic executive committee remained in the hands of men who had loathed the Democratic president, but had no intention of giving up their power base. Before the general election, the state Democrats passed a resolution "to stamp out Republicanism before it gets to first base."

The state Democratic officials took no public notice of Aaron's insurgency, which involved mock elections in the basements of black churches where men and women cast ballots even though they were not registered to vote. To the party bosses, the Mississippi Freedom Democratic Party was a joke, as laughable as the notion that blacks would someday hold office in the state.

CHAPTER 8

"A publicity stunt"

★ ★ ★ ★ ★

Nothing distinguished the Hi-Hat from any other white honky-tonk. A cheap, one-story structure built with board and cinder block, it nestled beside Highway 51 just north of Summit, near the Lincoln County line. On Friday and Saturday nights, hundreds from "dry" Lincoln as well as neighboring Walthall and Amite Counties flocked to Pike County, where beer was legal. Rowdy crowds, eager to mate and ready to fight, filled roadhouses like the Hi-Hat, where relief flowed from long-necked bottles of Jax and Falstaff, country music spilled from the jukebox, and couples danced the Texas swing.

Growing up in Pike County, I considered these places zoos for badass rednecks. If I dared venture inside the Hi-Hat, I made sure it was in the company of my older friends Lew Barnes and William Paulk, who provided a measure of security. I would never have considered taking a date there. Violence was palpable in the Hi-Hat, so I was not surprised to hear about the events that took place there on a Saturday night in late April in 1964.

With a big crowd on hand, a beer truck driven by James White pulled into the parking lot to replenish supplies. At thirty, White's glory years were already behind him. I remembered him as a star athlete at Liberty High School in Amite County; Liberty invariably squashed Summit in football. He went on to become a valuable player at Southwest Junior College, whose games I once covered for the McComb newspaper. A decade later, he remained a popular figure in Amite County—even though some folks believed he had taken up the devil's work with the beer distributor.

Inside the Hi-Hat there was a confrontation: a bump, an old grievance, an angry word, some kind of spark that triggered an argument between James White and Haskell Boyd. I knew Haskell, too. He was my age and had always been a bully. As a boy, he had a reputation for flying into sudden, unprovoked rages, pounding schoolmates with his hard little fists. James White was also known to be able to take care of himself. When he refused to back down, Haskell pulled a pistol and shot him. The football hero died in the portal of the Hi-Hat while a mournful Hank Williams number played on the jukebox.

Haskell Boyd was charged with murder. After a series of threatening telephone calls, the sheriff decided to move his prisoner from the county jail to an undisclosed location. Unable to reach the murderer, vigilantes from Amite County chose other targets. On the following weekend, they torched three honky-tonks north of Summit. The Hi-Hat and the nearby Friendship Club burned to the ground. The Briar Patch, tucked into a hollow on the other side of the highway, was saved after its manager used a garden hose to put out the fire.

The Amite County night riders used gallon jugs filled with gasoline as their weapons. Their strike against the roadhouses had nothing to do with race; it was purely revenge. But it proved a practice run for the violence that would consume Mississippi that summer during our most terrible year since the Civil War.

In Clarksdale, the establishment braced for conflict. A civil rights bill, unacceptable to the white community, was slowly making its way through Congress under the guidance of President Johnson. The measure called for the desegregation of public accommodations across the country, which meant that every restaurant, hotel, and theater would be forced to offer access to Negroes. To the bitter-end segregationists—and even to many moderates—the idea seemed preposterous; it flouted constitutional freedoms that they believed gave businesses the right to choose their own customers.

The Coahoma County Bar Association organized a letter-writing campaign to oppose the bill. Since members of Mississippi's congressional delegation were already deep-dyed opponents of the legislation and representatives from other states disregarded correspondence from outside their districts, the appeal seemed useless to me. But the lawyers who encouraged the letters recognized the importance of maintaining some kind of offensive. As students of Civil War history, they knew Shiloh had been lost when the Confederate army paused after the first day of fighting and failed to push the Yankees into the Tennessee River.

Though Clarksdale had no Citizens Council per se, the city was home to a pair of lawyers who belonged to a network of segregationists around the state. One of the men who crafted Clarksdale's tactics was Leon Porter, a pinch-faced, middle-aged attorney whose sour disposition reflected his antipathy toward blacks. His distaste for reporters was manifest, too, and he rarely spoke to me. His associate, Semmes Luckett, was infinitely more interesting. Polished and cynical, Luckett was blessed with a majestic crown of silky white hair and bore a resemblance to the movie actor Claude Rains. An examplar of Eric Hoffer's "true believer," Luckett devoted the latter part of his life to the struggle to preserve Southern tradition with all the vigor of a Confederate officer defending the Lost Cause.

Luckett lived in a big house with columns, around the corner from the courthouse. It was a gothic household. One of his daughters, a young woman named Money, spent most of her hours lying inside an iron lung, a victim of polio since childhood. Money read religiously, Catholic tracts and John Birch Society material, and her bedside seemed to be attended regularly by conservative Irish priests and members of the United Daughters of the Confederacy, who feared a Communist takeover was imminent. A son, Semmes Jr., had been my roommate at Ole Miss for a semester and remained my friend. On New Year's Day, 1964, Semmes Jr. invited me to watch the Sugar Bowl, a contest between Ole Miss and Alabama, at the Luckett home, which had one of the first color TV sets in town. Ole Miss lost the game, and I lost my entrée with the Lucketts after Money and her mother, Celeste, determined during our conversation that I was insufficiently enthusiastic about their suspicions of a Negro-Communist conspiracy.

Nonetheless, the father was unfailingly courtly. He talked with me whenever I saw him, though never divulging any of his plots to maintain segregation in Coahoma County. He carried out his legal battles with guile and improvisation, even as each of the barriers he tried to erect crumbled under court orders over the years. Knowing he was an eloquent exponent of the Southern way of life, I steered visiting reporters to see him. Luckett told me he was glad to talk to them; he felt he could articulate the cause of segregation far better than the bumbling county attorney, an over-the-hill athlete known as "Babe" Pearson. Luckett spoke ex cathedra, as attorney for the Clarksdale school district. From the day an NAACP suit in the spring of 1964 accused the local schools of operating a "compulsory biracial system," Luckett fought the case with brazen tactics and artful duplicity. He became known as one of the most skillful managers of segregation in the state, and his name was mentioned in the same breath as that of Hardy Lott, a seg lawyer from Greenwood who twice saved Byron De La Beckwith from conviction that year for Medgar Evers's murder.

As summer approached, the *Press Register* carried a wire story with the headline "State Faces Race Agitation." Several hundred student volunteers from outside the South were preparing to come to Mississippi to assist local blacks in their campaign against Jim Crow. The idealistic concept had been developed by Al Lowenstein, the man who had phoned Franklin Delano Roosevelt Jr. from the Clarksdale jail, and Bob Moses, the intellectual directing the protest in Pike County.

The operation was sponsored by the Council of Federated Organizations (COFO), a coalition of civil rights groups. With its nonthreatening name, COFO had been formed in 1961 as a vehicle to send a delegation of black leaders, including Aaron Henry, to meet with Governor Barnett. Three years later, COFO was revitalized to support the summer project. The organizations that formed COFO included the NAACP, Martin Luther King's SCLC, the Congress of Racial Equality (CORE), and the Student Nonviolent Coordinating Committee (SNCC). Because the NAACP had the largest membership in Mississippi, Aaron served as president. Since the four groups differed in philosophy and competed for membership and donations, it was a fractious arrangement. But the coalition managed to stay intact as a show of unity against segregationist forces.

Even though I was relatively new to the scene and slow to pick up on the infighting, I detected friction. When Dr. King came to Clarksdale, Aaron acted as his host, but there were undertones of a rivalry. I eventually learned that Aaron's boss in the NAACP, Roy Wilkins, could not stand Dr. King. But for a season, the organizations set aside their squabbles in deference to the project that would be called Freedom Summer.

There were suggestions that civil rights activists sought white volunteers for the project because of a belief that if whites were subjected to atrocities in Mississippi, it would draw more attention than the everyday sufferings of blacks in the state. There was even talk of the need for white martyrs.*

---

*In 2000, Constance Curry, an Atlanta writer and former SNCC board member, assembled Aaron's papers into a valuable book, *Aaron Henry: The Fire Ever Burning*. In it, Aaron talked of the worth of the white volunteers. The bitterness of Mississippi blacks, he said, "began to subside as they saw these white college students sacrificing everything in order to help them . . . the fact that whites from the rest of the country—the same color and looking

For white Mississippi, however, the influx gave new meaning to the term *outside agitators*; it seemed tantamount to a Communist invasion. Many of the student volunteers were Jewish, a prospect that bothered Rabbi Schultz, the John Birch Society cat's-paw, as well as some members of his Temple Beth Israel. The Jews of Clarksdale had worked hard to be assimilated. Theirs was a Reform congregation, and yarmulkes were rarely seen outside the synagogue. Were it not for their names—including such prominent families called Levy, Magdowitz, Shankerman, Hirsberg, Ehrich—one might not have known these citizens were Jewish. As lawyers, doctors, merchants, and accountants, they were very much part of white Clarksdale. Except at the Clarksdale Country Club.

The country club, where members dined and drank at an elegant building off the eighteenth hole of a golf course, did not accept Jews or others of suspect background. Clarksdale Jews and those with Mediterranean heritages—notably the Italians, Greeks, and Lebanese—used a public golf course south of the city, a facility the local aristocracy called the United Nations.

The prospect that a new foreign element was about to be injected into the community troubled Clarksdale's establishment. Already besieged by NAACP lawsuits, street demonstrations, and a civil rights bill gathering strength in Congress, the city sensed the potential for a major disturbance. Joe Ellis published an editorial titled "With Dignity and Restraint." He criticized the idea of a Freedom Summer, but closed with an admonition to his white readers: "While there is much to resent in this summer-long program, there is nothing to fear and, most certainly, nothing to justify intemperate action or reaction on the part of any citizen of Clarksdale, the Delta or Mississippi."

About twenty volunteers were deployed to Clarksdale, students from California, the upper Midwest, New York, and New England. They broke a taboo on their first night in town—sleeping in the homes of local black families. In the Delta, some whites might shake a black man's hand, call him "mister," even drink a Coke with him outside a country store, but the fellowship of a shared meal and an overnight stay in a Negro home was considered out of bounds.

---

a lot like the ones already here—continued to work with us and live in our houses, even when they were bombed and shot into, gave Mississippi Negroes a new image of the white man."

Shortly after the group arrived, the *Press Register*'s senior reporter, Bill Skelton, asked me join him for a talk with a couple of the white students. To avoid the stigma of being seen with the volunteers, we met our guests at a lunch counter at a downtown drugstore rather than at our usual venue, the coffee shop at the Alcazar Hotel, a watering hole for Clarksdale's white leadership.

Skelton was thoughtful, and he taught me much about human nature and newspapering in the years we worked together. He loved books and music, and he was progressive in his politics. But he was concerned about the presence of the white students in the black community, and I think he asked me along because he felt the visitors would feel more comfortable with someone their age. One of the students whom I got to know better as the summer progressed was a senior at UCLA, Lew Sitzer. Lew told us he had no qualms about living with Negroes. He considered his volunteer work a small gesture by a privileged white student. "We hear about people who are suffering, but we are too self-interested to do anything about it," he said.

Skelton wrote a sympathetic piece about the students and their philosophy, and Harry Abernathy, the managing editor, ran the story on the front page along with a couple of photographs. Harry's politics were progressive, too, and he liked to sneak things past Joe Ellis when Joe failed to monitor the layout for the newspaper. When Joe saw the display, he exploded over the tone of the story as well as its prominent placement. The *Press Register* would continue to cover Freedom Summer, he declared to his staff, but the stories would be consigned to the interior of the paper, unless there turned out to be significant developments.

A couple of days later, Freedom Summer was back on the front page. Three civil rights workers had turned up missing in Neshoba County, in tough, redneck territory on the other side of the state. While the students' colleagues feared the worst, Mississippi officials were skeptical. There were suggestions that the boys had skipped down to Havana to enjoy Cuba libres and cigars with Fidel Castro. Senator Eastland called their disappearance "a publicity stunt." Governor Johnson said, "I have no reason to believe that these people have been killed."

Despite the excitement, it was a lonely season for me. Jane Pelegrin, my girlfriend, had gone on a European holiday with a group from Ole Miss. I spent many evenings by myself, listening to radio broadcasts of the St. Louis Cardinals. The announcers, Harry Caray and Jack Buck, were like old friends. Buck was sober and straightforward, with a steady approach to the game. The dominant personality belonged to Caray. He was excitable and highly partisan, and I could imagine him guzzling the Anheuser-Busch products he advertised between innings. From the time I was a boy, I had gone to sleep on summer nights listening to Harry Caray and the Cardinals; for a high school talent show, I once mimicked his accounts of Cardinals games, which included his trademark shout "Holy cow!" But listening to the Cardinals was a long-suffering habit. The team had not won a pennant since 1946. Still, their fans greeted each season with the belief that this might be the Cardinals' year, and after the team acquired a flashy outfielder, Lou Brock, from the Chicago Cubs on the June 15 trading deadline, I nurtured the hope that the 1964 season would result in a pennant.

One night when the Cardinals were not on the air, I invited several Freedom Summer workers to my house to meet a few Clarksdale friends who were curious about the project. I planned to provide hot dogs and beer and thought the conversation might lead to some rapprochement on both sides. Although a few of the volunteers in Clarksdale were black, I made a conscious decision to invite only white students. My neighborhood was not ready for colored houseguests, and neither was I.

I arranged to pick up the students at the "Freedom House," their headquarters in Clarksdale's black section, and drive them across the railroad tracks to my house. Filled with good intentions, I presided over the evening and felt it went well. There was debate among my guests, but no harsh argument, and as we made our way through a couple of cases of beer, the atmosphere grew downright chummy. Then the telephone rang. The leader of the volunteers was calling, a young woman from Minneapolis with big-city street smarts and the demeanor of a labor organizer. She was mad as hell. It was past curfew, she informed me, and she had been desperate because several of her charges had not returned to their homes at the proper hour. Their absence was especially distressing because of the missing volunteers in Neshoba County. After making several calls, she had learned they were at my house. She wanted them back across the tracks immediately. Sheepishly, I drove the volunteers home. The next day, she bawled me out again, this time for hosting a segregated gathering.

Jim Silver's book came out that summer. As a professor at Ole Miss, he was already a notorious figure. He had been one of the few people on campus to befriend James Meredith, and he loved to write provocative letters to editors, jeremiads railing against the Mississippi establishment. One of Clarksdale's representatives in the state legislature, a John Bircher named Malcolm Mabry, had been calling for the professor's head long before Silver's book made headlines. In one speech, Mabry said Silver should be fired for "spreading untruths about the state." Silver's "damnable distortions of the truth are going to cause parents to stop sending their kids to Ole Miss," Mabry predicted.

With the publication of *Mississippi: The Closed Society*, Silver cemented his reputation. It was a bold dissertation on the state's tendency to suppress heretical thought, and he blamed Mississippi's political leadership, its press, its educators, and its clergy.

I did not know Silver, but I liked his book and reviewed it for the *Press Register*. I wrote that the author took "a number of well-deserved jabs at the Jackson press" while he lashed out at others equally deserving of criticism. "Most vigorously, he assails the white Citizens Council, guardians of the 'closed society' of which Silver speaks, and their leader, W. J. Simmons, 'a suave, sophisticated zealot.'"*

Despite the letter-writing campaign whipped up by the Coahoma County Bar Association, the U.S. Congress passed the Civil Rights Act of 1964, and President Johnson signed it into law in time for Independence Day. Clarksdale recoiled in horror. Untouchables would now be loosed on the city's cafés and hotels, into the public swimming pools and parks.

It would be necessary to destroy Clarksdale in order to save it from the Negroes.

A saying is attributed to Edmund Burke, an eighteenth-century British statesman: "The only thing necessary for the triumph of evil is for good men to do nothing." In twentieth-century Clarksdale, the failure of the city's moderates to challenge the decisions made by the segregationists led to a series of self-destructive steps. As they whipped up visions of blacks ransacking the city's cherished institutions, Semmes Luckett and Leon Porter operated in a vacuum, supported wholeheartedly by Clarksdale's elected officials.

On July 5, Clarksdale closed its public swimming pool. Commissioner

*Several months later I met Silver. He said my review was one of his favorites because it had appeared in an unlikely place, the Clarksdale newspaper. He thought of the review as a chink in the closed society. But a couple of years later, Silver was finally driven from the state and joined the faculty at Notre Dame.

Hudson Bell said the action was taken in "the best interests of the people of Clarksdale."

The city also made plans to sell Anderson Park, the center of its recreational program for white youngsters, to the American Legion. The deal was consummated before the end of the year for a mere $30,500.

On July 6, Aaron Henry and Floyd McKissick, the national president of CORE, were turned away from two motels on Highway 61, the Southern Inn and the Holiday Inn. Alerted by Aaron, I arrived at one of the motels in time to witness a strange pushing and shoving match. A CBS camera crew accompanying the two civil rights leaders dropped any pretense of objectivity, joining the effort to pry open the door to the lobby. Through the glass, I could see members of the Holiday Inn staff straining to reinforce the lock. After an unsuccessful struggle to get inside, the group moved to other battlements.

The next day, after five young Negroes obtained library cards at the Carnegie Public Library, all chairs were removed from the reading room and the reference room. I was surprised by the action because George Maynard, one of Clarksdale's leading moderates, was head of the library board. He explained to his family that the rest of the board wanted to shut down the library altogether. A compromise was reached. Blacks would be allowed inside, but in a concession to the segregationists, none would be able to sit down with whites.

That evening in Pike County, a bomb blew out the front of a home in the colored section of McComb where civil rights workers were living. Two volunteers were wounded, a young black man named Curtis Hayes and a white student from Oregon named Dennis Sweeney.*

On the seventh day of July, a delegation of blacks attempted to register at the Alcazar Hotel, a Delta landmark. Rather than accommodate Negro guests, the hotel closed its doors forever.

The following day, Lew Sitzer, the UCLA volunteer, and a chaplain from the National Council of Churches were picked up by Clarksdale police and instructed to leave town.

Later that day, seven blacks tried to enter the Elite Café in downtown Clarksdale. They were rebuffed by the owner, George Polles. That evening,

---

*Sixteen years later, deranged by mental illness, Sweeney would shoot and kill Al Lowenstein.

Polles was admitted to the hospital for treatment of a heart ailment.

Twenty-four hours later, a white man named George Jenkins brandished a pistol when a couple of black men attempted to integrate his barbershop on Issaquena Street. The county attorney, Babe Pearson, said Jenkins would not be charged. "I thought Jenkins was justified in using a gun to protect private property," Pearson told me.

In spite of the provisions of the new Civil Rights Act, three Negro girls were arrested a day later when they sought service at another Clarksdale eatery, the Hamburger Café.

Although they had failed to win acceptance at the cafés and hotels, a spirit of victory prevailed at a freedom rally that night in Clarksdale. The crowd sang James Weldon Johnson's grand old hymn "Lift Every Voice and Sing," and they swayed, with linked arms, through several verses of "We Shall Overcome." With the élan of a conquering general, Aaron Henry took the pulpit. "Clarksdale," he shouted above the chorus of "Amen's" in the congregation, "is on its way to becoming a ghost town if every business does like the Alcazar."

On the second Sunday in July, groups of blacks showed up for worship services at several white churches. At each church, deacons and elders—some of them armed—told the visitors they were not welcome. The incidents took place at the First Baptist Church, the Oakhurst Baptist Church, the Clarksdale Baptist Church, the First Methodist Church, the Church of the Nazarene, and the First Presbyterian Church.

That same day, two hundred miles south of Clarksdale, my stepfather convened a special meeting at the Summit Presbyterian Church. With a small and aging congregation that diminished each year, the little church hardly seemed a target for integrationists, but the elders believed it was important to establish a policy. With little debate, the congregation voted to seat any visitor, regardless of color, who came to worship there. "But where will they sit?" wailed one parishioner unhappy with the decision. My mother rose from her pew. "They can sit with me," she said.

Later that week in Pike County, two black churches were leveled by fire. One of the buildings, the Mount Vernon Missionary Baptist Church, had been standing for sixty years on a road near the entrance to Percy Quin State Park. Built by members who had toiled lovingly to construct a house of worship, the church was destroyed in an hour after a firebomb was lobbed through a window.

Before the summer ended, more than twenty Negro churches would be bombed or burned in the area. In national news reports, my old home was dubbed "the church-burning capital of the world."

Similar dramas played out elsewhere in the South. The historian C. Vann Woodward described the time in *The Burden of Southern History*:

"The experience of evil and the experience of tragedy are parts of the Southern heritage that are as difficult to reconcile with the American legend of innocence and social felicity as the experience of poverty and defeat are to reconcile with the legends of abundance and success."

In Greenwood, one of Clarksdale's sister cities in the Delta, officers of the law took over from the Klan. In the middle of July, helmeted police swinging clubs waded into a group of demonstrators in front of the Leflore County Courthouse. They threw 111 Negroes in jail.

The next night, Silas McGhee attempted to test the Civil Rights Act at the Leflore Theatre. Before he reached the ticket window, the black man was abducted at gunpoint, forced into a truck, and hauled to an auto repair shop where he was badly beaten. After McGhee filed a complaint, the FBI made three arrests. The suspects, including a man named Willie Belk and his teenaged son, were brought to Clarksdale, where the Coahoma County Jail served as a federal facility.

These were the first arrests made for a violation of the new Civil Rights Act, and the wire services were eager for a photograph of the men in custody. The Associated Press contacted me at the *Press Register*, promising to pay $10 if I could produce a picture. With that incentive, I picked up a camera and trundled across town. The jail was familiar territory to me; I stopped there on my rounds every morning and enjoyed good relations with the sheriff and the jailer. But when I walked through the front door of the jail, I saw no one I knew. The sheriff was gone, and the jailer had disappeared. The lobby was filled with strangers, men from Greenwood who had come to bail out their buddies. They weren't wearing sheets, but they looked like the Klan to me.

One of them spotted the camera. "What do you want?" he asked.

"I'm from the *Press Register*," I volunteered cheerfully. "I thought Mr. Belk and his son might like to have their picture taken."

"Mr. Belk don't want his picture took."

"Very well." I tucked the camera under my arm and left as quickly as possible.

That night, after a television station in Greenwood carried a report of the arrests, men wearing Halloween masks burst into the studio and wrecked equipment while the station's employees watched in fright.

The hunt for the missing men in Neshoba County went on for weeks. FBI agents dragged miles of the Pearl River with grappling hooks, and teams of military personnel searched the east-Mississippi swamps without success. Then, in the first week of August, acting on a tip that had reputedly come at the price of $30,000, a group of FBI agents dug the three bodies from a makeshift grave on the farm of Olen Burrage, a few miles outside of Philadelphia, the Neshoba County seat.

The discovery occurred the same week that officers aboard a U.S. Navy destroyer in the Gulf of Tonkin reported they had come under fire from North Vietnamese Communists. The incident led Congress to authorize President Johnson "to take all necessary means" to repel future attacks. The administration had been given carte blanche to wage war in Vietnam, but in Mississippi the news was dwarfed by the grisly affair in Neshoba County.

It was as if the deaths of James Chaney, Andrew Goodman, and Michael Schwerner confirmed the existence of demons in Dixie. First, the Birmingham church bombing, and now this. I had been a teenager when the body of Emmett Till, weighted down with a gin fan, was thrown into the Talla-hatchie River; a freshman at Ole Miss when a posse had taken Mack Charles Parker from a Pearl River County jail and lynched him. I had thought of the cases as instances of random, aberrant behavior. But the deaths of the four little girls in Birmingham appeared to be part of an insidious pattern, and the Neshoba County murders seemed to bear a stamp of approval from Mississippi authorities, the officials who had insisted all summer that nothing awful had happened. I was sickened by the deaths and the deceit, and when I heard an account of how those young men had died, I felt nothing but revulsion. From the confessions drawn from suspects in the case, we learned that the two white volunteers were executed first, causing one of the assassins, who had not yet fired his gun, to complain, "Y'all didn't leave me anything but a nigger."

The Neshoba County case triggered strong reactions: shock, sorrow, embarrassment, and dismay. Plagued by guilt and squirming over our horrible image, many white Mississippians began silently to question our commitment to the politics of Never! At the time, change was still imperceptible. But we had reached a turning point, moving toward our watershed.

*   *   *

The deaths in Neshoba County had a dispiriting impact on the civil rights volunteers, who were winding up their assignments in a climate of sadness and unfulfilled dreams. A few had dropped out of the program, inhibited by the violence. Others conducted workshops with a sense that they were accomplishing little, that it was impossible to make a difference in Mississippi in a summer's time. The visiting students talked with me, quite candidly, about their frustrations, and I tried to capture the mood in a final piece I wrote about Freedom Summer after observing classes for a couple of days at the Freedom School in Clarksdale.

The newspaper ran the story on page 12 under a headline I thought a bit gratuitous: "Freedom Schools Made Little Headway."

"They sat in a circle in the still heat of the Silent Grove Baptist Church," I began, writing about a discussion between the three student-teachers and their class of a dozen young Negroes. Their topic concerned racial strife that month in Harlem, and the class was asked to speculate on the causes for the unrest. It was apparent the children had little knowledge of the outside world or any interest in events in Harlem.

I wrote of the volunteers' plight: "There is very little middle ground. While they encounter hostility and disdain from most of the white community, they face apathy and ignorance with many of the Negroes. And there is distrust on both sides." One of the volunteers, a Yale graduate named Joe Youngerman, confided to me, "The other night we just sat around and had a depression session." When I asked him what he had accomplished, he said, "Not as much as we hoped."

But another worker, Kate Quinn from the University of Washington, told me of a young girl who had checked out a book on existentialism, read it, and returned to ask if the Freedom School had any other volumes on the subject. My story closed by suggesting that the girl's brush with existentialism represented an accomplishment, and in my final line I quoted Youngerman: "This is good."

Before Youngerman left town, he complained in a letter to the editor that my story had overlooked many accomplishments at the Freedom School, plays that had been produced, books that had been read, uplifting lyrics that had been sung.

In the end, the summer visitors I had befriended felt I had let them down.

*   *   *

As the students left Mississippi, the rump movement that had provoked derisive laughter when it had begun in Clarksdale in 1963 mushroomed into a national cause célèbre. The Mississippi Freedom Democratic Party (MFDP), led by Aaron Henry, pitched camp in Atlantic City, where they intended to challenge the official state delegation for its seats at the Democratic National Convention.

Aaron had first tried to win election as a delegate by ordinary means two months earlier. He had arrived unexpectedly at a Democratic precinct meeting in Clarksdale in the company of more than a dozen other Negro voters. Normally, their numbers would have been enough to elect him to a spot on the county delegation because few people bothered to attend the meetings and delegates wound up being appointed by the Democratic chairman. A party official, panicked by the sight of Aaron's group, delayed proceedings while a call for help spread through the white community. As I wrote in that afternoon's paper: "A hastily assembled group of 49 white voters today turned back a bid by a group of 15 Negroes to name Aaron Henry as South Clarksdale's precinct delegate to the county convention."

Attempts by blacks to win delegate slots failed around the state, leaving the party under the control of reactionary forces loyal to Senator Eastland and Governor Johnson. The outcome resulted in the usual all-white delegation to Atlantic City. Though they called themselves Democrats, they had little allegiance to the Democratic president or the national party's policies. To challenge the Mississippians' claim to be Democrats, the Freedom Democrats formed a counterdelegation at a meeting in Jackson a few days after the bodies had been found in Neshoba County and took their case to the national Democrats' credentials committee.

As the drama built in Atlantic City, I followed the action on television back in Clarksdale. Aaron testified about the long history of white dominance in the state party. I felt he made an effective case, but the appearance of Fannie Lou Hamer, a black woman from Sunflower County, electrified the hearing. Though she spoke with grammar and diction that indicated little formal education, Mrs. Hamer's story of repression in Mississippi was so powerful that she mesmerized a national TV audience. She explained how she and her husband had been evicted from their home on a white man's plantation because she had tried to register to vote. "Sixteen bullets was fired" into the home of another Negro couple, she said. When state troopers intercepted Mrs. Hamer and her friends on a voter registration mission, she said, "I began to hear the sounds of licks and screams."

The Freedom Democrats created a ticklish problem for President Johnson, who wanted to sail through the convention and win nomination for a full term without controversy. He instructed his prospective running mate, Senator Hubert H. Humphrey of Minnesota, to find a compromise—or else. Humphrey delegated the task to a protégé, a young attorney general from Minnesota named Walter F. Mondale.

After a series of frantic meetings in a seedy Atlantic City hotel room, Mondale's subcommittee proposed a resolution to the controversy: the regular Mississippi delegation would be seated, with the stipulation that racial discrimination would not be tolerated in the future. In addition, the MFDP would be given two seats as "delegates at large." Aaron and Ed King, his white running mate during the symbolic gubernatorial campaign in 1963, were awarded the spots.

The decision would have great impact on the complexion of future conventions, but that summer, the compromise satisfied no one. All but three of the white Mississippi delegates walked out of the convention, leaving rows of empty chairs in the hall. The settlement also caused a rift within the MFDP. Angered over their failure to unseat the governor's delegation and embittered by the murders in Neshoba County, several of the more radical members of the MFDP accused Aaron of accepting the compromise and selling out to the white power structure. They called him an Uncle Tom, an insult that would often be used during the power struggles to come. Shaken by the discord inside their delegation, Aaron and Ed King declined to take their seats at the convention, and the MFDP challenge ended on a bitter note.

The fissure in the movement, perceptible in the petty fighting between the NAACP and SNCC during the summer project, widened as the two sides returned to Mississippi and went their separate ways. Aaron's camp would continue to work within the system, seeking political accommodations with whites. Other blacks felt betrayed and no longer sought any compromise. In a couple of years, they would stir to a new siren's call: black power.

Despite the summer upheavals, Clarksdale's white community remained unyielding in the face of a school desegregation order due to take effect in September. According to a decree from a federal judge, the integration plan would begin immediately for first-graders in every elementary school in the city. The order was as objectionable as the Civil Rights Act, and the school board turned to Semmes Luckett and Leon Porter to find means of escape.

The lawyers devised a plan that would minimize the number of white children affected by the order, a simple scheme that drew upon the racially divided housing patterns in the city. Although Clarksdale had one natural barrier, the Sunflower River, which meandered through the heart of the city and divided a large white residential neighborhood from the commercial districts, the city was also bisected by railroad tracks. Only a handful of blacks lived in a pocket of run-down homes north of the tracks. The southern half of Clarksdale was predominantly black; just a few white families—most of them working class—lived in that part of town.

City officials carried out the Luckett-Porter plan as easily as cutting pie. The corporate limits were changed to move the black enclave in north Clarksdale outside the city's jurisdiction. Then the school board created new districts along a north-south divide, ensuring that no blacks would be eligible to attend classes in now all-white north Clarksdale. The few whites living south of the tracks, poor families with little influence, found themselves in Negro school districts. A phrase was used to describe these white families' dilemma—they had been "thrown to the wolves."

Because the south Clarksdale whites pulled their children out of the public school system rather than enroll them in the Negro schools, the Luckett-Porter plan succeeded in keeping the elementary schools segregated and thwarted the intent of the court order. But the most controversial element of the master plan to maintain the racial purity of Clarksdale's schools involved the joint city-county high school. Two years earlier, the city had consolidated its white high school with three other white high schools in outlying Coahoma County, creating a single, excellent facility.

Because it would be impossible for Luckett and Porter to extend the racial lines of demarcation through the rural areas, where whites and blacks lived in plantation settlements, the city abrogated its agreement with the county. Clarksdale–Coahoma County High School, constructed at great cost just outside the city limits, would be abandoned by Clarksdale before the integration order reached the upper grades. Under the new plan, the city students would retreat to the old building that had previously housed Clarksdale High School. And white children living outside the city limits would also be "thrown to the wolves."

Joe Ellis's family, who lived near the country club north of town, were among those "thrown to the wolves." So were the families of a number of other plantation owners and managers whose children attended public schools in the county. After the plan was revealed, these angry parents formed a committee to protest the city's action. They were joined by moderates living inside the city who disapproved of the school plan. Among local whites, it was the first public reaction against the politics of Never!

The controversy pushed the *Press Register* off its conservative course. With three children enrolled in the county school system, Joe Ellis broke with the segregationist establishment and editorialized against the Luckett-Porter strategy. He quarreled with old friends, and I could overhear hissing behind the partition shielding Joe's desk. Sometimes the office air was rent with the sound of flying papers and notebooks that Joe sailed across the room.

Emotions were strained throughout Clarksdale and Coahoma County as the white population broke into factions. Unusual alliances emerged from the school dispute, and one of them led to my friendship with an unorthodox pair of brothers nearly a generation older than me, Oscar and Andy Carr.

Both men were wealthy, articulate, and members in good standing of Delta aristocracy. Both had attended the Naval Academy, which attested to the proper political connections necessary to win appointment to the school. Overall, the Carr family owned a couple of plantations and farmed more than six thousand acres. Each brother had five children enrolled in the public schools. Though the Carrs were known as moderates, the growing racial conflict in Coahoma County spurred them to make drastic departures from the mores of the Delta.

Andy told me his racial views had actually been altered years earlier by a gentle black woman, a Dilsey-like character hired by his parents to care for his invalid sister. The nurse became a veritable member of the Carr family, writing Andy letters with biblical citations while he was in the navy. Uncomfortable with the tradition that called for blacks to show deference to whites, Andy urged her to stop calling him "mister." She was too bound to Southern custom to address a white man by his given name, however. She agreed to drop the "mister"; until the end of her life, she called him "Manager" instead. Andy said he could never fathom how his contemporaries in the Delta could treat meek blacks as a lower order. But he was not a confrontational character, and for a long time he kept his beliefs largely to himself.

Oscar was a few years older than Andy and more outspoken. He did not hesitate to criticize the local leadership during the school controversy. I first met him when he drove in from his plantation home on New Africa Road to deliver a scathing letter to the editor. Oscar was furious over the backroom manipulations by Semmes Luckett, and Joe published Oscar's epistle on the front page. "The decision to divide the school system does not aid or abet the pursuit of academic excellence in any way whatsoever," Oscar wrote. "In a state that ranks near the bottom of the totem pole academically, the divisive decision can only take from the general welfare."

Oscar's comments were dismissed by the segregationist leaders as the ravings of a nutty white man. The pleas of Clarksdale's ad hoc committee to maintain the joint school district also went unheeded. The city school board issued a statement confirming its withdrawal from the Clarksdale–Coahoma County arrangement, a decision that was reached, the bulletin said, "after a careful and prayerful consideration of all the factors involved."

Back in Pike County, racial terrorism continued unabated. On the last night of the summer of 1964, dynamite damaged two buildings in a black section in McComb, waking the neighborhood and causing hundreds of residents to run from their homes. The size of the Negro crowd, wandering in anger and confusion on the streets of McComb after midnight, attracted more police interest than the actual bombing. When officers tried to disperse the gathering, blacks vented their displeasure for the first time by pelting the police cars with bricks and bottles. Twenty Negroes were arrested and accused of "criminal syndicalism," an archaic charge originally aimed at labor unions.

The targets of the bombing that night had been a black church used in a voter registration campaign and the home of a civil rights activist, Alyene Quin. Two children and a baby-sitter were injured in the explosion that wrecked Mrs. Quin's eight-room frame house.

Three nights later, two more houses in McComb were hit with dynamite, including the home of Ardie Garner, who had testified earlier that day in Jackson before an advisory committee to the Civil Rights Commission. The attacks brought the number of bombings in Pike County in a single month to ten.

An appeal was sent to Washington for martial law in Pike County, where, a civil rights group said, "violence and terror are the daily companions of Negroes."

* * *

During this dark period, we seized on one piece of good news. After years of failure, the St. Louis Cardinals were making a sustained drive for the National League pennant, and every household in the region seemed to pause from the turmoil to listen to Harry Caray and Jack Buck describe each night the furious three-way race between the fading Philadelphia Phillies, the Cincinnati Reds, and the surging Cardinals.

In late September, I clung to my radio past midnight. The Cardinals had already won their game, but Caray refused to sign off the air. By telephone, he reached an announcer in a press box in Cincinnati during a critical sixteen-inning game that the Reds would lose 1–0. When the final out was recorded, the voice from Cincinnati declared, "You're in first place, Harry." The words produced an ecstatic reaction from Caray, whose own voice had become slurred as the game lengthened. "Hey! Hey!" Harry Caray shouted. I went to sleep happy, and I can still hear him now.

Stan Musial had retired a year earlier, and the stars of the Cardinals were now black men: Bob Gibson, the intimidating pitcher; Lou Brock, the fleet outfielder; Curt Flood, an agile center fielder; and Bill White, the powerful first baseman. Race did not factor into their heroics. When Brock stole second base, it was not a black man's exploit, but a triumph by a member of the Cardinal team. Even as we bickered over school integration in Clarksdale, whites and blacks were united in the Cardinals' pursuit of the championship.

The Cardinals won the pennant on the last day of the season, a showdown game that was not available on TV. We depended on Harry Caray for the news. His play-by-play broadcast over the radio triggered my imagination, the same way that *Amos 'n' Andy* had delighted me a decade earlier. When the Cardinals' catcher, Tim McCarver, squeezed the pop fly that ended the game, I could see it in my mind, and there were celebrations across the battle lines in Clarksdale.

That fall, the Solid South came apart. The regional coalition that had given its electoral votes to the Democratic candidate in practically every presidential race in the century transferred its allegiance to a Republican candidate, Barry Goldwater.

There had been earlier disruptions. Southern delegations had bolted from the national Democratic convention in 1948 to protest a civil rights plank in the party platform and a passionate speech by Hubert Humphrey, then mayor of Minneapolis. A Dixiecrat ticket, led by Strom Thurmond, the governor of South Carolina at the time, and his running mate, Mississippi governor Fielding Wright, took a majority of that year's votes from states of the old Confederacy. In his famous 1949 study, *Southern Politics,* V. O. Key Jr. noted that the electorate rallied to the voices of Thurmond and Wright, who "spoke fundamentally for the whites of the black belt and little more, at least if one disregards their entourage of professional Ku Kluxers, antediluvian reactionaries, and malodorous opportunists."

Mississippi, which had remained steadfastly Democratic in 1928 despite the presence of Al Smith, a Catholic, at the top of the ticket, had turned its back on John F. Kennedy in 1960, although religion had little to do with it. Ross Barnett, who had had himself nominated for president during a ludicrous moment at the national convention, organized a slate of unpledged electors to deny the state's electoral votes to either Kennedy or Richard Nixon. Both candidates were considered too liberal. Four years later, Mississippi made its divorce from the Democratic Party complete.

After the national party rebuked the state's delegation in Atlantic City and settled on a ticket that included the South's old nemesis Senator Humphrey, voters in Mississippi rallied behind Goldwater.

I covered Goldwater's visit to Memphis—my first taste of a presidential campaign. Though I intended to vote for Johnson, I was impressed by the size of the crowd greeting the Republican candidate. In my article, I drew a parallel with another phenomenon touring the region:

"New Orleans had the Beatles, but Memphis had Barry Goldwater, and it's doubtful that the hairy lads from Liverpool would have gotten a better reception than the Republican candidate for president in the Bluff City."

Joe Ellis, the longtime Republican, felt that his party had finally won parity. The *Press Register* endorsed Goldwater. "For most Mississippians and for any Americans dedicated to individualism and constructive conservatism," he wrote, "the decision must favor Barry Goldwater."

In November, Goldwater carried five Southern states plus his own Arizona. Mississippi voted six to one for Goldwater. In Coahoma County, where most blacks were unable to vote, Goldwater won 81 percent. Mississippi also elected its first Republican congressman since Reconstruction, a chicken farmer from south Mississippi named Prentiss Walker. Although Walker had defeated a member of the old Democratic guard, the state's political establishment failed to reckon with the news. "Can you think of anyone more nonuseful than a Republican congressman from Mississippi?" Governor Johnson asked.

Johnson and his henchmen did not understand the full dimensions of the 1964 election. But after eighty years of dominance, their conservative version of the Democratic Party was doomed in our state.

CHAPTER 9

"We don't have to beg anymore"

★ ★ ★ ★ ★

By the end of 1964, the first tentative steps had been taken to rein in the terror, and a few white voices were finally raised to challenge the climate in Mississippi.

In Pike County, the FBI made a series of arrests in connection with the bombing attacks. Many of the suspects belonged to the Klan and held jobs with the Illinois Central Railroad. Reviewing their names in news stories, I saw that several defendants were relatives of people I knew. In an effort to show that a more reasonable element existed in the county, a group of moderates organized a campaign to repudiate the violence. After more than six hundred white citizens signed a manifesto calling for a return to law and order, the *Enterprise-Journal* editor, Oliver Emmerich, published the document and the long list of names. Today, the language seems innocuous, but during that period it constituted a significant break with the Mississippi mind-set:

"We believe the time has come for responsible people to speak out for what is right and against what is wrong. For too long we have let the extremists on both sides bring our community close to chaos. There is only one responsible stance we can take, and that is for equal treatment under the law for all citizens regardless of race, creed, position or wealth. . . ."

In a speech a few months later to a Jackson audience, Emmerich urged the state to come out from under its racial spell. "For seventy-five years," he said, "Mississippi has had but one major political issue. Candidates have used it to rise to power, our people have been misled by it, frightened by it, and tormented by it."

Other citizens appalled by the carnage caused by the politics of Never!

began to stir from their lassitude to contest the reactionary forces that had commanded the state for years.

While public expressions of goodwill were helpful, tantalizing offers of reward money proved instrumental in breaking the back of the Klan.

Though the FBI succeeded in infiltrating the klaverns and arresting scores of backwoods terrorists, the manner in which the Bureau went about its mission was not nearly as glamorous as how it was depicted in Alan Parker's 1988 film about the Neshoba County case, *Mississippi Burning*. When several hundred FBI agents descended on Mississippi following the disappearance of the volunteers, there had been rejoicing in the civil rights community. Black people, fearing local law enforcement officers, looked upon the FBI arrival as divine intervention. But the reception soured after FBI officials made it clear that their mandate was to investigate crimes, not to protect civil rights activists. The distrust deepened after it became apparent that J. Edgar Hoover, the FBI director, was hostile to many of the movement's leaders. Yet the FBI and the civil rights community had a common enemy—the Klan.

The federal agents had special methods to deal with the secret organization. President Johnson, one of the agents later told me, was outraged by the burst of Klan activity; LBJ told Hoover that money should not be considered a problem, that a vast reservoir of funds would be available to pay informants.

As soon as the agents arrived in Mississippi, they selected their targets and began to exploit the weaknesses of a number of sad, troubled souls— men with turbulent home lives, unsuccessful in business, and resentful of the federal government. In some cases, the informants were dismayed to have been caught up in operations turned murderous. Generally speaking, they were all malcontents and were willing to sell out their fellow Klansmen for a few thousand dollars.

The arrangements the FBI worked out with the Klan turncoats would never show up in crime-fighting manuals. The informants proved to be slippery characters, almost as unsavory as the ringleaders of the Klan, and in some cases, their behavior while taking the FBI money was outrageous.

After a Detroit housewife, Viola Liuzzo, was shot to death transporting volunteers for the Selma-to-Montgomery civil rights march in the spring of 1965, the FBI learned that one of their most important sources, an informant named Gary Rowe, had been riding in the car with the Klansmen who ambushed Liuzzo. The FBI was embarrassed further by another Alabama case involving a Klansman named Henry Alexander, who was paid to keep the Bureau up-to-date on Klan activity. It was later learned that Alexander escaped prosecution for the murder of a black man because of his FBI connections.

In fact, there was evidence that Hoover—whose hate for Martin Luther King goaded one of Hoover's lieutenants to send an anonymous letter to King suggesting that he kill himself—failed to give Justice Department prosecutors information on the Birmingham church bombing because he did not want his informants compromised.

It was a seedy business. Chuck Morgan, an Alabama lawyer who represented the American Civil Liberties Union in a number of famous civil rights cases, once told me he deplored the FBI tactics and considered the informants "the sorriest human beings in the world. Judas did that kind of thing." Many of those who talked to the FBI turned out to be unreliable. But during the long investigation, agents were able to accumulate enough information to move against the Klan on several fronts.

In McComb, FBI evidence resulted in numerous arrests, though a local judge released the bombers with sentences no tougher than probation.

In the Neshoba County case, FBI money produced tips that led not only to the bodies of the three civil rights workers but to the arrest of twenty-one Mississippi men, including the local sheriff, Lawrence Rainey, his deputy, Cecil Price, and the imperial wizard of the White Knights of the Ku Klux Klan, Sam Bowers. When state prosecutors showed no thirst to press murder charges, federal authorities moved the case into their jurisdiction, charging the defendants with violations of the civil rights of the murdered men.* It was the strongest charge that could be brought in federal court, but it turned out to be the only way to get convictions for several members of the group.

Years later, I learned that one of the key FBI informants in the Neshoba case, Delmar Dennis—a young Southern Methodist minister who worked after hours as chaplain for the Klan—had also implicated Byron De La Beckwith in the murder of Medgar Evers. During an interrogration, Dennis

---

*Rainey was acquitted, but Price and Bowers were convicted.

said he had heard Beckwith boast at a Klan rally, "I killed that nigger." But the FBI was so eager to solve the Neshoba murders that they sat on the information about Beckwith to preserve Dennis's cover.

At the time, Dennis was controlled by a single agent, who dealt with him alone. To protect the informant's identity, even at the state FBI headquarters, Dennis was known only by his code number: JN74. His information cost the federal government $100 a week.

Three decades later, during a break in Beckwith's third trial in 1994, I drove out to the Mississippi Highway Patrol headquarters to talk about the informants with Jim Ingram, who had become the state commissioner of public safety. Ingram is a big, bluff man; I've known him for years and respect his rectitude. In 1964, Ingram had been one of the FBI agents supervising the network of informants in Mississippi.

Early in their work, the FBI determined that more than twenty Mississippi state highway patrolmen and local law officers were active in the Klan. After a list of their names was given to Governor Johnson, Ingram said, the state took steps to remove the men from the law enforcement ranks.

But years after the murders in Neshoba County, Ingram was still disgusted that Mississippi law enforcement officers had been involved in the conspiracy there. Breaking that case transcended all else. Looking back, Ingram professed no regret that Dennis's information on Beckwith had not been turned over to prosecutors. "The end justified the means," Ingram told me. "There was no way the FBI wanted to blow Dennis's cover. Delmar Dennis, no doubt about it, was one of the major informants the FBI had worldwide. Certainly the killing of Medgar Evers was of great importance, but with Delmar Dennis, we knew he would tell us all about the Neshoba case."

After I finished talking with Ingram, I went back to the Hinds County Courthouse, where Dennis finally took the stand as a major witness against Beckwith. The informant was middle-aged by this time, paunchy and twitching. I approached him during a recess in the trial, but he said he had no interest in elaborating on his testimony. He twisted his hands, obviously uncomfortable over his role. Within a couple of years, Delmar Dennis dropped dead.

Despite the breakthroughs in other areas of the state, progress seemed slow in Clarksdale. Even among the clergy. In a bid to create at least one biracial council in town, the Presbyterian minister, Preston Stevenson, proposed that the local ministerial association invite three or four black pastors to join the group. His motion was tabled before a vote could be called. The preacher at the Clarksdale Baptist Church, L. B. Marion, said he was "apprehensive that the Negro ministers might attempt to propagandize the civil rights movement."

Stevenson, a maverick, had alienated members of his own congregation long before his biracial initiative. He fancied a clerical collar disdained by most Protestant ministers, and expressed interest in events outside the parochial world. Stevenson showed up at the *Press Register* punctually at 2 P.M. each day to buy a paper fresh from the press run and to chatter with anyone in the office. He spoke loudly and cackled like a hyena. Joe Ellis would roll his eyes in exasperation. But after the presses had disgorged the last of the day's papers, the editor would usually join the minister and other members of the newspaper staff for coffee at the Alcazar Hotel.

Knowing that I was a stepson of a Presbyterian minister, Stevenson often talked to me in confidence. He considered me a sympathizer, and he let his frustrations bubble over. Fired as city hall chaplain for his earlier exercise in race relations, Stevenson expressed annoyance over the timidity of his clerical colleagues on the issue of integrating the ministerial association. When his church's elders offered to make the Presbyterian church annex available to a group planning to establish a private school for white children affected by the desegregation order, Stevenson became more aggravated. Clarksdale was in the grip of fools and sheep, he said, and in the manner of a biblical prophet, he warned that the city was following a path to disaster.

Few members of his flock heeded his message, however. White Clarksdale wrote him off as a nuisance, an obnoxious outsider who did not appreciate the way of life in the Delta. Eventually, Stevenson gave up his ministry in Clarksdale and moved to Bristol, Virginia.

To no one's surprise, a federal hearing found that the Clarksdale schools remained segregated, months after the desegregation order had been issued. When Semmes Luckett was questioned, he denied that his school district plan had been drawn up to keep blacks out of classes with whites. He insisted that those families whose homes had been cast outside the new city limits could easily become eligible to send their children to the all-white elementary school in the neighborhood. All they needed to do, Luckett claimed, was to move a few blocks, inside the city limits. The plaintiffs' attorney, a high-powered black lawyer named Derrick Bell, repeatedly asked Luckett about the difficulty these families might encounter in finding housing in the white zone. He never got a straight answer.

The police chief, Ben Collins, was also hauled into court to give a deposition in a separate lawsuit filed by the Mississippi Freedom Democratic Party. Accustomed to giving testimony supporting the prosecution of civil rights demonstrators, Collins wriggled in his seat when he was grilled about allegations of abuse at the city jail. Collins testified he had never mistreated any of his prisoners. He said he had never turned up the heat in the women's cell in the summer of 1963. He denied, categorically, that he belonged to the Citizens Council, the John Birch Society, the Ku Klux Klan, or a spin-off of the Klan, the Americans for the Preservation of the White Race. But when the police chief was asked if he was a segregationist, he declined to answer.

Like the plagues set upon Egypt, disaster seemed to visit Clarksdale in retribution. Terrible spring storms and tornadoes raked the Delta, flooding the fields and imperiling cotton-planting season. At the end of March, Clarksdale lost its last passenger train. The Delta Express, which carried passengers daily between Greenville and Memphis, stopped running without notice. In another development, members of the City Parks Commission, gutted by local officials after passage of the Civil Rights Act, quit abruptly. In their announcement, the commissioners stated the obvious: "We have no duties to perform, no responsibilities to discharge, and no funds to disburse."

Under the threat of court action, some of the chain franchises in Clarksdale, such as the Holiday Inn, had begun admitting blacks. But other motels and restaurants still refused to open their doors to Negroes. The Elite, a popular downtown spot, was hit with a federal injunction ordering the café to observe the Civil Rights Act. The owner built a new restaurant deep in the all-white neighborhood of West Clarksdale, far away from any Negroes. The Alcazar Hotel kept its overnight rooms locked and circumvented the law by turning its coffee shop into a private club.

I regret to report that I joined, paying the one-dollar membership fee. Though I had sworn off organizations that practiced discrimination after my days as a fraternity boy at Ole Miss, I didn't want to lose my place at the twice-daily coffee breaks. I broke personal principle to ensure that I wouldn't be left out of Clarksdale society at a time when I thought I was moving up in the world. Bill Skelton had moved to Jackson, and I was now the *Press Register*'s senior reporter, presiding over a staff of two—myself and a newcomer—and gloating over my title: city editor.

* * *

In the summer of 1965, I married Jane Pelegrin. It was a marriage made at Ole Miss, if not in heaven. In my senior year, we had met at a party and discovered we had lived next door to each other in Sardis when I was a first-grader. Jane later found a photograph from her fifth-birthday celebration that showed me standing in the group with the same look of mischief I had seen in my father in the old family photo of the Wilkies.

Our first date took place the weekend after the riot over Meredith's admission. We rode a student train to Jackson to attend a football game that had been moved from Oxford because of the military occupation on campus. Jane was on crutches; she had torn up her knee a week earlier, the Saturday night of Ross Barnett's speech, while experimenting with a new dance step—the twist—at a postgame party. I moved clumsily, too, because of the beer I'd consumed during the long train ride. We had sneaked a six-pack into the student section under Jane's raincoat. When the Ole Miss band, decked out in their phony Confederate uniforms, broke into "Dixie," drowning out the scores of other games being announced over the public address system, I sailed an empty can into their midst. Moments later, the band director confronted me with the news that I had damaged a valuable tuba. I told him to piss off. Jane intervened. She told the director that I had not thrown the can; that I, in fact, loved the Ole Miss band. The director left, unmollified. Our romance was off to an interesting start.

A week later, I was summoned to the office of my grandfather's successor, the chief of campus security at Ole Miss. I thought the chief's men might have found my bike, stolen during the rioting. Instead, the chief read me the accusation that I had grievously damaged a tuba in Jackson.

"Chief Tatum," I said, lying artfully, "I know all about this. That guy accused me of throwing a beer can at the game and I told him I didn't do it." I fingered "some rednecks from Mississippi State" as the culprits.

"Do you mean to tell me you weren't drinking at the game?" the chief asked incredulously, for it was not the first time that I had appeared in his office for a violation of the dry laws.

"Oh, no, Chief Tatum, I was drinking. But I was drinking whiskey. Only rednecks would drink beer at a football game."

The chief seemed satisfied with my explanation. Besides, he said, he thought the band director was an odd duck.

Jane and I dated for three years. She was a tall, pretty brunette and I loved her zany ways. I was fond of her parents, too. Her father was a cotton buyer, her mother a marvelous cook, and they embraced me with a warmth I rarely encountered outside my own family. The Pelegrins were Catholics, tolerant of pleasures frowned upon by Baptists; they threw merry parties at their house after midnight mass at Christmas. They were also moderate in their politics. After Jane graduated from Ole Miss in 1965, she took a job as a Spanish teacher at Coahoma County High School, which meant she would be moving to Clarksdale. Getting married seemed as natural to us as the turning of the seasons. Since I had doubts about the Presbyterian belief in predestination and had gone so far as to list myself as an "existentialist" on a hospital form, I had no problem committing our unborn children to the Catholic Church. No problem at all. When the mass was said in Latin, the language used at the time we started dating, the service carried an air of mystery that seemed to honor God better than the Welch's grape juice that served as Jesus' Communion blood at the Presbyterian church.

Jane's work went well at the county school, which had been cut out of the compact with the Clarksdale district, its students "thrown to the wolves." Instead of reacting to the situation with despair, a sense of esprit de corps developed among the faculty and the student body at Coahoma County High, and they prepared to accept integration as an inevitable consequence, with little of the rancor that characterized the city's approach.

As the son of a New Deal mother, I realized that I had been the beneficiary of many government programs. From the time of my father's death until I was eighteen, my mother saved my monthly Social Security survivor's checks to use for my tuition at Ole Miss. During my childhood, our school lunch program had been heavily subsidized with Department of Agriculture commodities; it may have given us a regimen of red beans and rice at the Summit school cafeteria, but no one went hungry, and the assistance enabled us to buy unlimited half-pints of milk for a penny each. Taking advantage of a voluntary government program, Mother enrolled me in an experiment to treat children's teeth with fluoride; the John Birch Society may have disapproved of federal aid as well as fluoride, but I have gone through life without a cavity.

Inasmuch as the New Deal programs helped pull the rural South out of the Great Depression, I could never fully understand the hatred the federal government engendered in the region. As I grew older, I learned that some of the animosity was inherited from the Scots-Irish, with their history of enmity toward central authority. Some of it was simply spite.

Yoknapatawpha. Grandfather Bob Black, holding a pistol, talks with a couple of neighbors on a road near Oxford around 1910. *(Courtesy of Dr. Robert R. Black)*

Mississippi gothic. The Wilkie family in 1915. My grandfather and grandmother with their children *(from left)*, my father, Curtis; my uncle, Jimmy; my aunt, Virginia. *(Author's collection)*

"A voice of sanity." My mother, Lyda, in 1935, after she had graduated from Ole Miss and met my father in the Delta. *(Author's collection)*

The Great White Chief. A century ago, Mississippi's politics were dominated by James K. Vardaman, who described the Negro as "a lazy, lustful animal." *(Mississippi Department of Archives and History)*

The man. Theodore G. Bilbo, the flamboyant racist who served as governor of Mississippi as well as U.S. senator before being denied his seat because of corruption. *(Mississippi Department of Archives and History)*

Hacksaw Mary. A campaign leaflet for Mary Cain, editor of the *Summit Sun,* who twice ran unsuccessfully for governor of Mississippi in the 1950s. *(Courtesy of the* McComb Enterprise-Journal)

Missionary's son. My stepfather, John Leighton Stuart Jr., at home in Summit. *(Author's collection)*

School days. Our ragtag Summit basketball team, circa 1950. In the front row, kneeling, Lew Barnes is second from the left; Fulton Beck, my partner in mischief at the Fox Theater, is fourth from the left; and I am at the far right. William Paulk is standing next to the coach at the left of the back row.
(Author's collection)

Southern hospitality. A Freedom Rider, Tom Hayden *(lower right)* cowers from blows delivered by a Pike County man on the streets of McComb in 1961. *(Courtesy of the McComb Enterprise Journal)*

Confrontation. Mississippi lieutenant governor Paul Johnson *(left)* blocks U.S. marshal James McShane and James Meredith *(right)* from entering the campus of the University of Mississippi in September 1962. The next year, Johnson used photos of the incident in his successful gubernatorial campaign. *(Department of Special Collections, J. D. Williams Library at the University of Mississippi, with permission of the Mississippi Highway Patrol)*

Spoiling for a fight. Ole Miss students, with state troopers standing by, gather to protest Meredith's arrival on campus shortly before a nightlong riot breaks out. *(Department of Special Collections, J. D. Williams Library at the University of Mississippi, with permission of the Mississippi Highway Patrol)*

Mopping up. Wearing tear-gas masks and poised with bayonets, troops interrogate a student in the ghostly aftermath of the riot. *(Department of Special Collections, J. D. Williams Library at the University of Mississippi, with permission of the Mississippi Highway Patrol)*

"Never." Ross Barnett, who, as governor of Mississippi, defied the federal government and helped set off a calamitous insurrection on the University of Mississippi campus, loved to appear at the Neshoba County Fair. *(Mississippi Department of Archives and History, with the permission of the* Clarion-Ledger*)*

Officers of the law. Members of the Clarksdale Police Department react to a group of civil rights demonstrators in 1963. *(Photo by Danny Lyon, Magnum Photos)*

Freedom Democrat. Aaron Henry heads a symbolic ticket of black candidates in Mississippi in the 1964 election. *(Mississippi Department of Archives and History)*

Target. James Meredith, the man who broke the color barrier at Ole Miss, is wounded on a Mississippi highway during his one-man march in 1966. *(Photo by Jack Thornell, Associated Press)*

Money talked. Two weeks before his death, Martin Luther King Jr. is startled by a gift of a $100 bill from a Delta farmer, W. B. "Money" Mobley, moments before their encounter degenerates. *(Photo by the author from his collection)*

Loyal Democrats. During a visit to Clarksdale by former vice president Hubert Humphrey in 1969, members of a biracial group that had successfully challenged the Mississippi delegation at the national Democratic convention in Chicago the year before hold a luncheon. At the head table *(from left)*: George Farris (partially seen), elected mayor in 1969; Humphrey; Aaron Henry; Billie Carr; Hodding Carter III; early black legislators Charles Young and Robert Clark; Fannie Lou Hamer; and the author. *(Author's collection)*

Conscience of Mississippi. Former Mississippi governor William Winter at his home in Jackson in 1996, holding my new puppy, Binx. *(Author's collection)*

Hero. Civil rights leader Aaron Henry, who overcame years of discrimination and a stay in the Clarksdale city jail to serve nearly two decades in the state legislature. *(Mississippi Department of Archives and History)*

Terror in South Boston. A cab-driver clings to a railing, attempting to escape a mob that had pulled him from his car after he drove near an antibusing demonstration. *(Photo by John Blanding, courtesy of The Boston Globe)*

Assassin. Byron De La Beckwith, accompanied by his wife, Thelma, arrives in Jackson for his final trial in 1994 for the murder of Medgar Evers. *(Photo by David Rae Morris)*

Crusader. Jerry Mitchell *(center)*, the Mississippi journalist who gave momentum to the campaign to bring justice belatedly to murder cases from the civil rights era, watches as reporters interview Forrest County district attorney Lindsey Carter *(right)* before the first day of the Sam Bowers trial in 1998. *(Photo by David Rae Morris)*

People are kinder here. The author *(left)* at dinner in Jackson with Eudora Welty and Willie Morris in 1994. *(Author's collection)*

But growing up, I had seen a side of the federal government that helped people, and as a young reporter, I realized that if we were to obtain relief from poverty and injustice, the action would have to come from Washington.

Local governments were in the hands of bitter-end segregationists such as Kat Kincade, district attorneys were unwilling to prosecute civil rights cases, and public offices seemed to be controlled by a general assembly of demagogues. To wit, shortly after leaving office in 1964, Ross Barnett joined Alabama governor George Wallace and Calvin Craig, the grand dragon of the Ku Klux Klan, at a Fourth of July "Patriots Rally Against Tyranny" in Atlanta. The event was sponsored by a strange little man named Lester Maddox, who had earned a regional reputation for himself by using an ax handle to chase Negroes from his Pickrick chicken café. Two years later, Maddox would be elected governor of Georgia. With men such as Wallace, Maddox, and Barnett's successor, Paul Johnson, in charge of a swath of states running from Savannah to Natchez, Negroes in the Deep South had nowhere to turn but the federal government.

After Washington had produced the Civil Rights Act and federal authorities had obtained a measure of justice in the Neshoba County case, the ground was broken for more ambitious offensives by President Johnson's "Great Society." In Clarksdale, I watched LBJ's initiatives grow to fruition in two areas: the registration of black voters and, later, the war against poverty.

With the support of strong Democratic majorities in both houses of Congress, the president put the Voting Rights Act of 1965 at the top of his domestic agenda. His efforts were aided considerably by "Bloody Sunday" in Selma, another moment of mayhem in Alabama. John Lewis, the courageous SNCC activist who went on to become a congressman from Georgia, wrote about the incident in his autobiography, *Walking With the Wind*. As the predominantly Negro group set out from Selma, marching across the Edmund Pettus Bridge, Lewis remembered the scene awaiting them:

"There, facing us at the bottom of the other side, stood a sea of blue-helmeted, blue-uniformed Alabama state troopers, line after line of them, dozens of battle-ready lawmen stretched from one side of U.S. Highway 80 to the other. Behind them were several dozen more armed men—Sheriff Clark's posse—some on horseback, all wearing khaki clothing, many carrying clubs the size of baseball bats. On one side of the road I could see a crowd of about a hundred whites, laughing and hollering, waving Confederate flags. Beyond them, at a safe distance, stood a small, silent group of black people." As Lewis recalled, "all hell broke loose."

The Alabama law officers swarmed into the marchers, presenting the nation with another indelible portrait of savage beatings, an attack that turned out to be as counterproductive to the segregationists as Bull Connor's police dogs two years earlier.

The incident in Selma gave LBJ the moral momentum to win the passage of the Voting Rights Act, and within days we began to see the legislation's effect.

When the act passed, only 12 percent of the adult Negroes in Coahoma County were registered to vote. The number seemed abysmally low, yet in other Delta counties the voting rolls contained practically no blacks. Our longtime circuit clerk, J. W. Smith, had guarded Coahoma County's rolls diligently, allowing just enough blacks to vote to prevent the numbers from looking ridiculous. Now the responsibility had been taken out of his hands.

Federal registrars set up headquarters in Clarksdale's federal building, and by the end of the year, nearly three thousand blacks had been added to the voting rolls in Coahoma County.

It was apparent that the Voting Rights Act would transform politics in the predominantly black Mississippi Delta, even though the evolution would take years.

In response to the new realities, city hall, the courthouse, and the hospital were quietly desegregated. Chairs were also returned to the library.

Buoyed by their sudden strength, hundreds of blacks trooped to a church rally in October 1965 to demand that the city and county hire black policemen and deputies, and to call upon the chamber of commerce to recommend blacks for sales jobs at local stores.

Aaron Henry, forever conciliatory, told the crowd he hoped Clarksdale would resolve its black-white differences through negotiations. But his partner in the NAACP state leadership, Charles Evers, was uncompromising. After enduring a lifetime of discrimination that included the murder of his brother, Evers wanted to wait no longer. He took over the pulpit to urge his audience to impose "a one hundred percent boycott" of Clarksdale's white businesses if their hiring practices were not changed. "We don't have to beg anymore," Evers shouted. "We're in the driver's seat."

Just when terror seemed to be ebbing in the state, night riders attacked the home of Vernon Dahmer, a well-known black leader living near Hattiesburg in south Mississippi. At the time, Dahmer was in charge of a voter registration campaign aimed at obdurate officials in Forrest County, where the circuit clerk, a hulking three-hundred-pounder named Theron Lynd, prided himself on having refused to register a single Negro for years.

In the euphoria that followed the Voting Rights Act, Dahmer established an auxiliary center for potential voters at a country store he operated outside town. As a light-skinned independent farmer, he had always been known for his boldness, but his efforts to enfranchise the blacks of Forrest County made him a marked man.

While Dahmer and his family slept on the night of January 9, 1966, a gang of masked men hurled Molotov cocktails into his store and his home. He died of burns a few hours later.

That summer, James Meredith strode out from Memphis with a pith helmet on his head and an African walking cane in hand to make a one-man "March Against Fear" through Mississippi, an enterprise that seemed quixotic from the first step. An eccentric whose politics befuddled others in the civil rights community, Meredith moved like a lone wolf, criticizing movement leaders and voting Republican.

On the second day, as he tramped down old Highway 51, Meredith's only companions were a few marchers, a couple of news reporters, and Jack Thornell, a photographer for the Associated Press. Just south of Hernando, a man rose from the roadside bushes, called Meredith's name, raised a shotgun, and fired three volleys of buckshot.

I was watching the evening news when the anchorman interrupted the broadcast to announce that Meredith had been shot and killed on a Mississippi highway. Stunned by the news, and with the same sinking sensation that had followed the news of other civil rights catastrophes, I prepared to rush to the scene, some seventy miles from Clarksdale. Then I heard the report corrected. Meredith was merely wounded.

He had been struck with dozens of pellets, but the wounds were not critical. Thornell captured the incident in dramatic photos of Meredith, spread-eagled on the blacktop and howling in pain, while his assailant, an unemployed Memphis man named Aubrey Norvell, hovered in the background, still aiming the shotgun. Thornell won the Pulitzer Prize for his pictures. His news agency was not so lucky.

Months later, a correspondent for the Associated Press told me how the wire service had come to be stuck with the name "Assassinated Press."

Moments after the shooting, a *Commercial Appeal* reporter traveling with Meredith had called his Memphis office with news that Meredith had been shot and wounded in his head. A young AP summer intern, working in the *Commercial Appeal* newsroom, eavesdropped on the conversation and thought he heard that Meredith had been shot dead. The intern sent a bulletin to the New Orleans AP office, which relayed the news to AP headquarters in New York. AP had been the source for the grim report I'd heard on TV. After an interval of a few minutes, my friend said, AP New Orleans received a terse telex message from the general manager of Associated Press in New York concerning their rival wire service, United Press International: "UPI does not have Meredith dead." At this point, the AP staff in New Orleans fell upon their knees, praying only partly in jest, "Die, Meredith, die."

Meredith did not die, but the attack generated an expanded march through Mississippi. Virtually every star in the civil rights constellation rushed to Meredith's bedside. Taking up his fallen standard, an army of demonstrators, ranging from such established figures as Martin Luther King and Floyd McKissick of CORE to Stokely Carmichael, the fiery new chairman of SNCC, paraded down Highway 51 while dozens of reporters and cameramen followed in their wake.

The march coiled through north Mississippi like a headless snake, out of the control of any single civil rights organization. After a carnival-like stop in Grenada, where hundreds of local Negroes were encouraged to register to vote, the marchers branched off into the Delta, making their way to Greenwood. When Carmichael attempted to pitch tents on the grounds of a school, he was jailed. The incident triggered a demonstration at the Leflore County Courthouse. Free on bail, Carmichael appeared before hundreds of cheering followers. "I ain't going to jail no more!" he told the crowd, adding that "every courthouse in Mississippi ought to be burned tomorrow to get rid of the dirt." Then he shouted a new term: "black power." The words seemed to catch on, so he asked a rhetorical question. "What do you want?" The crowd responded, "Black power!" The expression entered the American lexicon.

My friends in Clarksdale were troubled by the threat of black power. When they expressed fears at dinner parties that our white society might soon be overwhelmed, I tried to reassure them. Black power, I said, simply referred to a call for equality. Not even belligerent Stokely Carmichael would attempt to impose absolute black power, I said. After more than three years covering the movement, I still didn't get it.

At the end of the year, Carmichael expelled all whites from the Student Nonviolent Coordinating Committee, dismissing a dedicated cadre of young men and women who had risked their lives in the movement.

It took a struggle in the Delta over federal funds for the antipoverty program for me to realize the full scope of the conflict between traditional Negro leaders such as Aaron Henry and the militant activists.

When LBJ established the Office of Economic Opportunity, the agency that would channel millions of dollars into his War on Poverty, he unwittingly touched off a flurry of skirmishes among groups competing for money and legitimacy. Complicating the battles inside the black communities were attempts by white politicians in Mississippi to grab control of the funds.

The biggest fight involved the Child Development Group of Mississippi, an operation that ran Head Start programs in twenty-four counties, including much of the Delta. The leadership of CDGM was made up of many of Aaron's adversaries in the movement: a few white organizers left over from Freedom Summer, blacks who felt betrayed by the Freedom Democrats' compromise at Atlantic City, and radicals associated with the Delta Ministry, a project giving aid and organizational advice to poor farmworkers.

CDGM became a convenient target for opponents of the antipoverty program. The *Daily News* in Jackson compared Head Start to "Hitler's Germany," warning in the same breath that the preschool activities were a precursor to "ultimate mongrelization." Senator Eastland said the OEO funds were being given to "extreme leftist civil rights and beatnik groups in our state, some of which have definite connections with Communist organizations." Senator Stennis was also sharply critical of the program after it was learned that CDGM officials had used federal money to pay the fines of staff members arrested during civil rights demonstrations in Jackson.

When CDGM applied in the summer of 1966 for $41 million to run its program the coming year, Sargent Shriver, the head of OEO, choked on the political pressure. Separately, he summoned Aaron and Hodding Carter III, a young liberal who had taken over operations of the Greenville newspaper from his father, to Washington to explore the possibility of finding another group to run the Head Start programs in the Delta. "Sarge said, if we can't create an alternative, we're going to lose the whole program," Hodding told me. Aaron and Hodding returned to Mississippi to recruit several moderate black leaders and a few prominent white men—including my friend Oscar Carr of Clarksdale, LeRoy Percy, a descendant of the Greenville Percys, and Owen Cooper, an industrialist in Yazoo City—to serve on the board of a new nonprofit corporation, Mississippi Action for Progress.

The bruising battle for OEO funds was joined. Long books have been written about the struggle, but John Dittmer offered the best synopsis of the affair in *Local People*, his history of the movement days in Mississippi: "This coalition of Delta whites and old-line NAACP leaders . . . were genuinely concerned about keeping Head Start alive in Mississippi. Still, they must have been aware that control over millions of dollars of Head Start funds would give them political patronage and power, enhancing their position as a credible alternative to the Freedom Democratic Party," which had, by this time, forsaken its founding father, Aaron Henry.

When it appeared that the new group would capture the funds from CDGM, several thousand blacks rallied in protest in Jackson. Fannie Lou Hamer declared, "We aren't ready to be sold out by a few middle-class bourgeoisie and some of the Uncle Toms who couldn't care less."

Hodding told me he, too, felt the sting of Aaron's former associates. "Al Lowenstein called me and up said, 'If you don't get out of this, we'll have to destroy you.'"

In the ensuing uproar, Shriver responded to counterpressure from the CDGM advocates and wound up funding both groups for a couple of years, a decision that satisfied no one but kept the Head Start programs afloat. Of the controversy, Dittmer concluded: "Whatever its original intentions, the poverty program in Mississippi had divided the black community into warring factions, often pitting the poor men and women who had become politicized in the early 1960s against the old, traditional middle-class leadership."

In Clarksdale, the central figure in a separate squabble for antipoverty money was a mysterious character named Jesse Epps. A diminutive man with a Napoleonic complex, Epps had a smooth speaking style and a lust for publicity. When I described him in one story as a "stormy petrel," he liked the characterization. Epps's rivals pointed out that his background was not entirely clear, and my interviews with him failed to establish fully his qualifications. It seemed that Epps had grown up in the Clarksdale area, attended Syracuse University, and served an apprenticeship with organized labor before reappearing in the Delta, where he snagged federal funds as adroitly as the protagonist in *The Music Man,* who worked over River City.

Epps, who was black, set up something called the Southern Education and Recreation Association and won the county's first grant from OEO. To the consternation of Aaron as well as local white officials, Epps's operation was awarded $200,000. To put antipoverty funds in more "responsible" hands, the Coahoma County Board of Supervisors actually cooperated with Aaron, setting up a "community action program" to apply for more OEO money. The group named itself Coahoma Opportunities, Inc. Overseeing the operation was a twenty-eight-member board. Half were conservative white men who had more interest in blocking funds from the likes of Epps than extending aid to the poor, men such as Semmes Luckett, Leon Porter, and my editor. Aaron appointed the other half of the board. His faction was NAACP-oriented but included a few progressive whites—the most notable being Andy Carr, Oscar's younger brother.

Andy was governed by the words of Thoreau: "If a man does not keep pace with his companions, perhaps it is because he hears a different drummer. Let him step to the music which he hears, however measured or far away." Andy took those lines to a framing shop only to find that Ione Brewer, a Clarksdale woman known for her rabid conservatism, had had the same quote framed for herself. His discovery demonstrated, Andy told me, that no single philosophy held a franchise on principle, that conservatives could be deeply committed, too. So he was able to work with the conservatives to find enough middle ground to get the antipoverty program going in Coahoma County.

The group received a $336,000 grant from OEO and hired a white investment broker, Gus Roessler, and a black educator, Bennie Gooden, to run the program. Because Coahoma Opportunities' salaries were higher than the average wages in Clarksdale, white legal secretaries defected to the agency. Black women, who had earned no more than $3 a day on the farm, were hired as teacher's aides and trainees for $50 a week.

With the prospect of millions of dollars in future OEO grants, Coahoma Opportunities expanded. As the antipoverty officials developed plans to set up a legal aid office and a vocational training program, the county's Board of Supervisors became convinced that they had helped create a monster. Their representatives on the Coahoma Opportunities board all quit, complaining that "some of the projects which have been proposed are of a nature and size that will prove detrimental to the county." Andy scrambled to find a few white moderates willing to replace them to keep the program biracial.

The agency thrived without the imprimatur of the elected officials and succeeded in co-opting Jesse Epps. The "stormy petrel" went to work for Coahoma Opportunities for a while, but after questions arose during an audit of his operations, Epps left town to take a major role in the ill-fated garbage workers strike in Memphis in 1968.

Clarksdale's antipoverty program was not without its bureaucratic problems, and the agency weathered charges that it squandered money. Critics complained that Coahoma Opportunities had no impact. But the agency left a couple of important legacies: it elevated salaries in the local job market and encouraged a simple policy—even the poorest supplicant for help had to be addressed as Mr. or Mrs.

By the spring of 1967, civil rights activists focused concern on yet another aspect of poverty—hunger—and lured Robert F. Kennedy, now a senator from New York, and a couple of his colleagues to come to Mississippi to conduct hearings. On the last day of their stay, Kennedy and Senator Joseph Clark of Pennsylvania embarked on a tour of the Delta set up by Marian Wright, a skillful young lawyer who had sparred with Semmes Luckett in a couple of courtroom duels I'd covered.

I was on hand when the Kennedy entourage stopped in Cleveland, a college town near Senator Eastland's plantation. "The first home visited was a wretched little shack where 15 persons lived," I wrote for the next day's *Press Register.* "A group of Negro children were huddled in front of the house, bewildered at the commotion. 'What did you have for lunch?' Kennedy asked one of the children. The boy murmured a reply. 'You haven't had lunch yet,' Kennedy remarked, patting his head. 'What did you have for breakfast?' 'Molasses,' the boy said."

Kennedy went to a second house, and I witnessed a scene stored, like treasure, in my mind for more than thirty years. He encountered a small child in soiled diapers, crawling across a dirty room and picking at chunks of corn bread and grains of rice scattered on the floor.

"Flies were swarming," I wrote. "Kennedy knelt by the child and gently stroked his face for about two minutes without saying a word. The boy just looked at him with wide eyes."

Outside the house, Kennedy was confronted by Cliff Langford, the editor of the weekly newspaper in Cleveland. An Eastland crony, Langford was still annoyed over Kennedy's speaking engagement at Ole Miss the year before when the senator had given a detailed account of the deals Ross Barnett had tried to negotiate during the Meredith crisis. As a result of the warm reception given Kennedy by the students, the state's old guard was at work purging the faculty of the Ole Miss law school, which had sponsored the speech. Langford wanted to ensure that Kennedy's second visit to Mississippi would not be as friendly.

He rebuked Kennedy for coming to the Delta, telling the senator that equally poor conditions could be found in Harlem. He accused Kennedy's host, a local civil rights leader named Amzie Moore, of bringing Kennedy to the worst hovel in town. He also carped about allegations of starvation that the congressional committee had heard in Jackson the day before. "I don't know of anybody starving down here," Langford said.

"Step over here and I'll introduce you to some," replied Kennedy, waving toward a clutch of children.

After that encounter, the motorcade sped toward Clarksdale, but Kennedy asked for an impromptu stop as we passed through the all-black town of Mound Bayou. With no advance notice, Kennedy, his aides, and a few reporters burst into a shack occupied by an elderly man named Andrew Jackson and his wife. "Jackson's house had a tattered ceiling," I wrote. "A photo of the Glorybound Singers and a calendar hung on the wall. His wife apologized. 'This house sho ain't clean.'"

There was also a picture of John F. Kennedy on a wall, and the old man seemed incredulous that the late president's brother was a guest in his house. "Is you really Mr. Bobby Kennedy?" he asked.

"Yes." Kennedy smiled and took the man's hand. "And are you really Mr. Andrew Jackson?"

There would be few gestures of goodwill in the race for governor that summer. It was, in fact, the state's last openly racist campaign—blacks had not yet taken full advantage of the Voting Rights Act—and the spirit of Theodore G. Bilbo seemed corporeal in the oratory of several of the candidates. "Insult, insinuation and invective. These are the hallmarks of Mississippi's 1967 governor's race," I wrote in the *Press Register*.

Leading the parade were two of our enduring demagogues, Ross Barnett, struggling to make a comeback after the Ole Miss debacle, and Congressman John Bell Williams, whose apostasy in 1964 on behalf of Barry Goldwater had cost him his seniority in the House Democratic caucus—a punishment that had elevated him to martyr's status back home in Mississippi. "White power" was the theme of a third candidate, Jimmy Swan, an obscure rabble-rouser who became the darling of the Klan by declaring that the schoolchildren of Mississippi "will not be sacrificed on the filthy, atheistic altar of integration." It was said that every pickup truck in south Mississippi carried a Jimmy Swan bumper sticker.

Bill Waller, the district attorney who had twice prosecuted Byron De La Beckwith without success, entered the race as a moderate, but he was outflanked by William Winter, the eloquent state treasurer who had begun to assume leadership of the anti-Eastland bloc in the state Democratic Party. Winter was the favorite not only of the *Press Register,* but of virtually all my friends and family. My parents respected him as a prominent Presbyterian layman; I liked him because he had been one of the few state officials who had stayed out of the nonsense at Ole Miss in 1962. Winter was clearly too good to be elected governor.

The race would be Barnett's last hurrah. When I asked the former governor about the "Kennedy tapes" that were said to exist, evidence that would implicate him in the agreement that had brought Meredith to Ole Miss, the old politician peered at me without comprehension and answered, "The Kennedy assassination, did you say?"

"No, Governor, the Kennedy tapes. The tapes of the conversations between you and John and Robert Kennedy."

"Oh," Barnett said, and paused for a moment. "I don't know anything about that."

Barnett was a harried candidate. Jimmy Swan had tied up the votes of many hard-bitten racists by calling urban riots the work of Negro tools of a "Communist-inspired revolution" and promising that "should this ugly Communist monster raise his head in Mississippi, I will respond with such force and determination that a riot will never have time to materialize." Such rhetoric left Barnett competing with John Bell Williams for the favor of those segregationists who were somewhat wary of Swan's call for a racial Götterdämmerung.

Williams came out of the "empty sleeve" school of Mississippi politicians, those who flaunted war wounds as though they were qualifications for public office. Williams had lost an arm in a plane crash during World

War II; even though the accident had occurred on a training mission, he made the most of it. An acerbic man, Williams also used his mean sense of humor to great effect on Barnett.

"Mr. Ross!" Williams shouted derisively at his political rallies. "Mr. Ross! He opened his campaign in Pontotoc. Now, an organ grinder and a monkey can get a crowd in Pontotoc on Saturday. But when Mr. Ross opened his campaign, he got all these trucks and carried three thousand box lunches up to feed the multitudes. And when it was over, they had to carry twenty-six hundred box lunches back to Jackson. I hope the old folks' homes enjoyed those lunches, but I bet they're getting tired of chicken."

Barnett retaliated by calling Williams a "sick turkey," but he filled the air with so many malapropisms—accusing Winter of resembling "one of those scorpions you see sitting on a fence, changing colors"—that the former governor became an inviting target for ridicule. The whole state laughed at Barnett, and reports of his gaffes grew funnier as the campaign progressed.

At the Neshoba County Fair, an annual festival where several thousand Mississippians spend a week in cabins at a country campground and expect political speakers to provide some of the entertainment, Barnett observed that Congressman Williams worked in Washington and thus was "close to the left-hand side," consorting with "Kennedy, Katzenbach, and Kowatski." Nicholas Katzenbach had been Robert Kennedy's deputy at the Justice Department, but who was Kowatski? Barnett later confessed he didn't know. He said he thought the name sounded good.

My favorite anecdote was Barnett's story of how he, as governor, had wooed and won a Standard Oil refinery for the Gulf Coast. I heard the tale at a political rally in Tallahatchie County, where Barnett tried to entice his listeners from the shade of a couple of trees, to come into the sun, closer to the stage, to hear an account of his brilliance:

"I invited the president of the Standard Oil Company to the governor's mansion for breakfast," Barnett confided as he began his story. "So the day before, I gathered the servants around me. They were all nigguh boys from Parchman"—the state prison—"who worked as trusties. They had never done nothing bad, just killed their wives or something. Heh, heh, heh. So I said, 'Boys, previously, when you have served the grits, you have served them in one big bowl. The grits get cold and lumpy before they can be passed around the table. Tomorrow, the president of the Standard Oil Company is coming, and I want each place setting to have an individual bowl of grits.' Well, the day came, and the president of the Standard

Oil Company and his lackeys arrived. We sat down for breakfast, and I want to tell you, those nigguh boys did a splendid job. We fed the president of the Standard Oil Company piping-hot grits and biscuits with ham and red-eye gravy and Leake County molasses. And at the conclusion of the meal, the president of the Standard Oil Company looked at me and he said . . ."

The crowd waited to hear a pronouncement that the refinery would be located on the Mississippi Gulf Coast.

". . . he said, 'Governor, the system of feeding in Mississippi is a wonderful system.'"

End of speech. Members of Barnett's Tallahatchie County audience looked at one another in bewilderment, puzzled over the moral of his shaggy-dog story.

Old Ross finished fifth in the first Democratic primary that August. Jimmy Swan claimed in excess of one hundred thousand votes, more than three times as many as Beckwith got in his campaign that same year for lieutenant governor. Williams and Winter ended up facing each other in the "second primary" runoff. Although Winter had the support of moderates and newly enfranchised blacks, it was not much of a contest, not even when the good, moderate candidate felt compelled to tell one forum, "I was born a segregationist and raised a segregationist. I have always defended this position. I defend it now."

To paint a contrary picture, Williams's sympathizers circulated a leaflet headlined "Awake White Mississippi." Illustrated with a photo of Winter speaking to a group of blacks, the leaflet warned, "For the first time in our history we are faced with a large NEGRO MINORITY BLOC VOTE. . . . Winter's election will insure negro domination of Mississippi elections for generations to come."

John Bell Williams, of course, won the election, an outcome the Associated Press called "a smashing conservative victory that left Negro voting hopes wrecked."

CHAPTER 10

"Don't laugh folks, Jesus was a poor man"

★ ★ ★ ★ ★

L ike a debilitating virus, the rivalry among civil rights groups sapped energy from the movement just at the time their followers were finally reaching the gates of city halls and courthouses across the South.

Aside from the quarrels over antipoverty funds, the organizations competed for political dominance in black communities. In Mississippi, the NAACP jealously guarded its position and had little to do with SCLC, CORE, and SNCC. The days of the Council of Federated Organizations, the steward of Freedom Summer, were over. When Martin Luther King Jr., by this time a winner of the Nobel Peace Prize and acclaimed throughout the world as the leader of the black revolution in America, ventured into the state, he was not guaranteed a hearty welcome from his own people.

As spring came to the Delta in 1968, King arrived with little notice to begin preparations for his latest offensive, a Poor People's Campaign that would start in Mississippi and end in the nation's capital. Though there was not much local enthusiasm for the idea, any visit by the charismatic leader was newsworthy, so I interviewed King, and my *Press Register* story began:

"Dr. Martin Luther King has a dream. In it, he envisions waves of people descending on Washington. They are arriving aboard buses. Some are riding horseback. Others via a mule train that will make the journey from Mississippi in three weeks. Many more will make the pilgrimage on foot. . . ."

I, too, was skeptical about the project and King's ability to mobilize the masses for his campaign. Using a bylined column I had been given on the editorial page, I expressed reservations in another piece headlined "He's

Not the King in Mississippi." Noting that King occupied a position some-where between the old-fashioned NAACP and the "far left," I speculated about his political problems, pointing out that Aaron Henry might be will-ing to go to Washington for a one-day demonstration but disapproved of King's plan for a prolonged siege by the poor people. I concluded that the NAACP would "never be willing to hand over to Dr. King control of their strength" in the state.

Clarksdale's black leadership, loyal to the NAACP, allowed King one afternoon rally in the city, which drew a large crowd. But for most of his trip to the Delta, King was forced to drum for support for the march in dusty patches. One such outpost was Marks, a small town surrounded by cotton fields, fifteen miles east of Clarksdale.

To measure King's reception, I went to a rally at the Silent Grove Bap-tist Church in Marks where an audience of two hundred colored people—most of them women—stirred the muggy March air with cardboard hand fans supplied by a local funeral home. The only other white person in attendance was Jack Thornell, the AP photographer who had been on hand for the Meredith shooting. Just as King began to speak, a disheveled white man stormed through the front door of the church. Reaching in his hip pocket, he lurched up the aisle toward King. Jack and I looked at each other. I had a camera, too, and wondered, for a split second, whether I should try to win the next Pulitzer Prize for photography or attempt to dis-arm the intruder. With relief, I saw the man pull a $100 bill from his pocket instead of a gun.

King's eyes swelled in disbelief as the stranger approached with his gift. They had a soft conversation at the pulpit, and King identified his benefac-tor: W. B. "Money" Mobley, a Marks farmer. "Brother Mobley says he's been here thirty years, and he's got more colored friends than white ones," King trumpeted. The crowd applauded, a bit uneasily. "Anybody who gives a hundred dollars can say a word," King said. That proved to be a mistake.

Gripping the pulpit with both hands, Mobley declared, "Ain't nobody hungry down here in Mississippi."

An impromptu chorus shouted back, "We is, too, hungry!" and "Shut your mouth!"

King's chief lieutenants, Ralph Abernathy and Hosea Williams, grappled with Mobley, while the white man yelled something about "the goddamn Kennedys." He also addressed Abernathy as "boy." Fuming, Abernathy informed the visitor, "I'm not a boy, I'm the Reverend Abernathy."

Mobley shouted another insult, then stumbled out a side door.

The church was buzzing with disorder as Abernathy got in the last words: "We appreciate the hundred dollars from this white brother, but we've got to get him straight—he owes us more than a hundred dollars."

Afterward, I talked with King outside the church. He was sitting in a car with a couple of his aides, calmly eating a piece of cold chicken before heading toward his next stop. I asked if he was ever frightened.

"No, I'm not frightened," he said. "I move without fear because I know I'm right. I'd be immobilized if I was afraid. Besides, the climate of violence is gradually decreasing in the South."

That night, the first official day of spring, a freak storm deposited more than a foot of snow on the north Delta. Two weeks later, Martin King was dead.

Word of the shooting came, again, on an early-evening newscast. I hoped the report would prove to be as inaccurate as the exaggerated bulletin of Meredith's wounds, but King's death was quickly confirmed. In a reaction duplicated in cities across America that night, vandals smashed the windows of white-owned stores in Clarksdale's black neighborhood.

Unleashing my own anger, I composed a front-page editorial the next morning, beginning with a familiar quotation from Hemingway: "If people bring so much courage to this world, the world has to kill them to break them, so of course it kills them." As the managing editor, Harry Abernathy, and I completed final preparations for the front page—the type was already set in place—Joe Ellis decided to check the page proof. He flew into his own rage, yanking the editorial out of the mold minutes before the press run. He owned the goddamned paper, he reminded me, and he determined the paper's goddamned editorial policy. I could write news stories, but by God, I didn't have the authority to insert my own inflamatory bullshit in an editorial in his paper. Certainly not on the front page.

Admonished, I drove across town to Aaron's drugstore to commiserate. Despite his differences with King, Aaron seemed distraught. He showed me a small glass vial a friend had just brought from Memphis. It contained smears of blood scraped off the second-floor walkway of the Lorraine Motel, a touchstone from Martin Luther King already as prized as a splinter from the true cross. In the span of a few hours, the prophet of the civil rights movement had attained apotheosis.

An epidemic of looting was sweeping the big cities of the nation. In

Clarksdale, Aaron helped tamp down trouble with a statement: "The anguish of the Negro community is rampant, but I urge Negroes and white Americans of goodwill to avoid violence themselves."

Clarksdale groped for an appropriate response. After discussions between Andy Carr and Aaron, a Sunday-afternoon biracial memorial service at City Auditorium was agreed upon. Only one man objected openly to the idea. The mayor, Kat Kincade, ordered the doors to the auditorium locked in an attempt to prevent the service. But Andy obtained keys from another source, and at the appointed hour, the auditorium filled to its capacity with an integrated audience of nearly two thousand people. Whites sat beside blacks for the interdenominational service. A choir from all-black Coahoma Junior College sang. Several ministers spoke and offered prayers. Presiding over the event was Rabbi Schultz, turned from his anticommunist endeavors to racial reconciliation.

King's lieutenants in the Southern Christian Leadership Conference chose to begin the Poor People's Campaign in Marks a month later, but their leader's last dream dissolved into low comedy there.

As the heavens inundated the Delta landscape with torrential rains, dozens of marchers gathered on the grounds of a Negro school, accompanied by several covered wagons and mule teams. Though the wagon train would give the crusade verisimilitude, no one seemed quite certain how to handle the mules. While King's associates milled about, a couple of men— purported to be blacksmiths—tackled the mules in an attempt to shoe them. The struggle developed into an unusual style of mud-wrestling. After the men took several hours to shoe one beast, I wondered about their credentials as blacksmiths.

The marchers were stuck in Marks for days. Disorganization, compounded by the weather, pushed back each scheduled start. The campus had been transformed into a quagmire. Self-important SCLC workers barked unheeded commands at the mules as well as at their human charges, the Poor People, who had grown balky themselves, because of the rain and delays. King's aides issued daily bulletins of the wagon train's imminent departure from Marks, but I came to believe none of their promises.

The only SCLC official with credibility was a young minister named Andy Young. Philosophical and endowed with a sense of humor, Young observed each day's disastrous developments with equanimity. "By hook or crook," he said, "these mules are going to get to Washington."

The procession finally pulled out of Marks in a downpour. The side of one rickety wagon carried a handwritten poster: "Don't laugh folks, Jesus was a poor man." As volunteers in the Poor People's Campaign assembled in Washington from other corners of the country, sightings of the mule train petered in from rural villages in Mississippi. Chaos attended the journey. One mule perished from tetanus after a nail pierced his hoof while the poor animal was being shod; another died from a broken neck. An animal lover obtained an injunction against the SCLC, and state troopers intercepted the wagon train outside Winona, about eighty miles from Marks, two weeks after it had set out. The caravan never reached its destination.

In Washington, several thousand demonstrators staked out a "Resurrection City" on the mall between the Lincoln and Washington Monuments. But Robert Kennedy was assassinated in the first week of June, and the nation again plunged into mourning. The encampment of unruly, muddy demonstrators developed into an open sore in the nation's capital. Police and National Guardsmen dismantled Resurrection City before the month was out, and the Poor People dispersed back to their homes.

Andrew Young, of course, went on to become a congressman from Georgia, U.S. ambassador to the United Nations, and mayor of Atlanta. Years after the Poor People's Campaign, Young reflected in his 1996 autobiography, *An Easy Burden*:

"We didn't hold many illusions about the success of the Poor People's Campaign. Without Martin, it would be very difficult to convey our message. Truthfully, without Martin, keeping the staff focused on our message would be almost impossible. Not unexpectedly, in the confusion and tumult following Martin's death, the Poor People's Campaign got completely out of hand."

The drama of 1968 continued to unfold like ragged sequences in a nightmare. Under siege by antiwar protesters, Lyndon Johnson had announced he would not run for reelection in the face of Kennedy's decision to challenge him, and now Kennedy was gone, too. By the summer, the battle for the Democratic presidential nomination had narrowed to two men, Vice President Humphrey and Senator Eugene McCarthy of Minnesota, a peace candidate. Senator George McGovern of South Dakota, another figure from the party's peace bloc, made himself available as a symbolic stand-in for the Kennedy interests, but the momentum of the antiwar movement now belonged to McCarthy.

Although a resident of jingoistic Mississippi and removed from harm's way by my 4-F deferment, I had soured on the American adventure in Vietnam a couple of years earlier. The *New York Times* was not available in Clarksdale, but I had heard of David Halberstam's critical reporting for the newspaper, and even the wire service stories by Peter Arnett and Neil Sheehan sounded notes of warning about the American mission. Writing the obituaries of Clarksdale men killed in the conflict, I tried to give their lives heroic meaning. But a speech by Arthur Schlesinger Jr. at Ole Miss and a book by a doomed French journalist, Bernard Fall, finally convinced me of the folly of foreign intervention, and I became a dedicated opponent of the war, one of the few people holding such views in Clarksdale.

I sided with Gene McCarthy from the beginning of the campaign, sending his national headquarters a check for the grand total of $5, my first political contribution. I suppose it represented a breach of journalistic ethics, but I didn't really care. I was fixated on the subject. Since I had failed to be a brave advocate for civil rights, I was determined not to show the same weakness on the war issue. Emboldened by Jack Daniel's, I delivered boring tirades against the war at dinner parties. I badgered friends. It seemed that my only ally was Oscar Carr, who had served as Robert Kennedy's cochairman in the state.

But across town, opposition to the war had begun to grow. Blacks were being conscripted to die in disproportionate numbers at the same time the military effort drained funds from the federal budget that could have been used for social programs.

Aaron was troubled by the war, but he remained loyal to President Johnson—and especially to Humphrey. He and Humphrey were soul mates—pharmacists and civil rights crusaders. Aaron had been able to bring Humphrey into Mississippi a couple of times, and he had parlayed Humphrey's friendship into support for a number of initiatives in the state. As Humphrey closed in on the presidential nomination, he may have had no stronger supporter than Aaron.

Aaron invited me to debate him at a couple of political forums he convened in black churches. I was a reporter, not a public figure, and I had no authorization to act as a surrogate for McCarthy. Yet I appeared at the events to make long-winded condemnations of the administration's war effort. When I saw members of the audience nodding in approval, I realized that I had allies other than Oscar, and that they lived across the tracks in Clarksdale.

My political involvement deepened when Aaron asked if I would be willing to join an insurgent Mississippi delegation challenging Governor John Bell Williams's all-white group at the Democratic National Convention in Chicago. My allegiance to McCarthy had nothing to do with my invitation; I was picked because I was white. Aaron and his group were determined to send a forty-four-member delegation to Chicago that was half-black, half-white, and they were having difficulty finding twenty-two whites willing to take part in the coup.

I was acquainted with many of those involved in the plot to unseat the regular Mississippi delegation. Hodding Carter III, the leading white strategist, was a good friend. Though Hodding was five years older than me and far more worldly, I had gotten to know him as a fellow newspaperman in the Delta. We had covered several events together, including Robert Kennedy's trip to Mississippi, and we attended some of the same Delta parties. With his background as a Princeton graduate, marine, an LBJ campaign aide in '64, and a Nieman fellow at Harvard, Hodding stood out like a prince among the provincials. When he took control of his father's paper, the *Delta Democrat-Times*, he actually raised the paper's liberalism by several degrees.

As an outspoken national Democrat and an exponent of government programs to aid the poor, Hodding had joined his father as an archenemy of the state's political establishment. He was one of a small group of white men in the Delta who supported the domestic agenda of the national Democratic Party, a group that included several Greenville lawyers, Wes Watkins, Frank Hunger, and Doug Wynn; one of Hodding's reporters, Bob Boyd; the Carr brothers; and Bill Pearson, a planter from Tallahatchie County. We were all friends—sometimes driven to socialize together by our political isolation—and most of us wound up on the slate of delegates chosen by Aaron and Hodding.

Joe Ellis would have been justified in firing me, but he tolerated my political activity, just as he had accepted our other differences over the past six years. He gave me time off to go to Chicago, but he made it clear I would not be paid for any days I missed at work.

Brimming with idealism, I was proud to be part of an integrated delegation poised to strike down John Bell Williams's racist group in Chicago. But once again, I underestimated the divisions within the civil rights community. Our delegation, called the Loyalist Democrats, represented a hodgepodge of interests including remnants of the Freedom Democratic Party, organized labor, the NAACP leadership, and an assortment of white liberals. Many of the black delegates despised one another. That became evident at our state convention in Jackson.

We gathered at a Masonic temple on a sweltering Sunday afternoon in mid-August. Plans called for the carefully balanced delegation to be ratified; Aaron and Hodding were to be elected cochairmen, while Charles Evers would be named national committeeman at the same time that Patricia Derian, a white liberal from Jackson, became national committeewoman.

Rebellion, aimed primarily at Evers, erupted among the blacks. As an NAACP official, Evers automaticaly attracted animosity from radicals in the movement. They felt he was an establishment figure, too quick to cut deals with whites. Evers made matters worse with his personal style. After moving back to Mississippi, he had settled in Fayette, a small town near Natchez, where he had orchestrated economic boycotts by black residents. When local stores were driven out of business, Evers had opened his own commercial enterprises, including a shopping center in Fayette. "I want all of you, if you want me to be your leader, to keep me in business," he once told a group of local blacks. To men and women who had never owned a bank account, Evers appeared to be a greedy capitalist, behaving like a white autocrat.

Evers's opponents yearned to deny him the role as national committeeman. They also demanded rejection of the forty-four-delegate slate. With the national press watching, the Mississippi challenge appeared to be breaking up before we could even get to Chicago. Rising above the snarling exchanges, Harry Bowie, a minister from McComb whose loyalties lay with the Freedom Democrats, made an earnest appeal for unity. Even though Bowie and some of his associates—who had toiled for years in the most dangerous vineyards of Mississippi—had not been given places on the delegation, he said it was more important to unseat the segregationists than to break up our black-white coalition. After Bowie appealed to his friends to set aside personal vendettas, the delegation was saved. Evers won election, too, though the roll call featured rancorous demonstrations by competing groups, a preview of divisions that would eventually separate Evers from the movement.

The governor's delegation was led by Leon Bramlett, a Clarksdale planter long active in conservative affairs. Handsome and straitlaced, Bramlett had created Coahoma County's first seg academy following the school integration order and served as one of John Bell Williams's chief financial supporters. Despite our differences, I had been able to maintain a civil relationship with Bramlett, even though I knew he considered me a left-wing kook. Like Semmes Luckett, his close associate, Bramlett was always coolly cordial when dealing with me as a reporter, though my participation in the challenge against his group produced further strains.

As a result of the national party's decree against segregated delegations following the Freedom Democrats' challenge in 1964, the governor attempted to color his delegation by appointing three black men to the group. The trio refused the seats, leaving a team of segregationist lawyers to defend yet another all-white delegation before the national party's credentials committee. No compromise would be possible this time. A few days before the convention began, the committee voted to certify the Loyalist Democrats as the official Mississippi delegation, the first time in history that an entire delegation had been unseated.

As the governor's state party chairman, Bramlett was left presiding over an organization no longer recognized by the national Democrats. He warned of repercussions, and he, of course, was right. After a flirtation with George Wallace that fall, the old guard of Mississippi, the spiritual children of Vardaman and Bilbo, moved into the Republican Party.

In the last week of August 1968, I did not care about the ramifications of the political struggle in Mississippi. I was Chicago-bound, riding aboard an overnight train with a group of civil rights heroes and a handful of white upstarts, to cast my vote for the peace candidate, Gene McCarthy.

The week remains a blur, with scenes of Brueghelian conflict spilling through the streets of Chicago. Our delegation was bivouacked in the Loop at a run-down hotel favored by leftists. I think a sympathetic foundation paid the bill. To save money, we doubled up. Andy Carr was my roommate, though I spent only a few hours a night at the hotel.

Excitement negated the need for sleep. With only $50 in my pocket, I subsisted on adrenaline and free buffets laid out daily by Chicago businessmen supporting the antiwar movement. The Carr brothers took me to lunch one day at the swank Cape Cod Room in the Drake Hotel. Otherwise, I prowled the sidewalks with bands of antiwar protesters in the hours before we were required to be at the Stockyards, the site of the convention.

The old amphitheater at the Stockyards was an appropriate place to hash out the conflict in Vietnam; the neighborhood evoked blood and terrorized livestock. In "Miami and the Siege of Chicago," an account of the 1968 conventions he wrote for *Harper's* magazine, Norman Mailer offered a magnificent description of the setting:

". . . Chicago was a town where nobody could ever forget how the money was made. It was picked up from floors still slippery with blood, and if one did not protest and take a vow of vegetables, one knew at least that life was hard, life was in the flesh and in the massacre of the flesh—one breathed the last agonies of beasts." In Chicago, Mailer wrote, "they did it straight, they cut the animals right out of their hearts—which is why it was the last of the great American cities, and people had great faces, carnal as blood, greedy, direct, too impatient for hypocrisy, in love with honest plunder."

Even in the wars and revolutions I covered later in my life, I never again experienced the raw fury that permeated Chicago. It was as if every grievance alive in America visited the city that week. The convention floor was a seething surface of angry delegates. Although McCarthy's cause was hopeless, there were symbolic votes. During the debate over a peace plank for the party platform—a measure opposed by Humphrey—in our delegation only Aaron and another ardent Humphrey supporter voted against it. As the votes from Mississippi, arguably the most reactionary state in the union, were announced to be overwhelmingly in favor of the peace plank, thunderous roars rose from the antiwar forces in the galleries above us.

When a delegate from Ohio objected to my vociferous support of the peace plank, I told him to fuck off. His delegation, I said, was composed of "ward heelers and warmongers." We had to be separated. With a couple of other dissidents from Mississippi, I went to stand with the Wisconsin delegation, the rowdiest antiwar group on the floor, jeering at speakers representing the Johnson-Humphrey administration and the Chicago mayor, Richard J. Daley.

Our own little delegation fell apart in private caucuses. An argument between Hodding and another white liberal had to be broken up before they came to blows. The Freedom Democrats' faction objected to any motion by the "Uncle Toms." Most of them voted for McCarthy, if for no other reason than the knowledge that Aaron Henry supported Humphrey.

On the third night, the convention was thrown into further turmoil by news that the Chicago police had again attacked demonstrators downtown. Hundreds of antiwar delegates held a caucus at the Stockyards to consider a response to the police action. The room was sprinkled with celebrities: the actor-folksinger Theodore Bikel, the poet Allen Ginsberg, and popular political gadflies such as Al Lowenstein and Dick Goodwin. I saw Norman Mailer taking notes. Paul O'Dwyer, a peace candidate for a Senate seat from New York, called for a march on the Loop until he was told that it was a distance of several miles through some tough neighborhoods. Instead, we were bused to a point a few blocks north of the Conrad Hilton Hotel, ground zero for the disturbance. Humphrey, as well as McCarthy, had headquarters in the hotel, and thousands of demonstrators—licking their wounds—were positioned across the street in Grant Park.

I was given a red candle and a print of Ben Shahn's peace poster with its red, white, and blue dove. Holding both, I took part in my first protest demonstration, marching down Michigan Avenue with hundreds of other delegates. As we approached Grant Park, the police lobbed tear-gas canisters into the crowd, and we fled in the opposite direction, toward Lake Michigan. Trapped by gas, we looped back toward the hotel, weeping and screaming insults at Humphrey and the police. I spent the night in the park, joining the crowd in chants of "Dump the Hump!"

We were still there the next day, the convention's last, when McCarthy emerged from the hotel to address "the people of the government in exile." During McCarthy's appearance, Robert Lowell read poetry and Peter, Paul, and Mary sang mournful ballads. I thought the moment elegiac, far more inspiring than Humphrey's coronation that night at the Stockyards, where opponents of the war had been routed from the galleries, replaced by city workers bearing freshly minted "We Love Mayor Daley" signs and paying loud tribute to their boss and the new Democratic ticket.

Leaving Chicago, I vowed I would never vote for Humphrey. Then I considered the alternatives. The Peace and Freedom Party headed by the black radical Eldridge Cleaver was not on the ballot in Mississippi, so if I ruled out Humphrey, I was left with either Richard Nixon or George Wallace.

There was no suspense to the campaign back home. The Alabama governor might as well have been running unopposed. Since it was obvious Wallace would claim Mississippi's electoral votes, the fall campaign played out in anticlimax. I supported the Democratic ticket after all.

The contest was close nationwide, and television was chockablock with commercials for the candidates. Jane and I taught our two-year-old son,

Carter, to cheer when Humphrey's spots appeared, and to boo when Wallace was mentioned. Carter developed a routine. When he heard cheering, he would clap and shout spontaneously, "Yea, Humphrey!" Then he would shake his little head in distaste and yell, "Booooo, Wallace." When we took Carter to a high school football game, our little boy took his cue upon hearing the crowd roar for a touchdown. "Yea, Humphrey!" he shouted, following with the cry, "Booooo, Wallace!" We were unable to hush him. Even after the grandstand quieted, he kept up his cry: "Yea, Humphrey! Booooo, Wallace!"

On the night of the election, we gathered at Oscar and Billie Carr's home to watch the returns. We were a glum group, resigned to the belief that Wallace would carry the Deep South while Nixon would win the election. Our expectations were borne out late in the evening.

As Oscar and I sipped our drinks, I tried to rationalize the results. As long as I could remember, the people of our state had hated whoever occupied the White House. They hated Truman, I said, because he integrated the armed forces; they hated Eisenhower because he integrated Central High School in Little Rock; they hated Kennedy because he integrated Ole Miss; and they hated Johnson because he had integrated the entire nation. "Now," I said, "at least, they will have a Republican to bitch at."

In making this observation, I failed to reckon with Nixon's craftiness. Our victory over the governor's delegation in Chicago would be just one of the building blocks in the new president's initiative to convert white Southerners into Republicans, a brilliantly Machiavellian scheme that became known as Nixon's Southern Strategy.

CHAPTER 11

"Free at last!"

★ ★ ★ ★ ★

Shortly after Nixon's inauguration, I found myself in court in the hill town of Grenada, being judged by my peers—twelve white men from Mississippi—in my lawsuit against a local contractor.

The case arose from a wreck the year before when a long, flatbed truck pulled out of a roadside ditch and attempted to cross the highway in front of my car. The cab of the truck made it safely, but in a terrifying moment of grinding brakes and skidding tires, I collided with the truck trailer. My passenger, Bob Boyd, and I were hurt, but not seriously.

Bob, who worked for Hodding Carter, and I were on our way to a meeting of Mississippi journalists in Jackson. Following us in another car were two other reporters for the *Delta Democrat-Times*, Lew Powell and Ed Williams. I might as well have had Karl Marx, V. I. Lenin, and Leon Trotsky for my witnesses.

Before agreeing to settle my claim, a lawyer respresenting the contractor's insurance company spotted a vulnerability. Though the truck driver, an employee of the contractor, had been faulted in the accident report, the attorney decided I had a problem, too. He did not use the explicit expression but hinted that my history as a nigger lover might be used against me. I did not consider myself litigious, but I didn't want to act like a chump either. So I retained my friend Jack Dunbar to represent me.

Though he was a law partner with Charlie Sullivan, the conservative Clarksdale lawyer who had twice run for governor and had finally been elected lieutenant governor in 1967, Jack's own politics tended to be moderate. We played tennis together and sometimes enjoyed a beer after work. I also knew, from covering the courts, that he was a crackerjack lawyer.

Jack, who called me Scoop, explained the realities of the case. The rival attorney had not only intimated that my record as a young man with views inimical to the state of Mississippi would be exposed in any trial, he also expressed doubts about the credibility of my witnesses, inasmuch as they worked for Hodding Carter III. There was further difficulty. If the case went to trial, it would either have to be held where the wreck took place, in Raymond, the home of Governor John Bell Williams, or in Grenada, the home of the contractor. White citizens of Grenada had attacked black schoolchildren with baseball bats a couple of years earlier.

"Scoop, there's one bright spot," Jack said, grinning for the first time in our discussion. "The defendant is a Negro man with a Jewish name"—Willie Jacobs.

Of course, the real defendants were the Grenada contractor and his insurance company. Instead of intimidating me, their threat aroused my ire. "Fuck 'em," I told Jack, and we prepared for battle in Grenada, where I opted to file the suit. As luck would have it, the trial judge was a fierce conservative; he had once pitched a couple of civil rights lawyers in jail for contempt of court after they had had the temerity to make a motion to transfer a case from the judge's jurisdiction to federal court.

In spite of mounting evidence of my disadvantages, I pushed forward bullheadedly. I asked for $6,000, hoping a jury would award me a respectable percentage of that figure, since the highway patrol report indicated the truck driver had caused the accident. I felt satisfied justice was on my side.

Our first witness was the trooper who had investigated the wreck. Under cross-examination, he testified that I had been speeding, a statement he had never made before. Jack later discovered the trooper had become one of the governor's handpicked escorts; like most associates of John Bell Williams's, the trooper held strong views on the inferiority of Negroes.

My witnesses from the *Delta Democrat-Times* were not helpful, either. Each time Jack rose to strike irrelevant questions concerning Hodding Carter's politics, he was overruled. When I testified, the jury soon learned that I had been part of the integrated Mississippi delegation to Chicago. They glared at me as though I were a confessed child molester.

In his closing argument, the opposing attorney suggested that the hand injury I had suffered in the wreck could have been caused "chunking rocks at the police in Chicago."

The jury deliberated for a few minutes and returned with a verdict of $600—for the defendant. Bewildered, the judge explained to the jurors that they could not award a defendant money in a civil case. He sent the jury back to reconsider their verdict. It was growing dark outside. Cocktail time beckoned. The jurors, in spite of their obvious abhorrence of me, reversed themselves and gave me $600 to put an end to our day in court.

As Mississippi quivered in the death throes of segregation, the place grew almost comical.

Lew Powell and Ed Williams, my friends and witnesses, decided to publish a monthly newspaper to document the absurdities. After Hodding agreed to print the four-page gazette at cost, Lew and Ed recruited writers from a widening circle of young Mississippians willing to attack the status quo.

They named their journal the *Mississippi Freelance* in a deliberate parody of the old newspaper the *Mississippi Free Lance,* published by Bilbo during his political wars fifty years earlier with Fred Sullens, the editor of the *Jackson News.*

Although Sullens shared a bond of racial prejudice with Bilbo, it was not enough to paper over their personal hatred of each other. In editorials, Sullens branded Bilbo "the miserable little moral pervert . . . a self-accused bribe taker, a self-confessed grafter, a foul tongued slanderer, an unmitigated liar and contemptible crook." After Bilbo was elected governor, Sullens declared "a majority of the voters, fooled, deluded, blinded, lost to all reason, have said . . . that they would rather wallow in filth than walk on clean ground." He proposed substituting "a carrion crow" for the eagle on the state seal and replacing the eagle atop the state capitol dome with "a puking buzzard."

Bilbo used the pages of his *Free Lance* to dismiss Sullens. "Cast him out upon the lonely seashore of despair," Bilbo wrote, "where the howling winds of divine retribution will bite and cut him to the ignoble death that he so justly deserves; and where like a dead mackerel in the moonlight he will, forever, of his own corruption lie stinking and shining, shining and stinking."

We could never hope to duplicate such eloquence, but we had a good time trashing our own adversaries. I used the *Mississippi Freelance* to attack right-wing ministers as well as Clarksdale's mayor and police chief. The monthly encouraged equal-opportunity in its polemics, so I lampooned one of the first blacks elected to public office in the state, a clownish justice of the peace in the little Delta town of Friars Point. Impressed by the Duvaliers of Haiti, the official aspired to set up a dictatorship, but lurched instead from one mess to another.

Lew and Ed, meanwhile, raked the governor, the legislature, our alma mater, Ole Miss, and the racist policies at the Jackson television stations. In the days before CBS carried NFL games, each pro football franchise had its own TV network. Rather than telecasting the powerful New York Giants, which had a number of former Ole Miss stars on its roster, a Jackson station subjected Mississippi to the weekly follies of the league's lowliest team, the Washington Redskins, because the Redskins remained the only all-white squad in the league. During the Ole Miss crisis, the Jackson stations serenaded the state with endless choruses of "Dixie." Ed wrote of the attempt by a biracial group, including Aaron Henry, to wrest the license of Channel 3 from the present owners, an effort that would prove successful.

Lew, meanwhile, uncovered an astonishing story that had been ignored by the establishment press in the state. For an article in the *Journal of Mississippi History,* the president of the University of Southern Mississippi had plagiarized a paper written by a historian at Georgia Tech.

In another piece, titled "Up from Sis-Boom-Bah," the *Freelance* took note of cheerleaders who had risen to political prominence in the state. The list included Senator Stennis and an ambitious congressional aide named Trent Lott. Biting the hand that printed it, the *Freelance* pointed out that Hodding had also been a cheerleader in high school.

One of the *Freelance*'s favorite targets was the Mississippi Sovereignty Commission, the agency set up to safeguard segregation. Since its inception, its office had been controlled by a succession of Citizens Council leaders; Governor Williams perpetuated the agency's narrow outlook by appointing Semmes Luckett to the commission. Ostensibly, the Sovereignty Commission maintained a speakers bureau of Mississippians prepared to travel around the country extolling the virtues of segregation. Less was known about the agency's network of spies and detectives.

The Sovereignty Commission collected information on "subversive" activities around the state and reputedly kept dossiers on the most dangerous citizens—Negroes and their sympathizers. To spin their web, the commission used paid informants in the black community; the agency also ruined the reputations of individuals involved in the civil rights movement by planting false stories in the Mississippi press.

During the reign of director Erle Johnston, a former flack for Ross Barnett, the commission compiled a list of its accomplishments. In one case, the commission crowed, "We established that a very prominent female civil rights worker in the Delta had a long record of activity with an organization that had been cited as subversive. We gave the press information about her background. Stories were printed locally and in Delta newspapers and her influence was so reduced that she left."

Citing another accomplishment, the report continued, "When a man from a northern state came into Mississippi and set up an organization financed by donations from his home state, we sent a complete report of his activities in agitation and troublemaking to his home town newspaper. The story was published and resulted in so reducing his contributions that this organization could not exist."

The operation was meant to be quite sinister. Fortunately, the commission detectives, in practice, were such klutzes that their product more closely resembled the work of the Keystone Kops.

Years later, when the files of the commission were opened after a protracted lawsuit, we learned how shoddy their work had been. They dumped newspaper clippings and membership lists stolen from NAACP and ACLU activists into the files, willy-nilly. Unsubstantiated reports gathered from sources around the state were so riddled with mistakes that the commission memos made the FBI's infamous raw files glow, by comparison, with accuracy. When I finally obtained records about myself in 1997 from the old Sovereignty Commission files, I saw the poverty of their research. I was branded as a member of the delegation to Chicago, but they missed all the other stuff—my membership in the NAACP and the ACLU, my speeches on behalf of Gene McCarthy, my efforts to elect blacks to public office. They even failed to collect my seditious columns, printed for all to see, in the *Press Register*. It was an indication, I concluded, either of my insignificance or the Sovereignty Commission's incompetence. Probably a combination of the two.

But in 1969, the Sovereignty Commission still banked the fires of the aging segregationists, and the *Mississippi Freelance* decided to have some fun at the commission's expense. Luther Munford, a Princeton undergraduate working for the *Delta Democrat-Times* for the summer, was dispatched to the commission's Jackson office to interview the director, E. Webb Burke, a retired FBI agent. During his mission, Luther noticed several blank pieces of stationery and envelopes bearing Sovereignty Commission letterheads that had been discarded. In the spirit of the commission, he filched the material.

Luther wrote a tragicomic story for the *Freelance*. Comparing the agency to the witch-hunting House Un-American Activities Committee, the piece was headlined "Incompetence, Thank God, Helps Keep Our Mini-HUAC from Its Appointed Rounds." Luther also turned the stationery over to Lew and Ed.

Patt Derian, Mississippi's national committeewoman for the new Democratic Party and a loyal subscriber, was in London at the time, so Lew thought it would be amusing to send her the latest copy of the *Freelance* in a Sovereignty Commission envelope. He failed to put adequate postage on the communication, however, so it was returned to the Sovereignty Commission offices, triggering a major investigation.

It took the commission gumshoes a couple of months to break the case. Agent Burke, the director, filed a report with the state attorney general, A. F. Summer, that was replete with errors. He had Lew's and Ed's backgrounds reversed. He also deduced that Ed, rather than Lew, was the guilty party.

The document, which survived in the Sovereignty Commission files, details how "it was learned that both of these men do some work for the *Delta Democrat-Times*." According to the director, "The *Freelance* is well known to [the police chief] and the FBI in Greenville, as is the extremely liberal nature of the *Delta Democrat-Times* and Mr. Hodding Carter, III."

Armed with this intelligence, Burke and Mac Mohead, a commission investigator from Clarksdale, drove to Greenville to interrogate the pair. The director found Powell "obviously the 'smart alec' of the two," according to his report to the attorney general. With sorrow, the official also reported that Lew and Ed "expressed the feeling that they thought . . . Mrs. Derian would get a big laugh at receiving the paper in a Sovereignty Commission envelope."

The director said he "explained to these young men, quite emphatically, that such an act on their part definitely was not the least bit amusing. It was also explained that any further activity of this nature, after their having been advised of our objection, would certainly result in further action."

Actually, the commission's days were numbered. After Bill Waller was elected governor in 1971, he cut off its funding. "They didn't do much but clip newspapers and lobby for conservative causes," Waller told me years later. "It was Mickey Mouse, but it was a stigma on state government."

The forces of segregation still controlled Mississippi in 1969, but they were on the defensive, and in some places, on the way out.

In Clarksdale, the mayor was embattled. The *Press Register* received a tip that Kincade had been taking prisoners from the city jail to work as laborers at a home he was building for himself. Our new reporter, Vincent Lee, had no formal training as a journalist, but he possessed a knack for digging, and he tracked down several of the workers after they had been released from jail. They confirmed that as many as a dozen men a day were moved from their cells to work details at Kincade's construction site. They were paid nothing. After other inquiries, Vincent learned that one prisoner, awaiting prosecution for rape, had escaped from the detail and remained at large. At last, the newspaper had its nemesis in its crosshairs. The police chief referred all questions to the mayor, and Kincade refused to comment.

Vincent began his story:

"Clarksdale taxpayers should take an interest in Mayor W. S. Kincade's new residence under construction in Country Club Heights—if only to see if it suits their fancy—because it would seem they are indirectly paying for part of it."

The taxpayers were interested, all right. Within twenty-four hours of the story's publication, the district attorney said he would investigate. The next day, the mayor announced he would reimburse the city $3 for each shift worked by a prisoner. Chief Collins claimed he kept a log of the workforce, but said he could not show it without the mayor's permission. When I asked Kincade to make the log public, he snarled, "I ain't giving you any kind of authorization."

After the newspaper pointed out that, according to state code, prisoners "cannot be leased or hired by any individual," Kincade went into uncharacteristic silence for several months before bumbling into the news again. After a car wreck involving his brother-in-law, Kincade appeared at the hospital bed of a woman injured in the collision and issued her a ticket. He also waived his brother-in-law's $8 fine in the same case.

The mayor decided not to run for reelection in 1969, and his chum, the police chief, fell into a deeper hole himself.

Collins wrecked a police car late at night in a neighboring county. He said he had been pursuing a "suspected bootlegger" and explained he had been unable to call for assistance during the chase because his car radio did not work. We checked the car, awaiting repair at a junkyard, and reported that the radio worked just fine. Collins, wearing a neck brace to demonstrate his injuries with the same panache that John Bell Williams wore his empty sleeve, threatened to take action against the *Press Register.*

While Collins floundered in the police car controversy, we applied the coup de grâce. The newspaper got another tip that the police chief had gone into jukebox distribution as a side business and was muscling owners of local cafés to use his equipment. Collins had been seen, in uniform, lugging one of his jukeboxes into the El Matador Lounge. On April Fools' Day, the Board of Mayor and Commissioners fired Collins for "conduct unbecoming an officer." Kincade voted to keep him, but two new commissioners agreed to the ouster.

One of the commissioners, a likable Lebanese-American businessman named George Farris, seemed especially upset after learning that Collins's partner in the jukebox business was an ex-con named Carl "Towhead" White, whose exploits were known throughout north Mississippi. Towhead unwittingly cooperated with the investigation by getting murdered in Corinth, Mississippi, the next night. In the wire service obituary, the FBI helpfully described White as "one of the top hoods in the Southeast."

Collins hired Semmes Luckett as his lawyer and appealed to the Civil Service Commission, an approach that had saved him from dismissal earlier in the decade after he had been accused of interceding on behalf of a girlfriend under arrest in another county. Instead of being buffaloed, the new city commissioners refused to flinch. To the "conduct unbecoming" charge, they added public drunkenness, improper use of a police car and telephones, and undue brutality in the operation of the jail.

When the commissioners indicated they had evidence that Collins, who was married, had been riding around with another woman rather than chasing a "suspected bootlegger" when he'd wrecked the car, the chief dropped his appeal.

We celebrated discreetly at the *Press Register,* but across the tracks, on the black side of the city, there was open jubilation.

Clarksdale had changed dramatically since I'd moved there in 1963. Not only had its racist leadership been routed, a campaign by local moderates succeeded in changing the city charter to create a full-time mayor and four commissioners, an arrangement that would provide political openings for black candidates.

Coahoma County High School, where my wife taught, had been fully integrated, and no one had been eaten by "the wolves."

Despite Semmes Luckett's myriad strategies, the city schools were also desegregated. Many disgruntled whites moved their children out of the public schools and into seg academies, but the fight had gone out of the old guard.

Blacks, on the other hand, had become more assertive. Once I had been welcome to attend, as a reporter, their rallies and to sit in on their private discussions of tactics. As Aaron's friend, I had been trusted. Now, Aaron was being challenged by a younger generation that distrusted whites. When I attempted to cover meetings in the black community, I was sometimes expelled by new leaders determined to establish their independence. One night, while I watched a parade of blacks protesting in downtown Clarksdale, a rock pitched by one of the demonstrators nicked my head and drew blood.

In spite of the new tensions, relations between the races had improved considerably. The Carr brothers first broke the social barrier, hosting integrated dinner parties at their homes, and others followed. Jane and I shocked our neighbors when we invited black guests to our home, but after a while they grew accustomed to the sight.

Because the Catholic Church remained effectively segregated in Clarksdale, a few whites left St. Elizabeth's parish and began attending services across town at a church for blacks, Immaculate Conception. A thoughtful Dutch priest, Father John Kirsten, said mass there, and a spunky group of nuns ran a parochial school for the black community. Though Andy Carr remained a St. Elizabeth's parishioner, he sneaked over to IC, as we called it. Jane and I attended mass there, too. After our daughter, Leighton, was born, we wanted her christened by Father Kirsten, but an aging Irish monsignor at St. Elizabeth's forbade the priest for the black congregation from conducting the ceremony. So we decided to wait until we left town.

I had received a Congressional Fellowship from the American Political Science Association, and we would be going to Washington in the fall. It was time to move on. Not because of the anonymous crank telephone calls urging me to love white Clarksdale or leave it, but because I was weary of the struggle. I was tired and in a position to escape. I knew the hardships encountered by my black friends in Clarksdale eclipsed my own, and I admired them for their perseverance. But at the age of twenty-nine, I felt like a burnt-out case. Besides, I was intrigued by the promise of a job on Capitol Hill and the prospect of living in a big city. It would be good, I thought, to dwell in a place where race was not a preoccupation.

* * *

Before we left, Clarksdale held its first election under the new system. George Farris, the reform-minded commissioner, campaigned for mayor and openly sought black votes. He was expected to be elected easily. Two black men ran for commission seats—Charles Stringer, a soft-spoken funeral-home owner, and Henry Espy Jr., the son of another prominent family of undertakers. I thought one or both of them could be elected.

I worked covertly with Aaron and several others to pick an integrated slate of candidates that would be satisfactory to black voters as well as to the growing number of white moderates willing to share political power. If Joe Ellis had known about my backroom dealing, he should have fired me. But I had a rationale concerning the alliance with Aaron: it was important to bring blacks into city government, and I was about to give up my job anyway.

The black voters in Clarksdale were not sophisticated and many relied on sample ballots handed out in their neighborhoods by the NAACP before elections. After white candidates discovered the practice, some of them attempted to sow confusion by distributing bogus sample ballots in the Negro quarters. In fact, some of Aaron's black adversaries sabotaged his efforts by promoting candidates with yet another sample ballot purporting to appeal to black interests. But Aaron's slate carried the most clout, and we knew it was essential to manufacture the most legitimate sample ballot.

Aaron came to our house one night, armed with material to prepare the ballot. He and I sat at the dining room table, pressing a ballpoint pen hard onto the stencil for mimeographed copies. The wood table still has the marks from our effort. Faintly, one can make out the names Farris, Stringer, Espy, inadvertently etched into the mahogany.

When the votes were counted, Farris was an easy victor. Stringer fell short by a hundred votes out of more than fifty-four hundred cast. Espy also lost. The Clarksdale board remained all white for one more term, but the city and Coahoma County were on the threshold of remarkable political change.

Politics took an unprecedented turn in Summit, too. My friend Lew Barnes, now managing his father's furniture store, decided to run for the town council. He had turned thirty and given up his mischievous ways to take his place as a local businessman. But as his cousin, and my friend, William Watkins later wrote me, "Shortly after Lew's announcement, the family realized his candidacy was not automatically destined to be a success. In many ears, the echoes of 'Red Hot Boogie' still reverberated, and others thought the stains of wild turkey shit still besmirched the pews of the First Baptist Church. Some of Summit's most respected citizens considered Lew's decision an affront to common decency and vowed to oppose him in any way they could."

Another factor was at play in the election. Blacks in Summit were restive for a spot on the council and had their own candidate for one of the seats. Lew was a moderate on racial matters. I remember, as a youngster, that he always used "sir" and "ma'am" when talking with older blacks. His relatives were well-known moderates, too. His uncle, Frank Watkins, was a national Democrat; after the Summit schools were consolidated into the McComb system, he led the school board's efforts to desegregate peacefully. To ensure Lew's election as well as the success of a black candidate named Hezekiah Swanigan, Billy Barnes and his brother-in-law, Frank, calculated the mathematics required to build a winning black-white coalition, a compact that would have been unimaginable a few years earlier.

In Summit, a handful of votes could make the difference, so Lew's family went to work collecting commitments across both sides of the racial divide. They faced a daunting task. As William Watkins said, "Some of the Baptists in town would have rather had the reincarnation of Malcolm X on the council than Lew Barnes."

The Barnes family had little problem rounding up support for Lew in their discussions with black ministers who commanded the votes of their congregations; local blacks knew the Barneses, had treated their community decently through the years. But Lew's relatives had a difficult time delivering their end of the bargain—forty white votes that Swanigan would need to win his seat on the council. Billy and Frank struggled for weeks to find whites willing to perform this unnatural act—to vote for a black man. In the end, however, they succeeded by calling in their IOUs among the white voters. When Lew took a seat on the council, Hezekiah Swanigan joined him and became the first black elected official in Pike County since Reconstruction.

Back in Clarksdale, Oscar and Billie Carr hosted a dinner-dance for Jane and me a couple of weeks before we left, and dozens of people from across the Delta came to see us off. It was a lovely, melancholy evening. We circulated through the Carrs' garden past midnight, enjoying the company and reflecting on the bittersweet memories of the decade. As it turned out, several of our friends there—Oscar and Wes Watkins and their wives, Hodding and his reporters from the *Delta Democrat-Times*—would leave the state before long themselves.

On one of our last nights in town, Aaron and his wife, Noelle, invited us to a farewell dinner at their home. We had a quiet, simple meal, musing about the events—funny and sad—that had taken place during my years in Clarksdale. I promised to stay in touch.

Autumn was at hand when Jane and I drove away. Our young son and infant daughter slept in the backseat. As we crossed the state line at Memphis, I felt a sense of liberation. I was leaving Mississippi, and I would never go back, I thought.

Clutching the steering wheel, I invoked Martin Luther King's words on the last full night of his life. "Free at last!" I shouted, trying to make my voice soar. "Free at last! Thank God Almighty, free at last!"

CHAPTER 12

Backlash

★ ★ ★ ★ ★

Marching with a half million others, I thought we had found a refuge. Less than a month after we arrived in Washington, Jane and I took part in America's most massive antiwar protest yet. On a biting-cold Saturday in November the demonstration twisted slowly through the streets of Washington like a giant beast. Unlike in Chicago, the columns of the march kept order. Looking at thousands of my generation in jeans and parkas, long hair and beards, their breaths rising in gray puffs, I felt a rush of camaraderie. In delayed reaction to the youth culture of the 1960s, I had neither shaved nor cut my hair since leaving Clarksdale.

Washington opened all sorts of new opportunities. We smoked dope, drank Chianti out of straw-covered bottles, listened to Led Zeppelin, and attended a production of *Hair*. There were dozens of movies to see, including Pontecorvo's revolutionary *Battle of Algiers* and *Easy Rider*, an odyssey through the South set to a druggy sound track. Washington boasted fine restaurants, though the best we could afford were a Greek place on L Street and A.V.'s Ristorante Italian, with its garden of cheap statues off New York Avenue.

Most fascinating were our new friends, dozens of other young people drawn to the nation's capital. Though the only Southerner in my Congressional Fellowship class, I never suffered from isolation. Virtually every member of our group marched against the war. Working on Capitol Hill, I discovered other liberated Southerners, young Washington lawyers such as Steve Engelberg from Memphis, Ruff Fant from Holly Springs, Mississippi, and Mickey Kantor from Nashville. Graduates of Eastern law schools, they had already broken from home. At last, I thought, I had become part of Willie Morris's "genuine set of exiles."

From the confining politics of Never! I found myself in a world energized by sharp debate. In the years of the Nixon administration, Capitol Hill served as a battleground. Democrats controlled both houses of Congress, but the war subdivided the two parties into other wrathful factions. In that hothouse atmosphere, Nixon's Southern Strategy germinated.

In the fall of 1969, the president named a South Carolina judge, Clement F. Haynsworth, to an opening on the U.S. Supreme Court. The nomination touched off a bitter fight in the Senate, and after Haynsworth was tarred by reports that he had held stock in companies affected by his judicial decisions, he failed to win confirmation.

Southerners were incensed over the rejection, and Nixon seized the chance to play to the region's paranoia. He told his South Carolina aide, Harry Dent, a manager of the Southern Strategy, to "find a good federal judge further South and further to the right." They found G. Harrold Carswell of Florida. One of Nixon's aides later admitted that the White House thought Carswell was "a boob, a dummy." No matter. He was a Southerner.

The court battles took place during the first phase of my fellowship, when I was working for a forty-two-year-old senator from Minnesota, Walter F. Mondale. I'd first met Mondale when he came to Mississippi to support our insurgent delegation in 1968, and I liked his civil rights record and his style. At one of our staff meetings, he reflexively dismissed Carswell. "I don't like the way this guy smells," Mondale said, instructing his press secretary to put out word that Mondale opposed the nomination, even before hearings were held.

Carswell came to Senate consideration carrying the weight of a lifetime of opposition to Negroes, and a coalition of civil rights and labor interests volunteered to help liberal senators in their research. Combing through old newspapers in Florida, they found a report of a white-supremacy speech Carswell had delivered in 1948. Marian Wright Edelman,* who had moved from Mississippi courtrooms to run the Children's Defense Fund, uncovered Carswell's role in converting a public golf course in Tallahassee into a private club to escape a desegregation order.

The fight over Carswell boiled to the last day. A head count before the vote showed a deadlock among members of the Senate who had committed one way or the other; a few senators were undecided. Carswell's fate would

*By this time, Marian Wright had married Peter Edelman, a Robert Kennedy aide who had accompanied the senator on his Delta tour in 1967.

be decided in one of those rare roll calls where the outcome was not known beforehand. To watch the drama, I wormed my way into the Senate staff gallery.

Inspecting the Senate floor, I saw Jim Eastland for the first time. He had held a Mississippi seat for most of my lifetime, yet he rarely made public appearances in the state. News photos made him look Buddha-like; I was surprised to see he was relatively tall and trim, moving about the chamber with the authority of a committee chairman and one of Carswell's chief supporters. The vice president, Spiro Agnew, prepared to cast a vote to break any tie, sat unsmiling in his seat at the top of the podium.

The roll call followed expected lines. Then one of the undecided senators, Marlow Cook, a Republican from Kentucky, voted no, and gasps sounded as though air had been released from a large balloon. Winston Prouty, a Republican from Vermont, followed with a no, precipitating a short burst of cheers in the gallery. When Margaret Chase Smith, a Maine Republican, whispered no after her name was called, the defeat of Nixon's nominee was assured. I clapped as if I were at a baseball game, and so did dozens of others.

The chamber "exploded in applause and whistles," wrote Fred Graham in the *New York Times*. "Normally, the slightest rustle in the galleries is quickly silenced by attendants, but today the demonstration continued for two minutes despite demands from the Senate floor for order."

I remember seeing the powerful senator from Georgia, Richard Russell, his face reddened with rage, rising to demand that we be cleared from the chamber. Agnew, visibly upset over the outcome, pounded his gavel like a bludgeon, calling for the sergeant at arms to eject us. But we were already leaving, shaking hands and clapping shoulders in triumph.

Nixon characterized Carswell's defeat as another slap in the face of the South by Democratic liberals. I celebrated with other Mondale aides back at the Senate office building, but I overlooked the seismic political shift taking place. Even as the Democrats succeeded in blocking Nixon's Supreme Court nominations, they were driving hordes of Southern voters into the Republican Party.

Nixon collected converts like an evangelist. Roll calls were taken on bills to provide funding for the American presence in Vietnam, and each vote by antiwar Democrats resounded badly in the South, where support for the military remained strong.

Although the landmark Civil Rights and Voting Rights Acts were faits accomplis, new battles developed in Congress on ancillary issues. The Senate was the scene of a clash over the use of federal funds to bus schoolchildren to achieve integration, and Mondale led the civil rights forces while John Stennis, the Mississippi Democrat, carried the fight for Nixon and the segregationists.

Stennis had always been an interesting study. An aging, quintessentially Southern gentleman, he epitomized the moderate wing of the old Democratic Party in Mississippi. At the same time, he was a fervent defender of the Southern way of life and became one of Nixon's most reliable friends in the Senate. He and Mondale, the brash, youthful senator from the North, engaged in sharp arguments on the Senate floor.

One day, as I crossed from the Capitol to the Old Senate Office Building, I realized I was standing beside Stennis as we waited for a traffic light to change. I introduced myself as a Mississippian. He brightened and asked what I was doing in Washington. I admitted that I was a Congressional fellow, working for "your good friend Fritz Mondale."

The old senator smiled. "That Mondale's a good, young booger," Stennis told me. "If they don't treat you right, all those folks from Minnesota, then you come down to our office and see us."

Actually, Mondale and his people treated me fine. A few weeks later, when my Senate fellowship period expired and I was due to transfer to a House office, Mondale hosted a small going-away gathering. He followed a Capitol Hill custom, autographing an eight-by-ten photo of himself for the departing aide. But when I looked at it, I saw he had scribbled whiskers on his clean-shaven cheeks to salute my beard and had scrawled across his forehead, "You and John Stennis have been a great comfort to me," before signing it simply, "Fritz."

That spring, Nixon attended the annual Gridiron Club dinner, a white-tie event sponsored by a select group of journalists. Invitations to the dinner were more coveted than tickets to a Redskins game, and virtually every heavyweight in the capital could be counted on to be there, feasting on an elaborate meal and laughing at the satirical skits.

A newspaper reporter playing the part of Robert Finch, Nixon's secretary of health, education, and welfare, delighted the audience with lyrics sung to the tune of "A Dixie Melody":

Rock-a-bye the voters with a Southern Strategy;
Don't you fuss; we won't bus children in ol' Dixie!
We'll put George Wallace in decline
Below the Mason-Dixon Line.
We'll help save the nation
From things like civil rights and integration!
Weep no more, John Stennis!
We'll pack the court for sure.
We will fight for voting rights—
To keep them white and pure.
A zillion Southern votes we will deliver;
Move Washington down on the Swanee River!
Rock-a-bye with Ol' Massá Nixon and his Dixie strategy!

The president joined in the gales of laughter. As the evening neared its climax, he had an opportunity to lead the fun. When the curtain pulled back on the final act, the audience saw Nixon and Agnew, sitting at two pianos.

In his study of racial politics, *Nixon's Piano*, Kenneth O'Reilly described the scene:

"Nixon opened by asking: 'What about this Southern Strategy we hear so often?'

"'Yes suh, Mr. President,' Agnew replied. 'Ah agree with you completely on yoah Southern Strategy.'"

Roger Wilkins, a prominent black figure in Washington and a guest at the dinner, noted that Agnew's Negro dialect "got the biggest boffo," O'Reilly wrote.

"After more banter with the 'darky' Agnew, Nixon opened the piano duet with Franklin Roosevelt's favorite song ('Home on the Range'), then Harry Truman's ('Missouri Waltz'), then Lyndon Johnson's ('The Eyes of Texas Are Upon You'). Agnew drowned him out a few bars into each with a manic 'Dixie' on his piano, and the Gridiron crew got louder and louder."

When it was over, O'Reilly concluded, "those Gridiron members and their distinguished guests laughed and sang and cried not because they considered the president's Southern Strategy in the nation's best interest. Many in fact condemned his politics as opportunistic, divisive, even immoral. They cheered the president because they respected the electoral results. Simply put, Southern Strategy worked."

Nixon cultivated the white South with frequent visits and assuaging words of commitment to the American fighting men in Vietnam. He created new divisions between the region and the Democratic Party by excoriating liberal excesses; at the same time he comforted conservatives by withholding funds from the Great Society programs.

From the disgruntled ranks of the Citizens Council and the ambitious orders of the Jaycees, Nixon's agents recruited the leadership for a new, indigenous Republican Party in the South. In many locales, the GOP chairmen were glib, well-scrubbed lawyers who knew better than to use racial insults in public. But in some peckerwood counties, the Republican converts held views so extreme that they were merely scrubbed-up equivalents of the Ku Klux Klan.

The party was built with Babbitts and boosters, doctrinaire conservatives and fundamentalist preachers, American Legionnaires and ladies from the United Daughters of the Confederacy, used-car salesmen and closet racists. From my vantage point in Washington, I heard that many of my contemporaries, young men and women who had been apolitical at Ole Miss, were joining the Republican Party because it had become new and fashionable.

As the historian Dan Carter observed: "For nearly a hundred years after the Civil War, politicians had manipulated the racial phobias of whites below the Mason-Dixon Line to maintain a solidly Democratic South. To Nixon it seemed only poetic justice that the tables should be turned. The challenge lay in appealing to the fears of angry whites without appearing to be an extremist and driving away moderates."

With emotions running high on Capitol Hill over race and the war, a visit by Governor Lester Maddox of Georgia jangled nerve ends. Appearing for lunch at a cafeteria serving House members, he began handing out souvenir ax handles, the weapon he once used to drive away black customers from his restaurant in Atlanta.

Congressman Diggs of Michigan, who had escaped the firebombing at Aaron Henry's home and suffered other indignities over the years, was irate over the intrusion. When he complained, Maddox was dismissive. The governor said Diggs was acting "more like an ass and baboon than a member of Congress."

* * *

In the congressional elections of 1970, Agnew helped Nixon promote a "law and order" campaign designed to paint Democrats as soft on crime and weak on national defense. Liberals were targeted for defeat in a number of states, and several Southern Democrats who had defied Nixon on civil rights and the war seemed at risk.

After my stint with Mondale, I had gone to work for John Brademas, a young congressman from South Bend, Indiana. He had attended Ole Miss for a year on a special program following military service, though I was attracted to his office by his causes rather than his Ole Miss credentials, which he rarely invoked anyway. Brademas had graduated from Harvard and gone on to become a Rhodes Scholar, studying the leftist movement in the Spanish Civil War. On Capitol Hill, he was a leading advocate for funds for education as well as the arts and humanities. He was also a Democratic partisan, a liberal supported by the United Auto Workers, the most important union in his district.

I had first heard of Brademas six years earlier when he had come to Clarksdale to attend a wedding. As a Northern congressman supporting President Johnson in the 1964 election, he had been something of a skunk at a garden party. As he later told me, near the end of the evening someone had pointed out to him another "Johnson backer" across the dance floor at the Clarksdale Country Club.

The congressman approached the local Johnson man, introduced himself, and remarked, "I believe we may be the only two Johnson supporters here."

With a glint in his eye, the Clarksdale man replied, "You don't think I'd vote for that goddamned Jew Goldwater, do you?"

By 1970, Brademas was one of those marked for political extinction by the Nixon administration, and I made arrangements to work in his campaign in Indiana in the fall after my fellowship ended. To prepare for the effort, Brademas, his administrative aide Nye Stevens, and I went shopping for a TV consultant.

The atomic power of television commercials had become apparent in 1964 with a famous LBJ spot, produced by Tony Schwartz, that fanned fears of a nuclear holocaust should the hawkish Goldwater be elected. The ad showed a little girl peeling the petals from a daisy, with a countdown in the background that ended in a nuclear explosion and a warning: Vote for Johnson.

"In millions of living rooms, people wondered just what they had seen," wrote Jon Margolis in *The Last Innocent Year*. "Was this a political advertisement? Obviously it was, considering its concluding tag line. But it was unlike any political ad they had ever seen before. Until then, political commercials had been about candidates."

One of the filmmakers we visited was Charles Guggenheim, a talented Democrat who had helped Brademas in 1968. He told us a cautionary tale. Earlier that year, a populist Texas senator, Ralph Yarborough, had been challenged by a conservative, Lloyd Bentsen, in a Democratic primary; a wealthy Republican congressman from Houston, George Bush, waited in the wings in the general election. Before Yarborough could get past the primary, however, he was waylaid by Bentsen's TV spots linking the senator to rioting in the streets in Chicago at the Democratic convention.

Seeking rescue a few days before the primary, Yarborough and his top aide had come to Guggenheim's studio to see examples of the spots that had helped John F. Kennedy and other liberal Democrats in campaigns past. Yarborough was impressed. "Gene," he said to his aide, "we got to get ourselves some of these." It was too late to produce a counterattack against Bentsen, Guggenheim explained, though he said he would be willing to help in the general election. Yarborough never got that far, however; he lost his seat in the primary.

Brademas finally settled on a bright young filmmaker named Bob Squier and survived an ugly campaign in Indiana. Outside of South Bend, with its big UAW membership, the congressman had to deal with three rural, Republican-leaning counties. Our campaign bible became *The Real Majority*, a book by Richard Scammon and Ben Wattenberg, which had persuaded many Democratic candidates to chart a centrist course to avoid antagonizing the blue-collar vote. Brademas muted his disapproval of the war and his criticism of Nixon. His most effective TV spot was a simple endorsement by Ara Parseghian, the popular football coach at Notre Dame.

The Democrats managed to hold their majority in Congress, but the country was littered with casualties. An antiwar senator from Tennessee, Albert Gore, went down in a campaign where he had been attacked as a traitor and the "third senator from Massachusetts." He was replaced by a smooth, well-groomed man named Bill Brock, an heir to a candy fortune and a prototype of the new Republican politicians in the South.

* * *

News from Dixie:

—Mother called on a Sunday morning that fall. After we spent a couple of minutes chatting, I realized she had something more serious to say. The night before, Lew Barnes had been killed in a car wreck. After surviving a capricious adolescence, escaping serious punishment for his sorties against the Baptists and other powers in Summit, Lew had finally come undone. There would be no more turkeys tucked into the balcony of the Baptist church, no more tricks played on the town marshal. Lew left a widow and three young daughters, and the news of his death left me awfully sad.

—A couple of months later in Summit, Mary Cain resigned her positions at the First Baptist Church as secretary of the congregation, Baptist Training Union director, and member of the choir. She did so, she wrote in a letter to the congregation, "with a heavy heart" because the church intended to make Social Security payments on the janitor's salary. "I have steadfastly refused to accept a Social Security number and am willing to go to jail for my conviction that it is evil."

—On a frosty morning in Atlanta in January 1971, a new governor took the oath of office, replacing Mr. Ax Handle, Lester Maddox. In his inaugural address, Jimmy Carter told the people of Georgia, "The time for racial discrimination is over." When the throng recovered its collective breath, Carter continued, "No poor, rural, weak, or black person should ever again have to bear the additional burden of being deprived of the opportunity for an education, a job, or simple justice." Then he closed with a quotation from William Jennings Bryan. The future, Carter said, "is not a matter of change, it is a matter of choice. Destiny is not a thing to be waited for. It is a thing to be achieved."

Just as Southern politics appeared to me to be taking an encouraging turn with the election of Carter and several other progressive governors, the rest of the country seemed to be moving in another direction.

The grand alliance that had once existed between blacks and Jews, a force for liberalism that had nurtured organized labor and the civil rights movement, was disintegrating. Negro mobs, fired by frustration and fanned by allegations of usury, had looted many Jewish-owned stores during the urban riots that had spread across the country following the King assassination in 1968. Before his own murder in 1965, Malcolm X had warned followers of a Jewish conspiracy. "In America," Malcolm X said, "the Jews sap the very lifeblood of the so-called Negroes to maintain the state of Israel,

its armies, and its continued aggression against our brothers in the East."
On another level, black scholars complained that Jews had suppressed the
intellectual development of Negroes by hogging leadership in various
fields. The most vivid example of the rift took place in Brooklyn, where
Jewish teachers and black parents competing for control of the Ocean
Hill–Brownsville school district exchanged accusations of racism and anti-
Semitism.

In Manhattan, gangs of construction workers wearing hard hats
attacked antiwar demonstrators with the vehemence of Bull Connor's
police dogs. Philadelphia elected Frank Rizzo mayor. He had gained fame as
a police commissioner who brooked no nonsense from blacks. To demonstrate his pugnacity, Rizzo posed in a tuxedo with a nightstick tucked into
his cummerbund. Louise Day Hicks, a South Boston opponent of racial
integration, was elected to Congress three years after she had unsuccessfully run for mayor of Boston with a slogan that left little to the imagination: "You know where I stand."

A phenomenon that sociologists described as a "backlash" spread
through the working class in the North, fed by competition between blacks
and whites for jobs and inflamed by resentment when hiring policies gave
preference to minorities. Archie Bunker, the protagonist of the popular TV
series *All in the Family,* came to represent a bigoted, white Everyman, upset
with pushy blacks and court-ordered desegregation. Instead of Magnolia,
Mississippi, the show was set in the New York borough of Queens.

Nixon's reelection seemed secure in 1972, but George Wallace burst out of
Alabama again, exporting his critiques of pointy-headed bureaucrats and
pigheaded judges and promising to run down any Gandhian protester who
might lie in his path. "One of 'em laid down in front of President Johnson's
limousine," Wallace once crowed. "The first time they lie down in front of
my limousine, it'll be the last one they'll ever lay down in front of."

Wallace was the last primitive in Southern politics, soon to be supplanted by a new breed of more respectable Republicans, cultured men
with lacquered hair and scripted speeches, rolled out of GOP assembly
lines like the latest models of Lincoln Continentals, sleek and fully packed
with polls and advice from political scientists. But in 1972, Wallace was not
yet ready to yield the stage. For him, politics was not a science; it was a living organism, snorting laughter and mockery.

Wallace was a one-man riot to cover. At his rallies, he used reporters for the *New York Times* or "the *Time* magazine," as he called it, as foils, pointing them out to his listeners as flunkies of a biased Eastern press. He reduced audiences to giggles, telling the story of how officials once employed "recapitulation" to rob him of votes in a Maryland primary. "If you ever hear somebody say they're going to recapitulate you, don't let them do it," he yelled. After setting up his crowds with laughter, he moved them to anger with harangues about federal decrees and court-ordered busing.

The first time he ran for president, in 1964, Wallace shocked the nation by collecting a third of the vote in Democratic primaries in Wisconsin and Indiana before abandoning his symbolic effort. In 1968, Wallace conducted a full-fledged campaign under the banner of the American Independent Party, carrying 14 percent of the national vote and capturing forty-six electoral votes from Deep South states. He might have done better had it not been for the bravado of his running mate, former air force general Curtis LeMay.

During a press conference, LeMay spoke of his willingness to use nuclear weapons to win the Vietnam War. Fears of nuclear fallout were unfounded, the old general said. "I've seen a film of Bikini Atoll after twenty nuclear tests, and the fish are all back in the lagoons, the coconut trees are growing coconuts, the guava bushes have fruit on them, the birds are back." To be truthful, LeMay added, a problem had arisen with crabs on the island. "They get minerals from the soil, I guess, through their shells, and the land crabs are a little bit hot." But to round out his happy assessment, the general observed that "the rats are bigger, fatter, and healthier than they ever were before."

LeMay helped immolate the Wallace campaign that year, but Nixon remained troubled that Wallace had carried the Deep South. Those forty-six electoral votes could make a tremendous difference in a close election, and the prospect that another Wallace effort in 1972 might divide conservatives prompted the president to use the same sort of underhanded tactics that later ensnared him in the Watergate affair.

At the time, the White House moves to discourage Wallace were only rumors, but the tactics were eventually documented during the Watergate investigation. As J. Anthony Lukas wrote in *Nightmare*, a comprehensive study of the scandal: "When it became clear that Wallace's ambitions were as grandiose as ever, the White House set out with determination to throw some roadblocks in his way." Drawing from a secret fund, Nixon aide Herb Kalmbach funneled $400,000 in cash to the campaign of

Albert Brewer, Wallace's adversary in a 1970 gubernatorial election. Brewer, originally elected lieutenant governor, had ascended to the governor's office after the death of Wallace's wife, Lurleen. Because he could not succeed himself, Wallace had sponsored Lurleen's candidacy in 1966. Now the "fighting judge" wanted the office back. Overcoming the infusion of Nixon cash, Wallace won easily.

Having failed to derail Wallace in the Alabama election, the Nixon White House took a new approach, encouraging the Internal Revenue Service to investigate the tax records of Gerald Wallace, the governor's brother and confidant.

"The best the White House could hope for," Lukas wrote, "was to divert Wallace's bombastic energies from his crusade to mobilize the independent conservative forces in the South into a series of bruising Democratic primaries" that would further fracture the Democrats. Although an indictment was said to have been prepared for Gerald Wallace, a well-connected political fixer in the Alabama capital, Nixon's Justice Department announced on January 12, 1972, that the federal investigation had been dropped and the grand jury, which had spent eighteen months looking into corruption in Alabama, had been dismissed. A day later, the governor held a press conference to reveal that he would compete for the Democratic presidential nomination rather than lead a third-party effort in the fall.

In 1971, I had pushed a bit farther north, taking a reporting job with the *News-Journal* papers in Wilmington, Delaware. Because my stint as a Congressional fellow led the editors to believe I knew something about national politics, they assigned me to cover the 1972 presidential campaign.

By the spring, the primaries had worked their way to Michigan and Maryland, and Wallace was trailing only George McGovern in the race for convention delegates. Wallace had already outlasted the original favorite, Senator Edmund Muskie of Maine, and was running ahead of Hubert Humphrey. It was a profound embarrassment to the Democratic Party, but one hell of a news story.

I drove to Cambridge, on Maryland's Eastern Shore, to see how Wallace appealed to voters in a border-state town with a history of racial problems. Cambridge had a strong overlay of Southern culture. It had been a hotbed of Confederate sympathizers during the Civil War, and those attitudes had carried over into the twentieth century. In 1964, the town had been put under martial law after civil rights demonstrations had led to gunfire and street fighting. A Wallace visit there during his first presidential campaign had provoked a protest by local Negroes that drew a tear-gas attack by National Guardsmen.

Against that backdrop, Wallace returned to Cambridge eight years later to speak before a crowd of whites. I scribbled notes as police held a group of jeering blacks at bay a couple of blocks down the street. The situation was tense, but the candidate was able to leave town before another incident took place.

The next day, I cornered Wallace for a quick interview as he campaigned at a suburban strip mall. He appeared to be on the verge of victory in the Maryland primary and was thoroughly enjoying himself. He told me of his gratification that the message from Alabama was being received, loud and clear, in the North. He predicted more triumphs as the primary season played out across the heartland of America. He was at once funny and sarcastic. Detecting my Southern accent, he joked about Yankees being slow learners. He thought I was from a newspaper in Wilmington, North Carolina. I never corrected him.

Up close, Wallace resembled a beetle. He had dark, thick eyebrows and facial warts. His hair was slicked with pomade, and while we talked, his wife, Cornelia, picked flecks of dandruff from his shoulders. I was surprised by her beauty. I had been expecting Wallace's new wife to have the coarsened features of someone traveling with the hard-rolling stock-car-racing crowd. Instead, Cornelia looked lovely, even though she towered over her diminutive husband.

Wallace's courtship could have been a chapter in *All the King's Men*. After he had been widowed, a number of women had campaigned to become the next first lady of Alabama. One of them, Ruby Folsom Ellis, already had experience at the governor's mansion. She was the sister of a former governor, "Kissing Jim" Folsom, and following the death of Folsom's wife, she had served as her brother's official hostess. "Big Ruby," as she was known around Montgomery, stood nearly six feet tall and had a strong liking for bourbon, which she drank in gulps from an iced-tea glass at the Elite Café downtown. She had lost two husbands to cancer and pined for a new mate. In an interview with the Washington writer Myra MacPherson, she confided, "I never wanted a face-lift, but my children wanted me to have one. My friends said, 'Big Ruby, you don't need a face-lift, you need a body-lift.' You know, they're right. I looked in the mirror the other day, and my titties looked like two gourds hanging over a barbed-wire fence."

Big Ruby realized she would be no match for her own daughter, Cornelia, in the competition for George Wallace. Still, Big Ruby continued to flirt with Wallace and other men. When Cornelia expressed concern over her mother's behavior, suggesting that people might think her mother wanted to steal Wallace's affection, Big Ruby had a tart reply. "Honey," she said to Cornelia, "no way would I want George. He don't stand but titty-high." Despite Big Ruby's put-down, Cornelia married George just before Wallace reassumed the governor's office in 1971, and she accompanied him on almost all of his campaign trips.

At the conclusion of my brief exchange with the governor, Wallace agreed to a more extensive interview later and passed me off to his press secretary, Billy Joe Camp. I made an appointment to meet with Wallace in a few days in Annapolis, on the night before the Maryland primary.

Returning to Maryland on the morning of that engagement, I perused the schedules of the candidates and saw that Humphrey had a midday press conference in Towson that conflicted with a Wallace rally at a shopping center in Laurel. I thought, If you've seen one Wallace shopping center rally, you've seen them all. I went to hear Humphrey.

Afterward, driving toward Annapolis for my interview with the Alabama governor, I listened to the car radio. The music was interrupted by a bulletin. George Wallace had been shot in Laurel, and my blood ran cold.

With Wallace critically wounded and on the sidelines, Nixon cruised to reelection. The president made only three campaign outings in the fall, and I covered two of those trips. They struck me as carnivals of phony patriotism, larger-than-life-size models of the rabble-rousing political rallies I had seen in Mississippi.

The Democratic campaign, with Senator McGovern as the antiwar nominee, was an inspired but doomed enterprise, dogged by trouble from the outset. The South represented especially hostile terrain for him. Nevertheless, in the face of polling numbers that showed Nixon far ahead in the region, a band of Democratic loyalists tried to attract Southern support with a whistle-stop trip from Washington to New Orleans aboard a train called the Grassroots Grasshoppers' Special.

The Southern excursion was as cursed with bad luck as the McGovern campaign. The night before the group set out, Aaron Henry was arrested in a Washington park by undercover police and charged with soliciting a homosexual act. The policemen reported that when they went to Aaron's hotel room, they found narcotics; he was charged with that as well.

Questions about Aaron's sexuality had been around ever since his arrest on a morals charge involving the hitchhiker in Clarksdale a decade earlier. As far as I knew, the issue had never hindered his leadership role; though many of his friends suspected he had a gay side, few really cared about his sexual orientation. But the arrest in Washington came at an embarrassing time, and Aaron's colleagues aboard the Grasshoppers' Special tried to keep the news out of the papers. Word of Aaron's arrest leaked out, however, by the time the train reached New Orleans, and an Associated Press reporter tracked him down at a Democratic reception in the French Quarter. Aaron acknowledged he had been arrested on drug charges—no morals count was ever filed against him—and predicted that the case would be dismissed because the drugs were prescribed for him.

The next month, on the eve of the election, the U.S. attorney's office in Washington dropped the charges. But that represented the only good news of the week. Nixon piled up one of the biggest electoral college advantages in history, and it seemed as though the nation were adopting the politics I had grown up with.

There seemed to be no escape, unless I could get to Boston, the cradle of the abolitionist movement and the center of protest against the Vietnam War. Massachusetts had been the only state to reject Nixon. Not only did Massachusetts give its electoral votes to McGovern, a majority of the people in the state refused to accept Nixon's claim on the presidency. After Watergate grew into a serious matter, I envied the bumper stickers that said, "Don't blame me, I'm from Massachusetts."

In the fall of 1973, shortly after the Saturday Night Massacre, in which Nixon fired the Watergate prosecutor, Archibald Cox, I traveled to Boston. Across the river, Harvard Square was teeming with anti-Nixon demonstrators. For a souvenir, I bought a risqué bumper sticker, "Impeach the Cox-Sacker," from a student vendor. Boston was obviously the nirvana I had been seeking.

A year later, Nixon was gone, and Watergate had been replaced in the national headlines with stories of Boston's struggle to implement a federal court order requiring the city to achieve racial balance in its schools. The first phase of the order called for busing between two of the city's most combustible neighborhoods, predominantly black Roxbury and the white, working-class peninsula of South Boston. When yellow buses carrying black schoolchildren rolled into South Boston, the neighborhood erupted in an orgy of curses, rock-throwings, and random beatings.

The Wilmington newspaper, anticipating court-ordered busing in Delaware, sent me to cover the conflict. I spent a week in Boston, but barely scratched the surface of the controversy. To an outsider, it seemed largely writ in black and white. Black schoolchildren were being tormented by white bigots. But that was merely one small element of a complicated story involving historic racial patterns in Boston's neighborhoods, the "Southie pride" that survived in the warrens of three-decker homes and public housing units of South Boston, the legacy of militance in Roxbury that had produced Malcolm X and Louis Farrakhan, the racist oratory of many of Boston's political leaders, the weak role played by the Catholic Church in its failure to prepare the city for the ordeal, and the sense—alive in the toughest white districts of Boston—that the court order would never have to be obeyed.

Boston's imperfections were not yet evident to me when the *Globe* offered me a job. In January 1975—the same week that our second son, Stuart, was born—I accepted with alacrity.

The city was still roiled by the busing dilemma when I moved there, and practically every reporter on the *Globe* staff was thrown into the effort to keep up with the story. Violence had spread from South Boston and Roxbury to other parts of the city. Fistfights broke out on subways, and taxi drivers with the wrong-color skin became fair game if they strayed into hostile neighborhoods. For the first time, I heard a gerund applied as an adjective to supplement the word *nigger*. Blacks were not simply niggers; in the parlance of South Boston they were "fuckin' niggas."

As a new reporter, I had weekend duty at the *Globe*. So when federal judge W. Arthur Garrity issued the second phase of his desegregation order, an edict that paired the upper-middle-class Irish neighborhood of West Roxbury with a black district, an editor dispatched me to "feel the pulse" following Sunday mass at Holy Name Catholic Church, the massive red-brick anchor of West Roxbury.

As the parishioners streamed from the service, I identified myself as a *Globe* reporter and attempted to elicit their thoughts on "Phase Two" of the busing order. I was told, rather forcefully, by several of the worshipers—whose mouths had just accepted the Communion host, the body of Christ—what I could do with my newspaper and where I could stick it. Because of its editorial support of the court order, the *Globe* had become the enemy of the antibusing movement. After shots were fired into our newsroom, the publisher installed bulletproof glass throughout the building. Nails were sprinkled in front of our delivery trucks, and our newspaper sales were boycotted. To disrupt the *Globe* further, leaders of the South Boston uprising carried their demonstrations to our front door. If I did not already fully appreciate the hostility, it became quite clear that Sunday that the *Globe* was despised by much of the white population of Boston. And in spite of Boston's liberal image, I realized the city was a stronghold of racial conservatives.

A couple of the communicants at Holy Name agreed to explain to me their objections to the latest court order. They insisted that race was not their motivation. It made no sense, they said, to destroy neighborhood schools, to take children who could walk to their classes and bus them across town as pawns in a social experiment. Even a simple reporter from the *Globe* should understand that, I was told. I was relieved when I'd collected enough quotes to leave Holy Name parish.

News from Dixie:

—On July 5, 1975, business returned to normal on Robb Street in Summit after the Independence Day holiday, but an unusual incident took place shortly after William Watkins dropped by the furniture store to see his uncle, Billy Barnes. They became witnesses to a melodrama featuring such characters as Weewoe Norton, the village idiot; Johnnie Woodall, my old school-bus driver; Woody Seale, "Man Brown's" successor as town marshal; and a young black visitor from Chicago.

William is a gifted storyteller, like so many of my friends, and he provided me with a narrative:

"Three loafers—Weewoe, Johnnie Woodall, and Howard Adams—were sitting just outside the Barnes store, under the sidewalk overhang. One could discern no conversation between the three, as if all news and speculation about events had long since been done with. As Billy and I watched, this young black boy from Chicago rode his bicycle up and down the sidewalk. With each trip, he got closer to Johnnie Woodall's toe.

"The trio never scattered. They waited silently and unemotionally. The lad surely realized his activity was irritating them. Finally, the kid could wait no longer. On his next swipe, the bicycle nipped Woodall's toe and threw the boy off his pace. He paused to balance the bike. With the speed and stealth of a cottonmouth moccasin, Woodall grabbed a hickory stick from Weewoe and struck the young man across the back of his head. Blood spurted everywhere. The sound of the blow, the bleating of the injured boy, and the general commotion brought an immediate crowd out of the stores.

"The loafers scattered. The boy struggled toward the Bottom, knowing that although Chicago was too far to reach, some protection could be found there.

"The town marshal, Woody Seale, arrived at the scene with blue lights flashing and siren blaring. (Woody was one-legged, like Woodall, prompting Billy Barnes to brag that of all the towns in the world, Summit's police force had only one leg to stand on.) After obtaining eyewitness accounts, the marshal decided to pursue the boy, not the assailants. Armed with a twelve-gauge pump shotgun loaded with a tear-gas shell, he set off for the Bottom, his siren blowing and blue lights ablaze again.

"Following a trail of blood toward Mingo's Pool Hall, Woody parked abruptly in the middle of the street and propped his shotgun on the door of the police car. A crowd of blacks had already gathered, and out of their midst charged the boy, who appeared crazed with pain and humiliation.

"Without so much as a split second of restraint, Woody let loose a blast of the shotgun directly into the boy's chest, sending him tumbling back, unconscious, on the hot pavement. The tear-gas canister did not go off, and the shell did not cause too serious an injury. But the amount of blood convinced the crowd that the boy had been murdered.

"As rumors spread quickly through Summit's black community that another young black man had been dispatched by a white law-enforcement officer, an impromptu march was begun by the blacks, moving over the hill separating the Bottom from the white-owned businesses.

"Concurrently, a white crowd gathered along the main street. Though they were outnumbered by the blacks, the whites looked far more ominous. Several stood silently in front of J. T. Lilly's old store, with obviously malevolent intent to maintain peace and tranquillity. Many of the white men were dressed in long raincoats, which no doubt concealed weapons, probably shotguns and clubs. In his review of the incident, Billy called them 'the minutemen.'

"Black leaders and members of the state highway patrol succeeded in keeping the two factions apart, but I believe there was another reason that the blacks lost enthusiasm for a confrontation. These were people who, for the most part, did not leave the South in the 1930s, 1940s, and 1950s. They represented the remnants of the conservative blacks who found the South, with all its injustice and lack of opportunity and suffrage, acceptable and even comfortable. Others had gone off because they could not live within the system, but these people had stayed at home. The boy from Chicago was the only one of his race in Summit that day who had the daring to sport up and down Robb Street with mischief on his mind.

"The blacks retreated to the Bottom. After the boy was released from the hospital, he returned to Chicago and was never seen in Summit again."

A month later, I was again on Sunday duty at the *Globe* building in Dorchester, a working-class neighborhood on the edge of South Boston. From the deck outside our cafeteria, one could see Southie's crown, a hill topped by South Boston High School, the setting for much of the busing turmoil. Below lay one of the bays in Boston's harbor, fringed by a stretch of sand called Carson Beach.

After several weekends of intermittent fighting between blacks and whites along the beachfront, an assortment of black organizations and leftist groups called for a mass demonstration to assert the rights of Negroes to swim in the South Boston waters.

As one of the reporters sent to the scene, I staked out a spot near a bathhouse, between South Boston and a black housing project across the bay on Columbia Point. I did not have to wait long to begin taking notes. An effort by neighborhood officials to divert gangs of South Boston boys to a "Southie Pride Day" rally at another park failed to attract a crowd; the teenagers chose to defend Carson Beach against groups of blacks who had begun filtering into the area from the housing project.

Two young black men, ignoring taunts and threats, walked into the midst of a South Boston group until the crowd blocked their progress. One of the black men carried a camera, and he began snapping pictures. A Southie man wearing a "White Power" button posed sarcastically. Another spit on the photographer. For a few seconds, the black man and the white man stood their ground, spitting into each other's faces until police officers cleared the area. As the black pair turned back, dozens of Southie whites raised their middle fingers triumphantly.

"Just stay there," another burly black man yelled. "There's more niggers coming." Indeed, blacks were pouring into the area, and within minutes they overran a thin police line on the beach, setting off a series of fistfights and clashes in which wooden staves were used like swords. While police helicopters bobbed back and forth overhead, an amphibious police craft reared out of the water and onto the beach in an effort to reinforce the line.

The crowds surged against each other. Stones and bottles arched through the sky. The air also seemed to be filled with wild noise. Blacks were chanting, "Turn this motherfucker out! Turn this motherfucker out!" Rocks bounced off cars parked along Day Boulevard. Mothers holding small children cringed behind an ice cream truck. The rise and fall of sirens sounded as if the day had been scored by the composer Philip Glass.

To subdue the pitched battle, mounted police and members of Boston's special Tactical Patrol Force marched on the beach to derisive cheers from spectators on both sides. The skirmish continued, and I stayed behind the black lines, figuring I would be safer as a *Globe* reporter among the protest group than among Southie residents. As the police began herding the black demonstrators toward Columbia Point, a separate, vicious battle broke out between the occupants of the black housing project and a group of leftist whites. Although the whites wore T-shirts identifying themselves as members of a Committee Against Racism, the blacks concluded they were provocateurs. Men wrestled in the sand while a young white woman, wearing one of the T-shirts, fled into the bay, pursued by a mob of blacks. In the thrashing melee, her assailants pulled her head underwater. I thought she might drown.

A black woman told me, "You've got a lot of nerve." At first, I thought it was a compliment. In fact, it was a threat. Whites were no longer welcome on the black side of the brawl, so I edged away from the water to a neutral position near the police lines.

Before the battle at Carson Beach could be put down, eight hundred policemen had to be deployed. Officers estimated that four thousand whites and two thousand blacks were involved at the height of the disturbance. At least forty people were treated at hospitals for wounds and ten were arrested.

Thirteen years after the Ole Miss riot, I had made my way to the promised land of Boston and found another race war.

CHAPTER 13

"I love Mr. Carter as
a white man"

★ ★ ★ ★ ★

Following a period of national despair marked by Watergate, defeat in Vietnam, inflation, and racial discord, an apostle of love offered to lead the country. Jimmy Carter had completed one term as governor of Georgia and believed he was ready to create a government that would be "just as decent and honest and competent and filled with love as the American people." He also promised, "I'll never lie to you."

He had a face to fit his message, with the piercing blue eyes of a prophet, cheeks as fair as the skin on a Georgia peach, and a big, engaging grin that became a cartoonist's delight.

Carter was untroubled by the knowledge that no president had been elected from the South for more than one hundred years. In fact, he listed his Southern background as an advantage in his odd campaign book, *Why Not the Best?*: "Political analysts said that Southerners would never vote for an Irish Catholic from Boston," he wrote, "but when the returns were counted in 1960 John Kennedy got a bigger margin of victory—not in Massachusetts but in Georgia!" Voters in a predominantly white district in his state, Carter noted, had also elected Martin Luther King's former aide Andrew Young to Congress in 1972. The candidate appeared to be composed of more parts optimist than egotist, convinced that he could assemble an unprecedented coalition of Southern whites, Northern liberals, blacks, and union members.

Carter was also stalking the white supremacist George Wallace with the zeal of Captain Ahab, determined to put an end to his presidential ambitions. Though Wallace's biographer Dan T. Carter wrote, "There had never been any likelihood that he [Wallace] would be elected president of the United States; he was too raw, too crude, too Southern," Jimmy Carter felt that an educated moderate with pleasant manners, such as himself, could serve as an appealing alternative.

Three months before the 1976 New Hampshire primary, the *Globe* parceled out its assignments. As the largest newspaper in New England—and the liberal antidote to the right-wing *Union Leader* in Manchester—the *Globe* took its political coverage seriously. The top candidates were put in the hands of the most experienced reporters. Because I was the house Southerner with the least seniority on the political staff, I was given responsibility for covering the obscure candidate from Georgia. I was grateful, nonetheless. The assignment, which promised to keep me in motels for months, seemed a godsend because my marriage was coming apart, and I no longer had a home.

I spent days following Carter through northern New England in lonely little caravans made up of no more than the candidate, a couple of his aides, and his Secret Service detail. Sometimes I rode with Carter and found him all business. He had no interest in small talk, and unlike another candidate I occasionally covered, Congressman "Mo" Udall of Arizona, he had little sense of humor. But I was impressed by Carter's intelligence, earnestness, and his record on racial issues, and I liked the funny, irreverent Georgians who served as his chief lieutenants, Hamilton Jordan and Jody Powell. After watching Carter relate to the Northern audiences, I concluded he might wind up with a place on the Democratic ticket—as a Southern vice-presidential nominee providing regional balance.

But the more I saw of Carter, the more he seemed to be the antithesis of the friendly, folksy Southern politician. He moved like an automaton, from dawn to nearly midnight, to reach a public outside the Deep South. And behind that big smile—already the subject of caricature—lay a cold and calculating mind. In the wake of Watergate, he knew he had the proper message, and as he traveled across the continent, his simple call to goodness seemed to be catching on. With the New Hampshire primary approaching, the press began to take him more seriously.

In his book, Carter described his political weaknesses. "I don't know how to compromise on any principle I believe is right," he wrote, proudly pointing out that one state official had called him "as stubborn as a south Georgia turtle." With that in mind, I went to Atlanta to talk with some of the people who had dealt with Carter when he was governor. I found boosters who took pride in the candidacy of a native son; but I also located a number of Georgia politicians who said Carter had been quite difficult. They debunked him as bullheaded, obstinate, and self-righteous.

One of his conservative adversaries, House Speaker Thomas Murphy, told me, "Jimmy has no compromising ability at all. It's his way or no way. When you've got one hundred eighty House members and fifty-six senators with varying opinions, there has to be compromise. But with him it was no compromise. He liked to run the state like he was still commanding a submarine." Julian Bond, the young civil rights leader who had become a state senator, said, "I have never seen a man so rigid, and it was not on a question of high principle. Carter just wouldn't give in." Fearing retribution from Carter's friends in state government, a couple of the critics asked that I not use their names.

A month before the New Hampshire primary, the piece appeared across the top of the front page of the *Boston Sunday Globe*, headlined: "Carter: Strong on the Road, but Weak at Home." The candidate flew into Boston that evening on his way back to New Hampshire, and I met the plane to rejoin the campaign. My friend Jim Wooten, a reporter for the *New York Times*, was traveling with Carter, and as they disembarked, Wooten warned me, "Watch out, he's on the warpath."

Moments later, Carter spotted me and turned my way. His grin had a cutting edge. "Hello, my friend," he said. "I see you've been down in Atlanta talking with some of my other friends." He paused for a second to let his scornful pronunciation of *friends* settle over the conversation. "Let me tell you about those sources of yours." He named one of the legislators and said, "His brother had been feeding at the state trough for twenty years until I threw him off the payroll. Of course he hates my guts." Carter named another legislator and called him a crook. After lambasting several other Georgia politicians—some I had interviewed, some I had not—he turned his back and stomped off.

A few days later, it was my bad luck to receive a bit of intelligence from another *Globe* reporter: Carter was said to have had a secret meeting with William Loeb, the publisher of the far-right newspaper in Manchester, the *Union Leader*. The two men had supposedly reached some sort of unholy compact. Loeb would withhold an unfavorable story about a member of Carter's family if Carter would agree not to criticize his newspaper. It all sounded vague to me, but I had orders from Boston to ask Carter about it. Rather than raise the question in a press conference—an approach that would either give away the scoop if the story proved accurate or embarrass me if the information appeared erroneous—I arranged to talk privately with the candidate. We sat down at a small table in the dining room of a New Hampshire inn vacated by its lunch crowd.

"Governor," I began, "I need to ask you about a meeting I'm told you had with William Loeb."

Carter acknowledged seeing Loeb several months earlier, describing an obligatory session between a visiting presidential candidate and the boss of New Hampshire's biggest daily.

"That's not the one," I said, and sketched out allegations of a subsequent meeting that the two might have had.

"I had no meeting with Loeb," Carter said icily.

"Okay. I just wonder where this story came from. Did any member of your staff meet with Mr. Loeb? Have there been any telephone calls between Mr. Loeb and your campaign?"

"I told you: I had no meeting with William Loeb."

"I understand that, Governor. I'm asking if some member of your staff might have talked with Mr. Loeb."

For the first time, I saw the laser qualities of Carter's clear blue eyes. He had picked up this intimidating tactic from his mentor in the navy's nuclear-submarine program, Admiral Hyman Rickover, an officer renowned for his withering treatment of subordinates. Carter's eyes were burning a hole through my forehead.

"Curtis," he hissed, "I am not a liar. I do not tell lies." He pushed away from the table and marched from the room. His motorcade drove away quickly, leaving me stranded in the rural New Hampshire town. I never found out if he had that meeting with Loeb.

Driven by his relentless schedule and aided by hundreds of Georgians who came north to campaign for him door-to-door, Carter won the New Hampshire primary, beating a field of better-known Democrats. In the *Globe*'s election-night account, I wrote that Carter's victory demonstrated that there were no longer political shackles for a Southerner.

Sensing that momentum was on his side, Carter chose to compete a week later in the Massachusetts primary—thinking he could deliver a quick knockout punch before the campaign headed south to Florida. However, Boston was still at war over busing, and Carter underestimated the racial animosity in the air. Wallace did not. The fighting judge from Alabama decided to make one of his last stands in the city that considered itself the Athens of America.

With Wallace denouncing busing, the people of South Boston embraced him with a fervor they usually reserved for toasts to the late Irish patriot Michael Collins. The *Globe* artist Paul Szep drew a cartoon of a serpent with Wallace's head, coiled about the body of the commonwealth of Massachusetts. The day the cartoon appeared, Wallace held a rally in a ballroom of the old Statler-Hilton Hotel in downtown Boston. I had the night off, so Szep and I thought it would be fun to attend.

We avoided the press section and sat, as inconspicuously as possible, in folding chairs amidst the Wallace supporters jammed onto the floor of the ballroom. Above us, the balconies were boisterous. Before the program could be convened with prayer, a black TV cameraman caused a stir. As he walked up the aisle, a spectator whacked him on the back of his head. Blows were exchanged by several others before Wallace, clinging to his wheelchair, was maneuvered to the rostrum by bodyguards. His followers settled down.

"I saw that picture today, in the *Boston Globe*, of me dressed up like a snake," Wallace began, laughing contemptuously. The crowd roared its hatred of the newspaper. I slunk in my seat; Szep squirmed. Above us, a heckler shouted an insult at Wallace and was instantly attacked. While one man held the protester's arms, others threw punches at him. Blood wet his shirt, and the audience cheered.

Wallace saw the place was near pandemonium. "Hey!" he shouted. "Y'all, stop! Pay attention to me! I'm the main attraction here." Gesturing to the man being pummeled, Wallace said, "That fellow up there, he's just an undecided voter." Laughter and loud hoots swept the ballroom as the wounded heckler escaped.

The ferocity of the Wallace event may have been an omen. A blizzard struck on the day of the primary. With a fleet of four-wheel-drive vehicles, Senator Henry Jackson's AFL-CIO supporters had the most reliable get-out-the-vote operation and carried the pro-union candidate to victory. Udall finished a close second, a pattern he would follow throughout the campaign. Wallace carried Boston, the city whose statehouse Oliver Wendell Holmes once called "the hub of the solar system." Though he wound up third statewide, Wallace would boast for the rest of his life of how he won "the Boston primary." Carter ran a distant fourth in Massachusetts, getting only 14 percent of the vote, and I figured he would blame my newspaper and me.

Although Florida is situated in the South on the map, its state of mind doesn't resemble that of its neighbors. There are still enclaves of Protestant fundamentalism in the Florida Panhandle, but over the years an influx of new residents has overwhelmed the rest of the state. The Miami area has become a land of lox and bagels, Cuban black beans and coffee. The west coast is largely populated by the "snowbirds," who motored down in recreational vehicles from the Midwest on vacation and decided to stay. The interior is cluttered with gaudy theme parks. Orlando reminds me of Anaheim, as soulless as a suburban emporium. Nevertheless, political writers depicted the 1976 Florida primary as a regional showdown between two Southerners. So when Carter won handily in Florida, the national campaign of George Wallace was crushed forever.

The last time I saw Wallace as a candidate came during the Michigan primary. Thousands once came to hear him speak when he appeared in the state, their numbers so great that Wallace conducted doubleheader rallies. But by the spring of 1976, he was reduced to raking embers at a rally in a cheap airport motel near Detroit. About twenty people showed up.

Wallace was too proud to admit defeat. Mired in his wheelchair, holding a microphone to his lips, Wallace tried to snarl. Carter had deceived the American people, he said, and he warned his listeners to beware of "those with their grins and their smiles." He vowed to keep battling. But his voice sounded faint and the motion of his hands had lost its vigor. "I've been in the valley of the shadow," he admitted at one point.

At the end of his speech, Wallace's followers approached him. They wanted to shake his hand. Remembering the outstretched hand that had shot him in Laurel four years earlier, Wallace clutched the microphone as if it were a life preserver. He explained that he could not touch them. Instead, he extended his palm from a distance. "I hope you will take this as a handshake," he said. "I love you folks." As his aides wheeled him from the room, the fighting judge looked as though he wanted to cry.

In spite of his advantage, Carter seemed constitutionally incapable of cruising without blunder. During an interview with a *New York Daily News* reporter, Carter's views were elicited on the tendency of ethnic groups to congregate in big-city neighborhoods. "I see nothing wrong with ethnic purity being maintained," he said. "I would not force a racial integration of a neighborhood by government action." It sounded like something Wallace would say, even though Carter added that he "would not permit discrimination against a family moving into the neighborhood." His rivals were quick to pounce on his remarks as proof that Carter was just another Southern bigot. The *Globe* went further, publishing a dark Szep cartoon of a smiling Hitler wearing a Carter campaign button.

The candidate managed to extricate himself from the "ethnic purity" flap by staging a rally with several black leaders. "Daddy" King, a prominent Atlanta minister and father of Martin Luther King, called Carter's comment "a slip of the tongue that everyone knows does not represent his thinking." As the integrated crowd at a downtown Atlanta park applauded, Daddy King added his benediction: "I have a forgiving heart, so, Governor, I'm with you all the way."

Carter got back on track, but he did not forgive the *Globe*. The next time I interviewed him, sharing a row with the candidate on his campaign plane, Carter cited the Szep cartoon and informed me that I worked "for the only newspaper in this country that's prostituted itself in this campaign."

The mutual suspicions that existed between the *Globe* and Carter represented a microcosm of North-South misunderstandings. Although Carter's views on most issues rarely differed from the *Globe*'s editorial line, the newspaper subconsciously linked him with the obstructionist Southern governors of the 1960s. Carter, meanwhile, associated the *Globe* with Harvard and the Kennedy family; he considered the newspaper a voice of an elitist Eastern establishment that would never support a Southerner.

Carter had some grounds for his complex. Arthur Schlesinger Jr., an Eastern intellectual and leader of the liberal Americans for Democratic Action, had publicly inveighed against Carter's candidacy because, among other things, he was a Southern Baptist. Others on the East Coast who had never even met the candidate denounced Carter as a redneck.

Regional tension remained taut through the spring. After Carter scored a primary victory that put him within reach of the nomination, he expressed satisfaction that he had done so without the assistance of that well-known figure from the Northeast, Senator Edward M. Kennedy. "I don't have to kiss his ass," Carter said.

Despite my Southern background, Carter regarded me as a spear-carrier for the Yankees. At one point, he became so unhappy with my stories that he called Tom Winship, the editor of the *Globe,* to complain. Like other reporters assigned to his campaign, I picked at Carter's discrepancies to refute his claim that he would never lie to the American people. There were several examples. Carter referred to himself as a nuclear physicist when he was merely a nuclear engineer; he listed his height as close to six feet when he fell at least four inches short of that mark—the kind of things Steven Brill described in the article "Jimmy Carter's Pathetic Lies" in *Harper's* magazine. After a few months, Carter concluded I was a smart-ass; there was truth to that. But his request that Winship take me off the beat was made in vain. The *Globe* editor, a high-spirited liberal who enjoyed nothing better than a good, unpopular cause, had become something of a father figure to me. Winship had no intention of relieving me of duty. Instead, he encouraged me to zap Carter anytime I felt it was warranted.

The Carter campaign was the biggest assignment of my life, and I wanted to show I could measure up to it. One day, as Carter talked with a group of reporters on his campaign plane, I asked the candidate why he never used self-deprecating humor—a style employed so effectively by Mo Udall, his chief competitor. Carter glared at me and replied, "I don't know. I would have to check my character analysis in the *Boston Globe* to find out."

The next day, however, Carter told a couple of jokes on himself. The punch lines were lame and failed to draw much laughter. He quickly dropped the new routine, but not before some members of his staff found humor in the exercise. As one of his aides confided to me privately, "Jimmy's idea of self-deprecating humor is to shit on his staff."

In most presidential campaigns, reporters keep the candidate at arm's length, but a symbiotic relationship develops between the press and the candidate's staff. As we traveled thousands of miles together, friendships grew up in the Carter campaign. In the recesses of Carter's plane, behind the first-class compartment the candidate occupied, we debated strategies and exchanged private thoughts. Most of us were single—never married or divorced—and our group evolved into a large, unwieldy family of brothers and sisters flying from coast to coast.

Two years before Carter had begun his quest, his chief of staff, Hamilton Jordan, had suggested in a long and prescient memo that news organizations would tend to assign Southerners to cover the Georgian, a move that Jordan predicted would be helpful to the campaign.

Greg Schneiders, Carter's aide-de-camp, developed a dissenting view as the primary season hurtled to its conclusion. Carter's harshest critics in the press corps, he said, were Southern liberals who desperately wanted Carter to shatter the political shibboleths of Dixie, who tried to push the candidate further to the left than he was willing to go. Frustrated by Carter's moderation, the Southern reporters seized on any opportunity to write critical stories about him, Greg said.

Schneiders had become a good friend during our long days on the campaign, and he expounded on his theory in a conversation we had one night on the plane. He told me that I was one of three Southerners using a liberal meter to judge Carter unfairly. The other two, Greg said, were Eleanor Randolph, a native of Pensacola who wrote for the *Chicago Tribune,* and the *Times'* Jim Wooten, who also had Southern roots.

Wooten was unremittingly tough but fair, I thought; Eleanor dealt honestly with the question of Carter's unorthodox personality. As she wrote in one dispatch: "The Nixon presidency helped create a whole breed of political journalists, who appeared in great numbers in 1976 to explain the character of presidential candidates. It was kind of Teddy White–ism gone wild, and yet for all of us out there trying to explain what kind of person Jimmy Carter was, most of us didn't or couldn't and opted to call him an enigma. Perhaps that was the easy way out. Maybe it was better to say that Carter was an enigma than to say directly, in the middle of the campaign, that he wasn't a particularly nice guy."

Schneiders may have been right about me. I found myself conflicted over my professional requirement to be objective and my desire to see a Southerner succeed in national politics, to show the world that we were not a region of boors.

Assured of the nomination, Carter fell back to Plains, his hometown in southwest Georgia, to spend most of the summer husbanding strength for the general election in the fall. It would be my first prolonged stay in the South in seven years, and I was not sure I was glad to be back.

Plains lay in a red-clay belt where kudzu, the roadside vine, grew faster than the local crops of peanuts and cotton. Gnats swarmed by day, mosquitoes and moths by night. The heat was stifling. Yet it was reminiscent of home. During one of Carter's daily get-togethers with his press corps, I tried to establish rapport by remarking that Plains was just like my hometown—except Summit had stores on both sides of the street. He laughed.

In fact, Plains, a hamlet of six hundred citizens, was half the size of Summit, and the little row of stores lining the south side of the road that ran through town looked as though the buildings had been left over from the nineteenth century. Typical of a rural Southern settlement, more than half the population was black. Two or three influential white families exerted political control over the town, a situation in which petty jealousies grew up as naturally as johnsongrass.

In Plains, the Carters were one of the important families. They had lived in the area for generations and owned a peanut warehouse, the biggest operation in town, as well as hundreds of acres in the surrounding countryside. The matriarch, Carter's mother, "Miss Lillian," was a forceful woman with strong opinions. Carter's sister Gloria lived with her husband on a farm outside town; she was a smart, independent woman, too, known for her love of motorcycles. Another sister, Ruth, had gone into the service of the Lord in North Carolina. The candidate's first cousin represented the county in the state senate, ran a worm farm for fish bait, and owned a store he called Hugh Carter's Antique Shop. But the most colorful member of the family was Jimmy's younger brother, Billy.

Although he managed the peanut warehouse in the candidate's absence, Billy's favorite bailiwick was his service station, where most of the town's complement of rascals hung out after work every afternoon, drinking beer. The term *good ole boy* was bandied about a lot in 1976 by reporters who wouldn't know a good ole boy from a Georgia Tech graduate. They established their ignorance when they called Jimmy Carter a good ole boy. The candidate did not come remotely close. But the fellows at Billy's service station fit the description. As a general rule, good ole boys are good-natured, slightly dopey, ass-scratching, nose-picking guys who would prefer a six-pack of Pabst Blue Ribbon to a bottle of Veuve Clicquot.

When I arrived in Plains, Billy was the first person I sought out. He had been described to me as a "real character" who could provide "good copy" for stories. The advance billing was accurate; Billy turned out to be wonderful company. He was bright, funny, and profane. He liked to point out that his mother had joined the Peace Corps when she was nearly seventy, one sister rode a motorcycle, another was an evangelist, and his only brother was running for president. "Hell," he declared, "I'm the only sane one in the bunch."

Billy was a fount of folk wisdom and enjoyed sharing it with visitors. But he grew leery of some of the people flooding the little town. After one East Coast reporter put on a pair of overalls and a straw hat, and stuck a piece of straw in his mouth to stroll down the sidewalks of Plains—an act of ridiculous condescension—Billy turned to me and said, "Look at that asshole."

Fortunately, Billy appreciated my Mississippi background. I became one of the regulars at the service station, drinking beer with his buddies every afternoon. I went there on Sunday mornings, too, when the rest of the press corps attended the Plains Baptist Church services with the candidate. Since beer sales were forbidden in Georgia on Sundays, Billy gave the stuff away.

Billy was a mutant version of his brother. Though he had Jimmy's strawberry-blond hair and toothy smile, Billy's eyes were framed by heavy, horn-rimmed glasses and he dressed up in god-awful leisure suits when not wearing Levi's jeans. Compared to the candidate, Billy seemed to have no serious side. Sitting in front of his service station, across the railroad tracks from the row of stores, Billy spoke harshly of his cousin Hugh Carter, an avaricious merchant who had jacked up the prices at his "antique" store after tourists began coming to town. Hugh Carter was the kind of fellow who would rent out the roof of his barn for a "See Rock City" advertisement. Billy regarded his relative as "a sorry son of a bitch" and saluted him with a raised middle finger whenever he saw Hugh peering at him from across the way.

Hugh Carter's merchandise was mostly junk. The North Carolina novelist Reynolds Price came to Plains, commissioned to write a magazine piece about the candidate's hometown. I had dinner with him one night, and our conversation turned to Hugh Carter. "He calls his place Carter's Antiques," Price sniffed. "More properly, it should be Carter's Used Furniture."

One afternoon, as I sat with Billy and his companions—Randy Coleman, Leon "Hogpen" Johnson, and Bud Duval—they began to rag one of their friends for having an unusual family name. Because the fellow's name was Unger, they anointed him "the Polack."

"Let's hear it for the Polack," Billy chortled.

"Goddamnit, Billy," Unger shot back, "I'd rather be half-Polack and half-nigger than be kin to Hugh Carter."

That stopped Billy for a moment. Then he grinned—a smile as big as his brother's. "Goddamn," Billy said. "You know, you're right. That Hugh Carter is the worst son of a bitch that ever lived."

* * *

We watched as Plains was transformed from a quaint village into a den of greed. Souvenir shops replaced empty storefronts, a delicatessen sprouted along the state highway, a local man started selling guided tours of the place, and property values skyrocketed.

After a press briefing one afternoon at the Pond House, Miss Lillian's residence a couple of miles from town, Eleanor Randolph and I caught a ride back to Plains with one of the local volunteers in the Carter campaign. As we passed near the candidate's home, the driver glanced to her left and reported, "Oh, my, they're tearing down that old nigger house."

Eleanor and I looked at each other. We knew that a black family lived in a shack across the street from the Carters; we had seen them when we'd met with the candidate in his front yard. If they were being displaced, the move represented an ultimate parable of Plains's mindlessness.

Since we learned the news simultaneously, Eleanor and I agreed to conduct a joint investigation; we would not attempt to scoop each other. When we went to the Carters' neighborhood, we found that the black family had, indeed, moved. Their little wooden house was already being dismantled. After questioning other blacks in town, we learned that the Carters' former neighbors were Mr. and Mrs. A. Z. Pittman, a couple with seven children. It took us a day to track the Pittmans to a housing project in nearby Americus.

Mr. Pittman agreed to talk to us. He said that his landlord, a farmer from another county, had informed him that "Mr. Carter was going to be president and didn't want a house like that across the street." The landlord claimed "the Democratic Party came to him," Mr. Pittman said, "but to tell you the truth, I don't know about that. He said the house had to be tore down."

Mr. Pittman, who was sixty-seven, admitted it was not much of a house. The place had an outdoor toilet and rented for $16 a month. But he loved his garden in the front yard, where he tended peas, tomatoes, collard greens, butter beans, squash, okra, and green peppers. Sometimes, he said, he sold bunches of greens and okra to the Carters' young daughter, Amy, sent by her mother to buy fresh vegetables. The produce, he said, helped pay for the rent.

He would be able to keep the garden until the summer ended, he said, but the move required him to make long daily trips to work the vegetables and to slop a pig he had been forced to move out of sight of the Carters' home.

Mr. Pittman began to cry. "I don't like it, to tell the truth. I have to drive ten miles a day over there to work this land and feed my little pig. I might have been a little mistreated in the deal, but I love Mr. Carter as a white man. I know he didn't know nothing about this because he's a Christian gentleman. I hated to leave, to tell the truth. Mr. Carter wasn't an associate of mine, but he had my sympathies."

Before we wrote our stories, we privately asked Carter for comment. He said he had nothing to do with the decision to demolish the house and expressed regret that his candidacy was altering the face of Plains. Of the Pittmans, he said, "I hate to see them go."

The press corps lived that summer at the Best Western Motel in Americus, a town ten miles east of Plains. I kept a room there throughout the campaign, even when we were on the road; it became my mailing address.

A routine developed. Carter would make himself available for questions on the front lawn of his house in the morning. We filed stories. In late afternoon, we played softball on the grounds of the old Plains school. The candidate pitched for one side; Billy pitched for the other. One day Billy arrived with good news. His wife, Sybil, had just delivered their sixth child, a baby boy. A television reporter decided to do a spot about the birth. Interviewing Billy, he asked the child's weight. "Seven pounds," Billy answered, "and six and half pounds are dick and balls."

Evenings were spent at a double-wide trailer converted into a steak joint called Faye's Bar-B-Q Villa. An enterprising woman named Faye West ran the place. While her husband, Dave, grilled monstrous strips and T-bones over a bed of charcoal in a barrel outside, we sat at Formica tables, guzzling whiskey and wine from the liquor store down the street. The candidate and his family rarely came out to dinner, and Billy was good about going home to his wife and children at night. But Miss Lillian and her daughter Gloria often joined the crowd at Faye's. When she'd spot me, Miss Lillian would invariably rebuke me for failing to attend Sunday school.

Although Americus had a poor history of race relations, the town tolerated our rowdy, integrated group. One of those who broke local customs with great flair was Ed Bradley of CBS. An Americus businessman—probably not many years removed from the Klan—told me he was surprised how much he liked the black correspondent. In the middle of the summer Ed took a few days off to go to a prizefight with Hunter Thompson and Jimmy Buffett in Las Vegas and returned with greetings for me from another of his companions. I was astonished to learn that my old friend Semmes Luckett Jr. had been part of Bradley's group. The son of Clarksdale's most conservative family was running with an unconventional pack, fresh evidence of the change sweeping the South.

To appease Miss Lillian, I went to Sunday school on a day that Carter was scheduled to teach the class. The little room in the back of the white frame church was filled with local Baptists, reporters, and tourists who had made their way to Plains, like pilgrims, to worship with the man who might become president.

Practically everyone had a Bible. Spying my empty hands, Carter loaned me his. "Here," he said, "you probably need this more than anyone else." Flipping through the book, I saw that many pages were dog-eared; verses were underlined and margins annotated. I had once laughed at Carter's piety, but I found his Bible quite touching. Clearly he was a serious student of both the Old and New Testaments, and I regretted that I had ever mocked his faith.

On Labor Day, Carter resumed a pace that would keep him on the move for the final two months preceding the election. He made his first stop at Warm Springs, Georgia, the vacation home of Franklin D. Roosevelt, to underscore a Southern candidate's commitment to the national party. But another event later in the day gave a better demonstration of Carter's constituency.

The candidate flew to Darlington, South Carolina, for the start of an annual Labor Day event. I had heard Carter liked stock-car racing, but found it hard to believe until I followed him that afternoon as pool reporter. He visited the pits before the race and seemed to know many of the drivers and members of their crews. They hugged Carter and wished him luck. Trailing Carter across the infield, I saw an encampment of thousands of shirtless men, waving Confederate battle flags with one hand and holding cans of Budweiser with the other. They had brought their families in RVs and vans to set up housekeeping on the grounds of the track several days in advance of the race. By the time Carter climbed into the pace car, their faces and shoulders had been boiled crimson by the sun, and they were baying like hound dogs.

When I first saw the crowd I thought, These are Wallace people; they can't possibly support Carter. But I realized they were cheering enthusiastically. Public-opinion polls had indicated that the Carter campaign was reassembling the old Solid South. I had my doubts. Based on my Mississippi experience, I thought Southern whites had deserted the Democratic Party for all time. But Darlington was bursting with regional pride. As the pace car circled past the crowd, Carter was hailed by delirious roars from the infield and the grandstand, thick with rebel flags; the racing cars lent their thunder. I had never heard such noise. One hundred and eleven years after Appomattox, the South seemed to be rising up in an awesome, monolithic effort to put one of its own in the White House.

The crowds never diminished that fall, but Carter's advantage over President Ford dwindled in the polls. By the final weekend, the outcome of the election was uncertain.

On our last Sunday morning on the road, we woke in Dallas. It was Halloween, and before we left the city, we learned of a strange development back in Plains. Clennon King—the same man who had been thrown into a mental institution after trying to integrate Ole Miss eighteen years earlier— had shown up for services at the Plains Baptist Church. Rather than accommodate the black man, the deacons had canceled morning worship and shut the church.

As Carter moved through the hotel lobby toward his motorcade outside, reporters intercepted him to ask, What's going on at the Plains Baptist Church? He said he did not know; that he had just heard the news himself.

We flew to California, and after landing, I made a couple of calls to Georgia. One of Carter's friends confided to me that the candidate had known for several days that Clennon King might appear at the church. While Carter may not have approved of denying King a seat or closing the church, clearly he had failed to intervene on the visitor's behalf. I felt Carter had lied to us, and I was furious with his fellow Baptists back in Plains. Their Sunday-school teacher was on the brink of winning the presidency, and yet they had let their bigotry create an incident that might dash his campaign.

At his last event of the day, in San Francisco, Carter seemed oblivious to the story in Plains as he basked in the cheers of the most liberal city in the country. Afterward, I joined several other reporters for dinner in a restaurant in Sausalito, across the Bay. The food was excellent, and with the campaign winding down, moods were high. Except for mine.

I muttered about Jimmy Carter and loudly criticized "the fucking Baptist hypocrites" back in Plains. The Baptists, I declared, had held back the South for a hundred years, and now they were about to destroy the region's hope to regain political parity. If I never saw another Baptist, I said, I would be happy.

Charles Overby, a young reporter for the Gannett news chain, spoke up from the other end of the table. A Mississippian, he had attended Ole Miss after the Meredith affair and had been a voice for racial fairness as editor of the campus newspaper. "Curtis," he said. "I'm a Baptist. My whole family is Baptist. We go to church every Sunday. I even teach Sunday school."

I managed to stammer an apology: "Charles, I'm sorry. I was delivering a sweeping, collective indictment and that was unfair." Hell, most of my friends in Mississippi were Baptists. I had been gone only seven years, and I was acting like a judgmental Yankee prick.

At a press conference the next morning, I tried to word a question carefully for the candidate. I noted that some of his most eloquent statements during the campaign had dealt with racial justice and wondered why he had not spoken out against the decision by his church.

Speaking without equivocation, Carter said he disapproved of the deacons' action, and he succeeded in defusing the issue. I was not entirely satisfied, however. Carter's initial reaction to the incident reminded me of his reluctance to talk about Koininia, a controversial biracial collective in southwest Georgia. This bedraggled little Christian community struggled for existence a few miles from his home, yet Carter never mentioned Koininia in his campaign. I suppose he felt, as a Democratic candidate trying to regain the goodwill of the South, that some subjects were best left alone.

After a tumultuous rally in Los Angeles, we flew cross-country to Michigan for a joint appearance with Carter's running mate, my old boss Fritz Mondale, before heading for Georgia. It was a clear, cold night, and looking out my window on the campaign plane, *Peanut One,* I could see lights from dozens of small towns winking in the darkness. As we rushed from one side of the country to the other, I was struck by the majesty of the moment and recalled a passage from the beginning of Theodore White's *The Making of the President 1960.*

"It was invisible, as always," White wrote of the day the American people chose John Kennedy. "They had begun to vote in the villages of New

Hampshire at midnight, as they always do. . . . On election day America is Republican until five or six in the evening. It is in the last few hours of the day that working people and their families vote, on their way home from work or after supper; it is then, at evening, that America goes Democratic if it goes Democratic at all. All of this is invisible, for it is the essence of the act that as it happens it is a mystery in which millions of people each fit one fragment of a total secret together, none of them knowing the shape of the whole."

I wanted Carter to win, but I remained irritated over the Baptist church affair and couldn't completely enjoy the revelry of the campaign's last flight. Jim King, a Kennedy apparatchik from Boston who was in charge of *Peanut One*, had loaded a piano on board the plane and arranged a specially catered meal. The traveling party also conducted a facetious popularity contest. The candidate, who had caused problems for himself in September by talking about "lust in my heart" in a *Playboy* interview, was voted "most horny."

After dinner, Carter and others congregated around the piano, tucked into an exit row on the Boeing 727. Ben Brown, one of Carter's black supporters from Georgia, joined Jim Wooten at the keyboard. The group sang several old standards, then began a song I recognized immediately, "We Shall Overcome." Hearing it brought back memories of the civil rights movement, and I didn't feel comfortable standing alongside Carter. I walked down the aisle to the galley, where I opened another bottle of wine and sat with Jim King for the remainder of the journey.

On election night, we traveled to Atlanta to follow the returns in a cavernous convention hall. Massachusetts quickly gave its electoral votes to Carter, the first state to do so. But as the evening wore on, Carter and Ford traded states. On the color-coded maps used by the networks, Ford held the Midwest. Virtually all of the South was solid again, siding with its native son. Only Virginia had denied Carter its electoral votes, though Mississippi looked in doubt. In the hours after midnight, the results from Mississippi became critical.

The watch in Atlanta, which had begun with high expectations, began to wear down. The hour was late, and thousands of Georgians waited, tired and anxious. The floor of the convention hall was littered with bent plastic cups and the detritus of campaign posters and crepe paper. Carter's total was stuck, just short of the 270 electoral votes he needed for victory. Then sometime around 3 A.M., an announcement came. Carter had won Mississippi. The state's electoral votes put him over the top.

The crowd reacted with weary rejoicing, and Carter made a brief speech. Then we packed our typewriters and headed in a motorcade for the Atlanta airport. Carter was hell-bent to get back to Plains by dawn. Somehow, the press bus became separated from the rest of the caravan, and we arrived at *Peanut One* long after the candidate. We didn't realize we were late; we were too busy celebrating the end of the campaign.

As I reached my seat, Carter marched past me down the aisle to expedite loading. I heard later that he had been so impatient to get home that he'd wanted to leave us behind in Atlanta; Jody Powell and Greg Schneiders had succeeded in stalling him until the press bus had pulled up by the stairs at the rear of the plane. Once Carter had hurried everyone on board, he stomped back toward his first-class seat.

I was standing in the aisle, talking with Eleanor, Mary McGrory, Jim Dickenson, and his wife, Mollie. I thought this would be a propitious time to hail the victor.

"Governor," I said, "congratulations. It didn't take much to get Massachusetts, but I had to work like hell to deliver Mississippi."

The new president-elect of the United States looked at me with a familiar glare. "If it weren't for people like you," he said, "this election would have been over at nine o'clock last night."

CHAPTER 14

"From the deserts of the Deep South"

★ ★ ★ ★ ★

With every motel room within miles of Plains filled with campaign veterans, foreign commentators, future White House aides, television crews, and prospective officials in the new government, Billy Carter decided to add to the intrigue of the interregnum by running for mayor of Plains.

He had two planks in his platform: he would raise Hugh Carter's taxes and tear down a wispy, artificial Christmas tree the government of Taiwan had given to the town. "I never liked skinny women," he explained.

Winter was closing in on southwest Georgia, bringing cold, penetrating rain and icy conditions, and Billy's madcap race promised to be a welcome diversion. It began with the appointment of Leon "Hogpen" Johnson as campaign manager. Leon once told me how he got the nickname: "I was drunk coming back from Americus one night and drove Billy's pickup through somebody's hogpen. I didn't kill none of them, but they scattered, and the owners threatened to sue Billy because I aborted one of their sows."

In real life, Leon was a contractor of sorts. After he'd installed a new sewer line in Plains, a local woman tracked him down by phone at Billy's service station to complain that sewage was burbling into her yard from a leaky pipe. As we huddled over the heater, we overheard Hogpen's instant solution: "Hell, lady, put a rock on top of it."

Playing the role of an errant prince, Billy ran a campaign that consisted mainly of diatribes against his cousin—"a sniveling, sorry, self-made son of a bitch." In an effort to live up to his press notices as the pious president-elect's witty, hard-drinking brother, Billy grew even more outrageous. He made a transition from a few beers in the afternoon to heavy drinking, and his quotes were increasingly unprintable.

Cousin Hugh handled the attacks with equanimity. In the relative quiet of his store across the road, he made himself available for interviews as the "First Cousin," all the while preparing his autobiography. It would be called *Cousin Beedie and Cousin Hot*. Hugh had a childhood name, Beedie; young Jimmy had been called Hotshot. After the book was published, Cousin Beedie stocked hundreds of copies in his store, took the liberty of raising the jacket price because the books bore his autograph, and advertised the autobiography as a sure best-seller "soon to be a collector's item."

The swollen press corps followed Billy's campaign almost as assiduously as the president-elect's search for a new secretary of state. As the Plains election approached, the town assumed circuslike proportions. NBC's *Today* show came for a week of telecasts, inviting as one of their guests James Dickey, the Southern poet best known for his novel *Deliverance*. The night before his early-morning appearance, Dickey dined with Tom Brokaw and other members of the *Today* team at Faye's Bar-B-Q Villa. Sightings of the famous had become frequent there; in fact, some of the locals had attained celebrity status themselves. A couple of evenings earlier, Norman Mailer had come to taste the steaks, and when a customer had informed Faye that the author was in her midst, she'd asked, "Is that the fellow from the *Miami Herald* who wants to interview me?"

Dickey completed his meal without being asked for a single autograph, and when he finished, he approached a table where Miss Lillian, Gloria, and I were sitting with a couple of other reporters. Dickey was a big man with a robust appetite for whiskey, and the poet weaved as he stood chatting. Swinging his arms for emphasis, he knocked several drinks across our table. He apologized, then lurched from the double-wide trailer into the night.

Brokaw anchored the *Today* show at the time, and as he prepared for the program early the next morning, he wondered if Dickey would be in shape for his interview. Tom's fears seemed confirmed when the poet arrived. "He looked like hell," Brokaw told me later. "Like he had been in a fight. He had a cut on his face and his eyes were bloodshot." The wound, a red streak running the length of Dickey's nose, appeared to have been inflicted by a razor during an effort to shave. Dickey insisted he had been in a fight with a truck driver.

Brokaw said he thought it would be better to tape the interview rather than have Dickey appear on camera live. But during their talk, Dickey rallied. "We sat him down in an old rocker," Brokaw said, "and he was terrific. He told old Southern stories, and he was incredibly entertaining."

A few days later, Billy hosted the voters of Plains—and a few of his friends from the press corps—at a barbecue in the rear of his service station. After we helped ourselves to pork ribs, we picked our way through the muck of the backyard, cluttered with discarded tires and chunks of car engines. Since the president-elect was expected, the Secret Service set up a rope line to keep dozens of tourists, straining for a view of the spectacle, at a distance. One of Billy's buddies, Randy Coleman, prowled the perimeter, shouting an invitation to the tourists: "Naked women get to eat free! Naked women get to eat free!"

Jimmy Carter's arrival set off a buzz. He was dressed informally, in blue jeans, a plaid shirt, brogans, and a rain jacket. He seemed perfectly comfortable in his role as putative leader of the free world. With his own campaign over, he appeared removed from pressure. He and I had a brief conversation. Graciously, Carter told me he was glad I would be joining the White House press corps. I said it had once been a goal—when I'd interviewed for a Congressional Fellowship, I had described the White House job as my greatest ambition; though now I knew it was not as glamorous as I had thought. Nevertheless, I told Carter that I looked forward to covering him in the years ahead.

I inquired about his inauguration plans. Was he considering a poet for the program, the way John F. Kennedy had invited Robert Frost to read at his inauguration? Might he invite a son of Georgia, James Dickey?

Carter grinned and said, "We thought about that and decided it might be safer to have Dickey on tape."*

Despite the publicity, Billy Carter lost the mayor's race. One of his campaign promises was fulfilled, however, a couple of nights after the election. Someone lassoed the spindly Christmas tree, pulling the gift from Taiwan from its stand on a greensward next to the Plains railroad depot. Hitched to a speeding car, the tinfoil tree flew apart in a shower of sparks as it bounced

---

*Dickey was ultimately invited to appear at a gala the night before the inauguration. Without incident, he read a poem he had written for the occasion, "The Strength of Fields," which begins, "Moth-force a small town always has . . ." The poem was published by the 1977 Inaugural Committee.

to a dumping ground a half mile down the road. Georgia state troopers investigated the vandalism, but Billy had an airtight alibi.

The day before his brother's inauguration, Billy chartered a jetliner to carry members of his family and friends to Washington. When he asked me to join his group, I felt honored. I gave up my seat on the final flight of *Peanut One* to travel with the gang from the service station. We gathered early in the morning at the Albany airport, forty miles south of Plains, to board the charter. Knowing that Billy was coming, the airport manager arranged for the bar to be open. I bought the first round of drinks. When the Bloody Marys arrived, garnished with a stalk of celery, one of Billy's crew yelled, "Who put the fuckin' cabbage in my drink?"

The mood on board the plane grew festive in spite of the early hour. The passenger list was composed mostly of folks from Plains, white and black, and many of them had never flown before. When the pilot announced an altitude of thirty thousand feet and a cruising speed of five hundred miles an hour, sighs of wonderment filled the cabin. A champagne breakfast was served, and one of Billy's friends delivered a loud blessing. "Hooo, weee!" he shouted. "Us brier-jumpers is going to Washington."

We stumbled off the plane at National Airport. After putting his wife and children safely into a limousine, Billy jumped on a bus with the rest of the traveling party. Since I had a fifth of Jack Daniel's in my carry-on bag, he sat with me, swigging from the bottle as we rode into the nation's capital like members of a conquering army. I pointed out some landmarks. Billy spotted the marquee at Sans Souci, a fashionable French restaurant around the corner from the White House. "There's the Sand Suckee," he announced. "I hear they got good steaks."

After a long ride, Billy reeled into the lobby of his hotel. Reluctantly, I had to break off to go to the *Globe*'s Washington bureau to write about the Georgians' arrival. I shook hands with Billy. I told him I had enjoyed the trip, that I'd be talking with him soon.

In that giddy moment, it never occurred to me that I would never see him again.

Washington braced for the Southerners as if the Clampetts were coming. Pat Oliphant, the prize-winning cartoonist for the *Washington Star*, depicted the neighborhood of the Carter White House as Dogpatch North in a full-page drawing, giving the South Lawn all sorts of white-trash accoutrements—a junk car on blocks and a tire swinging from a tree. In the distance, the Sans Souci had a sign advertising "EATS" and people wandered the streets barefoot. "I got a lot of letters from the South," Oliphant told me years later, correspondence accusing the cartoonist of regional prejudice. He noted that his home was even farther south. Oliphant was born in Australia.

Writing in *The Nation*, the humorist Calvin Trillin claimed to have come across a 1928 fantasy by H. L. Mencken, the South's ancient scourge: "On those dark moments when I fear that the Republic has trotted before these weary eyes every carnival act in its repertoire, I cheer myself with the thought that someday we will have a President from the deserts of the Deep South. . . . The President's brother, a prime specimen of Boobus Collumnus Rubericus, will gather his loutish companions on the porch of the White House to swill beer from the bottle and snigger over whispered barnyard jokes about the darkies. The President's cousin, LaVerne, will travel the Halleluyah circuit as one of Mrs. McPherson's soldiers in Christ, praying for the conversion of some Northern Sodom's most Satanic pornographer as she waves his work—well thumbed—for all the yokels to gasp at. . . . The President's daughter will record these events with her box camera. . . . The incumbent himself, cleansed of his bumpkin ways by some of Grady's New South hucksters, will have a charm comparable to that of the leading undertaker of Dothan, Alabama."

After the quote gained wide circulation, Mencken scholars professed to be confounded; they could find no source for it. When I asked my friend Bud Trillin about the lines long afterward, he said, "I admit nothing." He also chuckled. Whether a legitimate Mencken barb or a product of Trillin's whimsy, the passage was typical of the ridicule heaped on the Carters.

Marshall Frady, a native Southerner, wrote in *The New York Review of Books* that Carter's "officious half-moon grin" resembled the "kind of freelance door-to-door hustler of his own homemade wares and notions in a neighborhood enclosed by Kmarts and Sears Roebucks."

Roy Blount Jr., who'd grown up in Atlanta, created new branches for the Carter family tree in a book called *Crackers*. One of the president's relatives was identified as "Martha Carter Kelvinator, 48, Bullard Dam, Georgia, who is married to a top-loading automatic washer. 'Yeah, I got the durn thing back here a few years ago and it washed my things s'good, I, well, I just fell in love with it. And my daddy, he's Jimmy's fourth or fifth cousin and all, why he had me marry it. And I haven't regretted it one day in this world.'"

* * *

While the nation laughed, the promise of the Carter years expired as quickly as a magnum of champagne left uncorked overnight. Although the new president struck a pose of egalitarian simplicity by walking with his family down Pennsylvania Avenue, from the Capitol to the White House, on the day of his inauguration, within a month Carter reverted to the uncompromising stance that had caused him trouble with the Georgia legislature. He antagonized members of Congress by eliminating, without advance notice, dozens of federal water projects that were pork barrel favorites. A few weeks later, when Carter wore a cardigan sweater to appeal to the nation to turn down thermostats and conserve energy, citizens snickered. His initiatives began to slide downhill.

Billy Carter's crash was more abrupt. In the early months of the Carter administration, Billy took advantage of his notoriety by selling himself to the highest bidder, promoting everything from a beverage called Billy Beer to belly-flop contests and hot-air balloon rides. His problems multiplied when he hired himself out as a goodwill ambassador for Libya, a North African nation regarded by the U.S. government as a terrorist state. After American Jewish organizations objected to Billy's arrangement with the renegade Arabs, he inflamed the controversy by observing, "There's a hell of a lot more Arabians than there is Jews." When the criticism continued, he delivered a message for Jews during a radio interview: "They can kiss my ass."

The president dissociated himself from his brother's remarks: "He is seriously ill at this point. I love him. I know for a fact that he is not anti-Semitic."

Billy's sponsors dropped him during the Libyan imbroglio, and his health deteriorated as his drinking escalated. The peanut operation in Plains fell apart. Two years after his brother's inauguration, Billy checked into an alcohol rehabilitation center in California. Hearing the news, I called a mutual friend to check on Billy's condition. "He has not been eating anything," I was told. "He was smoking four or five packs of cigarettes a day, and I mean inhaling them deep down. The last time I saw him, he could hardly breathe."

The innocence of the summer of 1976 in Plains had metastasized into something malignant. I felt sorry for Billy and guilty myself. By contributing to Billy's downfall by writing news stories glorifying his antics, I had been an accomplice to Billy's transformation from harmless good ole boy to a middle-aged wreck.

* * *

No serious observer held Jimmy Carter accountable for his brother's behavior, but Billy's case was symptomatic of the difficulties that the president encountered. He came to Washington not just as a Southerner but as an outsider, proud not to have been a product of the system inside the Beltway. As a result, Washington was less forgiving when things went wrong.

I thought some of the difficulties lay with Carter's personality. With his engineering background, he believed that problems would yield to logical solutions. He discounted the human elements involved in history, the imperfections and prejudices. With his slide-rule mentality, Carter felt he could find answers; he could not imagine that someone might have a rational, legitimate reason to differ with him. To make matters worse, he figured the members of Congress were cut from the same cloth as the bush-league legislators he had known in Atlanta.

Some problems were out of his control. In truth, Carter suffered a lifetime's worth of bad luck in four years. The oil-producing countries raised prices repeatedly, and long lines developed at gas stations across the country. On the economic front, interest rates rose exponentially and inflation depleted paychecks.

Six months after a foreign policy triumph—an agreement with Soviet president Leonid Brezhnev on the final terms of a strategic arms limitation treaty—the Soviets invaded Afghanistan. The pact was never ratified. Even Carter's greatest achievement, the Camp David agreement between Egypt and Israel, appeared ephemeral as hostilities continued in the Middle East.

Carter was pained by the loss of close friends on his staff. Bert Lance, a giant, affable Georgian, resigned as budget director during the first year, driven from Washington by charges that he had mismanaged a bank back home. Later, Andrew Young was forced to give up his post at the United Nations for violating U.S. policy forbidding contact with Palestinians.

From the moment Carter took office, unsympathetic gossip columnists pursued his chief aide, Hamilton Jordan, like hunting dogs. Hamilton had been the architect of Carter's campaign against Washington, and his reputation as a sarcastic Georgia playboy preceded him to the capital. Washington newspapers were quick to strike: Hamilton reportedly sucked an ice cube from a beaker of amaretto and cream and spit it down the blouse of a young woman at a bar on Pennsylvania Avenue; Hamilton was said to have leered at the cleavage of the Egyptian ambassador's wife and announced,

"Now I have seen the pyramids." Asked by a social climber how he pronounced his family name, Hamilton was said to have told her, "My friends say Jer-dun, but you can say Jor-dun." I enjoyed Hamilton. He was a wise guy, but smart and loyal. Late in the administration, he became the subject of a federal investigation of allegations that he had snorted cocaine at a Manhattan disco. No matter that Hamilton was exonerated, the story tainted the Carter administration.

The public anticipated breaches of etiquette by Carter and his associates. Lesser Carter aides were accused of demeaning the White House because they favored blue jeans or casual dress. When the columnist Rowland Evans invited Greg Schneiders, who had become Carter's media adviser, to a dinner party at his Georgetown home, he asked if Schneiders's wife was "presentable." Greg's wife, Marie, was a vivacious speech therapist.

The president's greatest crisis began on November 4, 1979, when followers of the Ayatollah Ruholla Khomeini overran the American embassy in Tehran and took dozens of hostages. Diplomatic attempts to free the hostages from the Iranian revolutionaries were unsuccessful. After the situation festered for five months, Carter approved a military rescue operation that ended in death and failure in a desert three hundred miles southeast of Tehran. A sandstorm destabilized part of the helicopter force, and in the turbulence an American chopper collided with one of the transport planes. Eight servicemen died, the mission had to be called off, and the grisly scene of burning wreckage became a symbol for the Carter administration.

Carter's decision to attempt the rescue caused a schism among his chief advisers. Secretary of State Cyrus Vance disagreed with the idea and told the president he intended to resign—even before the disaster in the desert. Vance's departure from the government was statesmanlike. But one of those who left with him would not go as quietly: Hodding Carter, my old friend from Mississippi.

Hodding had always been a champion of progressive Southern candidates. He once promoted the hapless presidential ambitions of Terry Sanford, a governor of North Carolina, and during the wacky 1972 Democratic convention Hodding had actually run for the vice-presidential nomination. Four years later, in 1976, he gave up his position at the *Delta Democrat-Times*, joined the Carter campaign, and wound up as Vance's spokesman in the new administration. A couple of years later, he married Patt Derian,

Vance's assistant secretary for human rights and another of our compatriots from the Mississippi Democratic challenge in 1968. In Washington, Hodding and Patt burnished their liberal credentials as members of a State Department faction that clashed frequently with Zbigniew Brzezinski, the president's hawkish national security adviser.

Vance's policy disputes with Brzezinski, who constantly called for confrontation with the Eastern bloc, had been the worst-kept secret of the Carter administration. Both sides leaked information in attempts to undercut their rivals, so when I heard from a mutual friend that Hodding would be willing to talk with me about the internecine dispute, I flew to his summer home in Maine shortly after his departure from the administration.

Hodding's frustrations poured out as we sat on a boulder overlooking Penobscot Bay. Brzezinski, he said, spent an inordinate amount of time whispering that Vance's team was "soft on the Russians." Hodding blamed Brzezinski for an incident the year before when the president had summoned eighteen top State Department officials to the White House and dressed them down because of a CBS News report, based on anonymous sources, that had predicted the fall of an interim government in Iran. "I felt it was a bum rap. I felt the procedure amounted to a kangaroo court," Hodding said. "It was a humiliation to Vance and destructive to the loyalty of those who had to sit there and be told, 'You are untrustworthy. You are my problem.'"

Although Hodding was hardly ready to rush into the arms of the Republican Party, his public break with the president reflected the erosion in Carter's support.

Hodding later wrote an account of his differences with Carter for *Playboy* magazine, an article that the president obviously felt was disloyal conduct by a former aide. When I had an opportunity to ask the president what he thought of Hodding's piece, he gave me a dark look I had not seen for a while. "It really pissed me off," he said. "I think Hodding is a creep."

Jimmy Carter's four-year term seemed to fly by like an out-of-balance pinwheel disintegrating with each rotation. Almost every story seemed to have a negative angle. Soaring energy rates. Three Mile Island. Congressional intransigence. Terrorism.

As I thumbed through the inside pages of the *New York Times* one day, looking for good news, I spotted a photograph of a familiar face. What's Oscar done now? I wondered. Then my eyes cut to the headline. My friend

Oscar Carr, Delta bon vivant and guide on our failed expedition to find Willie Morris in Manhattan a few years earlier, had died after a battle with cancer. I had been so preoccupied covering the White House that I had not known Oscar was ill.

By the fall of 1980, the base that Jimmy Carter had built four years earlier was collapsing around him. He had fended off a challenge for the Democratic nomination from Ted Kennedy easily enough, but Ronald Reagan was proving to be a formidable opponent in the general election.

Reagan appealed to white Southerners with his innate conservatism. His calls for sweeping tax cuts were soothing at a time when interest rates approached 20 percent and inflation sapped consumers. The former California governor's strong stance against the Soviet Union also played well across the South; a feeling that Carter was a bit wimpy persisted in a region that honored the military, particularly after a year of ineffectual efforts to free the hostages in Iran. Southern conservatives also objected to the Panama Canal treaty, which Carter regarded as one of his foreign policy triumphs.

At the beginning of September, the South looked like a major battleground. Carter opened his campaign on Labor Day in Tuscumbia, Alabama, in a corner of the state near the borders of Mississippi and Tennessee. Before the day ended, the Republican nominee, who often talked of a mythical "welfare queen" and claimed that trees caused pollution, made a new, interesting assertion. Reagan charged that Carter had chosen to begin his campaign "in the city that gave birth to and is the parent body of the Ku Klux Klan."

Reagan's comment, most charitably, could be called a stretch. No Klan had been born in Tuscumbia. The only local organization resembling the Klan was a bunch of right-wing extremists who had recently established headquarters in the town.

To stir regional pride, Carter fired back, "I resent very deeply what Ronald Reagan said about Alabama and about Tuscumbia. . . . Anybody who resorts to slurs and innuendos against a whole region of the country— based on a false statement or a false premise—is not doing the South or the nation good service. This is not the time for a candidate trying to get some political advantage to try to divide one region of our country from another."

Unfortunately for Carter, the issue turned out to be a one-day wonder, overtaken by other events. Even the most chauvinistic Southerners soon forgot Reagan's remark, and the Republican kept marching through Dixie, as surely as Sherman.

The last day of the campaign began with false rumors that the hostages would be released; it ended with a punishing 6,600-mile cross-country journey for Carter. After starting on the East Coast, the president worked his way westward to Seattle, where he held a final midnight rally in an enormous airport hangar where the noise of the crowd bounced off the vaulted metal ceiling. Outside, light rain blew in from Puget Sound.

The incumbent felt momentum on his side, and he maintained his spirits even as the event grew bizarre. When he spotted a heckler holding a sign that said, "Carter Blew His Four Years of Time," the president blew the boy a kiss. He appeared unfazed when another demonstrator tried to storm the stage. The man carried a placard saying, "Carter's Maternal Grandmother Is a Mulatto."

I figured the election would be close. On the flight to the West Coast, I sat with my pal Greg Schneiders. We decided to bet one dollar on the results from each of the fifty states. As we pondered a map, I saw Greg was projecting a comfortable victory for the president. I gave Carter much of the East, several of the big industrial states, and felt he would hold his own in the South. When I totaled those electoral votes, Carter won by a very narrow margin.

Following the Seattle rally, we flew overnight back to Georgia. The plane ride had none of the exuberance that had attended our homeward flight four years before. Carter traveled on *Air Force One*; the press and much of the staff, exhausted from the long day, struggled to sleep on board a separate, crowded charter. For old times' sake, Greg, Eleanor Randolph, and I shared a row of seats. We had traveled tens of thousands of miles together in 1976 and thought it appropriate to mark the end of the 1980 campaign in one another's company.

A few reading lights glimmered in the dark cabin. Most of the passengers rested in awkward angles of repose. On the East Coast, it was nearly 5 A.M. Polls would be opening in an hour. In the middle of our rambling conversation, Greg asked a question: "When are you going to write next?" Eleanor and I told him not until that evening, after the election results were in. Satisfied that we would not break the news, Greg revealed a secret he had learned at the last stop: "We're going to lose, and we're going to lose big."

On the flight to Seattle, Jody Powell, Carter's press secretary, had called the campaign pollster, Pat Caddell, back on the East Coast. Caddell had a grim report from a survey just completed. Voters in demographic groups the president had hoped to attract were breaking for Reagan in large numbers. Potential support for Carter had disappeared over the last weekend. He faced certain defeat. Greg said Jody had offered a simple, two-word assessment when they had talked briefly in Seattle: "It's gone."

Greg said he was glad to be traveling on the press plane. "They are going to have to tell Jimmy on the way home."

Carter's aides later described for me the scene on *Air Force One*. Jody reached Caddell by phone again, and the president asked for the polling results. "It's bad," said Powell, who had worked for Carter for ten years and had traveled a million miles with him. He handed the president the phone to hear the news for himself. Carter remained expressionless as he listened to Caddell's forecast of a Reagan landslide. When the conversation was over, Carter instructed Jody to work up a statement. "I think I'll take a nap," the president said.

Rick Hertzberg, Carter's speechwriter, and Stuart Eizenstat, an intellectual from Atlanta who served as Carter's top domestic adviser, were delegated to draft remarks for the president to deliver after he voted in Plains that morning. As they scribbled on a legal pad, the aides were weeping; their tears fell, blurring the ink.

The two jetliners landed in Georgia after dawn. The landscape was wrapped in a funereal ground fog; leaves from the pecan trees fell gently to the earth in rust-colored showers.

As *Marine One*, the White House helicopter, carried the president's party to Plains on the last leg of the trip, speechwriter Chris Matthews thought of the chopper as "a dying bird."

For another aide, Hertzberg, the trip was his first to Carter's Southern home. A writer for *The New Yorker* before he'd joined the administration, he had no natural affinity for the region. Yet on the way to Plains, Rick had found himself haunted by the lyrics of a song performed by The Band:

> Like my father before me,
> I'm a working man.
> And like my brother up above me,
> We took a rebel stand.
> We were just 18, proud and brave.
> But a Yankee laid him in the grave . . .

DIXIE

The night they drove old Dixie down,
and all the bells were ringing.
The night they drove old Dixie down,
and all the people were singing.

A couple of hours later, it was my turn as pool reporter when Carter went to vote at the school building he'd attended as a child. I was in a delicate position. I realized that the president now knew he would lose, but I was ethically bound not to use my inside information. He looked quite tired, and his complexion was blotched. He told the press pool he hoped to win. "We'll see."

His comment fell short of the expression I had heard so many times. "Mr. President," I said, "you always say, 'I don't intend to lose.'"

He smiled wanly. "All right. I don't intend to lose. Right on." Then Jimmy and Rosalynn Carter walked from the school to the old train depot.

I remembered the scene four years before, when Carter had bounded up the depot platform to address the people of Plains the morning he won election. He had gathered his brother, Billy, in an emotional embrace, throwing both arms around him. Billy's eyes were scarlet from the victorious, all-night vigil; the Carter brothers and many others in the throng were weeping tears of joy.

But this year, a smaller crowd waited to hear Carter. Billy was nowhere in sight. The president carried his prepared remarks with him, but once he began to speak, it was apparent he had no intention of following the script. He spoke as though he were grieving.

He said he had taken the values he had learned in the South to the White House, and he had made critical judgments "with the memory of my upbringing here in Plains, the fact that I'm a Southerner, the fact that I'm an American." His chin trembled. "We've tried to deal fairly with all people. With black people, with those who speak Spanish, with women, for those who've been deprived in life. Sometimes it's aroused the displeasure of others, and sometimes it's been politically costly."

He recalled the generosity of his neighbors in Georgia. "People from Plains, from Americus, from Richland, from Preston, from Schley County, from around this area, have gone all over the nation to speak for me and shake hands with people in other states to tell them that you have confidence in me and that I would not disappoint them if I became president."

The president looked as if he were about to break down.

"I've tried to honor your commitment to those other people," he said, fighting to complete the thought. "In the process I've tried to honor my commitment . . ." He stopped and bit his lips. When he began again, his voice quavered in falsetto. " . . . to you." His eyes glistened with tears. He swallowed, then finished with a benediction: "God bless you."

That night, Ronald Reagan carried forty-four states; Reagan even won Massachusetts, where the third-party candidacy of John Anderson peeled enough votes from the Democratic ticket to enable a Republican to claim the state's electoral votes. In Dixie, only Georgia supported the Southern president. The South had repudiated its son as cruelly as the rest of the country.

CHAPTER 15

"We have wasted too much time"

★ ★ ★ ★ ★

During the decade that began with Nixon's Southern Strategy and ended with Carter's presidency, several important developments took place that scrambled Southern politics so severely that I no longer recognized the system under which I'd grown up.

Black people, at first uncertain about participating in a democratic process long barred to them, began to exercise their right to vote in large numbers. Atlanta, the business-driven city that boasted it was too busy to hate, broke racial barriers in 1972 by sending Andrew Young to Congress; a year later, Maynard Jackson became the city's first black mayor. During the last half of the decade black candidates would win hundreds of local offices and claim congressional and legislative seats across the South. In many places, blacks won without white support, but in some instances whites were willing to work for a black candidate.

Young discussed in his autobiography, *An Easy Burden,* the wonder of his congressional victory in a district where only 38 percent of the voters were black. A group of idealistic whites, including my friends Paul and Carol Muldawer, as well as Stuart Eizenstat and Jack Watson—who later had important roles in the Carter administration—volunteered their assistance. But it took an outpouring of black votes to make the difference.

"Thanking the voters the morning after election day was one of the most memorable and joyous experiences of my life," Young wrote. "These were the hotel workers, the hospital workers, the custodians and janitors of Atlanta who were off to work early, and who changed buses downtown as they came from the black neighborhoods going to the white areas where they were employed. These were people who braved the rain to vote after they got off from work, and my guess is a goodly number of them had never before voted in their lives."

As blacks enlisted in the Democratic Party, the evolution of white voters became more pronounced. Like dinosaurs seeking to mate with elephants, members of the old guard—the curators of the politics of Never!—shuffled off to the Republican Party. They would not practice the politics of segregation as openly, but their influence would push the GOP further to the right on such issues as abortion, affirmative action, gay rights, gun control, and prayer in schools. The realignment that political scientists had been predicting for years finally took place.

But the shift did not occur simply because old right-wing Southern Democrats chose to consider themselves Republicans.* The region was undergoing vast demographic change, and in their 1975 book, *The Transformation of Southern Politics,* Jack Bass and Walter DeVries identified four categories of new Republicans:

"One group consists of migrants from other regions, usually business and professional families who moved into the South as part of the industrialization and economic expansion and brought their Republicanism with them. . . . A larger group consists of urban and suburban middle- and upper-middle-class migrants from farms and small towns, native Southerners who joined the middle class and who, often receiving poor public services, developed negative attitudes toward social programs and hostility toward government spending and taxing. . . . A much smaller group consists of reformers who are interested primarily in building a two-party system. . . . The final group, and a large one throughout the South, includes those who were attracted by the Goldwater candidacy in 1964, many of them ideologues who are conservative on racial and economic issues and who tend to be more interested in party purity—and they equate purity with conservatism—than party success."

While the GOP grew, a different version of the Democratic Party developed. The party that had produced Jim Eastland and George Wallace turned into a home for blacks and progressive whites. These Southern whites were slow to identify with the biracial party, but by the late 1970s many of the men and women who had watched passively during years of turmoil finally decided to take an active role in an effort to modernize politics. Their numbers were not large enough to be a countervailing force to

*Most Southern states have no party registration.

the white conservatives, but when coupled with black votes, this unlikely coalition could compete with the mossbacks who had ruled the region for most of the century.

Even as Nixon was luring Southern voters at the start of the 1970s, indigenous Democrats succeeded in rejecting the tradition of Faubus, Barnett, Wallace, and Maddox by electing a wave of thoughtful Democratic governors: Dale Bumpers in Arkansas, Bill Waller in Mississippi, Reubin Askew in Florida, John West in South Carolina, and Carter in Georgia.

In 1978, an urbane young politician whose support of civil rights and opposition to the Vietnam War was well known won the governor's office in Arkansas. Bill Clinton barely looked old enough to vote.

A year later, William Winter, a man I had admired since I was a young reporter in the Delta, was elected governor of Mississippi after carrying the state's progressive hopes unsuccessfully in two previous elections.

In his inaugural address, Winter told his fellow Mississippians, "We have wasted too much time. . . . We have spent too many of our years, too much of our energy, being against things we did not understand, being afraid of change, being suspicious of the intellectual, and being oblivious to our image and our reputation."

Finally, I thought to myself, it seemed safe to go back.

On the same day that Winter won, a heavy black vote in the Delta resulted in Aaron Henry's election to the Mississippi House of Representatives. Ten years after Aaron and I had scribbled out a sample ballot on my dining room table, the man who had been harassed and jailed for his civil rights activity took a seat at the same capitol that had once sheltered James K. Vardaman and Theodore G. Bilbo.

Aaron's political vindication seemed complete, though he had enjoyed influence for some time. Because of his role as leader of the newly constituted state Democratic Party, Mississippi Democrats in Congress had been forced to deal with him on matters of patronage for most of the decade. For some of them, it was a distasteful reality.

Nothing was stranger than the relationship between Aaron and Eastland. Since Eastland's chairmanship of the Judiciary Committee was controlled by the Senate's Democratic caucus, the senator had no choice but to cooperate with Aaron on party affairs in the state. Well aware of the growing strength of the black vote, Eastland also realized it would be impolitic to continue to antagonize a substantial bloc of Mississippians.

The situation displeased Eastland, but delighted Aaron. In the 1960s, when Aaron had journeyed to Washington to make appeals for help, he had been received in the highest councils of the Democratic administrations of John Kennedy and Lyndon Johnson, but never in the offices of his own state's senators and congressmen. Now he was able to negotiate directly with Eastland.

The meetings between Aaron and Eastland involved differing ideologies as well as personal styles. Aaron was an exuberant, affectionate man who used the Latin *abrazo* when greeting friends; he not only hugged acquaintances, he often rubbed the side of his head against theirs like a cuddly puppy. His mannerisms encouraged the suspicion that Aaron was gay. Eastland, on the other hand, was phlegmatic and rarely showed emotion. He did not like being embraced by Aaron—or any other male. When Aaron visited his Washington office, one of Eastland's associates once told me, the senator directed his staff to surround his desk with chairs to prevent Aaron from touching him.

In 1978, in his last year in office, Eastland asked Ted Kennedy to deliver the commencement address at Ole Miss. In a way, Eastland's friendship with the Kennedy family had been as strange as his arrangement with Aaron Henry. As a power on the Judiciary Committee, Eastland dealt with three Kennedy brothers at various times over a thirty year period. They seemed to be polar opposites, but the Mississippi senator and the Kennedys had not only arrived at a modus vivendi, they often reached their agreements over highballs in the cozy backrooms of the Senate.

Out of this unusual understanding had come at least one unfortunate bargain. In the early stages of John Kennedy's presidency, Eastland had asked the White House to nominate his college roommate Harold Cox to be a federal district judge in Mississippi. Cox was a well-known racist. Opposing the nomination, Roy Wilkins of the NAACP wired the president, "For 986,000 Negro Mississippians Judge Cox will be another strand in their barbed wire fence, another cross over their weary shoulders, and another rock in the road up which their young people must struggle."

Despite Cox's objectionable record, Eastland enjoyed a tactical advantage. Kennedy wanted to name Thurgood Marshall, the prominent black attorney who had successfully argued the *Brown v. Board of Education* case, to a position on a federal circuit court of appeals. Eastland could delay Marshall's nomination indefinitely.

In *Robert Kennedy and His Times*, Arthur Schlesinger Jr. wrote: "The famous story of Eastland's remark to Robert Kennedy—'Tell your brother that if he will give me Harold Cox, I will give him the nigger'—is perhaps apocryphal, but was true in some vaguer sense."

Both Marshall and Cox got the judicial positions. Marshall went on to distinguish himself as a justice on the U.S. Supreme Court. Cox disgraced himself in 1964 when he accused applicants in a voter registration case of behaving like "a bunch of niggers . . . acting like a bunch of chimpanzees."

Years after the Cox embarrassment and deaths of his brothers, Ted Kennedy still maintained the family connection with Eastland. Kennedy's agreement to speak at Ole Miss may have been the result of yet another quid pro quo; more probably it was simply Kennedy's tribute to an aging politician who would soon retire from the Senate. With Aaron and other black leaders in the state invited to the commencement exercises, Kennedy's trip to Oxford promised to be newsworthy as well as symbolic.

I flew to Mississippi with Kennedy along with a couple of other Southern journalists, Jack Nelson of the *Los Angeles Times* and Phil Gailey of the *Washington Star*. We toured the campus where John F. Kennedy's army had suppressed a revolt; sixteen years after that unpleasantness, his brother was treated as an honored guest. Ted Kennedy's speech got a warm reception, and afterward he and Eastland attended a reception at the Oxford Country Club. Aaron was there, with no chairs blocking his access. When he spotted Eastland, Aaron rushed to embrace him and planted an affectionate kiss on his cheek.

Returning to Washington on a commercial flight that night, I sat with Kennedy. We both had several drinks during a long layover at the Memphis airport, and the senator was in a playful mood. "You know, there are two things I would like to have from that reception," Kennedy said.

"What's that, Senator?"

"A picture of Aaron Henry kissing Jim Eastland," Kennedy said, convulsing in laughter. "And the second thing: a picture of Jim Eastland when he realized someone had a picture of Aaron kissing him."

When Eastland chose not to run for reelection, he opened a Senate seat in Mississippi for the first time since Bilbo's death in 1947. For most of my life, the same two men had served as senators. Eastland had always worked from the shadows, exercising his power back home through his organization of Citizens Council leaders, courthouse cronies, and conservative newspaper publishers.

His counterpart, John Stennis, also had a conservative voting record, but his style was quite different. Stennis made many public appearances, and his conservatism had an overlay of Southern gentility. He might argue against busing into the night, but he would do so politely. And compared to the Sphinx-like Eastland, Stennis was positively gregarious.

The two Mississippians were once invited to the White House during the Watergate investigation in an effort by President Nixon to shore up support in the Senate in his prospective impeachment trial. As Nixon pleaded his case, Stennis repeatedly interrupted him, assuring the president that no apology would be necessary. Nixon tried to explain his position again; Stennis insisted that he understood. Finally, Eastland had heard enough chatter. Motioning toward the president, Eastland told Stennis, "John, let the boy talk."

Over the years, Stennis had inherited informal leadership of the moderate faction that tussled with Eastland's organization for political control in Mississippi. In the one-party state, these political forces—divided behind the two senators—created the competition that Republicans had failed to provide for years.

All that ended with Eastland's retirement, though the change actually began in 1972 when a pair of young men switched parties and won congressional seats as Republicans. One of them, Thad Cochran, had been my friend since childhood. His parents had been in graduate school at Ole Miss in the summer of 1947, the same year my mother obtained her master's degree. Our families had lived in the same dormitory, and Thad, his brother, Neilson, and I had played together on the campus as kids. A decade later, Thad and I were undergraduates there. I also remembered Trent Lott from student days at Ole Miss; he had been a cheerleader and a constant candidate for campus offices. Trent and I had not traveled in the same crowd.

Thad came from a school of Mississippi moderates. He voted for John Kennedy in 1960; he even supported Lyndon Johnson in 1964, helping to account for the 13 percent LBJ managed to win against Goldwater in our state. But by 1968, Cochran began to pull away from the Democrats.

"I thought that under Humphrey the Democrats would go too far to immediately push the people in the South toward integration in a way that would provoke rebellion," Cochran told me years later. "I felt we needed to digest the Voting Rights Act, *Brown v. Board of Education,* and the other civil rights legislation that had been passed." He recalled that he had supported the Voting Rights Act and had naively written a brief upholding its constitutionality for a senior member of his law firm. Cochran's associate, who was preparing to testify before Eastland, wanted the opposite opinion.

To Cochran, the 1962 insurrection at our alma mater demonstrated that resistance to the law backfired against our state. But he also shared the belief of many white Mississippians that the state had come under a Reconstruction-like siege by the federal government. Richard Nixon, Cochran concluded, posed an acceptable alternative to Humphrey on the left and to Wallace—in the midst of his strongest campaign—on the right.

The Republican Party, knowing the South held football in the same awe as religion, tapped Bud Wilkinson to lead an operation called Citizens for Nixon that year. The former University of Oklahoma coach employed his recruiting skills on Southern Democrats. Cochran and Raymond Brown, a former Ole Miss quarterback practicing law in Pascagoula, were asked to direct the effort in Mississippi. Cochran's decision four years later to run for Congress as a Republican was the next logical step in his political development.

Trent Lott's conversion to the GOP seemed more visceral. After graduating from Ole Miss Law School, he took a job on the staff of William M. Colmer, a veteran congressman who served as chairman of the House Rules Committee. Colmer was a typical Southern Democrat of the day, an unyielding segregationist who used his seniority and committee assignment to thwart civil rights legislation. Colmer expressed no regret after Martin Luther King's death, only worry that the assassination would provide impetus for passage of a strong open-housing bill.

In 1972, Colmer decided to retire, and Lott ran for his House seat, vowing to oppose the Kennedys and to "fight against the ever-increasing efforts of the so-called liberals to concentrate more power in the government in Washington." There was nothing surprising in Lott's rhetoric, but the young candidate shocked even his closest friends by announcing that he would campaign as a Republican. His decision was calculated. Nixon won his greatest margin in Lott's district that fall, taking 87 percent of the vote. Lott drew only 55 percent, but it was enough to launch his political career.

On paper, it appeared the two congressmen were on parallel tracks. Compared to the senior members of the Mississippi delegation, both Cochran and Lott seemed energetic and articulate, more attuned to the last quarter of the twentieth century. They were part of a new Republican vanguard in the South. Their voting patterns were similar. Reflecting partisan values, they supported military spending, opposed liberal Democratic initiatives, and piled up favorable ratings from conservative organizations such as Americans for Constitutional Action. If one inspected their records closely, however, distinctions could be detected. Cochran, for instance, voted against a mean-spirited bill that would have required impoverished food-stamp recipients to pay for a portion of their monthly allotment. Lott supported the measure.

In fact, Cochran and Lott were never close, and the longer they served together in Congress, the farther they moved apart. When Eastland's Senate seat became available in 1978, Cochran declared immediate interest. Privately, he told Republican officials in Mississippi he was tired of running for reelection to the House every other year. He didn't care about Lott's ambitions. He would fight his colleague for the GOP nomination if necessary. If he failed, Cochran said, it would not be the end of the earth; he would move back to Jackson and practice law for the rest of his life.

Lott was not as determined. Mike Retzer, a leader in the Mississippi Republican Party, told me, "Trent loved Washington and didn't want to risk losing his seat." Lott kept his House seat and stayed out of the race. For years he was said to have regretted his decision.

Cochran had a relatively easy time. His Democratic opponent, Maurice Dantin, was hurt by the independent candidacy of Charles Evers. The Evers campaign was a maneuver familiar to those who had watched his career in the years since he'd returned to Mississippi following Medgar's murder. After establishing a duchy as mayor of the little town of Fayette, where he controlled federal grants and state contracts while building a business empire for himself, Evers had been indicted in 1974 on three counts of income tax evasion. He was charged with understating his income for one year by nearly $160,000. The doubts expressed years earlier by his detractors in the civil rights movement had finally come to roost in federal court. Evers escaped conviction, but his name was tarnished.

Evers evoked mixed feelings. Speaking of Evers, my friend Patt Derian told me, "He was a hero when we needed one." But most white liberals turned away from him. So did many blacks, loyal to the Democratic Party and leery of Evers's version of capitalism in Fayette. Still, he had a following.

During the campaign, disgruntled Democrats suggested that Evers stood to profit financially by taking blacks from the party's fold. The allegations were never proved, but the prediction of black defections was accurate.

Evers won 23 percent of the vote, and Dantin was reduced to 32 percent. With a plurality of 45 percent, Thad Cochran became the first Republican senator from Mississippi since Reconstruction.

Lott was bitter about being left behind in the House, and his antipathy toward Cochran, originally grounded in petty grievances involving campus politics at Ole Miss, grew more intense. One of the focuses for Lott's frustration involved an old friend of mine, a colorful Jackson lawyer named Grady Jolly.

Though Grady and I were at Ole Miss together, I got to know him better when he served as a young assistant U.S. attorney and I covered federal courts in north Mississippi. His wife, Bettye, was a journalist, and I have enjoyed their company for more than thirty years. Grady is irreverent and tart-tongued—characteristics that are not part of Lott's public persona—and Grady has perfected a Ross Barnett imitation that he uses to regale friends with tales featuring our former governor. In 1978, he went into politics himself—as Cochran's campaign manager.

Three years later, Mississippi's first modern Republican senator used his connections with the new Reagan administration to try to win Grady a seat on the U.S. Fifth Circuit Court of Appeals. Although Lott, a mere congressman, had no formal standing in the procedure, he began a protracted campaign to block the nomination. I wondered why. I heard one ridiculous reason. At Ole Miss, Grady had gained the enmity of Lott's fraternity by running for student body president and depriving one of Lott's Sigma Nu brothers of the post. But there was more. Lott felt he had been humiliated at a Washington dinner party for Mississippians that the Jollys had hosted in the late 1960s. At the time, Lott was a Colmer aide, Bettye Jolly worked for another Mississippi congressman, and Grady had a job at the dreaded Justice Department.

It was easy for me to imagine the scene. As a frequent overnight guest in the Jollys' home, I've been subjected to Grady's barbs about my liberalism many times. But he needles ideologues of all stripes. On the night that Lott came to dinner, according to friends, Grady ridiculed his guest for serving as an assistant to one of the most reactionary members of Congress. He called Lott's boss a "troglodyte," among other things. Lott did not forget.

More than a decade later, Lott used his contacts with the Reagan administration to try to undermine Cochran's choice of Jolly for the Fifth Circuit. Though Grady had become quite conservative in his politics, Lott portrayed him as a threat to perpetuate the liberal agenda of the Fifth Circuit.

It took Cochran a year of guerrilla warfare to prevail and win Grady's confirmation.

Lott was forced to wait to get a Senate seat for himself until John Stennis retired in 1988. Once Thad and Trent were in positions of power in the Senate, I recognized a pattern in the succession—from Eastland and Stennis to Lott and Cochran. The rivers that had once run through the Democratic Party now flowed in the GOP. Cochran represented the Republican moderate conservatives, the better-educated, country-club/chamber-of-commerce types who once viewed Stennis as their leader. Lott took over command of the Eastland crowd, the rawer, antigovernment camp that included the last practitioners of the politics of Never!

With the South's old political front in ruins, disorganization extended to the hardest core of the segregationists. The warriors of the Ku Klux Klan were reduced to the straits of those Japanese soldiers who had dwelled in caves on Pacific islands after World War II, disbelieving defeat had come to them. I knew the Klan suffered from disarray, but I didn't realize how badly their ranks were tattered until I traveled to Decatur, Alabama, in 1979 to cover a black-white dispute that had escalated into a gunfight on the streets.

The disagreement started with the conviction of a mentally retarded black man charged with raping a white woman. Activists associated with the Southern Christian Leadership Conference, the Atlanta-based organization that had dwindled since Martin Luther King's death, took up the defendant's cause with a series of demonstrations. The Klan staged counterdemonstrations, inspired by a prayer from their hooded chaplain: "We pray for the day when men in white robes riding white horses will come out of heaven following the white savior, the pure savior, Jesus Christ." Competition between the SCLC and the Klan led to scuffles and, eventually, shootings.

The citizens of the little city of Decatur, located on a peaceful bend of the Tennessee River, were distressed by the disorder. "It's like a bunch of people from Atlanta and a gang of Alabama rednecks came to fight in our playground," said Charles Finney, a stockbroker and president of the chamber of commerce.

The Klan of northwest Alabama seemed singularly inept. I sought out one of their leaders, Bill McGlocklin, at his service station on Highway 31. McGlocklin had a number of tattoos on his arms; otherwise, he looked normal. We had a pleasant conversation in which he volunteered the information that he had been the "grand klaliff" in Decatur. In the Klan hierarchy, he answered only to the grand dragon, he explained.

One of McGlocklin's problems was that he didn't know which grand dragon. His group had been affiliated with the Federated Klans out of Stone Mountain, Georgia, he said, but the Federated grand dragon refused to give approval for an attack against the SCLC. As a result, McGlockin's group switched to the Invisible Empire, Knights of the Ku Klux Klan, with headquarters in Denham Springs, Louisiana.

I asked if he had had to change emblems on his sheets as a result of the shift.

The friendly tone of his voice switched abruptly to a more hostile gear. "What'd you mean by 'sheets'?"

"I mean the things you wear at the rallies."

"Hell, them things ain't sheets, they're robes." McGlocklin began a dissertation on the quality of his Klan's vestments. Another fellow in Louisiana was purported to be a Klan leader, he said, a guy named David Duke, who made money peddling cheap Klan paraphernalia. "Duke's stuff is made of this raggedy-ass muslin," McGlocklin said. "Our robes are made of one-hundred-ninety-grain heavy polyester. It don't wrinkle. You can throw them in the wash and put them right back on."

He then changed the subject from fabrics to treachery within the Klan. His role had been usurped by one of his own acolytes, McGlocklin complained, and he felt cast adrift. "I think I have done a lot of good. If necessary, I'll form a citizens committee to fight the Klan and the niggers both." He scratched his curly head. "I have never been against the blacks. I'm against the Communists and the Jews." He identified Dorothy Schwochow, a member of the Decatur City Council, as one of his Jewish enemies.

Mrs. Schwochow, I learned later that day, was a Protestant who came from Pennsylvania Dutch stock.

The Klan disappeared altogether from my old hometown, Summit. My mother kept me posted on developments in long weekly letters. She was losing her hearing, and conversations over the telephone were hard for her. In an age when most people communicated by phone, she preferred written correspondence anyway, just as she would rather read a book than watch TV. She and Pa were both retired; their health was beginning to fail them. The town was changing, too. The elders of Summit—Jack Covington, the mayor, Billy Barnes, the merchant, Frank Watkins, the head of the school board—had all died within months of each other in 1976, and the Presbyterian church never recovered. The congregation was consolidated with a larger one in McComb. Pa did not give up his ministry altogether, however, and preached part-time at a small church in Osyka in the southern part of Pike County.

Because Pa had devoted much of his life to the Summit church, the presbytery allowed my parents to stay in the manse, next to the abandoned church. It pained them to see the building empty on Sunday, but they loved the surroundings. Mother gave me accounts of the birds visiting the backyard, the beautiful cardinals, the singing mockingbirds, the meddlesome jays, the obnoxious crows, the exotic bluebirds that made rare appearances. She wrote mostly about positive, happy topics.

She noted that after years of exile in New York, Willie Morris had returned to Mississippi to teach at Ole Miss. "He's come home, and he's writing nice things about the South," she said. Her implication was clear.

I made a point to visit the new governor of Mississippi. More than a dozen years had passed since William Winter had first run for the office as the candidate of blacks and moderates. He had renounced his expedient 1967 claim to being a fifth-generation segregationist; I'm sure he regretted he had ever made the remark.* Finally, he had triumphed over the old guard, and I was glad to see he still retained his enthusiasm and raconteur's gift. His voice carried the cadence of the Old South, deeply modulated, as though he had learned to speak at the foot of the pulpit at the Neshoba County Fair. But he was very much a modern man, and he understood the tides of Southern history.

I laughed at the stories Winter told me. Some involved his own political naïveté, others dealt with the follies of Ross Barnett. In 1967, after Barnett had been eliminated in the first Democratic primary, the old man had endorsed Winter. Barnett abhorred Winter's moderate politics, but he despised Winter's rival in the runoff, John Bell Williams, even more. During the campaign, Williams had waved copies of land deeds, charging Barnett with bestowing pardons for state prisoners in exchange for property. In their attempt to stymie Williams, Barnett and his relatives dragged Winter

---

*In the late 1990s, Winter served as vice chairman of the advisory board to President Clinton's Initiative on Race.

through the hills of east Mississippi, introducing him to wary cousins in places like Noxapater and Laurel Hill, making a good-faith effort to rally what was left of Barnett's troops. Winter's peculiar alliance with Barnett failed that year, but the new politics of Mississippi enabled Winter to triumph in 1979.

After Winter and I talked for a bit, the governor rose from his desk and said, "Come on, there's something I want to show you."

The capitol was being renovated, and Winter gave me a tour. He had taken advantage of the construction project to move some of the furniture around. For thirty years, a life-size statue of Theodore G. Bilbo had been the centerpiece in the rotunda of the capitol. The likeness of the old racist had dominated the chamber. With his hands stretched toward the sky, he appeared to be greeting visitors with either a blessing or a curse. Winter undoubtedly knew of Santayana's admonition about those forgetting history being doomed to repeat it. But he also realized Bilbo's days of glory were long gone. The governor showed me Bilbo's new home. He had moved the statue to a side corridor, just off a men's room in the basement.

A remarkable change was also taking place a few blocks away from the capitol, in the newsroom of the *Clarion-Ledger* and *Daily News*. Under the direction of a young Hederman, the newspapers were replacing racism with responsible journalism. The new editor, Rea Hederman, authorized muckraking stories that touched on hitherto forbidden subjects—poverty in the Delta, shady financing practices by a prominent homebuilder, and illicit gambling on the Gulf Coast. For those who had been weaned on the words of Jimmy Ward and Fred Sullens, it was a startling turnabout.

During my visit to Jackson, I met Rea Hederman at a small cocktail party at the Jollys' home. He was roughly my age, and I would have liked to talk with him about the newspapers' revolution. But the subject seemed awkward because any praise of Rea's work implied disapproval of the regime of his father, Bob Hederman, and other members of the family.

While one wing of the family controlled the printing side of the business known as Hederman Brothers, Tom and Bob Hederman had run the newspapers as if they were in-house publications for the Citizens Council. They had railed against integration, counseled resistance, advised Ross Barnett during the Ole Miss crisis, and opposed racial equity adamantly into the 1970s. But as they prepared to retire, they handed the reins of the newspapers to Rea, and he began a makeover of the papers' image.

"I think Rea decided to make them good newspapers because he was embarrassed by them," one of his friends told me later. "He hired the best graduates out of the University of Missouri journalism school. He brought in a total group of outsiders to report the news, and they really rocked the boat."

The new look diminished the aging racist voices, and Rea gradually replaced their commentary with investigative journalism. The tribune of segregation, Jimmy Ward, was stripped of much of his authority and reduced to writing a column that played inside the pages of the *Daily News*. "To all of us, Jimmy Ward was this wheezing, emphysema-ridden Marley's ghost who reminded us of what those papers had been," Raad Cawthon, one of the newcomers on the staff, told me years later. "He was an object of ridicule and derision."

While a newer generation of Mississippians approved of the transformation, consternation swept the ranks of the older Hedermans. Suddenly, a few months after my visit to Jackson, Rea left town. "He just vanished," one of his friends on his staff told me. "There was no farewell, nothing." Sometime later, his departure was linked to the breakup of his marriage. He turned up in New York, where he became publisher of *The New York Review of Books* and *Granta*, a respected literary quarterly. Like Willie Morris, he had left Mississippi to assume a place in Manhattan's social circles. But Rea Hederman left behind a legacy in Jackson that could not be reversed—though some members of his family tried.

For a period, Rea's brother, Bob Hederman Jr., tried to reassert control. In 1981, Karenna Cawthon, a photographer for the paper at the time, took a picture of a beautiful black child playing in a flooded street. After the photo was published, an edict came down from the editorial offices. "This was not to happen anymore," she recalled. "We were not to run pictures of black people or snakes because they made people uncomfortable."

After a short interval, the Hederman family decided to rid themselves of the troublesome operation, selling the papers to the Gannett chain. Charles Overby, the journalist who had gently chided me for my diatribe against the Baptists on election eve 1976, was brought in by Gannett as executive editor in 1982, and it turned out to be a serendipitous move.

Charles was a native of Jackson and understood the role he needed to play in the city. He had experienced his own personal epiphany as a high school student at the Calvary Baptist Church in the early 1960s.

"There were six or seven black people dressed in their Sunday finest," he recalled for me years later. "They said they wanted to worship with us. The deacons blocked the door and called the police. I watched all of this. The Jackson police came and grabbed these people and threw them in a paddy wagon." The police were rougher than necessary, and the suits and dresses of the black men and women were torn and dirtied. "This was when I came face-to-face, in a dramatic way, with right and wrong," Overby said.

A newspaper project, conceived by Rea Hederman, to review the deplorable state of Mississippi's public schools was already in the works when Overby arrived. It was timed to coincide with Governor Winter's plan to increase the state sales tax to institute kindergarten classes and make other reforms in the educational system.

The *Clarion-Ledger* carried a series of stories demonstrating "just how bad our public schools were," Overby told me. "We ran strong editorials to support Winter's program. We worked very closely with the Winter administration. We created a 'Hall of Shame' that featured legislators who opposed the education program. No one had ever covered these committee meetings before. No one knew how they voted. The governor and members of his staff—David Crews and Andy Mullins—would tell us who was wavering, who was trying to block it."

After a prolonged debate, the education program—designed to help a public school system with a disproportionately high percentage of black students—passed. As a result of the newspaper campaign, the *Clarion-Ledger* won a Pulitzer Prize for public service.

Overby was struck by the irony of his alliance with Winter. "Here we were, using the same phone lines between the *Clarion-Ledger* and the governor's office that had been used in 1962 to try to keep Meredith out of Ole Miss."

As Winter's term expired—state law then prevented a governor from a second consecutive term—I returned in 1983 to take a look at the field of candidates campaigning to succeed him at Mississippi's great political festival, the Neshoba County Fair. The event has been staged every summer since 1889, bringing prominence to the county long before the bodies of James Chaney, Andrew Goodman, and Michael Schwerner were discovered a few miles from the fairgrounds in 1964. Set in a clearing in pinewoods, hundreds of cabins have been built around a speaking gallery where generations of politicians and musicians have held forth. The numerous property owners, who have roots in Neshoba County, have cut a harness racetrack out of the red clay and created a midway for a traveling carnival. For one week each summer, thousands converge on the dusty fairgrounds, gathering on cabin porches to renew old friendships, nibble on fried chicken, and surreptitiously violate the county's dry laws. The oratory from the politicians is impassioned, and members of the audience sit in a tin-roofed pavilion, cheering their favorites and hooting at their opponents.

Barnett spoke at the fair every year. In his heyday, he vilified the federal government and dismissed Negroes with jokes about darkies and watermelons. But change in Mississippi had forced him to temper his language. His son, Ross Barnett Jr., was a candidate for the legislature one year, and the old governor confided to an acquaintance, "I can't talk about the nigguhs anymore, Ross Jr.'s got a bunch of 'em in his district."

Still, Barnett packed the pavilion. Hundreds wanted to see him for old times' sake; a new generation flocked to the performance as if he were a prehistoric relic, as remarkable as an exhibition of King Tut's treasures.

Watching the parade of politicians, I saw the former governor had given up his fire-eating sermons on race for a guitar, which he played poorly. He told a couple of pointless, rambling stories and strummed along, singing several verses of the old standard "Are You from Dixie?"

But even as I laughed at the old man, I was touched by the pathos of his appearance. Younger members of the audience egged him on, encouraging Barnett to make a bigger fool of himself. "Sing us another one, Ross!" they shouted. And the man who had not been governor for twenty years obliged; he was unwilling to give up the spotlight. He resisted entreaties from members of his own family to leave the stage, and he played on, thumping his guitar for emphasis.

It would be the last time I would see old Ross, but for the first time in my life I felt a bit of pity for him.

The 1983 race for governor narrowed to two candidates, the Democratic attorney general, Bill Allain, and Leon Bramlett, the Clarksdale planter who had been John Bell Williams's chairman in the Democratic Party when it was racist. As an illustration of the old guard's shift, Bramlett was now the Republican nominee. Charles Evers was running as an independent again, but his credibility had been washed away by his increasingly erratic political moves, which included an endorsement of Ronald Reagan.

Returning to Mississippi a few weeks before the general election, I bought a copy of the *Clarion-Ledger* at the Jackson airport and soon picked up a scent of Mississippi politics past. In a news story, Bramlett's wife was quoted as saying, "I'm running for first lady, and I'm unopposed." What was that supposed to mean?

I called Overby. The editor gave me a brief rundown of the situation. The Republicans had hired detectives to investigate the private life of Bill Allain, who was divorced and lived alone. The project yielded affidavits from several black transvestites who claimed to have had homosexual encounters with the Democratic candidate. Although the information was leaked to Overby, he said he refused to let the *Clarion-Ledger* be used as a conduit. He told the Republicans they would have to air the charges themselves if they wanted to make the information public.

"Are you going to be around tomorrow afternoon?" Charles asked me. "The Republicans are going to have their press conference, and you don't want to miss it."

The next morning I had breakfast with William Winter at the governor's mansion. He knew about the allegations and was uncomfortable. Although a lifelong Mississippi politician, he was also a man of some probity, and it was not easy discussing transvestite adventures over bacon, scrambled eggs, and grits. He thought it all sounded crazy. For the record, he denounced the Republican tactic as "the most scurrilous kind of political activity."

I wandered over to the state capitol, where the *Globe* tracked me down by telephone in the pressroom. A U.S. Marine installation in Beirut had been hit by suicide bombers the day before, and more than two hundred servicemen were dead. Our foreign desk wanted me to meet one of our photographers, Stan Grossfeld, in New York and rush to Beirut. For more than a year, the newspaper had been grooming me for the Middle East. I had spent weeks there in 1982, covering uprisings on the West Bank and the Israeli invasion of Lebanon. I suppose they thought I qualified for the assignment because of my experience covering racial conflicts. In fact, I was just beginning to understand the difference between a kibbutz and a settlement, to realize that the Arabs were not one big happy family. But the Middle East appealed to me. I told the editors I would be delighted to go to Beirut. "But I'm not leaving until after this press conference," I added.

In twenty years in journalism, I had never seen anything quite like it. A Jackson attorney, William Spell, conducted the news conference, distributing a set of lurid affidavits that would have made the Marquis de Sade blush. Speaking with assumed feminine names, the transvestites described in detail their alleged encounters with the Democratic candidate. One said that Allain enjoyed covering his mate's face with lipstick and eating it off. Another said Allain liked him to wear only socks and shoes during their trysts. Those were the mildest of the accusations.

Standing in the gaggle of Mississippi reporters, I thought we all needed a hot shower to wash off the slime. Spell acknowledged the investigation had been sponsored by William Mounger, a wealthy Jackson oilman who had been finance chairman for the GOP and one of President Reagan's staunchest Southern benefactors. The witnesses were being paid $12 a day for meals and $50 a day for "lost income," Spell admitted. One of the sources had been paid a $300 "finder's fee" for producing an additional witness. The transvestites were available for interviews at a motel across the river in Louisiana if anyone cared to talk with them personally, Spell said.

I could hear the ghosts of Vardaman and Bilbo applauding.

Allain called the charges "damnable, vicious, malicious lies." Two weeks later, although tagged as the consort of black homosexuals, Allain was easily elected the next governor of Mississippi. The trash tactics that had benefited demagogues for a century no longer worked in the state.

In Summit, Mary Cain did not follow the campaign with her usual energy. She was slowed by age, and the fire had gone out of her little newspaper. The *Sun* was no more than a pastiche of her commentary and canned John Birch Society columns. With her old press machinery obsolete, she relied on the printing shop of the *McComb Enterprise-Journal* to publish. Her husband, John, too old to work, shut down the garage next door.

Her first column of the new year, 1984, sang of a tired, broken heart. "My beloved John is gone," she announced. "I am numb and haven't begun to face that fact."

Three months later, her column was reduced to a single paragraph:

"I had a little fall Tuesday morning and have not been feeling real well since. I can't seem to shake off my weakness, but I am trying real hard to get well and get back into the swing of things in Summit and the rest of the world."

Her final column appeared in May. It began with her usual quote from Lincoln and her out-of-date photograph, but the rest of the space was left empty and bordered in black. "Hacksaw Mary" was dead, and another of the angry voices from my childhood had been silenced forever.

CHAPTER 16

Sahafi

★ ★ ★ ★ ★

Nothing about Jerusalem should have resembled the South; still, I found constant reminders behind its exotic façade. From my first trip there during an Israeli crackdown on the West Bank in 1982, I had been struck by scenes of Jewish settlers, M16s slung across their shoulders, swaggering through the cardamon-scented Arab souk in the Old City like plantation managers patrolling a row of tenant farmers' shacks. Reports of troublesome Palestinians being shot while trying to escape custody and the obdurate language of the Likud government also sounded like my old home. I knew it was simplisitc to compare the Israeli-Palestinian conflict with Southern racial strife, but the stories that were part of a reporter's daily diet in Israel and the occupied territories had a familiar ring. So did other, more happy similarities.

When I set out to begin a three-year tour of duty in the fall of 1984, I felt comfortable with the assignment. On the trip out to JFK for my flight, the taxi driver learned I was moving to Jerusalem. He eyed me warily in the mirror and concluded, "You don't look Jewish to me." To paraphrase the old advertisement for Levy's bread, you didn't have to be Jewish to love Jerusalem. In those days, before American-style suburban sprawl turned the beautiful, winding approach up the mountain into a drive through Levittown, Jerusalem sparkled like a heavenly city. In the early mornings and late afternoons, the creamy stone of its buildings took on a bewitching color; at midday, the city gleamed with blinding intensity. No rain fell on the Jerusalem plateau between early spring and winter, and except for the occasional *hamsin*—a desert sandstorm that enveloped the landscape in dull shades of gray and yellow—the skies were bright blue and the climate magnificent.

The weather did not remind me of Mississippi, but the Mediterranean pace of life certainly did. Nothing hurried. In Summit, shops closed at noon on Wednesdays for a half holiday each week. In Jerusalem, businesses shut every day for an afternoon siesta, and often they never reopened. Government offices effectively quit after lunch. The bureaucracy wheezed with inefficiency, and citizens needed *protezcia*—slang for knowing someone with clout—to cut through the red tape. In some ways, life in the Holy City was like revisiting my childhood. The Sabbath was strictly observed. Luxury consumer goods were in short supply. Telephones were unreliable, and a single Israeli television channel operated for only a few hours each evening.

If riveting news stories require conflict for a basic theme, then Jerusalem was a reporter's dream. The city was split by an invisible "Green Line" as emphatic as the railroad tracks that divided white and black Clarksdale. Although Israel had seized control of the entire city during the 1967 war, thousands of Palestinians still lived in sullen isolation in East Jerusalem, inside the walls of the Old City and in neighborhoods scattered around Suleiman Street and down the road to Jericho. West Jerusalem contained the newer city, starkly modern, with high-rise apartments and hotels breaking the beauty.

It may have been unfair, but it took little imagination for me to see Ariel Sharon, the Israeli general who had invaded Lebanon to crush the Palestine Liberation Organization, and think of Bull Connor. And Palestinians living under military occupation in the West Bank and Gaza toiled with the same desperation as blacks in the South twenty years earlier. Most families were poor, and the Palestinian men provided a pool of cheap labor for Israel, standing by roadsides at dawn in ragged groups, hoping to be selected for day work.

I spent a week in Gaza working on a magazine story. The squalor there made poverty in the Delta look tolerable. Rashad Shawa, twice deposed as mayor of Gaza by Israeli authorities, told me, "I think we have reached the bottom. We are enslaved by Israel. We have become servants of Israel. All of the street sweepers of Israel are from Gaza. Our young people are forced to work in degrading jobs. Even our breath is restricted."

During this period, the Palestinians had no voice in government and were subject to arbitrary laws, including a judicial instrument, "administrative detention," that gave Israeli authorities power to jail someone for months without any formal charges. It smacked of Southern "due process" in the old days. To challenge that authority, a small group of civil rights lawyers labored to defend the Palestinian minority. Many of these crusading attorneys were Israelis, just as Jewish lawyers had carried a disproportionate burden of the civil rights cases in the South.

There was a major difference, however. Unlike the South, where liberals and moderates had been silent and outnumbered during my childhood, a noisy opposition to the Likud policies existed in Israel. Hundreds of thousands of Israelis opposed the occupation in Gaza and the West Bank and regularly protested the military strike into Lebanon, an adventure that had led to massacres at Palestinian refugee camps in 1982 and continued to claim victims almost every day.*

On reflection, I eventually recognized another distinction between the American civil rights movement and the Arab-Israeli conflict. The most thoughtful civil rights leaders followed a "turn the other cheek" principle; in the Middle East, both sides practiced a vengeful "eye for an eye" approach. New Testament/Old Testament. Or to put it another way, the principles of Gandhi were displaced by the armed struggle.

On tourist maps, Israel is depicted as the heart of the Holy Land, a peaceful region of gentle lambs and biblical miracles. In fact, the region bottled up a volatile mix of bloody history, religious prejudice, official injustice, and ethnic jealousy. Western journalists working in the Middle East had a code name for the place: Dixie.

The origin of the nickname came from a period when it was dangerous to use the word *Israel* in Beirut, where many correspondents were stationed. Since Israel lay south of Lebanon, *Dixie* seemed a natural nom de guerre. In conversations in the bar of the Commodore Hotel in Beirut, a nest of spies and gunrunners and third world hacks, we never talked of events in Israel, a country that Arab states refused to recognize. The news we discussed came from Dixie.

I carried two passports—one that contained the stamps from my Israeli residential visa, the other to be used in places like Amman, Beirut, Damascus, Baghdad, and Riyadh. Outside of Egypt, which had reached an accord with Israel at Camp David, Israel's name was not to be uttered in public in Arab states. No passports with Hebrew characters were accepted. Armed with a business card that used a post office box on Cyprus as my home address, I traveled throughout the Arab world on assignment for the *Globe*. But I lived in Dixie.

* * *

*Not until 2000 did Israel complete its military withdrawal from Lebanon.

I tried to immerse myself in the surroundings, reading books and interviewing sages on various sides of the struggle over land, theology, and politics. I found the Jewish people to be tribal, proud, introspective, with an understanding of history and a knowledge of loss not unlike my people. Like Southerners, they had produced an impressive body of literature out of proportion to their numbers and cultivated a keen sense of irony. (But when I wrote about the apparent parallels, the *Globe* got several indignant letters from Jews in the Boston area objecting to the comparison with Southerners.)

As I studied the Middle East, I became acquainted with the multitude of Israeli political parties, the breakaway factions of the PLO, and the countless militias acting as belligerents in the civil war in Lebanon. I learned a bit about Judaism and Islam and discovered that many Palestinians were Christians. I went to ulpan school, taking a crash course on Hebrew. It was hopeless. My Southern tongue refused to curl around the *ch* pronunciations. My Arabic was equally atrocious, limited largely to *habibi* (friend), *sahafi* (journalist), *inshallah* (God willing), and *wahad birra* (a beer). After I had studied Berlitz tapes for weeks in a vain effort to master Italian—I spent most holidays in Italy—my friends in Rome said I mangled the language so badly that I should limit my practice to Calabria, a rural southern province.

When necessary, I hired interpreters. Most of the people I interviewed in the Middle East spoke English, but I encountered occasional problems. During the TWA hijacking in 1985, a standoff that went on for days in Beirut, I attended a press conference in the basement of the home of Nabbih Berri. The Shia Muslim leader was trying to work out the release of several dozen American hostages held by a fringe group of Shia terrorists, and dozens of multilingual reporters from around the world were on hand. Questions and answers flew back and forth in French, Arabic, and English. When I asked a question in my own language, the host looked perplexed. "Could someone translate this into English?" he asked.

Despite my difficulties with language, I got by with the help of many friends and associates. Once I posed as an Israeli "investor" to join the Israeli writer Amos Elon on an expedition. With Amos handling the Hebrew, we took a promotional bus tour arranged by Israeli con men selling vacation homes on a Gaza beachfront cheek by jowl with a dangerous Palestinian refugee camp. The scam was a bit like offering a plot of land in the Everglades.

A recurrent story I perversely enjoyed involved the Friday-night fights between ultraorthodox and secular Jews. On many weekends they battled each other in the streets of Jerusalem over attempts to show movies and open restaurants on the Sabbath. When police used water cannons to drive the religious protesters, sidelocks dangling from beneath their black hats, back into their neighborhood of Mea Shearim, my secular friends would cheer from the sidelines, "Spritz the curlies!" The controversy reminded me a bit of the Deep South's blue laws. But it took the bitter dispute between the Israelis and the Palestinians to bring the region really home to me.

My friend Ze'ev Chafets, who gave up his American name and Detroit home to make aliyah to Israel in 1967, complained that I used the civil rights struggle as my frame of reference for the Middle East. The Southern experience involved a colonialist attempt by white masters to preserve racial discrimination, he argued, while Israel's cause was just. Since the country was surrounded by enemies, a degree of control was necessary to contain Palestinians living under Israeli rule, he said; otherwise the Jewish state would be overrun and the only democracy in the Middle East—Ze'ev liked to call Israel "a good place in a bad neighborhood"—would be lost.

Ze'ev was the first Israeli I'd met when I obtained my press credentials at the government press office on my initial trip to Jerusalem in 1982. An aide to Menachem Begin, the prime minister at the time, Ze'ev ran the office, and I had been instructed to introduce myself to him. I expected an older, dour official, a contemporary of Begin's generation and a practitioner of the right-wing Jabotinsky ideology; I met someone slightly younger than me, with an engaging wit and a taste for Jack Daniel's.

We struck up a friendship that lasted through years of argument over Middle East politics, American basketball, and the merits of various rock 'n' roll recordings. Ze'ev told me he had been attracted to the Likud by the populism of Begin. The prime minister had won election by rallying the underclass in Israeli society, the poorer Sephardi Jews and others ignored for years by the Labor establishment. Ze'ev liked underdogs, and I did, too, though I considered the Palestinians more downtrodden than the Sephardim. After Ze'ev wrote a book, *Double Vision*, which suggested that American journalists were dupes of the PLO, we had another topic of dispute.

Despite our differences, Ze'ev served as my guide to the cultural demi-monde of Israel. Traveling down the mountain with him from Jerusalem to Tel Aviv, I became a regular at Bonanza, a bohemian bar a couple of blocks off the sea that served as a gathering spot for writers, artists, and musicians. Its kitchen was decidedly nonkosher. We hung out with Shai, the owner, Shaul, a humorous columnist for one of the Israeli tabloids, and a number of interesting women.

Moving among these friends, I navigated my way through a fractured society beset by the Palestinian question, political schisms between left and right, quarrels over religion's role, and ethnic mistrust between the older families from Europe and the newer immigrants from the Levant.

Ze'ev's own journey reflected the shifting patterns of the country. After Begin gave up his office, Ze'ev became disaffected with the Likud. He detested the ultrareligious parties that were part of the Likud's coalition, and he despised the young men in knit yarmulkes and black hats who used their religious status to escape military service mandatory for all others. He left his government job and took up writing full-time, and though Ze'ev would be loath to admit it, his politics moved to the left.

The only place Ze'ev would not go with me was to the American Colony Hotel in East Jerusalem, a favorite spot of Western journalists, diplomats, and Palestinian intellectuals. Earlier in the decade, while on temporary assignment to Jerusalem, I had stayed at the hotel for weeks and thought of the place as my second home.

To me, the American Colony represented an oasis, a sanctuary removed from the bustle and kitsch of West Jerusalem. The hotel had been a pasha's palace when the Ottoman Empire had ruled the Holy Land, and the old stone buildings were ornamented with marble, Armenian tile, Persian rugs, and inlaid ceilings. Its quiet courtyard, graced with citrus trees, a fountain, and bougainvillea, was my favorite spot in the world.

Right-wing Israelis called the hotel the PLO headquarters.

The owners, a British family named the Vesters, made no secret of their sympathy with the Palestinians. With the exception of a Swiss manager and chef, members of the hotel staff were all Palestinians. To many Israelis, a visit to the American Colony was a political statement, and they tended to avoid East Jerusalem altogether. For me, the trip crosstown, from my apartment in West Jerusalem to the American Colony, was reminiscent of visiting Aaron Henry at the Fourth Street Drug Store.

* * *

I tried to keep up with the Palestinian leaders in East Jerusalem and the territories. From time to time, I had lunch with Hanna Siniora, the editor of *Al Fajr*, a newspaper identified with Yasir Arafat's wing of the Palestinian movement, Al Fatah, or I drove to Jericho to see Saeb Erakat, an outspoken Palestinian who was in and out of house arrest. Two other Palestinians were also emerging as articulate voices: Faisal Husseini, who lived down the slope from the Mount of Olives, and Hanan Ashrawi, a professor at a West Bank university.

In the years since the 1967 war, the Palestinians had been demonized in American press reports as terrorists and child butchers masquerading in kaffiyehs. Over the years, Palestinian terrorists had contributed to the unfavorable impression by hijacking airliners, launching raids on Israeli villages, and most dramatically, carrying out a slaughter of Israeli athletes at the 1972 Olympics in Munich. With his perpetually unshaved face and rheumy eyes, Arafat looked the part of a villain. And it did not help that the Palestinians were often confused, in America, with Islamic fundamentalists creating havoc in Lebanon and waging their own war against Israel and the West.

Contrary to this image, I found the Palestinian leaders to be educated and well versed in Western values. They had the same commitment I had seen among American blacks in the civil rights movement. Carrying the parallel further, the Palestinian movement was splintered into many factions and afflicted with the same sort of personal and ideological disputes that split the civil rights crowd.

The PLO cause had seemed especially doomed and romantic in the autumn of 1983, when Arafat's forces had come under siege by renegade Palestinian militias and units of the Syrian army in Tripoli, a seaport in northern Lebanon where the PLO leader had been allowed to resettle after the Israeli invasion of Lebanon had driven him from Beirut the year before.

I had been in Beirut, covering the aftermath of the terrorist attack on the marines, when the trouble broke out in Tripoli. The conflict drew the attention of the group of journalists staying at the Commodore Hotel, and each dawn we commuted from Beirut to Tripoli, fifty miles away, in secondhand London taxis. Each evening we returned to Beirut to file our stories over the hotel telex.

I usually rode with my friend Don Schanche, a veteran correspondent for the *Los Angeles Times*. It was a strange, miniature war. The sky moaned with Katyushas and Grads, the Soviet-made rockets, and our driver often wept as we approached Tripoli. With the clatter of small-arms fire providing sound effects for a towering pall of black smoke billowing from burning oil tanks, the situation was "too hot," he said. Our driver longed to return to the peace of Beirut. His assessment seemed especially accurate when we passed an orange grove at the same moment Arafat's men fired a rack of Katyushas, the missiles screaming over our heads. Don and I allayed our own fears by washing down tablets of Valium—available over-the-counter in Beirut—with beer we brought from the hotel.

Bumping over cratered roads on our first day in Tripoli, we sought out Arafat, whom I knew only from press clippings. I expected to see a scruffy terrorist defending his last redoubt; instead, we encountered a charismatic leader, fastidious in an olive British field commander's cap and fatigues. Arafat was a study in determination throughout the battle in Tripoli and amenable to interviews. He also held daily press conferences to prove to the world that he was still alive.

One afternoon, Arafat arrived in the courtyard of a government building teeming with European paparazzi. His appearance created a mob scene. With the photographers jousting for position, Schanche, Herb Denton of the *Washington Post*, and I climbed on a ledge to escape the rugbylike scrum. Arafat saw our avenue of escape and joined us. In a wire service photograph I have treasured since that time, we formed an odd tableau.

Herb stood next to Arafat. As the press conference began, Herb told Arafat that the people of Tripoli were frightened and asked the PLO leader why he had pulled his troops from the front—a Palestinian refugee camp a few miles away—into the middle of the city, drawing fire on innocent civilians.

Arafat rolled his eyes. "Have you been authorized to speak for the people of Tripoli? Or are you a journalist?"

"I'm a journalist, of course," Denton said.

"Then you are not authorized to ask that question."

"Very well, I'll ask it as a journalist. Why have you retreated into the heart of a city, drawing fire on the people of Tripoli?"

"You are not authorized to ask this question."

Several other questions ensued. Then Herb asked Arafat again about his tactic.

Feigning indignation, Arafat looked at Denton and answered, "Don't be silly." He ended the press conference at that point, but the next day, when

Arafat spotted Herb, the PLO leader snorted, "Are you going to try to squeeze me again today?"

The PLO's defense of Tripoli was directed by Abu Jihad, Arafat's military commander. Like Arafat, Abu Jihad's reputation was that of a terrorist mastermind, a man responsible for murderous operations against the Israelis. In Tripoli, he seemed to be a polished, professional soldier rather than a mad dog, and his dedication to the Palestinian cause seemed to me heroic.

In the face of the ferocious attack by his erstwhile Arab allies, the Palestinian leader said he and his PLO men were prepared to "die hard" in Tripoli. Many of them did during the days that shells and rockets fell on the city. When the hospital morgues overflowed, refrigerated trucks were used to store the dead.

Eventually, international negotiators arranged a truce, and Arafat, Abu Jihad, and their fighters were able to leave Tripoli, scattering to different points in the Palestinian diaspora. Abu Jihad settled in Amman.

I saw him there a year later at his home, a large stone house guarded by Jordanian soldiers as well as Abu Jihad's men. The commander received guests in his living room, where the marble was softened by velvet sofas and rich Persian rugs. His wife, Intissar—known as Umm Jihad (Mother of the Struggle)—served coffee and Palestinian sweets before returning to the interior of the home, where I could hear the sounds of their children.

After learning that I lived in Al-Quds—the Arabic name for Jerusalem—Abu Jihad asked about events in "Palestine." Before his family was driven from the land, he said, he had lived as a boy in Ramleh, a village near Ben-Gurion Airport outside Tel Aviv. "Ah, my friend," Abu Jihad instructed me, "you must go to my home. The lemon trees I planted there as a child must be grown now. Go there and bring me a picture of it."

Though I visited Abu Jihad a number of times, I never attempted to find his old home in Ramleh, and he never really expected me to do so. Our exchange about the lemon trees was merely a diversionary aside. Conversations in the Arab world tended to take circular patterns, looping gradually toward the heart of the matter. Journalists called the extraneous patter "Middle East bullshit."

Abu Jihad was unfailingly polite. After we expended the first few minutes of our conversations in meaningless dialogue, the subject would eventually turn to the armed struggle against Israel. The Palestinian military initiatives often seemed like a doubtful enterprise. The PLO had lost face in the 1970s when their guerrilla attacks against Israeli civilians had drawn innocent blood and international condemnation. As a result, Abu Jihad had changed tactics. He made the Israeli military his target. The Israeli Defense Forces represented a legitimate enemy, he said, even though the decision pitted his raiding parties against a superior army.

By the early 1980s, he had begun to take the political consequences of PLO actions into account. During one of our conversations, he spoke critically of a terrorist operation. A band of guerrillas led by a PLO officer, Mohammed Abbas, had seized an Italian cruise ship, the *Achille Lauro*, and killed a Jewish tourist from New York while the captive vessel sailed aimlessly through the Mediterranean. The tactics were stupid and counterproductive, Abu Jihad said. He knew the Palestinian movement suffered from foolish tactics that fed its terrible image in the West.

On another visit, I asked Abu Jihad about a mysterious incident in the Mediterranean that had recently involved a ship named the *Ataviros*. According to accounts out of Cyprus, more than twenty Palestinian fighters had been killed when an Israeli gunboat sank the *Ataviros*. Without any hesitation, Abu Jihad confirmed the report and took responsibility for the deaths of the men. "This was my operation," he said with some pride. Gesturing with his hands, Abu Jihad outlined the mission's objective, a plan that sounded like a blueprint for disaster to me.

According to Abu Jihad, the commandos were to land on a beach below Tel Aviv, then move to a position on the coastal highway where they could hijack a bus. Using the Israeli bus as a Trojan horse, the PLO raiding party hoped to penetrate the city and attack the fortresslike Israeli defense ministry on the other side of Tel Aviv. Abu Jihad said the assault had been timed to humiliate Israel on the anniversary of its independence. "It failed," he said, "but another operation will take its place."

During one of his intermittent quarrels with Arafat, the Jordanian monarch, King Hussein, expelled Abu Jihad from Amman. I did not see him again. In the spring of 1988, Abu Jihad was murdered by an Israeli commando unit inside a compound where he had taken refuge in Tunis. The news did not shock me, but I felt he deserved more than an obituary highlighting his history as a terrorist. So I wrote a remembrance of him for the *Globe*'s Sunday magazine, describing his troubled pursuit of a Palestinian state. I closed by using an Arabic expression: "*Ma'assalame*, Abu Jihad. Farewell, and go in the peace you never knew in your lifetime."

The *Globe* was inundated with letters from the Jewish community in Boston. My reporting from the Middle East had never been popular, and I got lots of angry mail myself. More than a year after Abu Jihad's death, one of my critics wrote a letter to the *Globe*'s publisher, denouncing me as an anti-Semite and an associate of Abu Jihad—the man, my complainant charged, who had blown Pan Am 103 out of the skies over Scotland.

When the publisher passed the correspondence on to me, I replied with a letter of my own. I told my critic he had every right to disagree with me, but no right to call me anti-Semitic. As for Abu Jihad's role in the Pan Am bombing, that was hardly possible, I noted. He had been killed eight months before the Christmas sabotage of the Boeing 747.

During the ten years that I wrote, off and on, about the Middle East, the Israelis never once complained. Compared to the commentary in the Israeli press, my dispatches were tame. Freewheeling and democratic to a fault, Israel harbored almost as many newspapers as it did political parties in its noisy Knesset, and the voices were discordant.

Although the country was understandably sensitive about security matters—and attempted to impose censorship on stories dealing with military operations—I found Israeli officials invariably open and surprisingly accessible. Everyone in Israel had an opinion, and everyone talked. I tried to maintain a balance, seeking interviews with Likud leaders for each audience I had with Yitzhak Rabin, Shimon Peres, and other officers of the Labor Party.

Once I interviewed Ezer Weizman, at the time a Likud minister, in his spartanly furnished office, and noticed a picture of Jimmy Carter on the wall. Weizman had formed a bond with Carter at Camp David; he had even made an unauthorized trip to the United States to travel with Carter in an effort to give the president a boost during the 1980 campaign. Weizman waved at the photo. "I don't know why the American people didn't love this man," he said to me, a touch of annoyance in his voice.

If American politics represented a puzzle to Weizman, Israel remained something of a conundrum to me, too, though I worked to understand the place that I came to love and hate and love again as much as Mississippi. Over the years, I interviewed Jewish settlers on the West Bank as well as members of Peace Now; I talked with academics and diplomats, students and soldiers, rabbis and philosophers. Through my friends in Jerusalem, I got to know several literary figures and thought that one of them, the young writer David Grossman, best embodied the inner conflicts of Israel.

David looked as harmless as a botanist. He wore glasses and spoke so softly that at times it was difficult to hear him. But David was intense. As a sabra, a native son, he held strong allegiance to Israel, yet he was deeply troubled by his country's treatment of the Palestinians.

One night he talked at length about his misgivings over dinner at the American Colony—he had no problem going there. David seemed to be wrestling with the same sort of questions I had faced in Mississippi, but he confronted the dilemma more directly than I had. He hosted a morning show on Israeli national radio and regularly risked sanctions for publicly expressing his views. Once, interviewing Yitzhak Shamir, he asked the prime minister about "the price of occupation." David told me that Shamir's eyebrows jumped in shock; the Likud leader denied there was any occupation. Shamir insisted that Israel had a right of sovereignty over the West Bank and Gaza.

In the months before the *intifada* began, David was commissioned by a leftist Israeli magazine, *Koteret Rashit*, to travel through the West Bank and write about the mind of the Palestinians. David spoke Arabic fluently, and he conveyed the Palestinians' pain and wrath in an article that grew into a powerful book called *The Yellow Wind*.

He wrote about raids by Israeli soldiers on the homes of Palestinians suspected of insurrectionist activity, and he described the Israeli practice of demolishing the homes of suspects. He did not spare his country.

David also wrote of a conversation he had had with an old Arab named Abu Harb: "He asked me if I had heard about the yellow wind that would soon come, maybe even in his lifetime: the wind would come from the gate of hell . . . a hot and terrible east wind which comes once in a few generations, sets the world afire, and people seek shelter from its heat in the caves and caverns, but even there it finds those it seeks, those who have performed cruel and unjust deeds, and there, in the cracks in the boulders, it exterminates them, one by one. After that day, Abu Harb says, the land will be covered with bodies. The rocks will be white from the heat, and the mountains will crumble into a powder which will cover the land like yellow cotton."

I moved back to Boston as *The Yellow Wind* was being published in the United States. When I left the Middle East, I had no apocalyptic visions of upheaval. No doubt, the Palestinians were unhappy, but they seemed so broken that I saw few sparks of life.

A few weeks after I gave up my Jerusalem home, the first rocks were thrown in Gaza, a territory where I once had written, "The people have been beaten by circumstances into submission."

The *intifada* had begun. I would be called back to cover the conflict, off and on, over the next four years, but the Palestinians started their revolution without me.

CHAPTER 17

"We'd all love to see you again"

★ ★ ★ ★ ★

When the sun lights up Bulfinch's golden dome above the state-house, sailboats flit along the Charles River, and Pei's great glass tower on Copley Square mirrors the russet facade of Trinity Church, Boston looks incomparably beautiful. A swath of green covering the Common and the Public Garden softens the bustle of business downtown. Culture spills from the city's museums and symphony hall; it's the best of sports towns, too. With a strand of universities, Boston crackles with intellectual firepower. Tens of thousands of students give the place a youthful vibrancy, and high-technology outposts on the perimeter highway, Route 128, serve as New England's gateway to the twenty-first century. By almost any measure, Boston is one of the great cities in America.

I was a misfit there. Even though I had spent most of my career with the city's leading newspaper, I felt lost in Boston. Despite the best efforts of my friends and colleagues to integrate me into the local scene, I remained as much a stranger as the newest arrival off an Alitalia flight at Logan. For the first time in my life, I was homesick—and astonished to be missing Jerusalem.

As I tried to adjust to life back in the United States, Bostonians laughed at my accent. When I asked to buy ten subway tokens, the man in the booth sniggered, "Tay-yun! Is that how you say it in Tex-azz? Tay-yun!" When I opened my mouth in Boston, I became a cracker, a redneck, a frecklebelly, a country clod.

The cold made me miserable. Winters closed in shortly after Labor Day. Impatiens I planted hopefully in June, when frost finally let go of the soil, would be struck dead overnight, slumped in defeat by early September. More depressing than the snow and ice and numbing cold was the darkness. During the long winter, it seemed to fall over the city before lunch could be digested properly, gathering up New England in a curtain of gloom. Had my oldest son, Carter, finishing his studies at Boston College, not moved in with me, I might have bolted within months.

We lived around the corner from Holy Name Church, the parish where I had been berated during the busing controversy in 1975. It was a quiet, Irish-Catholic neighborhood, and I suspect that my vote for Michael Dukakis for president in 1988 may have been the only one our governor got on my block. Not many *Globes* were delivered on Bellaire Road either. My neighbors preferred the *Herald,* a conservative tabloid. I discovered the battle over busing had not been an aberration, that Boston had not yet realized John Winthrop's promise as "that great shining city on a hill." Centuries after the battle cries of patriots had rung from Faneuil Hall, the city remained deeply divided by race and class. And I felt gripped by spiritual coldness.

Melancholy, I would sometimes sit alone in the evening, listening over and over to a tape by the Irish group Moloney, O'Connell, and Keane performing "Kilkelly." The lyrics cite a sequence of letters over the years from a family in County Mayo to a son who has found work in America. Each verse ends with a plea for the son to come home. After the son's mother dies, the aging father writes:

> Thank you for sending your family picture
> They're lovely young women and men
> You say that you might even come for a visit
> What joy to see you again.

But the son never returns, and at the end he learns in a final letter that his father, too, has died.

> And it's funny how he kept talking about you
> He called for you at the end.
> Oh, why don't you think about your coming to visit
> We'd all love to see you again.

In the spring of 1990, I embarked on a trip that led me home. Patches of snow were worn gray with age when I left Boston, but flying into Atlanta, I could see the Southern countryside lit with a colorful profusion of azaleas and dogwood, and a familiar, humid warmth enveloped me as soon as I stepped off the plane.

Assigned to do a magazine piece on Jimmy Carter's work as former president, I planned to spend several days at the Carter Center in Atlanta. I had seen little of Carter since he left the White House, but knew that he and his wife, Rosalynn, spent much of their time working on behalf of the poor. Their labors on construction projects in American ghettos for Habitat for Humanity were well publicized; I was more interested in Carter's missions in Africa and Asia and his involvement in the Middle East peace process.

By this time, Carter was sixty-five, but looked younger than when he'd lost office ten years earlier. He still carried an air of certitude about him, but his political drive seemed to have been replaced with a mystic serenity. During the first couple of days in Atlanta, I tagged along with him to a luncheon and seminars at Emory University and was pleased when he introduced me as someone who knew almost as many people in Plains as he did. On my last day there, we sat down for a formal interview.

In my talks with Carter during his political years, he kept the conversation on point. This time, he drifted a bit. Not many months earlier, his brother, Billy, had died, a victim of pancreatic cancer, the same illness that had claimed all of the former president's other siblings. Some of the most indelible characters from that year in Plains were gone now: Billy, his sister Gloria, their mother, Miss Lillian. Carter appeared wistful talking about his family. When I asked about the Plains Baptist Church, Carter told me he now worshiped elsewhere. After the Clennon King fiasco, the Carter family and several others had formed a new church called Maranatha Baptist, where black worshipers were welcome. "We have a good congregation," he said.

He brought the interview back on subject by telling me that his mother's work as a nurse in rural Georgia had inspired him to invest the Carter Center resources into campaigns to eradicate guinea-worm disease and river blindness in Africa. He talked at length about his efforts to resolve a prolonged conflict in Ethiopia and to monitor elections elsewhere. It occurred to me that Jimmy Carter was one of the few prominent white Americans to show interest in the land mass we had been taught in school to call the Dark Continent.

I asked Carter about his relationship with Yasir Arafat. As president, he had been precluded by U.S. law from meeting with Arafat until the PLO recognized Israel and renounced terrorism. While he'd held office, he'd abided by the restriction, though it had always been clear Carter chafed at diplomatic protocol. Once he left government, Carter was free to meet with the PLO leader, and he had done so quietly on several occasions. Since Arafat was a principal figure in the Middle East, Carter said, it was obvious that no comprehensive peace could be reached in the region without him.

Carter dealt regularly with diplomatic pariahs around the globe. Relieved of official constraint, he seemed to enjoy circumventing State Department policies. Some of his freelance initiatives maddened Washington, and the Reagan administration had tried to undercut his efforts, Carter said. "They did everything they could to subvert what we attempted to do. I would go to a country, after making careful preparations and laboriously raising money, and arrive in the capital and find that all of my appointments had been canceled by the ambassador."

Still, he persisted in his efforts to build on the Mideast agreements he had negotiated at Camp David. His life seemed to be fulfilled. Instead of taking his 1980 defeat as an end to his career, Carter had accepted the political loss as humbling and moved on.

When we finished, I asked him to sign my copy of his book on the Middle East conflict, *The Blood of Abraham.* Afterward, when I looked at the inscription, I saw he had written, "Best wishes to Curtis Wilkie, an old friend."

After a long, adversarial relationship, I was flattered that he called me his friend, and I left Atlanta convinced I had misjudged him years ago.*

The next leg of my trip south took me to a reunion of journalism school graduates at the University of Mississippi—my first visit to my alma mater

---

*Eight years later, reading Douglas Brinkley's book, *The Unfinished Presidency,* I discovered that during the period I saw Carter in Atlanta the former president had been working at greater lengths than I realized to rehabilitate Arafat's image in the West. Secretly, Carter recommended negotiating positions for Arafat and went so far as to write passages for the PLO leader's speeches that were designed "to secure maximum sympathy" for the Palestinians. When I next saw Carter, we talked about Brinkley's book. I told him his commitment to unpopular causes and characters such as Arafat reminded me of Christ's work among prostitutes and criminals. "I thought the book made you out to be a kick-ass Jesus," I said. Carter startled me with a big laugh of approval.

in a decade. In the years since I'd moved from the state, I'd had little association with Ole Miss. My memory was jaundiced by the events of my senior year. I remembered Ole Miss as a place caught in time, the last stronghold of the old Confederacy. Instead of remembering strolls through the groves of academe, I had recollections of the acrid smell of burning cars and tear gas. Nearly thirty years had passed, but I was still resentful. With a few notable exceptions, the university's administration and faculty had been too meek to stand up to the politicians in 1962, and I felt estranged from the campus where I had first lived as a child and later as a student.

For the visit to Mississippi, all three of my children flew to join me, and their presence improved my disposition considerably. Visiting the campus, I realized the school was making a good-faith effort to change. The job obviously could not be done overnight; it might take decades, but Ole Miss finally seemed to be looking to the future rather than the past. Judging from the student newspaper, the bulletin-board notices, and the modern curriculum, the place had become relatively hip. Clusters of black students walked through the Grove, a setting of magnolias and oaks where Confederate soldiers and the irregular troops of the twentieth-century rebellion had once mustered. The journalism school, which had occupied classrooms in temporary World War II huts when I'd enrolled there, had grown dramatically, moving into a prime location overlooking the Grove. I was delighted to see that Jere Hoar, the professor who had flunked me in feature writing, was still around, giving a new generation of students an appreciation for writing and deadlines. Though I had feared him in the classroom, I now considered Jere an old friend.

I took part in a panel discussion with two other alumni, Rudy Abramson of the *Los Angeles Times* and Dan Goodgame of *Time* magazine. We were planning to harass the fourth member of the panel, our friend Larry Speakes, class of '61, for serving as a mouthpiece for the Reagan administration. But Speakes was a no-show. He was drawing heavy flak for his book *Speaking Out*, in which he acknowledged fabricating statements attributed to Reagan when Speakes served as White House spokesman. We supposed he stayed away to dodge further criticism. There was a certain irony to Larry's absence. A few years earlier, he might have found asylum at Ole Miss, but the school was no longer part of the "closed society."

A highlight of the weekend was a Saturday dinner, climaxed by an auction of memorabilia to raise money for the journalism school. I contributed an original cartoon by the *Globe*'s Paul Szep featuring Billy Carter. It had hung on my wall for years, but since Billy's death, I found it too depressing to look at. As the auction proceeded, I won the bidding for copies of the Memphis newspapers on the day Elvis died. But the item I really wanted was a photograph of Faulkner on horseback, taken by my classmate Ed Meek. The competition narrowed to two bidders, myself and a stout conservative I had never met. When I raised his second bid, he countered with a higher figure and shouted, "We can't let this Yankee take Mr. Bill above the Mason-Dixon Line."

Jesus, I thought, I stand guilty of many things, but I deny categorically that I am a Yankee. In the end, I won the bidding and packed Mr. Bill for New England. I would put him up against Hawthorne and Melville any day.

Our visit to Oxford was also the occasion for a small family reunion. My children and I visited my stepgrandmother, the old lady we called O, at a nursing home. She was nearing one hundred, still lucid and unreconstructed. She referred to her maid as Nigger Nancy to differentiate her from other Nancys she knew. Though O used the term without malice, we groaned and insisted that she stop using the word. But O was too old to change; she was our family's last link to the nineteenth century and still steeped in its customs. My son Carter, collecting oral history on a tape recorder, prompted her to tell stories of the early days in Oxford. O was not reticent. She talked in a rush—as if she knew her time was expiring—and a strand of saliva fell from her mouth. "Good Lord," she said apologetically. "I'm slobberin' like a mad dog."

Before we left Oxford, the rest of my relatives drove over from Tupelo, where they now lived. They represented the remainder of my mother's tribe: my uncle, Scott Black, looking healthy in retirement, and his two sons—my cousins Bob and Scott Jr.—and their wives and children. Three generations filled a long restaurant table as we chattered and gorged ourselves on fried chicken and mashed potatoes. It reminded me of the Thanksgiving dinners at our grandparents' home down the street when my cousins and I had been children. Afterward, we posed for group pictures with the Oxford square as the backdrop. Aside from my immediate family, these were my closest living kin, and their welcome of a relative who had rejected Mississippi touched me more than I believe they knew.

* * *

To complete our journey, my children and I rose early the next day to drive 250 miles farther south, to Summit. When we arrived at the manse, in time for Sunday lunch, the house was empty. A note pinned to the door fluttered like a small storm-warning flag. Pa had become ill a few hours earlier. My mother instructed us to meet her at the hospital.

Southwest Mississippi Regional Medical Center is a big, modern institution with an impressive staff of professionals, nothing like the drab infirmaries that had served the area during my childhood. I was not worried. Pa would get excellent treatment. When we found him in the intensive care wing, with my mother at his bedside, the sight of his grandchildren seemed to lift his spirits. Though his health had been sliding, he had rallied from earlier surgeries and seizures, and I assumed Pa would recover. But a few minutes later, in a private conversation with his physician, I learned Pa was unlikely to come home again.

I was grateful that at least we were all there. Two days later, Mother and I went to see Pa before breakfast. He was unable to talk. He pointed at his head, then at his heart, then at Mother. Three words: *I love you.* She held his hand, and after a while he simply seemed to go to sleep. When I looked at the monitor for his heart, the electronic line on the screen had gone flat. He was eighty-four.

My mother did not cry. She kissed him and told him she would be joining him soon. She would be eighty in a couple of weeks, and she seemed dazed. On that morning, the first day of May 1990, the indomitable will of my mother had been broken, too.

As we prepared for Pa's funeral, the little town responded with affection. Summit had been the only place where Pa had felt at home. He had come there as a stranger, a quiet man with the quaint manners of someone who had been raised a missionary's son in China, yet Summit had embraced him as if he were locally grown.

Over the years, I had learned some of the details of his isolated youth. When he was a teenager, Pa had been sent to a military school in Chattanooga; his parents had stayed behind in China. His adjustment to life in the United States had been hard. Outfitted in hand-me-down clothes—out-of-fashion knickers and jackets from parcels American Presbyterians shipped to their missionary families overseas—he looked foreign. Though Pa never claimed to have been lonely, I suspected he had few friends in school. His own father had been a Sigma Chi; Pa told me the fraternity did not offer him a bid at Washington and Lee. When he was twenty, working at a summer job at an amusement park in Massachusetts, he had received a telegram informing him that his mother had died in China. By the time he got the news, she had already been buried in that distant land. He asked for the afternoon off, he told me, and sat quietly by a lake to mourn.

In his own father's 1954 memoirs, *Fifty Years in China*, Ambassador Stuart wrote of his son: "Everything about his personality, to say nothing about my own prejudices, seemed to point toward his remaining in the South. He had imbibed from association with me and his Peking environment a somewhat broader outlook than if he had grown up under typical Southern conditions, and had learned to do his own thinking. . . . The result is that he appreciates truth on each side of the argument and puts the emphasis, where it belongs, on preaching to meet popular needs and on pastoral service. . . . Wisely, I think, in view of his own special qualifications and of changed conditions in China, my boy decided to work in the home country. . . . In him much that I once thought of for myself has been continued, first in Virginia and now in a church of the 'deep South' at Summit, Mississippi."

At one point in his career, my stepfather felt he had overstayed his welcome in Summit and took another pastorate in Mississippi. But two years later, in a rare move, the Summit congregation asked Pa to return. He accepted the call immediately. I was in college at the time, and I never saw Pa and Mother more joyful than the autumn they returned to Summit. It was there that Pa found the acceptance he had not known anywhere else, and on the day he was buried in the Summit cemetery, I thanked the townspeople for making the last half of his life happy.

Before returning to Boston, I reflected on my trip to the South. I had lost the man who had become my father, but in the span of a couple of weeks I had reconnected with several symbols from my past: the former president from the South, Ole Miss, my Mississippi family, and my old hometown.

My mother never recovered. Three months after Pa's death, she suffered the first of several strokes that disabled her. She bobbed in and out of consciousness, sometimes recognizing me as a little boy. "They call you Rabbit in school," she remembered, using a nickname I had not heard in forty years. Several times, she spoke of a "great explosion" that would soon take place. "Watch out," she warned. One of the last coherent messages she delivered to me was "Please, Son, don't put me in a nursing home."

From the hospital, I brought her back to the manse, to lie in as much comfort as possible in her own bed. For several years, she and Pa had been helped during the day by Lora Martin, an imposing woman who watched over them diligently. To care for Mother around-the-clock, I asked Lora if she could recruit a team of her friends to work at the house.

White Southerners have invariably turned to our black neighbors in times of need. The arrangement is as old as the South. Through two centuries, we denied black people their rights and standing, yet we entrusted them with the caring for our helpless, whether a newborn infant or an aging parent. Invariably, they responded to our appeals and devoted themselves to the task. In many instances, their loyalty created a bond almost as strong as shared blood.

Lora effectively moved into our house in Summit, ministering to my mother with cups of broth and words of encouragement. Lora supervised shifts of two or three other women to ensure that Mother did not suffer. In the Southern tradition, this black woman became part of our family.

I returned as often as possible, flying into New Orleans and renting a car for the short drive to Summit. My problems finding a hotel room in New Orleans planted a seed in my mind: why not buy a small place in the French Quarter, a pied-à-terre that would not only guarantee lodging, but put my toe back in Dixie? I had loved New Orleans from the time I was in elementary school, when Mother and I would board an early-morning train for day trips to the city. Though I disliked the shopping tour through Canal Street's famous department stores, Maison Blanche and D. H. Holmes, Mother would reward my patience with lunch at Galatoire's, a lovely French Quarter restaurant. Afterward, she would take me to the Saenger Theatre for a matinee before we'd catch a late-afternoon train back to Mississippi.

I knew New Orleans as well as any other Southern city. As a college student, I'd haunted the French Quarter, imagining myself a bohemian at large in the atmosphere that had inspired Faulkner and Tennessee Williams. I had used La Casa, a rowdy Latin bar on Decatur Street, as the setting for a sophomoric short story for my creative writing class and had enjoyed leading Ole Miss classmates to out-of-the-way neighborhood taverns when we'd visit the city on weekends. One Saturday morning we had become so caught up in the music and pageantry of a jazz funeral that we nearly missed the afternoon train to Baton Rouge for a night game with LSU.

Even though I had never lived there, I felt an attachment to New Orleans. Its culture is as exotic as Venice's; the city lies below sea level, flanked by a giant lake and the Gulf of Mexico and wrapped by the great river. Despite its French heritage, the heart of New Orleans beats in time with Port-au-Prince, not Paris. Voodoo rites and jazz funerals are common-place practices, and the basic cuisine is Creole. Though "The Big Easy" came into vogue a few years ago, I knew New Orleans by its earlier slogan: "The City That Care Forgot."

There is a Lorrie Moore short story in which two characters take a trip south, stop at a Civil War museum in Vicksburg, and learn that after its fall on July 4, 1863, the city refused to celebrate Independence Day again until 1971. "I like a place with a strong sense of grudge," one traveler says to the other. "But let's get on to New Orleans. I also like a place that doesn't give a shit."

New Orleans was not afflicted with a Civil War complex. The city sur-rendered at the first sight of Union troops and endured a federal occupation with the same insouciance that marked life under French and Spanish rule in the eighteenth century. The only resistance was led by women, who hired artists to paint a likeness of the Union commander, General Benjamin Butler of Massachusetts, at the bottom of their chamber pots. Each morning, the matrons of New Orleans would dump the contents of the pots from their balconies onto the heads of Yankee soldiers below. Butler was provoked to issue Order No. 28: "Any women (calling themselves ladies) who by word, gesture or movement, insult or show contempt for any officer of the United States, shall be regarded as a woman of the town plying her trade." The city responded by giving the general a nickname: "Beast" Butler.

At its core, New Orleans is as soft and seductive as a tropical holiday. New Orleanians will use any excuse for a party or a parade. Beginning with the Sugar Bowl at New Year's, the New Orleans calendar reels off two weeks of Mardi Gras celebrations, St. Patrick's Day, St. Joseph's Day, the French Quarter Festival, and the Jazz & Heritage Festival, before pausing for a breath in early spring.

When the Republican Party held its national convention in New Orleans in 1988, the *Globe* asked me to write a piece about the city. Each newspaper article must be given a word for identification in the computer; I slugged my story on New Orleans "lovesong."

* * *

Instead of finding a place in the French Quarter, I wound up wandering New Hampshire in 1991 during the early stages of the next presidential campaign. I liked traveling with Paul Tsongas, a former senator from Massachusetts who had given up his seat after learning he had cancer. He seemed to have beaten back the illness,* emboldening Tsongas to defy a losing precedent set by Dukakis, another Greek-American from Massachusetts who had run for president. Tsongas relied on a pro-business theme. When he talked of economics, he did not elicit a great deal of excitement, but I discovered he had a wry sense of humor. When I asked him what accounted for his rise in public-opinion polls, he had a quick answer: "My charisma."

I was also interested in another candidate challenging an unfortunate precedent set by Jimmy Carter. After Carter had lost the presidency, I remembered hearing Dale Bumpers, an Arkansas senator, say it would not be easy for another Southerner to succeed in national politics in the foreseeable future. Nevertheless, I thought the governor of Arkansas, Bill Clinton, had an excellent shot to win the Democratic nomination and an outside chance of toppling President Bush. From a distance, I had seen Clinton's political skills and been impressed with his intellect. Other than for a two-year interval between his defeat in 1980 and his victory to reclaim the office in 1982, Clinton had served as governor of Arkansas since 1979 and had matured into a preeminent Southern statesman.

Even more than the prototype "New South" governors of the early 1970s, Clinton represented a departure from the likes of Faubus and Barnett. Educated at Georgetown and Yale Law School, a Rhodes scholar as well, Clinton had an awesome mind. No one laughed at his accent. Physically imposing, with his height, bulk, and enormous hands, Clinton towered over other men and dominated any room he entered. He devoured books, loved conversation, and seemed utterly charming. His only political problem was widespread stories of his lust, but I figured he could control those urges.

My oldest son was interested in working for a candidate. Four years earlier, Carter Wilkie had dropped out of Boston College to join Senator Joe Biden's presidential campaign a few weeks before it went belly-up. Carter lost a semester, but it did not dampen his interest in politics. I suggested

*Tsongas died a few years later.

that he look at Clinton. At the time, Carter was working at the Kennedy School of Government at Harvard, so when Clinton made an appearance there in late October, we both attended the event.*

After Clinton's speech, students and faculty members pelted the candidate with questions that ranged from budget-balancing procedures to crises in places like East Timor. The candidate was dazzling; he responded knowledgeably on every subject. In an article for the next day's *Globe*, I wrote:

"Gov. Bill Clinton prepped for the first presidential debate of the season in New Hampshire by fielding, without obvious error, tough and sometimes technical questions from a Harvard University audience last night."

When I encountered Clinton the next day in New Hampshire, he asked me, only half-joking, "What do you mean 'without obvious error'?"

"Hell, Governor, you sounded good," I said. "But for all I know, you might have screwed up. I needed to cover my own ass."

The afternoon of the debate in New Hampshire, I got a call from the *Globe*'s national desk. Would I mind breaking off from the presidential campaign for a couple of weeks to go to Louisiana to cover the runoff in the contest for governor between Edwin Edwards and David Duke? The switch in assignments might have sounded to them like a step down, but I headed south before they could reconsider.

Growing up on the edge of Louisiana, listening to New Orleans radio stations and reading the *Times-Picayune*, I knew something about the state's strange politics. Compared to the Manichaean struggle in Missis-

---

*Carter Wilkie was so impressed he joined the Clinton campaign. After starting as a low-level aide in New Hampshire, he advanced to more important positions in the primaries that followed. In Jack Germond and Jules Witcover's book on the campaign, *Mad As Hell*, Carter is credited with helping to conceive the idea of the cross-country bus trips by Clinton. At the time of the Ohio primary, the authors wrote, Carter "was intrigued by the cultural roots that had buried themselves into the soil of Appalachia through West Virginia, Ohio, Kentucky, and Indiana—economic populism and social traditionalism—and thought he saw a kinship with Clinton's own roots and agenda." He proposed a tour by Clinton to "tell his life story, connect with ordinary Americans, and begin to define himself as a Democrat in touch with traditional, middle American values." The Arkansas governor did not take up the recommendation until after the convention, but when he and his running mate, Al Gore, embarked on a series of bus trips, the maneuver helped propel the Democrats to victory. By that time, Carter was working in the Little Rock headquarters, preparing the overnight briefing book for the candidates to study each morning. After the election, my son spent two years in the White House as a speechwriter.

sippi, Louisiana conducted its elections with the gusto of Mardi Gras. Years after his assassination in the hallway of the state capitol in Baton Rouge, Huey P. Long remained a legend, and he had been followed by an array of colorful characters in my lifetime, ranging from the "singing cowboy," Jimmy Davis, to the Kingfish's raffish brother, Earl Long.

In *The Earl of Louisiana*, perhaps the best political book I ever read, A. J. Liebling wrote:

"Louisiana politics is of an intensity and complexity that are matched, in my experience, only in the republic of Lebanon. . . . The grand gimmick of Louisiana politics, providing it with a central mechanism as fascinating as a roulette wheel, is the double primary system for gubernatorial nominations. The first primary is open to anyone who can get up the registration fee. . . . This brings out as many entries as the Preakness or the Kentucky Derby. If any candidate has more than 50 percent of the total votes, he wins the nomination. . . . If no one has a clear majority, the two top men have a runoff in a second primary held about a month later. It is unusual for a candidate to win first time around, and if one does he arouses a certain amount of resentment as a spoilsport."

In 1991, the Louisiana system had produced a runoff between Edwards, a notorious three-term governor who had twice escaped conviction for racketeering in highly publicized trials,* and Duke, a onetime wizard in the Ku Klux Klan who had written sympathetically of the Nazis. For a journalist, it was a contest too good to be true.

The Edwards campaign mobilized support with a bumper sticker carrying a unique message: "Vote for the Crook. It's Important." With his debonair manners, eye for young women, and a penchant for high-stakes poker games, Edwards epitomized the Southern rogue politician. He could not resist playful wisecracks, such as the line that both he and Duke were "wizards under the sheets."

His opponent looked like a poster boy for the Aryan race. Duke was fair and blond, and according to rumor his face had been fine-tuned by plastic surgery. The candidate was too clever to shout, "Nigger!" But his rallies contained all of the ugly, frustrated emotions of a Klan meeting, sans sheets.

By the time I got to Louisiana, Duke was under furious attack by the

---

*Edwards was finally convicted in 2000 on racketeering charges in connection with the award of casino licenses in Louisiana.

state's biggest newspaper, the *Times-Picayune*. As Tyler Bridges, one of their reporters covering the candidate, wrote later in his book *The Rise of David Duke*:

"The paper's editors met and decided that they would not treat this as a conventional gubernatorial election. Duke was an extraordinary candidate in American history—no other neo-Nazi had come close to being elected governor of a state—and the situation demanded an extraordinary journalistic response. The paper's editors decided they would launch a no-holds-barred assault against Duke, with hard-hitting news stories and slashing editorial columns."

A *Times-Picayune* editorial set the tone: "The limelight of the world is on our state, and we are not a pretty sight to behold—by many measures last or near bottom in education, literacy and living standards. And now we have a first: elevating an extremist of the caliber of Mr. Duke to direct contention for the governorship." One day, the newspaper carried five front-page stories dumping on Duke on a variety of subjects.

The campaign played out on racial as well as religious lines. Nearly 30 percent of the voters in Louisiana were black and needed little prompting to reject Duke. But the state is divided by a denominational fault line: south Louisiana is predominantly Catholic; the parishes north of Baton Rouge are as heavily Protestant as most Mississippi counties. In the closing days, the race between Edwards and Duke turned into a peculiar holy war.

To paint his opponent as a pagan, the Duke campaign circulated leaflets with a picture of Edwards, his arms outstretched in a crucifixion pose. Duke said Edwards had been "mocking Christ." In fact, Edwards had been performing a skit at a press club dinner to complain about negative stories. At the dinner, Edwards had smeared ketchup across his chest to emphasize the wounds. When Edwards learned of the charge by Duke, he tried to turn the argument. "If those skinheads knew anything about the Bible, they'd know Jesus was not stabbed in the chest," the former governor said.

Duke, meanwhile, stumbled over his own religious credentials. He said he attended the "Evangelical Baptist Church." Investigation showed the church didn't exist—or if it did, it housed an all-black congregation.

Mencken and Liebling would have loved this campaign.

I followed Duke to the heart of conservative, Baptist country in Monroe, where an auditorium was so jammed with his supporters that hundreds stood outside, whooping in the darkness. Later, he infiltrated Edwards's Cajun parishes with an appearance at a Lafayette racetrack that drew thousands more. A few days before the election, Duke held a frenzied rally in an auction barn in the woods of Livingston Parish, not too far from Pike County, Mississippi.

The audience needed little conversion, but Duke produced a man identified as a Lutheran minister without portfolio to buttress Duke's claim to be a born-again Christian. The reverend wore a wig that resembled a pecan pie, and he assured the assembly that their candidate was a friend of Jesus'. Hundreds of Duke's followers, who came in pickups and old Jeeps, lit matches or held flaming cigarette lighters aloft to demonstrate their belief in Duke. I thought the idiots were going to burn the place down and envisioned a *Globe* headline over my obituary: "Reporter Immolated Along with 500 Louisiana Kluxers."

By the closing days, however, it was clear that Edwards would win decisively, and I relaxed with friends in New Orleans. We had drinks at the Napoleon House, dinners at Galatoire's, and tried out a spiffy new place in the warehouse district called Emeril's. It was a week before Thanksgiving and the weather was glorious in the city that care forgot. I could feel New Orleans pulling with gravitational force.

CHAPTER 18

"A beautiful, fantastic experience"

★ ★ ★ ★ ★

I n the winter after Bill Clinton's inauguration, so much snow cascaded across New England that it seemed a protest against another Southern president.

I called the Realtor who had patiently showed me places in New Orleans, assured him I was really serious this time, and expressed a desire for a sunny balcony in the French Quarter. He described an old building being converted into condos near the river, on Governor Nicholls Street. I flew down that weekend and found the apartment better than I'd expected. It had bright skylights, two bedrooms, two baths, and a loft where I could write. Best of all, the third-floor balcony enjoyed all-day sun; the spire of St. Louis Cathedral and the buildings of the Vieux Carré lay in the foreground, the skyline of downtown New Orleans loomed in the distance. I bought it within twenty-four hours.

There was an intangible consideration to the purchase. After an absence of nearly a quarter century, I was taking back a tiny piece of my homeland. Though I felt the investment daring, there was nothing novel about it at all. I was merely one of thousands being lured back to the region. While I had grown into middle age as an expatriate, the South had been bursting out of its old traces. I had failed to notice it evolving into a showplace for commerce, recreation, and investment opportunities.

Remembering the South as isolated and rural, I was stunned to learn that the region now claimed one-third of the population of the United States. People were pouring into the sunshine spots of Florida and Texas, as well as such off-the-beaten-track places as Hattiesburg, Mississippi, and

Aiken, South Carolina, which had become retirement retreats. The complexion of the South was being changed by an influx of new citizens with Hispanic or Asian backgrounds, but more significantly, blacks were coming home. One survey found that at the end of the twentieth century, a steady migration of blacks, amounting to about one hundred thousand people a year, was taking place.

"Some black in-migrants move to the South to retire, some to care for elderly parents, and many simply to return to the region they call home," noted the North Carolina research organization MDC. According to the report, most of the new black residents "are of working age and have moved south for the jobs the region offers."

In my case, I rediscovered a place that fit me as comfortably as the proverbial old shoe. There is something about our accent, mocked in Boston as a bumpkin's twang, that seems lilting with hospitality. My voice no longer betrayed me. If I stopped at an Alabama gas station for directions, I was assured of a friendly reception. It reminded me of the joke about the Mississippian lost in Manhattan. After several failed attempts to find help, the tourist made one last effort. Approaching a cabdriver stuck in midtown traffic, the visitor asked, "Excuse me, sir, could you tell me how to get to the Empire State Building? Or should I just go fuck myself?"

I flew to New Orleans on many weekends and drove to see my mother. She lay in a pitiful state, in Alzheimer's condition. Mute, she could no longer feed or care for herself. She stared at me as though I were alien. Outside her window, dozens of mockingbirds, cardinals, and jays—descendants of the birds she had fed for years—fluttered and chirped, but Mother gave no sign of hearing them.

The backyard, where I had toiled over a 4-H Club garden and played pitch and catch, needed work. Ragged leaves fell from two pecan trees that no longer produced. Our pomegranate tree had died, and the camellia and azalea bushes begged to be pruned. Poking around the grounds, I was overwhelmed with nostalgia. The smell of burning leaves down the street brought back pleasant associations of long-ago autumns: the taste of fresh-cut sugarcane chewed to pulp, the Friday-night high school football games when the air bore the first hints of frost.

Like much of the South, Summit had changed—and yet it had not changed. Physically, Robb Street still resembled the place where I had walked as a child. With a couple of exceptions, the names on the storefronts were different, but the buildings still contained the ghosts of Joe Schluter, the hardware merchant, and Jasper "Jap" Fortenberry, the barber.

The office of the *Summit Sun* was deserted. The Fox Theater had been razed, replaced on the block by a new bank. There was no trace of our old school. After the Summit district was consolidated into the larger McComb system, the classrooms where I had spent ten years were leveled, the ruin as complete as Carthage's.

The town had not atrophied; it had merely endured a transplant. My generation had been replaced by new people, moving to the area to take jobs in McComb and buying homes in Summit, where dozens of Victorian residences, neglected for years, waited to be refurbished. The houses I had thought of as old-fashioned when I was a child had been rehabilitated into handsome mansions. It had never before occurred to me that Summit was a pretty little place.

Virtually all my classmates were gone, living in the Southern capitals of Jackson, Little Rock, and Nashville, or in new boomtowns in North Carolina and Florida. My old acquaintances were limited. Walking about town, I stopped at Barnes Furniture to chat with Lew's widow, Janet, now a grandmother and manager of the store, or had coffee with my mother's best friend, Ottomece, still spry in her eighties. I often had dinner with one of my few contemporaries left, William Watkins, an oilman, and his wife, Lynne. We spent much of the time reminiscing.

On some trips, I pushed on to Jackson, seventy-five miles north, to visit my "gang of six"—three couples, my friends since Ole Miss days. While I had bumped from one locale to another, through various romantic interludes, they represented stability to me: Bettye and Grady Jolly, Meredith and Jimmy Creekmore, and Pat and Butch Cothren. All of them were successful, yet none had an ounce of pretension. Grady, the Fifth Circuit judge, enlivened our dinner conversations with outrageous observations; Jimmy had a quiet sense of humor, and Butch, a trial lawyer, still used his childhood nickname.

Butch and I had been friends since we had held down the left side of the infield—not too effectively—for the McComb Manufacturing Tigers in Little League. We had gone on to Ole Miss, been groomsmen in each other's wedding, and when we got together, we reverted to Pike County backwards talk. Speaking of an acquaintance with an unsavory reputation, Butch might describe him as "one of the finest, upstanding men I have ever known."

In the fall of 1993, Butch and Pat proposed that I go with them to an Ole Miss football game. I had missed SEC football. In Washington, the Redskins were the only game in town, and in the six states of New England, only Boston College played a big-time schedule. Throughout my long exile, I had never forgotten the autumn Saturdays in the South, when football was king.

When we arrived on campus a few hours before the kickoff, I was staggered by the sight. Tens of thousands of people were already spread through the Grove, as far as I could see. From the University Avenue entrance, where Ross Barnett had intercepted James Meredith, past the Lyceum building, where the federal marshals were held under siege, people gathered around picnic tables loaded with fancy food and drink. In the years I had been away, the pregame festivities at Ole Miss had turned into a great happening. In the flow of the meandering crowd I ran into dozens of old friends I had not seen in decades. For good measure, Ole Miss roughed up a strong Georgia team.

Returning to Boston the next week, I made a proposal to the *Globe* editor Matt Storin. Since I was a national reporter, traveling the country rather than writing about New England, it shouldn't matter where I slept. Why not let me live in New Orleans, at least for the winter? I would come back in the spring, I promised, when the weather moderated and the Red Sox season started. Matt thought it a good idea. My presence in the South would give the newspaper a dimension it had not had before, he said.

When I set out by train for New Orleans with a couple of seabags full of clothing, I had every intention of returning to Boston. I left my car behind, kept my house in West Roxbury, and maintained my account at the Bank of Boston. Before leaving, I cast an absentee vote for the man who would become the city's new mayor, my friend Tom Menino. But within a few weeks, I knew I would never go back. The warm days wrapped themselves around me like a lover's arms. When my children visited on Thanksgiving, we dined on my balcony with the clop of mule-drawn French Quarter carriages ringing below.

The news stories were interesting, too. I wrote about the economic renaissance in Charlotte, North Carolina, a city transformed from a sleepy marketplace into a financial fortress guarded by skyscrapers. Charlotte's banks were challenging Atlanta's for regional supremacy, and the National Football League had just recognized the area's growth by awarding Charlotte one of its hotly contested franchises. To dramatize the Southeast's vitality, Jacksonville got the other new team in the NFL.

While I was in Charlotte, I had dinner with my old *Mississippi Freelance* pals and their wives. Ed Williams was now editorial-page editor of the *Charlotte Observer*; Lew Powell wrote a column. They were as smart-assed as ever. Both Ed and Lew had tweaked me, in the years since I'd left Mississippi, for my old declaration that I intended to spend the rest of my life within the Boston-Washington corridor. Now that I had come back, I was at their mercy.

A few weeks later, I encountered another economic miracle—in Tunica County, Mississippi, once the poorest spot in the nation. A classmate from Ole Miss, Billy Wood, now president of the Planters Bank in Tunica, served as my guide. As we drove over the levee, we were greeted by a dazzling concentration of neon and glitter rising out of the Mississippi River backwater like castles from Oz. Casinos had come to Tunica, bringing thousands of gamblers to the remote location. In 1960, the average citizen of Tunica had four years of schooling, the median family income was $1,260 a year, and unemployment rates were well into double digits. Now anyone who wanted work in Tunica had a job. When I'd lived down the road in Clarksdale in the 1960s, Tunica had one lonely motel on old Highway 61; by the end of the century, the county would have several thousand hotel rooms.

I found prosperity in Oxford, too. In my absence, the rural county seat that had been my mother's home had grown into one of the most attractive college towns in the country. Fashionable boutiques had sprung up on the courthouse square, and grungy cafés had given way to trendy restaurants and bars. Oxford had finally legalized liquor. There had been no bookstore in Faulkner's hometown when I went to Ole Miss, but in the interim Blaylock's Drug Store had been converted into Square Books, with a friendly, knowledgeable staff and a stock to rival bookstores in Boston.

Evidence of a "New South"—a term I never liked—was everywhere, but the old, conflicted South still existed. It was impossible to cover the region without dealing with race. One of my first assignments had given me a seat at the Beckwith trial. Soon I was dealing with other cases that reminded me of the 1960s. But I found a characteristic that had been missing in my days at the *Clarksdale Press Register*: a desire for reconciliation.

In an incident near my hometown, three young white men had burned down two rural black churches, thirty years after Pike County had been branded the "church-burning capital of the world." This time, however, the vandals did not get off with a reprimand from the judge, as had the Klansmen who were caught in 1964. These men were sent to prison, and members of several white congregations volunteered to help rebuild the churches. My friend David Feldman, an antiques dealer in Summit, worked on the project. When construction at the Spring Hill Freewill Baptist Church was finished, a consecration service was held there. "I helped lead a biracial choir," David told me. "It was a beautiful, fantastic experience, one of the highlights of my life."

The *Globe* liked my reports. Matt Storin asked me to write a regular piece on Southern idiosyncrasies that would appear each Monday under a standing headline. When he asked about a name for the weekly report, I suggested "In Dixie." Matt felt "On Dixie" more appropriate; it matched other *Globe* musings such as Peter Gammons's "On Baseball" and Marty Nolan's "On Boston." So "On Dixie" it would be. When I filed my first piece, Matt was out of town, and two midlevel editors objected to the word *Dixie*. I explained that *Dixie* was not a racist term. Although its origins were unclear, I understood the word derived from the period when the French had controlled the Deep South and the ten-franc *dix* note was used as currency. Travelers from the region, making their way upriver bearing *dix* notes, became known as Dixies, according to the version I had heard. At any rate, I said, *Dixie* was a legitimate synonym for the South. Today we drink Dixie Beer, sometimes out of Dixie Cups. In the New Orleans telephone directory, two columns are filled with businesses bearing names from Dixie Alarm Systems to Dixieland Tours & Cruises.*

No matter. The desk editors in Boston insisted the word was offensive. My piece did not run. But a few days later, Matt returned and "On Dixie" made its appearance in the *Globe*. I had a lot of fun with the space. I wrote about our various pests: armadillo, nutria, Formosan termites, and kudzu. I

---

*Cheryl Thurber, who wrote her doctoral dissertation on *Dixie* at the University of Mississippi in 1993, believes the *dix*-note version was promoted by a New Orleans bank when Dixieland jazz swept the country early in the twentieth century. She is convinced the word was actually popularized by the song "Dixie," written by Daniel D. Emmett, a minstrel impresario, in the year before the Civil War. In this case, Dixie was the name of a benevolent plantation owner who had sold the old home place and left behind his slaves, who longed to be back in his hands rather than owned by a cruel new master. The song became known all over America and the lyrics were altered over the years, but it was never intended to be racist, Thurber said. "It's had a bad association with the rebel flag," she told me. "It's become guilt by association."

gathered recipes for pecan pie and crawfish étouffée and wrote about Friday lunch at Galatoire's, where New Orleanians stay until dinnertime, drinking their way through boisterous afternoons.

When the *Globe* asked for an "O. Henry–type story" for Christmas, I rose before dawn to interview the people paid $200 by members of the Galatoire's lunch crowd to hold a place in line overnight. Tradition-bound Galatoire's does not accept reservations, so to get tables on the special Fridays before Christmas and Mardi Gras, regular customers hire stand-ins the day before and take over their places shortly before the restaurant opens. I asked the men and women, gathered in the darkness on the sidewalk on Bourbon Street, what they planned do with their money. One intended to buy his son a bike; another said he would get a case of whiskey for himself. But a fellow in an old overcoat had the most interesting idea. "You know," he said, "I'd like to use the money to buy myself a meal there sometime. I've always wondered what it looks like inside."

Sometimes I felt as if I were fighting a losing battle with preconceived notions about the South's violence and ignorance. After a shooting in a Mississippi school, the *Globe* sought the opinions of Ivy League intellectuals, who concluded the tragedy was a natural by-product of a gun-crazed society below the Mason-Dixon Line. The *Globe* did not conduct the same sort of regional introspection when a fanatic shot up a couple of abortion clinics in a Boston suburb shortly afterward.

My favorite example of Yankee condescension was a piece on the front page of the *New York Times*'s "Week in Review" section. Titled "Southern Curse . . . Why America's Murder Rate Is So High," the article was as dumb as anything I've read in that newspaper. The story quoted Roger Lane, a history professor at Haverford College, who declared with interesting syntax: "The whole American scandalously high homicide rates are Southern in origin." Other sources for the essay included Alexis de Tocqueville, whose death in 1859 came two years before the Civil War; Frederick Law Olmsted, who expired in 1903; Andrew Jackson's mother; and Benjamin Franklin, who was said to have described the Southern settlers as "white savages."

The article blamed the high murder rates in the South on hot-blooded descendants of the Scots-Irish. My people. One of the story's few living sources, David Hackett Fischer, a history professor at Brandeis University, said of the old settlers: "They had a penchant for family feuds, a love of whiskey, and a warrior ethic that demanded vengeance." I have quoted Fischer myself and think *Albion's Seed,* his study of the American folkways imported by immigrants from the British Isle, an outstanding book, but I'll be damned if I could see how his observation about nineteenth-century Southerners supported the *Times*'s thesis linking the region's modern murder rate with the Southern white man's code of honor that was "reinforced by slavery."

What the *Times* article ignored was the sad fact that most of the Southern murders were being committed by black people killing fellow blacks. After New Orleans became known as one of the nation's "murder capitals" in the 1990s, the city's newspaper, the *Times-Picayune,* devoted several pages to showing photos of every local victim in the past year. Virtually every face was that of a young black man, and in practically every instance the deaths were related to gang wars or drug trades gone haywire. In its own way, the layout was as stunning as the long-ago edition of *Life* magazine with pictures of all the young Americans killed in Vietnam during a single week. But the phenomenon of urban violence in the South was lost to the author of "Southern Curse."

While I was rediscovering the joys of life in the South, I fell in love. Butch Cothren introduced me to Anne Winter, a lawyer in Jackson. She was intelligent and lovely, with eyes as dark as her hair, and she reminded me of Audrey Hepburn, fresh off the set of *Breakfast at Tiffany's.* Though Anne was a dozen years younger, we had scores of mutual friends. Her father was William Winter, so it was natural that her politics dovetailed with my own. Though she spoke with a soft accent, Anne shunned the role of Southern belle and mocked the staid traditions of the Old South. She even dismissed Ole Miss. She said it had not been necessary to go there because she had already attended Ole Miss in high school; she went to Murrah High in Jackson at the time it had been a feeder school for the university. Although other members of her family matriculated at Ole Miss, Anne characterized any visit there as a "field trip."

She graduated from Southwestern at Memphis, a fine liberal arts school that has been renamed Rhodes, and the University of Tennessee Law School, where she led her class. Her intelligence was a bit intimidating; otherwise, she seemed as sweet and soft-spoken as a saint. Shortly after I met her, she won a new trial for a black man condemned to die at Parchman, the state penitentiary. The prisoner she represented had been convicted of murdering a white man in Neshoba County during a fight over a woman. Accounts of the case sounded, at worst, like manslaughter; certainly the incident should not have warranted capital punishment, and she saved the man's life.

Anne and I went out to dinner several times during the Beckwith trial, and she hosted the party that included Eudora Welty and Willie Morris. Inspecting her bookshelves, I saw we read the same novels. The works of talented Mississippi artists hung on her walls. I was also pleased she liked baseball. In the spring, we attended minor league games in Jackson and New Orleans. That summer, she went with me to Boston, where we took in a game at Fenway Park. We drove up to Maine to see Patt Derian and Hodding Carter at their summer home, then rode the ferry to Nantucket for a couple of days.

We decided to get married, and I put my house in Boston on the market. Just before Christmas, Anne and I bought a Creole cottage on Burgundy Street in the lower French Quarter, with a walled courtyard shaded by a magnolia tree, a live oak, and soaring banana stalks bearing heavy bunches of fruit. We set about renovating the old house, built in 1815—the year Andrew Jackson's troops defeated the British a few miles down the river. We ate meals alfresco. Chimes from a church on the other side of our courtyard wall rang gently each quarter hour.

I had given up Jack Daniel's, figuring I had already consumed my lifetime quota, but I still liked wine. One of the first gifts Anne had given me was a device to snip the covering from the top of a wine bottle. It was, she explained, a little something for the man who has everything. For a time, I thought I did. At home with Anne in New Orleans, I was happier than I had ever expected to be again.

The *Globe* officially authorized a New Orleans bureau, and though I was not restricted to the South, I found most of my stories there.

I filed a piece in 1994 about the sons of former president Bush who were running for governor in Florida and Texas. Though I enjoyed my visit with George W. Bush—he was a principal owner of the Texas Rangers and we talked more baseball than politics—I concluded, with my usual perceptive powers, that his brother Jeb had a better chance at being elected that year.

I covered the trial of a young man in Pensacola charged with the first American murder of a doctor at an abortion clinic. After talking with Michael Griffin in prison following his conviction, I explored the environment that had led him to kill, a religious community that supported an end-less Pentecostal revival and nurtured a fanatical antiabortion movement.

In a diversion for "On Dixie," Anne and I joined her parents for a tour led by Willie Morris into the backwoods of Mississippi. We were among a hand-ful of white spectators in a crowd of twenty-five thousand at Alcorn State to watch Steve "Air" McNair, the latest in a line of outstanding athletes—including Walter Payton and Jerry Rice—who came from humble back-grounds and attended predominantly black colleges in Mississippi before achieving national recognition.

When James Meredith announced that he intended to establish a foun-dation to fight ebonics—the use of slang among blacks—it represented another twist in his unusual career. The last time I had seen him, he was campaigning for Ross Barnett in 1967. Meredith had gone on to work for another hard-line segregationist, Senator Jesse Helms, and had proved quite unpredictable in the years since he'd broken the color barrier at Ole Miss.

I arranged to meet Meredith at his home, in the same neighborhood where Willie Morris and Governor Winter lived. Parking in front of his house, I noticed an Ole Miss bumper sticker on a Mercedes in the carport. Meredith greeted me wearing an Ole Miss sweatshirt and an Ole Miss cap. After we finished discussing ebonics, I told Meredith we had been in school together. I regretted, I said, that I had failed to offer him any moral support. I should have had the guts to sit with him at lunch, buy him a cup of coffee, or make some sort of gesture that might have made his experience there easier.

Meredith smiled. It was no big deal, he said, I should not worry. He told me, in his high-pitched voice, that people had always been mistaken about him. He said he had no apologies for his own strange political bedfellows. "I've been a Republican and conservative all my life," he said, laughing at the incongruity.

In 1996, for old times' sake, I traveled by train to Chicago for the Demo-cratic National Convention, following the same route our ragtag delega-tion had taken in 1968. The convention was orderly, and afterward I returned home on the same train, the City of New Orleans. At dinner, the steward happened to seat me at a table with two passengers I recognized, Benjamin Hooks and his wife. Hooks had been a prominent minister and judge in Memphis during the movement days, and after he'd gone on to lead the NAACP, I'd interviewed him several times over the years. We had a pleasant conversation, and just as we were getting our dessert, Aaron Henry—who had attended the convention as a delegate—walked into the dining car. Spotting our table, he shouted happily. He called me homeboy and hugged all three of us.

Riding through the darkened Illinois countryside, we talked for another hour. The year before, Aaron had lost his legislative seat. His friends told me he had been hurt by the defeat to a young man representing a generation of blacks who seemed to have little appreciation for the long struggle Aaron had led. Aaron, however, expressed no bitterness. He said he had lived to see many of his dreams realized, and he seemed optimistic about Mississippi's future.

Though his spirit seemed as strong as it was the day I had met him thirty-three years earlier, Aaron did not look well. He was approaching his seventy-fifth birthday. Bald patches spread over the crown of his head, and his eyes had a dull cast.

The following spring, I traveled to Washington to see another of my Mississippi heroes, the journalist Bill Minor, receive the first John Chancellor Award. It promised to be a happy reunion. The ballroom at the Mayflower Hotel was filled with people who had covered the civil rights movement or played a major role in it. But our celebration was tempered by bad news from Dixie. After a lifetime defying the most malignant forces in the South, Aaron Henry had been killed by a stroke.

Sometime later, I returned to Clarksdale and found that the city I had known had disappeared, as surely as Aaron had predicted back in 1964 when he'd warned that Clarksdale "is on its way to becoming a ghost town."

Fourth Street had been renamed Martin Luther King Boulevard, but the vibrant black businesses that had once operated like outposts of African civilization were now shut and covered with plywood. Fire had destroyed Aaron's drugstore, and nothing had been rebuilt on the lot. The only trace of the civil rights leader showed up on a fading sign on a boarded-up window around the corner: "Re-Elect Aaron Henry State Legislator District 26."

Issaquena Street, once filled with dry-goods stores owned by Jews catering to blacks, had been abandoned to dust motes. Most of the Jews of Clarksdale were gone, the old merchants dead, their sons and daughters leading their lives in cities elsewhere. Blacks still lived in Clarksdale in great numbers, but they had transferred their trade to cavernous discount stores out on Highway 61. An empty marquee in front of the New Roxy Theatre sagged in disrepair. The Greyhound bus terminal, where I had seen Jim Crow laws challenged in 1963, was empty. Only the churches where a young reporter had been baptized in the civil rights movement— Metropolitan Baptist, Centennial Baptist, and Haven Methodist— remained in place.

The scene in the white business district was almost as stark. The red-brick Alcazar Hotel, a favored destination for travelers in the Delta at mid-century, still stood, but its rooms had been empty since the passage of the Civil Rights Act in 1964. The McWilliams Building, the subject of a feature story I'd written about Clarksdale's "skyscraper"—all seven floors of it— was reduced to two tenants.

Business life had shifted to the outskirts of town, to a tacky strip of fast-food joints, motels, service stations, convenience stores, and supermarkets. Downtown seemed possessed by nothing but memory. My editors at the *Press Register,* Joe Ellis and Harry Abernathy, were dead; my other colleagues there had retired or moved away.

In my absence, I learned that Clarksdale had elected a black mayor, Henry Espy, whose name had been on the sample ballot Aaron and I had etched onto my dining room table. A white man now held the office, but blacks occupied many other elected positions.

I stopped by to see Bennie Gooden, one of Aaron's good friends. Bennie had aged, but looked prosperous. He gave me his assessment of local demographics. "We have sixty-five percent of the population, but we still have less than five percent of the wealth. We have two blacks in city government and two on the board of supervisors, but we still don't have a majority," he told me, a note of frustration in his voice.

God, I remembered the days when the black people of Clarksdale had nothing.

West Clarksdale, once all-white and inviolate, had now become home to an increasing number of black families. The public schools were totally integrated, though many white families sent their children to private Lee Academy. Two Catholic churches and parochial schools still coexisted, I learned, but blacks now took Communion at St. Elizabeth's.

The only thing unchanged was the land, the vast expanse of flat cotton fields, unrelieved by trees. Acres and acres and acres stretching across the horizon as far as I could see.

When the *Globe* asked me to write a series of articles on regional cultures in America, I departed from my preoccupation with Mississippi and picked South Carolina as the setting for my Southern piece. Although South Carolina was largely spared the racial violence that had flared across Dixie in the 1960s, the state always seemed peculiarly Southern to me, and the controversy over the Confederate battle flag that played out there later in the decade appeared to validate my choice.

The accents, especially in the Low Country where the Gullah influence is strong, are more pronounced; Protestant fundamentalism, embodied at Bob Jones University in Greenville, is practiced throughout the state; and a strong military tradition, extending from the time of the Revolutionary War, burns brightly. Over the years, the strict discipline of the Citadel encouraged the idea of military service, and many of the state's leaders either came from the school or have an armed forces background.

The first shots in the Civil War were fired across the harbor in Charleston, a city that preserves its Old South heritage as vigorously as Savannah, Natchez, or Richmond; indeed, the people of South Carolina hang on to the nineteenth century more tightly than in any other place I know.

Walter Edgar, director of the Institute for Southern Studies at the University of South Carolina, told me that an extraordinarily large number of South Carolinians remained devoted to the Lost Cause, honoring the Confederacy in song and prayer and reliving the war on old battlefields. "You can't have all these guys dying in vain," Edgar said of the thousands lost in the war. "There has to be some rationale behind their dying."

In South Carolina, the Civil War has an astonishing grip on many people, as if they believe remembrance of the conflict can transcend loss. In an essay in the *Encyclopedia of Southern Culture*, Emory Thomas wrote that "the Southern response to defeat, reunion, and Reconstruction inspired a myth-history that ennobled the destruction of the Southern nation. The Lost Cause mythology held that the Southern cause was not only undefiled by defeat, but that the bloodbath of war actually sanctified the values and mores of the Old South."

Even as the war recedes in history, hundreds of South Carolinians take delight in their roles as reenactors, regularly donning butternut and gray uniforms to pose as Confederate soldiers on the plains of old battlefields. Tony Horwitz wrote of the phenomenon in *Confederates in the Attic*:

"While battles remained the core event, reenacting now encompassed all the nonmilitary aspects of the Civil War, mirroring a similar trend in scholarsip on the conflict. Soldiers were joined by growing ranks of 'civilian' reenactors who played the part of nurses, surgeons, laundresses, preachers, journalists—even embalmers. A generation ago, a young person with a keen interest in the War would likely have joined a Civil War 'roundtable,' one of the hundreds of scholarly clubs nationwide. In the 1990s, the same person was more likely to join a reenacting unit, perhaps with his wife and kids. . . . Reenacting had also bred a vast cottage industry of tailors, weavers, and other 'sutlers,' a Civil War term for merchants who provisioned the armies."

Having dinner in Charleston one night with Barbara Williams, editor of the local newspaper, the *Post & Courier,* and her husband, Manning, an artist, I discovered that Manning was irate over the book. As an enthusiastic reenactor, Manning appeared in one of Horwitz's anecdotes. He felt he had been made to look silly, that the author had deliberately set out to parody the reenactors.

I thought it reasonable to find good humor in the spectacle of middle-aged men playing soldier in a war that had ended more than one hundred years ago, and we were able to laugh about it at dinner. But I discovered that any discussion in South Carolina that ventured into the realm of the Confederate battle flag triggered a verbal cross fire as vicious as the bloody Hornet's Nest clash at Shiloh.

During the 1990s, the flag issue required me to make several trips to Columbia. At one point, a Republican governor, David Beasley, sacrificed the goodwill of his conservative supporters by advocating that the flag be taken down from atop the state capitol, where it had flown since 1962, when it was raised in defiance of civil rights legislation.

Beasley was a bona fide member of the religious right, and his move had the backing of the business leadership in the state, as well as former governors and ageless old Senator Thurmond. For the first time in memory, these reactionary forces were taking a progressive step; ironically, they were depicting their opposition, the lions of the Lost Cause, as a bunch of revanchist yahoos.

But when I visited with Chris Sullivan, the state commander of the Sons of Confederate veterans, I heard an articulate argument instead of loony ravings. "We're being told the flag is evil, racist, just like the Nazis, bad for business, illegal, unconstitutional, even un-Christian," he said. "I disagree with that vehemently. It's not political science for us, not abstract theory. That flag represents our ancestry, our families, and all those who rallied around it."

I heard similar expressions of commitment to the flag from South Carolina legislators, who insisted that the banner stood for honor rather than slavery. Beasley's attempt to move the flag to a Confederate shrine on the capitol grounds ultimately failed in 1997, and he was defeated for reelection the following year.*

South Carolina was only one setting for the squabble over the flag, as other states were forced to grapple with the issue. A few years earlier, Alabama officials had agreed to take down the Stars and Bars from the state capitol dome, effectively eliminating the controversy there. But the Confederate symbol remained part of the state flag in Georgia and Mississippi and continued to cause conflict.

The crossbars representing the Confederate cause was formally incorporated into the Georgia state flag in 1956 to show official disregard for the *Brown v. Board of Education* decision. In the period leading up to the 1996 Olympic Games in Atlanta, defenders of the flag managed to fight off efforts to alter the banner, but in a stealthful move the Georgia legislature later approved a new, scrubbed-up state flag.

The Stars and Bars occupied a corner of the Mississippi flag even longer. Its presence goes back to the 1890s, the same decade that post-Reconstruction legislators drafted a state constitution that included a number of measures to hold back blacks. The old constitution, though amended, still stands today, and the flag still flies.†

* * *

*In 2000, after a long, contentious debate and a boycott of the state by the NAACP, the South Carolina legislature voted to bring down the flag from the capitol dome and move the banner to a Confederate memorial on the capitol grounds. No one seemed satisfied with the compromise.

†In 2000, Governor Ronnie Musgrove appointed a commission, headed by William Winter, to recommend a design for a state flag after a court ruling that found the old flag had never officially been approved. The group suggested replacing the Confederate symbol with a circle of stars, but in an April 2001 referendum, voters in the state chose, in overwhelming numbers, to keep the old flag.

Although I have developed some strong views on racial justice during my metamorphosis from youthful know-nothing to Southern liberal, my feelings toward the Confederate battle flag can best be described as ambivalent. I'm sure I must have displayed the flag as a gesture of Southern pride or rebellion as a youngster. It was our trademark at Ole Miss. I still think it is visually a beautiful banner, with its deep red field slashed by the blue crossbars and white stars.

If the old Confederate flag merely represented the South as a geographic region, I might feel some allegiance. But I ceased flag-waving years ago, after Richard Nixon used the American star-spangled banner for pseudopatriotic lapel pins to show support for the war in Vietnam. I came to realize that the Confederate flag had become identified with the South's unworthiest causes. When the banner that had rallied my great-grandfathers' generation began flying at Ku Klux Klan rallies, many Southerners felt that desecration had taken place.

Shelby Foote, the Civil War historian, deplored the appropriation of the flag in a 1970 letter included in *The Correspondence of Shelby Foote and Walker Percy*. The Klansmen, Foote wrote Percy, "are the scum who have degraded the Confederate flag, converted it from a symbol of honor into a banner of shame, covered it with obscenities like a roadhouse men's room wall."

I stopped having anything to do with the flag. It seemed insensitive to flaunt something that Beatrice Branch, who had replaced Aaron Henry as head of the Mississippi NAACP, once told me "signifies to us racism and hatred."

At the same time, I have been troubled by moves to sanitize our history, purging names and destroying symbols from the past. In my adopted city of New Orleans, where blacks have political control, public schools have been stripped of names honoring a local Confederate hero, General P. G. T. Beauregard, as well as George Washington. Because the men owned slaves.

The flag controversy was wrenching at my alma mater, though the chancellor, Robert Khayat, has succeeded in gradually pushing the Confederate banner off campus with gentle persuasion. Symbols, he told me when I talked with him about the problem, are too much with us in the South.

Khayat, as much as anyone, personifies Ole Miss at the turn of the twenty-first century. As a student, he was a popular figure, a football star, a member of our famous 1959 team; he was also my squad sergeant in the days when I bumbled through ROTC drills. Shortly after I moved back to the South, he was appointed chancellor at Ole Miss, and I knew of no one who could have better bridged the chasm between older alumni and the newer generations who believed the school had to change or die.

"Sometimes," Robert told me, "substantive change is easier than symbolic change. Our goal is to enhance our academic reputation, and it's been turned into a heated discussion of symbols." While working to attract more public school graduates from the state—which is to say more blacks—he led the drive, within the limitations of the First Amendment, to displace the battle flag from its mooring at Ole Miss.

As a result, students have largely given it up. When a well-known racist—a Northerner who moved to Mississippi several years ago in search of a cozy environment—showed up peddling the flag before a football game a couple of years ago, several of my former classmates chased him off campus. The only holdouts I see on my autumn visits are a few families who continue to raise the banner over their picnic tables in the Grove.

When I stopped by Robert's office on a Monday following one game, he began our conversation by asking, "Did you see any flags?"

Come to think of it, I said, I had not seen any in the stadium. It no longer occurred to me to look for them.

The Southern beat might not have been as newsworthy as Washington or as explosive as Jerusalem, but I enjoyed the job immensely. When I moved to New Orleans, two other reporters had a similar assignment, Adam Nossiter of the *New York Times* and Jim Yardley, then working for the *Atlanta Journal-Constitution*. One day we treated ourselves to lunch at Galatoire's to talk of our good fortune.

The South, we agreed, was full of marvelous stories, sorrowful tales of racial conflict, poverty, and violence as well as comic clashes between old and new. One of my favorites involved a battle between the keepers of Faulkner's flame in Oxford and the efforts by an innovative Ole Miss professor to institute an intellectual conference on Elvis. We were also regularly treated to crazy political stories, often set in Louisiana and steeped in corruption. But poignant pieces about unselfish actions by ordinary people also abounded. The stories cropped up in different places, in Alabama hamlets, Arkansas mountains, and Carolina capitals.

Like fortunate prospectors, we could dig almost anywhere in the South and find a good story, we decided. But our best stories, we concluded, always seemed to turn up in Mississippi.

CHAPTER 19

"Put a Code Four on him"

★ ★ ★ ★ ★

In the summer of 1998, I received an unusual call from Jerry Himelstein, the director of the New Orleans office of the Anti-Defamation League. When he asked if I could come see him about something he didn't want to discuss over the telephone, it piqued my interest. In the years since I'd moved to New Orleans he had been helpful in passing on information concerning white supremacists and hate groups monitored by his organization. His predecessor, A. I. "Bee" Botnick, had been Byron De La Beckwith's target when the old racist had been arrested with a bomb in his car on the outskirts of the city in 1973, so Jerry had an appreciation for his job. Having grown up in the Mississippi Delta, he, too, had firsthand knowledge of the region. He also had a keen sense of humor and an infectious laugh, and I enjoyed his company.

When I arrived at his office, Jerry outlined a fascinating story about a man living on the Mississippi Gulf Coast. Jerry did not identify his subject, but said the fellow had gone into debt gambling after casinos were established on the coast earlier in the decade. To curb a gambling addiction, he had enlisted in a program. As part of a twelve-step recovery process, he had been called upon to make amends to someone whom he had caused suffering. After a long debate with his conscience, the man had decided to contact the family of Vernon Dahmer, the NAACP leader murdered by night riders thirty-two years ago. At the time of Dahmer's death, the gambler had been working as an errand boy for Sam Bowers, a jukebox dealer whose larger role in life involved his activities as imperial wizard of the White Knights of the Ku Klux Klan. Shortly before Dahmer's house had been firebombed, the young man had overheard Bowers and other Klansmen talk about implementing a "Code Four" operation—Klan lingo for annihilation. More than three decades later, the case was being revived, and the man, now middle-aged, had offered to testify against Bowers in a forthcoming trial. Jerry told me the potential witness feared the Mississippi prosecutors were discounting his credibility, and he wanted to tell his story to ensure that his account would be made public before the trial opened.

"Would you be interested?" Jerry asked.

"How soon can we go?" I replied.

The next day we drove to a small office in an isolated Gulfport storage shed, guarded by a German shepherd, where Jerry introduced me to Bob Stringer. Though Bob was a big man, forthright and friendly, he had sad eyes and the skittish manners of an abused animal. Bob said he had been raised by grandparents who worked in a factory in Laurel, a hard-bitten Jones County town. As we talked, Bob put flesh on the bones of the story Jerry had started the day before:

"When I was about fourteen, I had to work to survive. I worked at a dry cleaner's in the afternoon and a newsstand at night. Carl Ford owned the newsstand. The Klan was formed in the back of it. Sam Bowers and Carl were big friends. This was around 1960, and Sam came around a lot. He was reading his favorite book, *Animal Farm,* and he called it 'the greatest book of all.' After a while, Sam took me in like a son. I ran errands for him, helped install pinball machines. When he learned I could type, he brought a typewriter to his office and I typed up these things called the Klan Ledgers for him."

Bob handed me a yellowed copy of one of the Ledgers, and I read the words he had typed:

> Now listen you COMMUNISTS and NIGGERS and JEWS.
> Tell all your buddies to spread the news.
> Your day of judgment will soon be nigh.
> As the Lord in his wisdom looks down from on high.
> Will this battle be lost? NEVER! I say.
> For the Ku Klux Klan is here to stay!!!

Bob continued, "I mimeographed the papers for Sam and passed them out in different locations, in restaurants, Laundromats. I dropped off stacks for others to distribute. I did a lot of hauling for Sam, too. I didn't know what I was hauling. It could have been dynamite or guns; I don't know. I never took an oath for the Klan, but I considered myself part of it. I never went on missions with them, but I was never asked. If they had asked me, I probably would have gone. Once I asked Sam why he never let me play a bigger role. He said it was my age. He said, 'You're putting out propaganda. I'm fighting a revolution to put out more propaganda.'"

Over the years, Carl Ford sold his newsstand, and the Klan members began to hang out at John's Café, which was owned by another Klansman, Devours Nix. Bob Stringer patronized the place, too, dropping by regularly for coffee and sandwiches. One night, sitting at a counter near the booths in the back of the café, he heard a conversation among Bowers, Nix, and a man named Henry deBoxtel.

"They were upset about this polling deal down in Hattiesburg," Bob said, referring to a voter registration drive headed by Dahmer following the passage of the Voting Rights Act. "They were frustrated that the Forrest County Klansmen hadn't done anything about it. Sam said, 'Something's got to be done about that nigger down south,' and he slapped the counter. Henry deBoxtel said, 'Put a Code Four on him.'"

I picked up the sequence of the story a couple of days later from Dahmer's son Vernon Dahmer Jr. and his stepmother, Ellie Dahmer, the widow of the NAACP leader. Several members of the Dahmer family still lived on their land in Forrest County, about thirty-five miles south of Laurel. Dahmer's son had a quiet, determined dignity about him. Now sixty-eight, he had been away in the service at the time of the attack, but returned home after retirement to lead the long fight to bring his father's murderers to justice.

Talking in the kitchen of her ranch house, built over the ruins of the home that had been burned, Mrs. Dahmer clearly recollected the raid:

"We had been getting threats over the phone. We knew the Klan was active. They would put up signs on the trees, and when Vernon would drive by, he'd stop and tear them down. They would call and ask for Vernon. They accused him of wanting to be white. Then they would use the N-word and tell him he was going to get killed."

Night riders burned down a hay shed on Dahmer's place, and several times they knocked out the windows of a store he operated adjacent to his house, so the couple slept in shifts during the early part of the 1960s to protect their home. But the threat seemed to dissipate, and by the frosty night of January 10, 1966, Mrs. Dahmer said, "we had started going to bed like ordinary people." Only to be awakened by the sound of gunfire and shattering glass. "I told Vernon, 'I believe they got us this time.' There were two carloads of them. One stopped by the grocery, the other by the house. They shot out the plate-glass window of our house and the display window of the grocery." Then they threw jugs of gasoline, lit with burning rags stuffed into the bottle necks, into the buildings.

Using a shotgun he kept close to his bed, Dahmer exchanged fire with the vigilantes while his wife and children escaped through back windows. After the raiding party sped away, Dahmer joined his family in the safety of a barn, where they watched their home and store burn to the ground. Though Dahmer was ambulatory, his lungs had been seared. He died in a Hattiesburg hospital twelve hours later.

Because of Dahmer's prominence in the NAACP, dozens of FBI agents were assigned to the case. They traced a pistol that had been dropped at the site to a Klansman named Billy Roy Pitts. In short order, Bowers and a dozen of his henchmen were arrested. Three of the men were sentenced to life imprisonment, but no one served more than ten years. One defendant had his prison sentence commuted after less than two years by Governor John Bell Williams in 1970.

Though Bowers was widely believed to have ordered the Klan attack, he escaped conviction in three separate trials that ended with hung juries. But Vernon Dahmer Jr. never put Bowers far from his mind. Encouraged when state authorities rearrested Byron De La Beckwith in 1991, the Dahmer family asked the local district attorney to reopen the case. In 1994, following Beckwith's conviction in Jackson, the mood in the state seemed receptive to pressing charges against Bowers again. Dahmer's son appeared on television and appealed to anyone who might have knowledge of the case to contact him.

Bob Stringer was watching. By this time he was approaching fifty. Since leaving Laurel he had gone through hard times. He had lost his latest job and his life savings of $30,000 because he couldn't stay away from the casinos. But something else gnawed on his conscience: the conversation he had overheard in the back of John's Café in 1966.

Step nine in his recovery program suggested that he make "direct amends" for those he had wronged if it was possible to do so without causing injury to others. "It was a tough decision," Bob told me. "I wanted to make amends to the Dahmer family, but on the other hand, I didn't want to injure my old friends," people such as Sam Bowers and Devours Nix. Henry deBoxtel was dead.

Bob decided to drive to Hattiesburg, where he looked up Vernon Dahmer Jr.'s number in the telephone directory. He used a pay phone to place a call that could not be traced. He told Dahmer he had once associated with Klansmen and wanted to help, but he refused to give his name or any details. During subsequent conversations Bob initiated by phone, trust developed between the two men, but more than two years lapsed before Bob Stringer and Vernon Dahmer Jr. met.

Bob finally asked an intermediary, known to Dahmer only as Frank, to arrange a face-to-face meeting. It took place in April 1997 in a Gulf Coast motel. Six men gathered in the room: Vernon Dahmer Jr. and his brother, Dennis Dahmer, the man who had identified himself only as Bob, his friend Frank, Jerry Himelstein, who pledged ADL resources to help Bob relocate his family, and Jerry Mitchell, a Mississippi newspaper reporter who had specialized in old civil rights murder cases before interrupting his career to return to college.

Bob spent the day discussing his experiences as Bowers's acolyte. Before the group dispersed, he agreed to cooperate with state prosecutors.

Although he eschewed publicity and refused to give interviews, Bowers had become a well-known figure in the state in the years since he'd assumed power over a network of local Klan groups. He was, by all accounts, a quiet man who conducted his affairs from a run-down building across the street from Laurel's biggest industry, the Masonite Corporation. Both his bare living quarters and his office were located in an unpainted frame house that emanated an air of depression. Using a contraction of his name, he had formed a word—insulting to blacks—to name his jukebox enterprise Sambo Amusement Company.

Bowers was not your average redneck, reacting instinctively against black people. He was well educated and clever, the grandson of a congressman, and he waged a doctrinaire war against those he perceived as enemies to the Southern way of life.

Jack Nelson described Bowers as a cold and calculating racist in *Terror in the Night*, Nelson's 1993 book about the Klan's campaign against Jews in Mississippi:

"He became a slave to an idea—the idea of an international Communist conspiracy, masterminded by the Jews. He believed the Kremlin was merely a front for a cabal of Jews attempting to bring down Christians throughout the world. In the United States, their chosen vehicle was the civil rights movement. Using Communists as their agents, the Jews sought to destroy white Christian society by mongrelization.

"In 1955, the year he was arrested for illegal possession of liquor, Bowers joined the Original Knights of the Ku Klux Klan of Louisiana after the group spread across the Mississippi River and established a klavern in Natchez. By the early 1960s, with the civil rights movement growing stronger and more insistent, Bowers concluded that the Original Knights were too passive. On February 15, 1964, at a meeting in Brookhaven, Mississippi, he convinced about two hundred members of the Original Knights to defect and join a highly secret Klan he was forming that would not hesitate to use 'physical force.'"

Bowers wrote directives for his new group. The White Knights, he said, would be "a nocturnal organization that works best at night. We must remember that the communists who are directing the agitators want us to engage in pitched battles in the streets so they can declare martial law."

He espoused a perverse form of Christianity, which he said was tempered by "kindness, generosity, affection, and humility." At the same time, he wrote, "as militants we are disposed to use physical force against our enemies. How can we reconcile these two apparently contradictory philosophies? The answer, of course, is to purge malice, bitterness, and vengeance from our hearts. . . . If it is necessary to eliminate someone, it should be done with no malice, in complete silence, and in the manner of a Christian act."

Under Bowers's reign, only he, as imperial wizard, could authorize a Code Three, which called for a firebombing, or a Code Four, which meant death. Subordinates could order lesser actions, such as a Code One for a cross burning or Code Two for a whipping.

Jim Ingram, the former FBI agent, told me Bowers "had his tentacles farreaching. He had separate units of the Klan in Jones County, in Amite and Pike Counties, in Natchez and Meridian, and he was smart enough that he didn't tell the others about his business." The Klan unit in Natchez carried out several murders in the 1960s. The Meridian gang was deeply involved in the Neshoba County killings, and Bowers ultimately spent six years in federal prison as a result of a conviction in that case. But after serving that time, he had been free for more than twenty years, living in the back of Sambo Amusement Company.

Armed with a new sense of resolve and a fresh witness, the state of Mississippi decided to move against Bowers. It was a natural outgrowth of the Beckwith case, but the decision to reopen the case was promoted by a source that would have been unbelievable thirty years ago—the *Clarion-Ledger*. To be more precise, the impetus came from the young reporter who had attended the first meeting between Stringer and the Dahmers, Jerry Mitchell.

In a profession characterized by cynics, agnostics, and heavy drinkers, Jerry Mitchell stood out like an apprentice saint. Aside from his bright red hair and beard, there was nothing flamboyant about him. He had been raised on the west side of Texarkana, a working-class city that lay on the state line between Texas and Arkansas, a place with a culture more Southern than Western. He had attended Harding University in Searcy, Arkansas, a Church of Christ school that harbored a number of right-wing professors and once sponsored a National Education Program to ferret out Communists in the civil rights movement. Jerry still belongs to a Church of Christ congregation in Jackson and is quietly devout, though he told me, "Some of what I grew up with I disagree with." The Christianity he embraces seems more inclusive than exclusive, more grounded in the precepts of Jesus than the preconceptions of conservative ministers. "It's hard to describe," he said, "but I think Christianity offers a lot for all people." From the time he joined the *Clarion-Ledger* in 1986 as a twenty-seven-year-old, it was obvious that his philosophy departed radically from the racist theories that had once guided the newspaper.

More than anyone else, Jerry Mitchell created the opening for prosecutors to tackle the Beckwith case and other unsolved murders. As part of a team interviewing figures from the Neshoba County case for a story on the twenty-fifth anniversary of the murders, he realized that prime suspects in the deaths of the three civil rights workers as well as those believed responsible for the murders of Medgar Evers and Vernon Dahmer were still alive and free.

In 1989, someone slipped Jerry hundreds of pages of documents from the files of the defunct state Sovereignty Commission, material that had been impounded by a federal judge while combatants in a civil case quarreled over whether the files should be made public. Going through the papers, the reporter discovered a folder tagged "Medgar Evers Race Agitator." Inside the file, he saw that a Sovereignty Commission investigator had prepared a report on the background of potential jurors in the second Beckwith trial in 1964. Concluding that the document provided evidence that the state agency had tampered with the jury, the *Clarion-Ledger* published Jerry's story on the front page. The news break prodded the victim's widow, Myrlie Evers, and Bobby DeLaughter, an assistant prosecutor in Jackson, to press for a new trial of Beckwith.

Jerry does not name his sources, but I have a theory of how he got the material. Late in his life, Erle Johnston, the former Ross Barnett aide and onetime director of the Sovereignty Commission, turned over about 2400 pages of commission documents to a friend—whose identity I think I know—who then made them available to Jerry. I once talked to Johnston about the commission's work and found him apologetic about his involvement with an agency whose purpose had been to deny rights to black people. His courtly manners were similar to those of his old boss, Barnett; not an innately evil man, Johnston was a product of a culture that had known nothing but segregation. Before he died, I'm convinced—and so are others—that Johnston wanted expiation for his activities, so he leaked the damning Sovereignty Commission files.

It took another five years to bring Beckwith to justice, and when that was done, Jerry took up the Dahmer case as a crusade. He found old FBI notes indicating that the Klan had tampered with Bowers's jury before his first murder trial. According to an informant, three potential jurors had been contacted. At least one assured the Klan he would vote to acquit Bowers; another said he would consider voting for Bowers's innocence. The trial ended in a hung jury.

When Bob Stringer agreed to testify, Jerry came back from his studies at Ohio State University to help the Dahmers prepare the case. By the time Bowers was brought to trial in August 1998, Jerry had rejoined the *Clarion-Ledger*. Bowers's attorney used his opening argument to denounce the journalist.

During the Beckwith trial in 1994, I had sat with Jerry and other reporters in the press gallery. We were together again four years later for the Bowers trial. I relied on him as a walking encyclopedia for information on the Mississippi cases.

On the first day of the trial, however, I wound up in an unusual position. The judge, Richard McKenzie, invited reporters to observe the prospective jurors being questioned, and I found myself sitting next to the defendant, the imperial wizard Sam Bowers, in a small room where the jury selection was taking place.

From a distance, I had thought Bowers looked surprisingly fit for a seventy-four-year-old defendant in a murder trial. He wore a cord suit and a fashionable striped tie, and his graying hair was carefully combed. But up close, he had the look of a down-and-out door-to-door salesman. The cuffs on his coat were frayed, and his suit had yellowed with age, as if it had not been cleaned in years. Bowers had been a bachelor all his life, and judging from his appearance, he could have benefited from a wife's care. I noticed he was also wearing two Mickey Mouse lapel pins. During the first break, I asked him about the pins. He looked at me, put a finger to his lips, and wordlessly shook his head. Silence was his rule.

Bob Stringer fretted over the prosecutors' preparation; he worried about their interest in convicting Sam Bowers after all these years. But after hearing the opening arguments, it became apparent that Bob's fears had been misplaced.

In his introductory remarks to the jury, Robert Helfrich, an assistant district attorney, laconically set the scene: "Two A.M. A cold January morning. Two cars with heavily armed Klansmen. Unit Four, Jones County White Knights of the Ku Klux Klan, attacked the Dahmer property. They came armed with pistols, shotguns, and twelve gallons of gasoline."

Across the courtroom, Bowers showed no emotion, sitting at a table with his attorneys. But at that moment he must have sensed freedom slipping away.

The prosecution assembled an impressive lineup of witnesses, tearful members of the Dahmer family who gave accounts of the raid, and aging, retired FBI agents who helped tie together details of the case. But the most compelling testimony came from Bob Stringer and a couple of old Klansmen.

A witness named T. Webber Rogers recalled that shortly before the raid he had attended a Klan meeting at a farmhouse where he had heard Bowers declare that "something's got to be done about that damned nigger." Rogers said he did not go on the mission, quit the Klan after learning of Dahmer's death, and moved away. He did not want to say where he lived.

The judge asked Rogers if he had been threatened. "Hell, yes," the witness said, and bowed his head. "I didn't want to have to go through with this."

Billy Roy Pitts, a star witness at the three unsuccessful trials in the 1960s, made a reappearance. He was the Klansman who had dropped his pistol from a quick-draw holster he had rigged for the raid, leaving behind evidence that had led to the mass arrests and earning him the enmity of Bowers. Pitts said he had begun talking to the FBI because he believed Bowers "wanted to annihilate me" for his clumsiness.

Pitts testified that after Bowers had been summoned in late 1965 to appear before the House Un-American Activities Committee, he had exhorted his followers to eliminate Dahmer "to show the people in Washington that the South means business." The formal order to kill Dahmer came at the farmhouse, he said. Pitts identified a dozen men who were on hand for the meeting. One of them was Bowers's attorney, Travis Buckley.

During the first days of the trial, I had thought Buckley merely inept. He seemed a bumbling country lawyer; his brown suit was rumpled, he cupped his ear to hear testimony, and his own questions were rambling and incoherent. Now he had been singled out as a Klan conspirator himself.

Jerry Mitchell filled me in on the lawyer's background. He had originally been indicted in the Dahmer case but was never convicted. He was, however, convicted in another 1960s case in which a wayward Klansman had been punished. According to testimony, the lawyer had held a knife while Billy Roy Pitts beat up the disloyal member of the Jones County Klan. The state Supreme Court eventually overturned the conviction, and Buckley was able to practice law again.

As evidence mounted against his client in the Bowers case, Buckley complained that it was a Communist-type show trial, inspired by the political ambitions of the state attorney general, Mike Moore, who was contemplating a race for governor. Moore had provided special investigators and lawyers to assist the local prosecutors, and he had come to Hattiesburg to watch part of the trial. During a recess, I asked Moore about Buckley's remarks. He scoffed and said they were not worthy of comment. Buckley, he said, was nothing but a broken-down "Klan lawyer."

After the prosecution rested, Buckley opened his defense on a blundering note. He called Devours Nix, who faced renewed charges of arson in the Dahmer case himself. When Nix had been arraigned that spring following his arrest, he had appeared in court in a wheelchair and was released without bond because of his poor health. A few weeks later, a *Clarion-*

Ledger photographer sneaked a photograph of Nix teeing off at a golf course. The next day, hours after the photo had appeared in the newspaper, Judge McKenzie had Nix rearrested and required him to post a $50,000 bail.

Nix was rolled to the witness stand in a wheelchair. Tubes dangled from his nostrils, providing a connection to an oxygen tank strapped to the back of the wheelchair. His hands trembled, he said, from an adverse reaction to medication that had been prescribed for cancer. It looked to me like a phony routine to win sympathy.

Nix called Bowers "a real, real nice man" and said he had been drawn to the Klan because it was a "benevolent" organization that handed out fruit baskets at Christmas. Snickers swept the courtroom. Even members of the jury laughed out loud.

During cross-examination, Nix was asked the color of his Klan robe.

"I didn't have no robe," he said.

Helfrich, the prosecutor, presented Nix with an old photo, seized at Nix's home during a search by authorities after Dahmer's death. "What does this person have on?" Helfrich asked.

"Looks like it might be a robe."

"With a hood?"

"Mmm-hmm."

"Holding a gun?"

"Yes, sir."

Nix insisted that it was not himself in the photo, but Helfrich countered with a note from old law enforcement files reporting that Nix's wife had complained to her husband, "They found that crazy, silly picture of you with a pointed hood on."

By the time Nix was rolled from the courtroom, his testimony had been completely discredited. But his illness was not a ruse. Devours Nix died a few months later, just before his own trial.*

As Bowers's trial neared its conclusion, I spotted Will Campbell in the courtroom. Though I had only known Will for a few years, I had heard of him for much of my life. Years before, the legendary minister had tended to flocks of civil rights activists at the same time that he labored to save the souls of the Klansmen. Before I enrolled at Ole Miss, Will had been run off

---

*Travis Buckley, the Klan attorney, died in 2000.

as school chaplain for playing Ping-Pong with a black man. He went on to a career as an apostate Baptist minister, a writer and teacher, and he had a reputation as one of the finest of Southern renegades.

During my first year on the Southern beat, I had sought out Will Campbell at his farm near Nashville and spent a morning with him in his log-cabin office, where he chewed tobacco and showed off jugs of white whiskey distilled from corn he grew himself. He used surplus cornmeal to feed dozens of birds on his farm. As we talked, I discovered Will had grown up in a tiny southwest Mississippi community, East Fork. He told me his family considered my hometown, Summit, a big city. It was the nearest incorporated town, and they had gone shopping in Summit every Saturday. In 1940, the year I was born, Will declared himself a Baptist minister at age sixteen, but his sermons proved incompatible with the conservative faith of his congregation. "They were going to defrock me, but they couldn't figure out how to do it," he told me. At one time, the Amite County Klan, which included a couple of his cousins, planned to murder him, he said. "I was like a family dog that had gone rabid and had to be killed."

He attended Yale Divinity School and served for a while as a pastor in north Louisiana until his sermons, he said, "got me in trouble. I moved on to Ole Miss, looking for a home. I didn't find it at Ole Miss either." During the civil rights movement, he worked as a troubleshooter for the National Council of Churches, an organization sympathetic to the black cause. He also explained his ministry to Klansmen by noting that they, too, were children of God.

Will dropped out as a Southern Baptist. He told me he now considered himself a "Seventh-Day Horizontal." But he continued to toil in the name of Christ, and over the years he had become a folk hero.

With the Bowers trial getting heavy news coverage in the South, Will decided to come from Nashville to Hattiesburg. During a recess, he met with members of the Dahmer family, who had been following the case from a balcony overlooking the defense table. They all greeted him warmly. Later, Will walked across the courtroom to speak to Bowers. For the first time in four days, I saw Bowers smile. He hugged the old minister and they spoke softly for several minutes.

For many of us, the trial was another station on a Southern Via Dolorosa. The effort to track down and convict the men responsible for the civil rights murders had become a ritual of atonement and redemption, an exercise almost religious in its nature. The sins of a segregated society could not be swept away in a single swoop, but it seemed clear to me that the people of my home state were committed to justice, and I was convinced Bowers would be found guilty.

The case went to the jury late on a Friday morning. At noon, I joined Will Campbell and a couple of others for a plate lunch at a nearby café. "We better eat quickly," I said. "The jurors are holding out for one more free meal themselves, then they're going to convict the old bastard." We hurried back to the courthouse before 1 P.M. Within minutes, the jury passed word that they had reached their decision. The courtroom audience rose as the six whites, five blacks, and one Asian-American filed into the chamber. Anticipating the verdict, Bowers began emptying his pockets. He took off his wristwatch and placed it with his billfold and other belongings in an attaché case on the defense table.

Bowers was found guilty. The imperial wizard had nothing to say before Judge McKenzie sentenced him to spend the rest of his life in prison. He was led away in the custody of three black deputy sheriffs.

In the balcony, members of the Dahmer family embraced one another and wept. Other pockets of celebration broke out in the crowded room. But when I saw Will Campbell, he seemed absorbed by sadness.

"Will," I said, "you may be the only person in the courtroom who feels bad for Sam Bowers."

"I do," he said, eyes wet. "Jesus never liked to see any man imprisoned."

As the noise inside the courtroom subsided, the Dahmer family and members of the prosecution team moved outside to conduct a press conference. Vernon Dahmer Jr. was especially eloquent. He had run a gauntlet in his own lifetime, hobbled by Jim Crow laws and stung by his father's murder. Yet he told us he had returned to Mississippi after retiring from the air force because he still believed in the state. "This is a new Mississippi," he said. "I came back home to be with my people, black and white. Mississippi has good people. I intend to die in Mississippi."

CHAPTER 20

"There was no meanness"

★ ★ ★ ★ ★

I have begun to find comfort in cemeteries.

Inhibited by a dread of graveyards as a child, I played hide-and-seek among the tombstones of the old Jewish cemetery only in my bravest moments during daylight. Summit's main cemetery, Woodlawn, was two blocks from our house, but I made detours to avoid it. Burial grounds were terrible, haunted places, I thought.

My friend Willie Morris had a different notion. He used cemeteries as props for practical jokes. William Styron likes to tell of the time Willie led him to a cemetery to discover a copy of Styron's first novel, *Lie Down in Darkness*, leaning against a headstone. Over the years, Willie enchanted schoolchildren with visits to the Yazoo City cemetery, which he described as bewitched in his tales. In *North Toward Home* he had written of its place in his own boyhood:

"The cemetery itself held no horror for me. It was set on a beautiful wooded hill overlooking the whole town. I loved to walk among the graves and look at the dates and words on the tombstones. I learned more about the town's past here, the migrations, the epidemics, the old forgotten tragedies, than I could ever have learned in the library."

Not until I returned to the South, by now more than fifty years old, did I make my own peace with cemeteries. Just as I had been drawn back to the land of my ancestors, I had developed an interest in visiting their resting places. Gradually, I began to consider the graveyards as lovely elysian fields, grounds that contained my family and my friends.

On a trip to north Mississippi, I sought out my father's grave. Though I had not visited Longtown Cemetery in nearly thirty years, instinct helped me locate the remote spot on the edge of the Delta where the Wilkies are buried. They are all there: my grandmother and grandfather, my aunt and uncle and cousins. Walking in the deserted cemetery, with a chill wind hurrying leaves over the earth, I located the headstone bearing my own name—the name of my father. The dates of his birth and death were bracketed below it, then a simple line: "God loved him best." Because he died young, I suppose. These may have been the loneliest ghosts in the world, yet there seemed to be an ineffable peace to the little knoll where they lay.

By contrast, St. Peter's Cemetery in Oxford has the feel of a park where lovers wander along paths, untroubled by worldly cares. St. Peter's is a shrine, in a way, because Faulkner is buried there, and for nearly forty years his devotees have been making pilgrimages to pour whiskey on his grave or to leave bottles in homage to the master. My maternal grandparents are buried just up the hill from Faulkner. When O, my stepgrandmother, died at the age of ninety-nine, the gravediggers at St. Peter's found that, a few years earlier, the coffin containing Mae, her spinster sister, had been placed too near that of my grandfather Bob Black. Our family had to get a court order to move Mae a couple of yards in order for O to lie beside her husband. My cousin Bob and I laughed over the storm O would have caused had she known Mae nearly took her place in perpetuity.

Not long ago, the day after a Thanksgiving reunion in Oxford, my children and I met Bob and his brother, Scott, for a tour of Toccopola. Little is left of the country village where our ancestors weathered the Civil War, only a gas station, several forlorn churches, and a couple of cemeteries. In one yard, across the road from the family homestead that burned on Christmas Eve, 1920, we found a headstone for the grave of our great-grandfather John F. Black, adorned with the letters C.S.A. According to the inscription, he served in the First North Carolina Cavalry, Company F, of the Confederate army before migrating to Mississippi after the war.

We also trooped through a neatly kept cemetery a mile or so away, next to the Old Lebanon Presbyterian Church. There were more Gilmers and Blacks as well as the graves of relatives who had perished during a nineteenth-century epidemic. After a bit, my cousins and I stumbled upon the grave of our grandmother, May Gilmer Black. We never knew her. Our grandfather was widowed twice before we were born. O was his third wife. All of Grandfather Black's wives had come from within a mile's radius of the Presbyterian church in Toccopola.

* * *

In the spring of 1997, seven years after Pa's death, my mother finally let go. Though I would miss her presence and lose my last link to Summit, I felt a certain relief. She had effectively passed on years earlier, occupying a body that had slowly withered away. She was buried next to Pa in a plot at the back of the Summit cemetery, under the shade of pecan trees. The skies were menacing—typical of Southern springtime—and few mourners braved the weather. William Winter—my mother's favorite governor—and his wife, Elise, drove down from Jackson, joining my family and a handful of Mother's friends at the graveside service.

As the morning grew darker, I spoke of how she had been a quiet, early champion for women's rights, and how she had taught me to respect our black neighbors. For laughs, I told the story of how Faulkner had named the madam in *Sanctuary* after Mother's friend. My eulogy was going smoothly until my daughter, Leighton, and Lora, who had cared for my mother in her final years, sobbed loudly. I could barely finish, my voice croaking as I recited the last verse of Mother's favorite hymn:

> Hold Thou Thy cross before my closing eyes,
> Shine through the gloom, and point me to the skies;
> Heaven's morning breaks, and earth's rain shadows flee,
> In life, in death, O Lord, abide with me.

Driving between New Orleans and Oxford, I often stop at the cemetery in Summit. Near my parents' graves is the home of an elderly black man who tends a vegetable garden. I don't know his name, but we always exchange waves. The cemetery is restful. The week that Mother died, my son Carter and I spotted a bluebird in her backyard, a rare sighting. In hopes of attracting the beautiful little birds, Carter found a bluebird box that I erected between the garden and the graves. A season later, I saw a nest inside the box, and it gave me great pleasure. On my visits, I clean my parents' headstones and tell the latest news of their grandchildren—and now, their great-grandchildren.

The Summit cemetery is a good place for my yellow Labs to break the trip, to stretch their legs as they race between the monuments, retrieving sticks that I throw. I don't think the ghosts would mind.

One day, as I cleared the graves in Summit, it occurred to me that all of my relatives are buried in Mississippi.

* * *

In my fourth year in New Orleans, Anne said she was unhappy and left my life as mystically as she had entered it. I had been discouraged before, but for the first time I felt beaten and old. I was reminded of the character in Mark Helprin's novel *Winter's Tale* who lost his mate "when the sky was full of darting crows and the world lay prostrate and defeated after winter. . . . It ruined him forever. It broke him as he had not ever imagined he could have been broken. He would never again be young, or able to remember what it was like to be young."

I closed myself in penitential solitude and had no desire to talk with anyone. My dog Binx became my only companion. We took long walks through the French Quarter. I did not think it possible to become so fond of a pet. He had come from a kennel in one of those south-Mississippi counties known for producing better hunting dogs than human beings, and I had given the puppy to Anne on our second Christmas together. We wanted to give the dog a short, flip literary name linked to New Orleans. That ruled out Ignatius J. Reilly and Stanley Kowalski, so we named him Binx Bolling, after the protagonist of Walker Percy's *The Moviegoer*. Later, we learned from our friend Billy Percy, the novelist's nephew, that the fictional character had actually been named for his father's dog Binx. Billy said his uncle Walker had written Billy's dad, LeRoy Percy, asking permission to use the name. Later, when Anne saw LeRoy Percy at a dinner party in Mississippi, she confessed we had named our dog Binx without his permission. Peering over his glasses in mock-seriousness, Mr. Percy replied, "My lawyer will be seeing your lawyer." I loved that story. It stamped our Binx with the Percy imprimatur.

On our walks, Binx and I strolled along the levee, a few blocks from the house on Burgundy Street. I have always been drawn to the river and, like many Southerners, draw some kind of sustenance from it. It rushes timelessly, like an immutable, indestructible force.

Aaron Henry, who survived the enormous flood in the Delta in 1927, wrote in a journal he kept during the movement: "That old Mississippi River has never had one ounce of racial prejudice. It will drown or wash away a white man just as quick as a Negro and never think twice about it. When it comes busting over those levees, it doesn't stop to ask where the colored section is, it just takes it all. There's a particular equality about the river, an equality that comes in something so great and powerful and so potentially good that no man can change it."

My friend and French Quarter neighbor John Barry also wrote about the river and the 1927 flood in his marvelous book *Rising Tide*. John likes the river so much he wants to establish a Mississippi River museum in New Orleans. "The river's sinuosity itself generates enormous force," he wrote. "The Mississippi snakes seaward in a continual series of S curves that sometimes approach 180 degrees. The collision of river and earth at these bends creates tremendous turbulence: currents can drive straight down to the bottom of the river, sucking at whatever lies on the surface, scouring out holes often several hundred feet deep."

The river awes me, too. It is as much a part of the South as our soil. Knowing that the Mississippi was nearby, and that I was surrounded by familiar accents and customs, proved a consolation. Eventually, the good fortunes of my children eclipsed my sorrow. Carter and his wife, Allison, presented me with two granddaughters. My younger son, Stuart, excelled in computer graphics, a field I never understood. And in a union of descendants of the Lamar Rifles, my daughter, Leighton, married Campbell McCool on a brilliant autumn afternoon. The wedding was held in New Orleans, and the cheerfulness of the gathering beat away my gloom.

Though Leighton and Campbell, who have now blessed me with two grandsons, live in Atlanta, they acquired a second home in Oxford, five blocks from the courthouse square. They have been generous in sharing it with me. I spend a lot of time there—my mother's home and my old college town—visiting friends, prowling through Square Books, dining out and sipping wine—a vice denied to us during my Ole Miss days—on the balcony of the City Grocery restaurant overlooking the stone Confederate soldier in front of the courthouse.

We have season tickets for Ole Miss home football games. The stadium is nearly twice the size that it was when I was a student. Most members of the starting lineup are black, and they are cheered as enthusiastically as we once yelled for the old, victorious Rebel teams. On these autumn weekends I look forward to picnics in the Grove with Pat and Butch Cothren. Leighton and Campbell host postgame parties for their own generation at their house in town. One of their friends is a local FBI agent, an Ole Miss schoolmate of Campbell's named John Atkins. I discovered John's grandfather was Ross Barnett and talked with John about the old governor one night. The grandson has understandable affection for him. I said diplomatically that Barnett was certainly "colorful" and told a couple of harmless Ross Barnett tales from my repertoire.

As I grow older, I am more forgiving. I have concluded that Barnett was never an evil man, merely a creature of the Old South who got bad direction from the Citizens Council crowd. A few weeks after my talk with John, I read that his mother now teaches at Lanier, the predominantly black public school in Jackson erected during the "separate but equal" days. The newspaper article cited the unique situation of two instructors teaching at the same school: Ouida Barnett Atkins, the old segregationist's daughter, and Bob Moses, the man who once led voter registration drives in Pike County. Disillusioned by the internal strife of the civil rights movement, Moses had changed his name and moved to Africa thirty years earlier. Now he had reclaimed his original name and was back in Mississippi, too.

Walking up Bourbon Street to have dinner with friends on the first Monday evening of August in 1999, I waved as one of my neighbors, Julia Reed, passed on a bicycle. Julia had grown up in Greenville, another Delta writer who had settled in the French Quarter. Seeing that I was in a good mood, she wheeled back and said, "I'm going to ruin your evening, but I need to tell you this: I just heard Willie Morris died of a heart attack." She added the hope that the news might prove erroneous, a product of Mississippi gossip. I hoped so, too, and managed to make my way through dinner, sustained by the idea that the news would be false. With his practical jokes and zest for life, Willie seemed immortal, a boy in his sixty-fifth year. But when I got home a couple of hours later, my telephone voice mail was clogged with messages from Mississippi.

I went to bed late, knowing my phone would not ring as often after midnight again; there would be no more late-night impersonations of celebrities or editors, no more comical hoaxes that had became so predictable that I answered any late call with the greeting "Hi, Willie."

The next morning I took a copy of *North Toward Home* from my bookshelf and sat down to read. A few years before, when Willie and his wife, JoAnne, had visited us in New Orleans, I'd asked him to sign it. "To my dear comrades Anne and Curtis," he'd written. "With thanks always for your friendship. Willie. P.S. Everything in this book is 98% true."

I searched for the passage where Willie, as a schoolboy, had played the trumpet at funerals for veterans at the Yazoo City cemetery. But when I finally found the words, I could not read them for my tears.

I drove to Jackson, expecting to speak briefly with JoAnne and attend the funeral in Yazoo City the next day. But when I arrived at their home, I found the place overflowing with friends from Willie's far-flung network.

Literary giants were flying in from the East Coast, but the glue that held the wake together came from Willie's eclectic circle of Mississippians: Peyton Prospere, a lawyer who had left one of the sobbing messages on my phone; Jill Conner Browne, who had written the ball-busting *The Sweet Potato Queens' Book of Love* at Willie's urging; Malcolm White, impresario of Willie's hangout, Hal & Mal's; Rick Cleveland, a *Clarion-Ledger* sports columnist, and his wife, Liz, whose children called Willie "Uncle"; William and Elise Winter, who lived across the street; John Evans, owner of the splendid Lemuria bookstore; Semmes Luckett Jr.; Josephine Haxton, who began using a pseudonym in the 1960s, "Ellen Douglas," to spare her family harassment for her novels' views on racial justice; the old newsman Bill Minor and his wife, Gloria; Raad and Karenna Cawthon, who had both worked at the *Clarion-Ledger* during its renaissance; and Bobby DeLaughter, the prosecutor who had put Byron De La Beckwith behind bars.

When I saw JoAnne, her eyes were swollen from weeping. She hugged me. "There's just this big, damned black hole," she said.

It *was* a big, damned black hole. Like benign farm animals, Willie's friends collected rather helplessly, in growing numbers, in the backyard that ran down to Crane's Creek. Inside, the kitchen counters were piled with pies, casseroles, fried chicken, potato salads, cheese dips, sausages, fruit cocktails, and black-bean dishes. We sent out for cases of beer and wine and whiskey and set up a bar outdoors, figuring that Willie's death should be observed in his fashion.

Instead of paying brief respects and departing, I wound up lingering for hours. There seemed to be a collective feeling that we could keep Willie's spirit alive with alcohol and anecdotes. For the better part of two days, we crowded the yard, crying and laughing and recalling his pranks. Rick Cleveland remembered the night Willie had telephoned David Duke's headquarters in New Orleans and paged Eva Braun. I recalled the time Willie had posed as an Associated Press reporter and elicited several sanctimonious observations from me about a Massachusetts politician.

None of us felt embarrassed by our tears. Willie had made crying a legitimate emotion. Late in the evenings, after helping demolish several bottles of whiskey or wine, Willie tended to get sentimental. He would weep quietly over memories of dogs long dead, or lost friends, and he would wipe at the tears and say apologetically, "Aw, shit."

We knew him as one of the most generous of men. After recruiting a remarkable stable of talent for *Harper's* magazine as its youngest editor, he was fired by owners who cared more about the bottom line. After a few years in New York's purgatory, he returned home to become a writer-in-residence at Ole Miss. He offered encouragement to a coming generation of Southern writers, always finding time to meet with anyone seeking advice or editorial guidance. Cleaning my desk one day, I discovered an old blank check from Willie, dating from one of the evenings we'd drunk too much and talked, perhaps too obsessively, about the South. Willie wanted me to write a book about coming home. On the back of the check, he'd scrawled four proposed titles we came up with for my nonexistent book: (1) *Code Word: Dixie*, (2) *Dixie*, (3) *South to New Orleans*, (4) *D'La to D'Lo* (D'La was De La Beckwith, D'Lo a small town in south Mississippi). He had also written down two phrases he wanted me to work into my manuscript: "shithead right-wingers in tuxedoes" and "a squalid arrogance."

Willie was a Yellow Dog Democrat who supported every progressive candidate. When I'd first met him, he was master of ceremonies at a rally for his friend Bill Clinton, outside the Old State Capitol in Jackson during the closing days of the 1992 presidential campaign. Following the Beckwith trial two years later, Willie had adopted the prosecutor, Bobby DeLaughter, as a candidate for judge and was deeply disappointed when the campaign failed.

As we conducted our postmortems in Willie's backyard, Peyton Prospere volunteered the best line. Willie, he said, had already given so much of his heart that nothing was left to save him when his own heart came under attack.

On the morning of the funeral, David Halberstam flew in from Nantucket, and I met my old friend at the airport. David had written for Willie at *Harper's* and had a wealth of stories about his former editor. Years ago, David had told me he feared Willie was squandering his talent. "We've got to get Willie to stop writing about these fucking dogs," David said. In 1995, when *My Dog Skip* was published, I wanted to write about the book for an "On Dixie" piece in the *Globe*. I called David and asked if I could use a censored version of his remark about Willie and dogs. "Only if it's done lovingly," he said.*

*Willie liked my dog Binx. The year after Willie's death, Binx fathered a litter, born in the French Quarter on Mardi Gras. I took the pick of the litter and named my second dog Willie.

As we drove into Jackson from the airport, David remembered the time he'd received a call from a "diet doctor" whose book had replaced *The Best and the Brightest* atop the *New York Times* best-seller list. The diet doctor proposed that he and Halberstam collaborate on a new title. "And what would that be, Doctor?" David asked. The diet doctor/Willie answered, "*The Best and the Fattest.*"

Governor Winter arranged for Willie to lie in state in the rotunda of the Old State Capitol building, only the third Mississippian to be so honored. All morning, hundreds of people, men, women, and children of both races filed past the bier. Inside the closed, shining wooden casket, I later learned, Willie lay clothed in his favorite knit shirt and loose-fitting pants. A suit would have been out of character. When JoAnne and Jill Conner Browne had made a last visit to the funeral home, they'd seen the undertaker had tucked Willie's shirt into his pants. That would not do either. His knit shirts always flopped outside his belt, so they instructed the undertaker to make the adjustment.

Though Willie's family made no public announcement, his corneas had been donated to two Mississippians with failing sight. Months later, one of the recipients, a black man, said the gift had enabled him to read again—and he wanted to read Willie's work.

To preserve Willie's sense of levity, his son, David Rae Morris, placed one of his father's old foils, a plastic roach, on the marble boot of a statue of Jefferson Davis in the capitol rotunda. Once I had been with the Morrises when Willie had tucked the roach into someone's salad at Galatoire's. David Rae also arranged special music at the burial. The musicians would play "Darkness on the Delta," a number identified with Willie's friend the late Jackson saxophonist Charlie Jacobs. A piece by the Grateful Dead would also be slipped into the ceremony.

At noon, we walked from the Old State Capitol to Hal & Mal's next door, where many of us had gathered five years earlier to celebrate Willie's sixtieth birthday. Fortifying for the afternoon ahead, we ate red beans and rice, the Southern staple; some of us complemented the lunch with Bloody Marys. Will Campbell, who would officiate at the services, sat at our table. Earlier in the day, he had stopped by the state archives to get a copy of his Sovereignty Commission file, and he proudly waved the sheaf of papers documenting his subversion vis-à-vis the old Southern way of life.

Once we arrived in Yazoo City, driving over the last hill and into the Delta, I thought I might start weeping again. But someone had had the wisdom to call the service "A Celebration of the Life of Willie Morris," and that was what it was. At the beginning, we listened to the majestic sounds of "Finlandia" and a beautiful a cappella rendering of "Amazing Grace" by a black singer, Jewell Bass.

I found myself laughing with others in the crowded Methodist Church as a series of speakers delivered their eulogies. One of Willie's high school teachers, Harriet DeCell Kuykendall, began by saying, "He always said he liked me better than algebra." She read from *North Toward Home*.

William Styron told the graveyard story, then the deep, stentorian voice of David Halberstam filled the chapel. Despite his New York background, I think of David as an honorary Mississippian. Fresh out of Harvard, David had joined the staff of the state's smallest daily newspaper in the 1950s, a time when race had begun its upheaval of Mississippi, and through the years he has been a witness to our best and our worst. From the pulpit, he saluted Charles Evers, sitting among the honorary pallbearers. Afterward, I told David I had had to bite my tongue over his recognition of the civil rights leader turned right-wing Republican. But I admitted that it was something Willie would have wanted David to do; Willie had always been inclusive.

Mike Espy, the first black congressman from Mississippi in the century, spoke. Recently acquitted in federal court—but not before the questionable investigation by a special prosecutor had cost him a place in Clinton's cabinet—Espy made one of his first post-trial appearances to speak of Willie: "He is—and will forever be—our region's greatest ambassador. Our avuncular bridge spanning the chasm from then to now."

I kept my composure until former governor William Winter spoke:

"For those of us who, like Willie, were—to use his word—'ineffably' affected by growing up in a Mississippi of myths and legends, of fantasy about what never was and hope for what might never be, of insufferable baseness and incredible goodness, he was the one who perhaps more than anybody else of our generation caused us to look within ourselves and discover there the joy and inspiration to sustain us through the good times and the bad.

"I know that was true for me back in the late 1960s when I first heard about Willie Morris and when I was looking desperately for some voices that would speak of what I thought the South was really about—of civility and courtesy and kindness and tolerance—not of rage and hate and bitterness and bigotry. I found in his writings the special insight of one whose affection for his home state was not only undiminished but reinforced by his recognition of our weaknesses as well as our strengths and especially of our need to reach out to more, indeed to all, of our neighbors, and to erase the barriers that separated us from one another.

"There was no meanness and there was no pretense in Willie Morris. While not a publicly religious man, his life personified what true religion is all about. He found it not in the usual places but in the places where his friends were—in his words—'at the ball games and bus stations and courthouses and the bargain-rate beauty parlors and the little churches and the roadhouses and the joints near closing time.'

"Willie found goodness and kindness in people wherever he met them. As an old Mississippi farmer said, 'He didn't cull nobody.'"

At that point, a tear dribbled down my nose.

Near the end, Will Campbell announced that Willie deserved a standing ovation. We rose, and applause beat across the crowded sanctuary like a warm summer rainstorm.

Afterward, we drove in a snaking cortege through the late-afternoon sun to the cemetery Willie had memorialized in *North Toward Home*. Grieving late into the night after Willie's death, JoAnne had searched to find the passage she wanted to have printed in his funeral bulletin.

"Death," Willie wrote, "in a small town deeply affected the whole community. For weeks or even years the physical presence of the dead person would be missed in specific places; his funeral itself would touch closely upon the life of the town. Years later, when I would go to small funerals in nondenominational funeral parlors in New York City, I would be appalled by the cramped impersonality of natural death. The service itself would be hurried, as if they wanted to get it over with as soon as possible; and outside, on the crowded streets, people would never give a thought to the meager little procession."

While echoing trumpets sang taps across the Yazoo City cemetery—in the same manner Willie had played for fallen veterans a half century ago—I was brought back to the question Willie had posed at that dinner in Jackson more than five years earlier: "Curtis, can you tell us why you came home?"

Just as Vernon Dahmer Jr. had said, I, too, believe I came home to be with my people. We are a different people, with our odd customs and manner of speaking and our stubborn, stubborn pride. Perhaps we are no kinder than others, but it seems to me that we are. I would never claim superiority over the people of Washington or Boston or Jerusalem or the other places I've lived and traveled, but I found during my long exile that we are surely no worse. We appreciate our history and recognize our flaws much better than our critics. And like our great river, which overcomes impediments by creating fresh channels, we have been able in the span of Willie's lifetime and my own to adjust our course. Some think us benighted and accursed, but I like to believe the South is blessed with basic goodness. Even though I was angry with the South and gone for years, I never forsook my heritage. Eventually, I discovered I had always loved the place. Yes, Willie, I came home to be with my people.

Index

INDEX

Democratic Party:
  black Southerners in, 145–46, 178–81, 250–51
  civil-rights divisions in, 150–51, 254
  congressional control and, 198, 203, 204
  federal vs. state, 131, 145–46
  generational shift in Southern state governors of, 251, 290
  Mississippi polarization within, 60–61, 170, 179–81, 254, 258
  Reconstruction-era allegiance to, 33, 50
  Southern biracial constituency of, 250–51
  white Southern defections from, 150–52, 181, 199, 202, 231, 250, 254–55
  see also elections
Dennis, Delmar, 23, 155–56
Dent, Harry, 198
Denton, Herb, 274–75
Derian, Patricia, 180, 190, 242–43, 256, 303
DeVries, Walter, 250
Dick, Isaac, 64
Dickenson, Jim, 234
Dickenson, Mollie, 234
Dickey, James, 17, 236–37
Diggs, Charles, 21, 202
Dimaggio, Joe, 73
Dittmer, John, 166
Dixie:
  as journalist code name for Israel, 269
  as term for South, 300
"Dixie" (song), 300n
Doby, Larry, 73, 74
Drake Hotel, 181
Draper, Lyman C., 28
Dukakis, Michael, 281, 290
Duke, David, 259, 291, 292–94, 331
Dunbar, Jack, 185–86
Duval, Bud, 227

Earl of Louisiana, The (Liebling), 292
Easter, Luke, 73, 74
Eastland, James O., 60, 137, 145, 165, 168, 169, 199, 250, 255
  Henry's negotiations with, 251–52, 253
  Kennedy family and, 130, 252–53
  on Mississippi elections, 91, 130
  racism of, 93n
  retirement of, 253–54, 256, 258
Easy Burden, An (Young), 177, 249
Easy Rider, 197
Edelman, Marian Wright, 168, 198
Edelman, Peter, 198n
Edgar, Walter, 307
Edwards, Edwin, 291, 292, 293, 294

Eisenhower, Dwight D., 62, 95, 184
Eizenstat, Stuart, 246, 249
elections:
  of 1964, 145–46, 150–52, 207, 254
  of 1968, 177–84, 207, 254–55
  of 1972, 206–7, 208–9, 210–11, 249–50, 255
  of 1976, 217–25, 230–34
  of 1978, 256–57
  of 1980, 244–48, 277
  of 1988, 281, 289
  of 1992, 290–91
Ellis, Joe, 121, 157, 306
  on civil rights activists, 116, 136, 137
  as newspaper publisher/editor, 115, 119–20, 175, 179, 194
  as Republican, 115, 151
  on school desegregation plan, 147, 148, 149
Ellis, Ruby Folsom, 209–10
Elon, Amos, 270
Emmerich, Oliver, 100, 153
Emmett, Daniel D., 300n
Encyclopedia of Southern Culture (Wilson and Ferris, eds.), 307
Engelberg, Steve, 197
Enterprise-Journal, 100, 153, 266
Epps, Jesse, 166–67, 168
Erakat, Saeb, 273
Espy, Henry, Jr., 194, 306
Espy, Mike, 334
Ethridge, Tom, 100
Evans, John, 331
Evans, Rowland, 242
Evers, Charles, 127, 162, 180, 256–57, 264, 334
Evers, Medgar, 21
  murder of, 15, 16, 22, 23, 25, 121, 126, 127, 135, 155–56, 256, 318, 319
Evers, Myrlie, 23, 24, 319

Fall, Bernard, 178
Fant, Ruff, 197
Farmer, James, 87
Farrakhan, Louis, 212
Farris, George, 192, 194
Faubus, Orval, 17, 95, 251
Faulkner, William, 81, 90, 285, 288
  burial site of, 326
  on liquor prohibitions, 82–83
  Oxford background of, 36, 299, 311
  Southerners depicted by, 18, 57, 67n, 327
Federal Bureau of Investigations (FBI), 192
  KKK informants of, 154–56
  Neshoba County deaths and, 143, 155, 156, 317